TKO STUDIOS

SALVATORE SIMEONE - CEO & PUBLISHER

TZE CHUN - PUBLISHER

CARA MCKENNEY - CREATOR OUTREACH

SEBASTIAN GIRNER - EDITOR-IN-CHIEF

SHAINA JULIAN - DIRECTOR OF OPERATIONS

ROBERT TERLIZZI - DIRECTOR OF DESIGN

GOODNIGHT PARADISE #1-6.

Published by TKO Studios, LLC.
Office of Publication: 450 7th Ave Suite 2107 New York, NY 10123.

TKOPRESENTS.COM

TKO PRESENTS A WORLD BY:

JOSHUA DYSART
WRITER

ALBERTO PONTICELLI
ART

GIULIA BRUSCO
COLOR ART

STEVE WANDS
LETTERER

SEBASTIAN GIRNER
EDITOR

JARED K FLETCHER
COVER & TITLE DESIGN

ROBERT TERLIZZI
BOOK DESIGN

CHAPTER 1

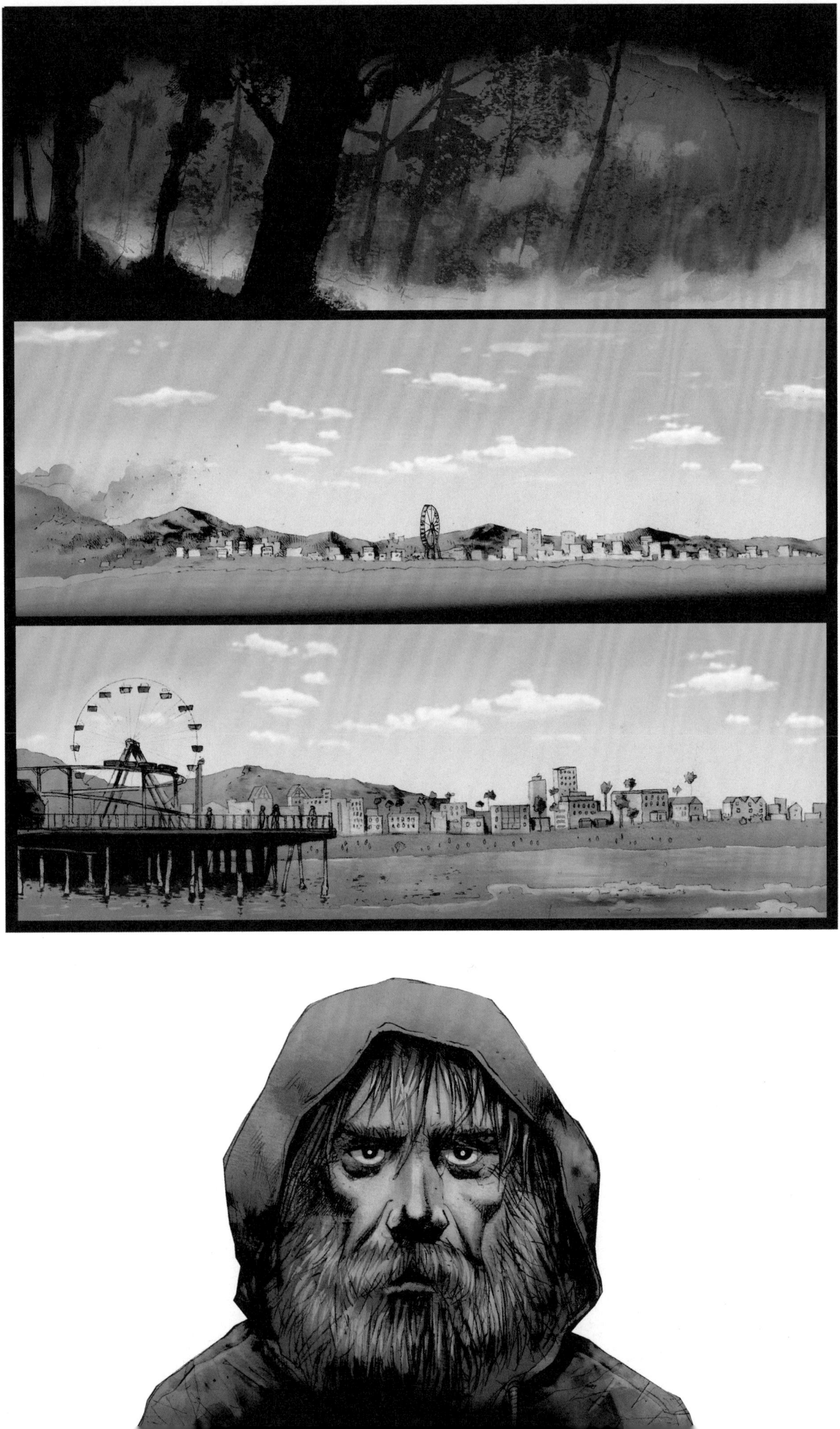

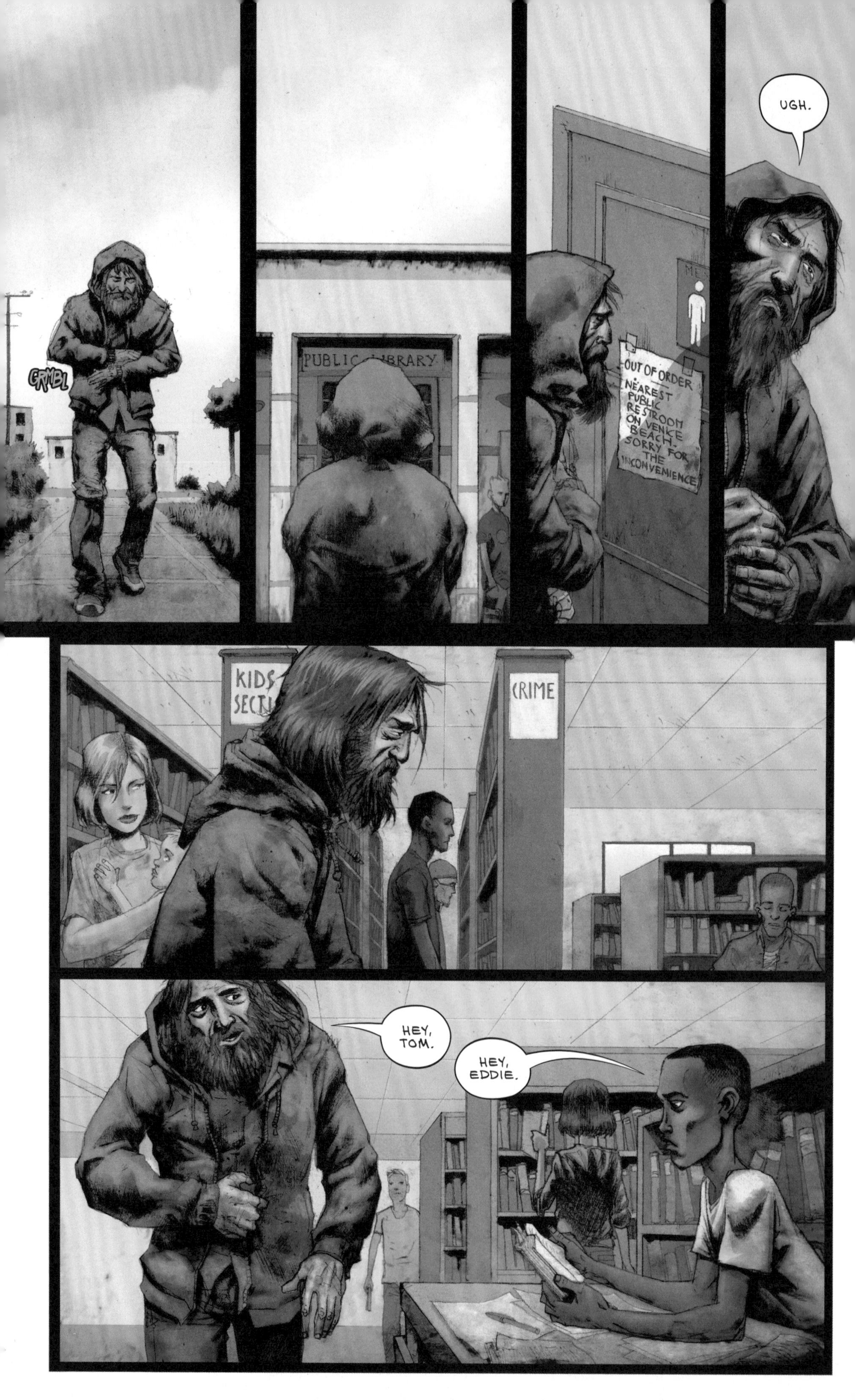
GRMBL
PUBLIC LIBRARY
OUT OF ORDER
NEAREST PUBLIC RESTROOM ON VENKE BEACH. SORRY FOR THE CONVEMIENCE
UGH.
KIDS SECTI
CRIME
HEY, TOM.
HEY, EDDIE.

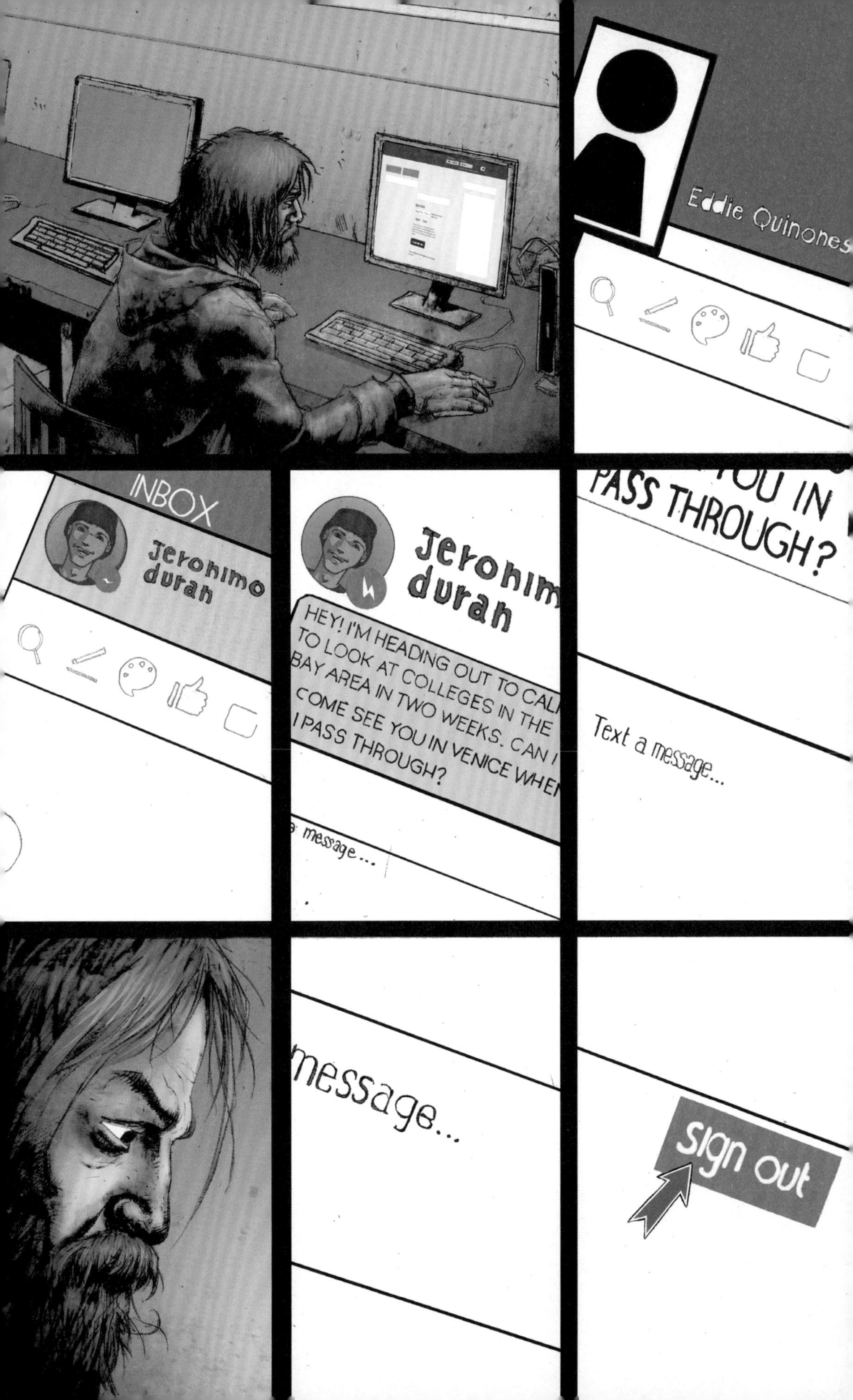
Eddie Quinones
INBOX
Jeronimo duran
Jeronim duran
HEY! I'M HEADING OUT TO CAL TO LOOK AT COLLEGES IN THE BAY AREA IN TWO WEEKS. CAN I COME SEE YOU IN VENICE WHEN I PASS THROUGH?
message...
YOU IN PASS THROUGH?
Text a message...
message...
Sign out

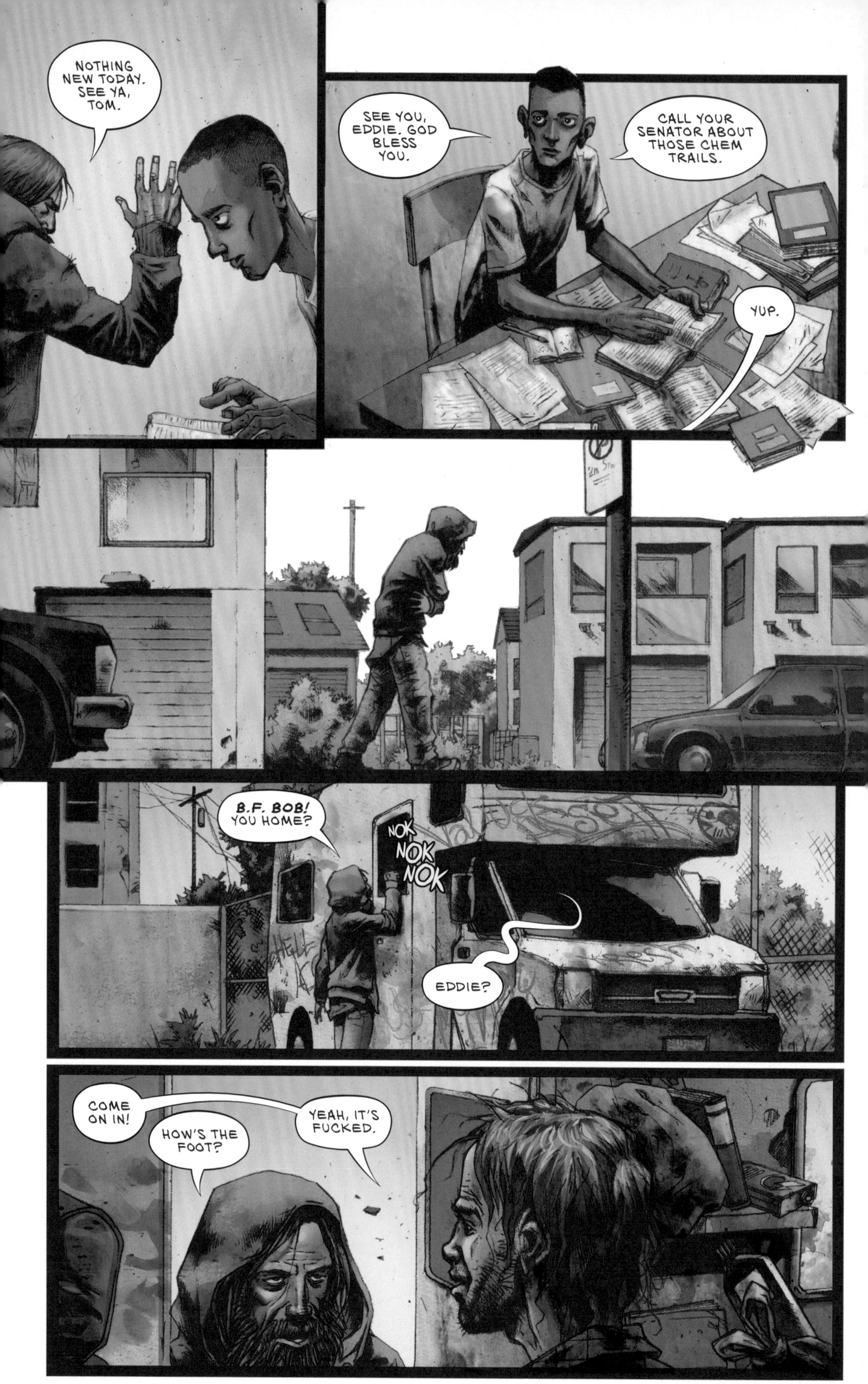
NOTHING NEW TODAY. SEE YA, TOM.
SEE YOU, EDDIE. GOD BLESS YOU.
CALL YOUR SENATOR ABOUT THOSE CHEM TRAILS.
YUP.
B.F. BOB! YOU HOME?
NOK NOK NOK
EDDIE?
COME ON IN!
HOW'S THE FOOT?
YEAH, IT'S FUCKED.

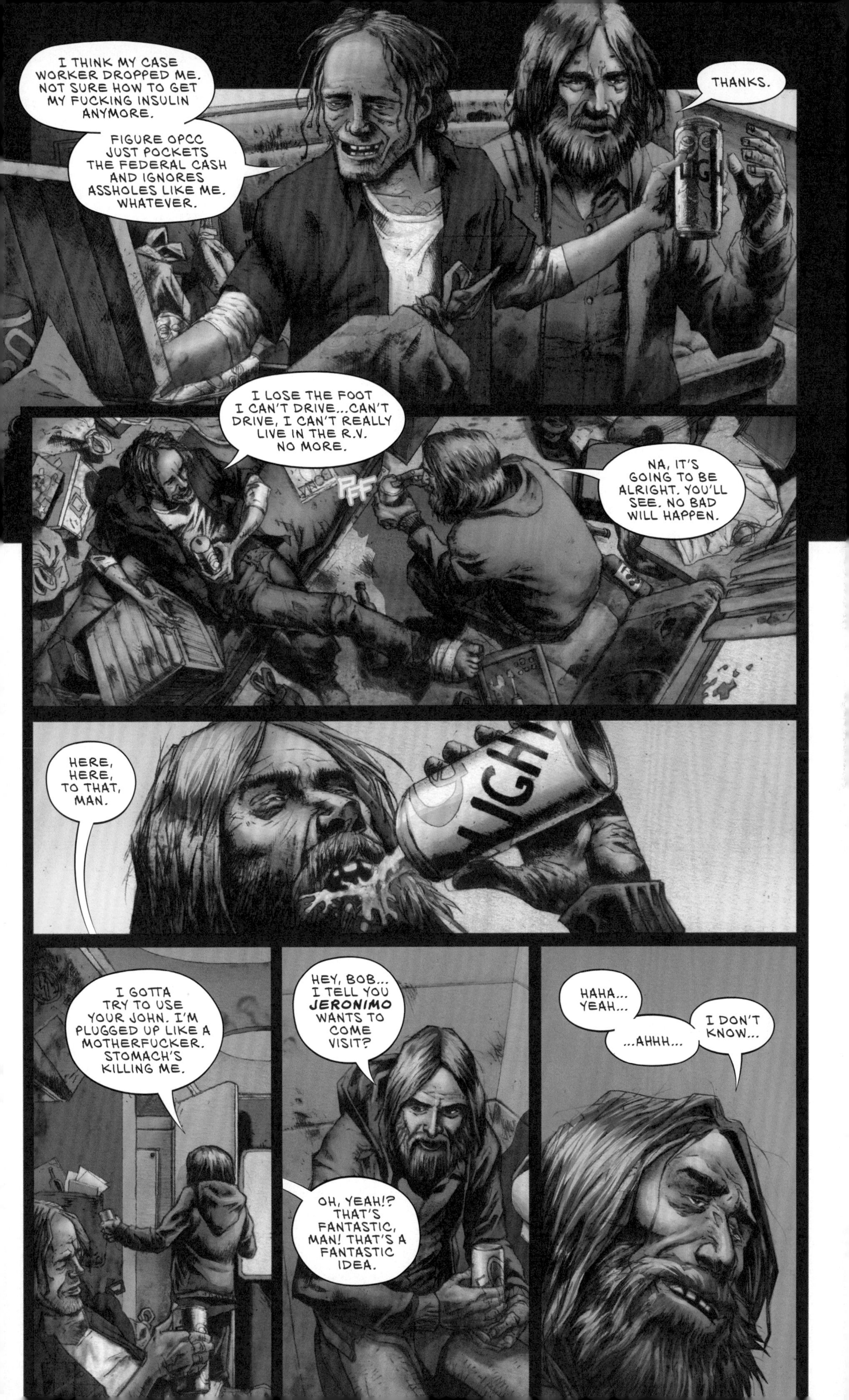
I THINK MY CASE WORKER DROPPED ME. NOT SURE HOW TO GET MY FUCKING INSULIN ANYMORE.
FIGURE OPCC JUST POCKETS THE FEDERAL CASH AND IGNORES ASSHOLES LIKE ME. WHATEVER.
THANKS.
I LOSE THE FOOT I CAN'T DRIVE...CAN'T DRIVE, I CAN'T REALLY LIVE IN THE R.V. NO MORE.
PFF
NA, IT'S GOING TO BE ALRIGHT. YOU'LL SEE. NO BAD WILL HAPPEN.
HERE, HERE, TO THAT, MAN.
I GOTTA TRY TO USE YOUR JOHN. I'M PLUGGED UP LIKE A MOTHERFUCKER. STOMACH'S KILLING ME.
HEY, BOB... I TELL YOU **JERONIMO** WANTS TO COME VISIT?
OH, YEAH!? THAT'S FANTASTIC, MAN! THAT'S A FANTASTIC IDEA.
HAHA... YEAH...
...AHHH...
I DON'T KNOW...

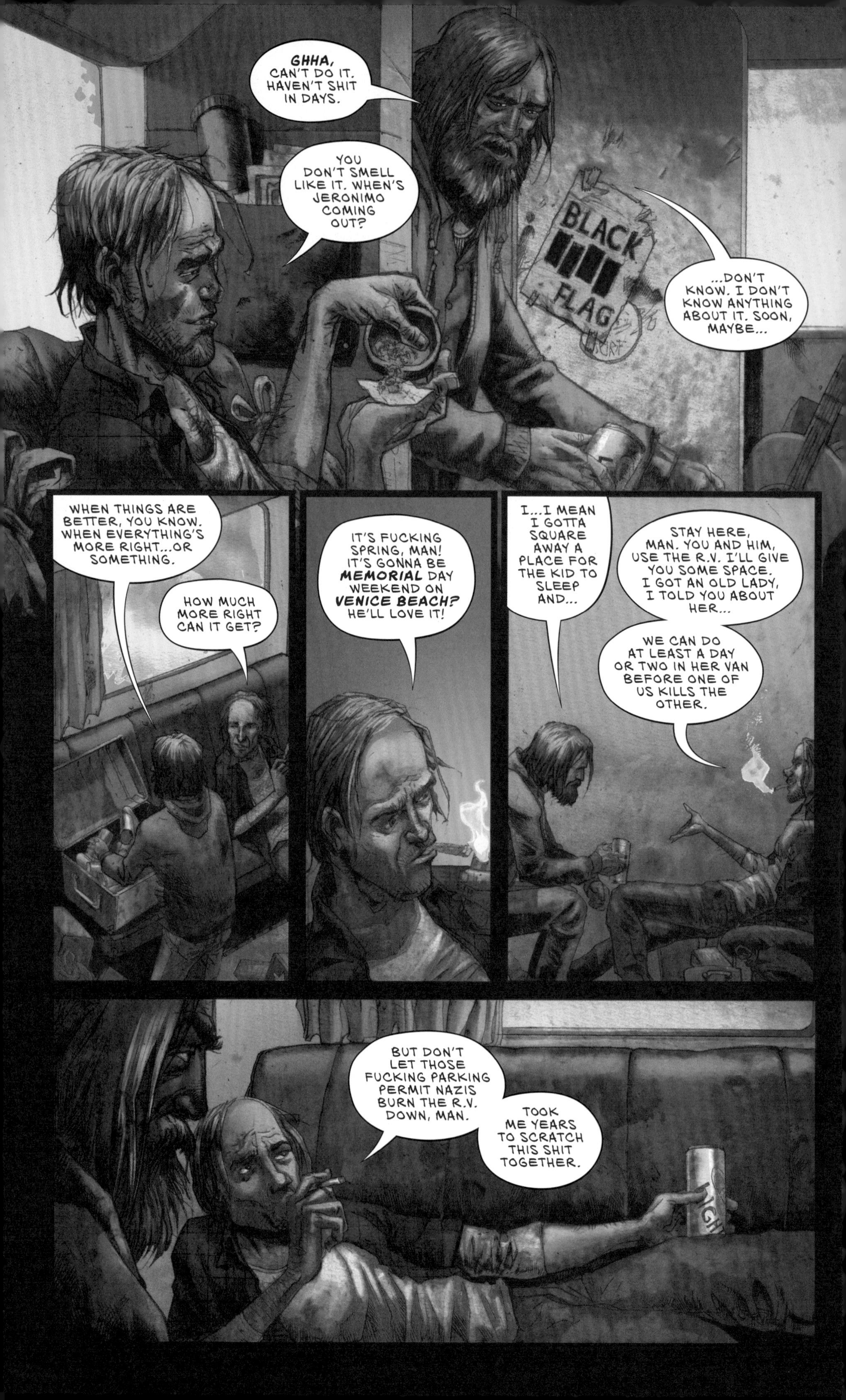
GHHA, CAN'T DO IT. HAVEN'T SHIT IN DAYS.
YOU DON'T SMELL LIKE IT. WHEN'S JERONIMO COMING OUT?
...DON'T KNOW. I DON'T KNOW ANYTHING ABOUT IT. SOON, MAYBE...
BLACK FLAG
WHEN THINGS ARE BETTER, YOU KNOW. WHEN EVERYTHING'S MORE RIGHT...OR SOMETHING.
HOW MUCH MORE RIGHT CAN IT GET?
IT'S FUCKING SPRING, MAN! IT'S GONNA BE MEMORIAL DAY WEEKEND ON VENICE BEACH? HE'LL LOVE IT!
I...I MEAN I GOTTA SQUARE AWAY A PLACE FOR THE KID TO SLEEP AND...
STAY HERE, MAN. YOU AND HIM, USE THE R.V. I'LL GIVE YOU SOME SPACE. I GOT AN OLD LADY, I TOLD YOU ABOUT HER...
WE CAN DO AT LEAST A DAY OR TWO IN HER VAN BEFORE ONE OF US KILLS THE OTHER.
BUT DON'T LET THOSE FUCKING PARKING PERMIT NAZIS BURN THE R.V. DOWN, MAN.
TOOK ME YEARS TO SCRATCH THIS SHIT TOGETHER.

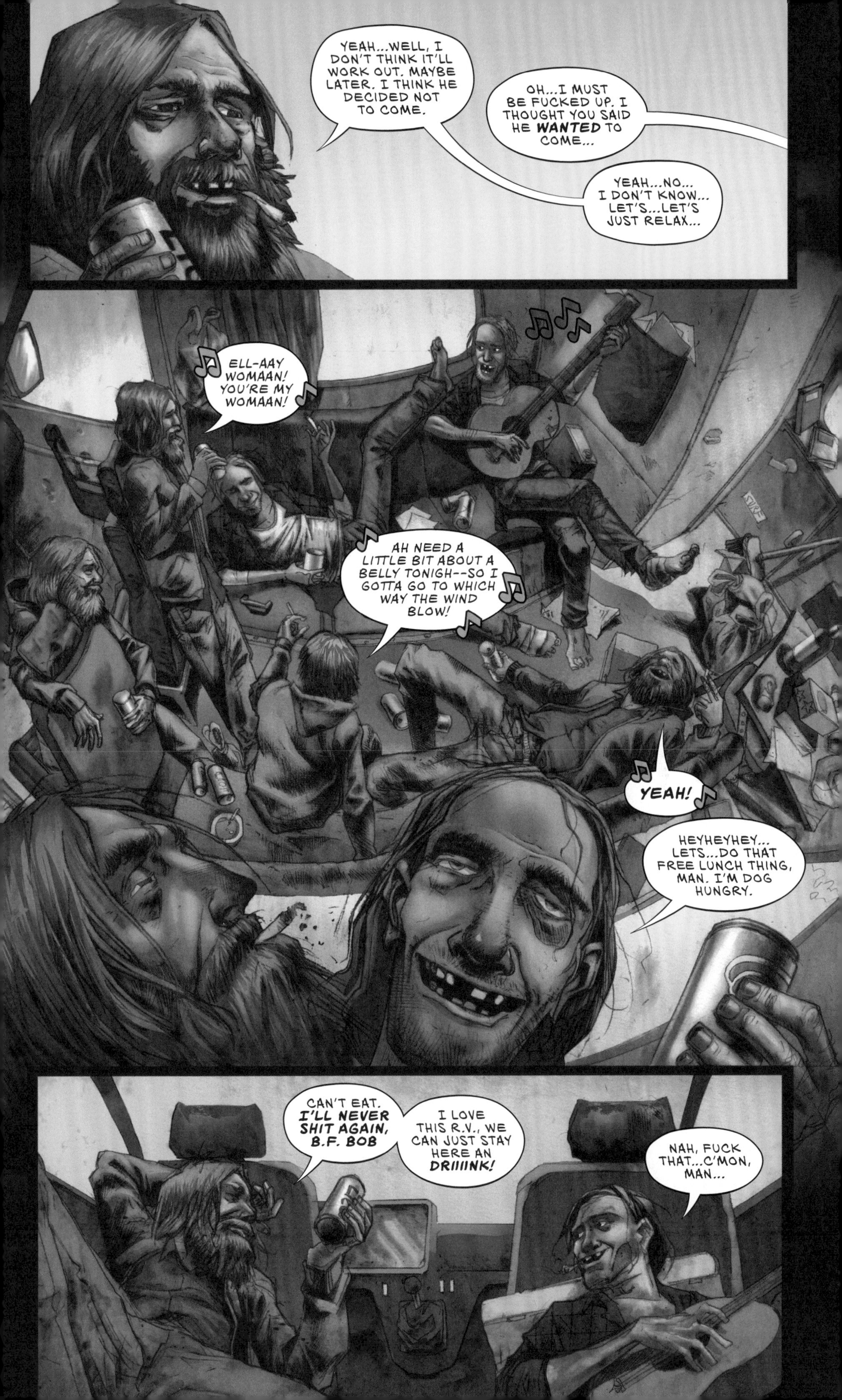

YEAH...WELL, I DON'T THINK IT'LL WORK OUT. MAYBE LATER. I THINK HE DECIDED NOT TO COME.
OH...I MUST BE FUCKED UP. I THOUGHT YOU SAID HE WANTED TO COME...
YEAH...NO... I DON'T KNOW... LET'S...LET'S JUST RELAX...
ELL-AAY WOMAAN! YOU'RE MY WOMAAN!
AH NEED A LITTLE BIT ABOUT A BELLY TONIGH--SO I GOTTA GO TO WHICH WAY THE WIND BLOW!
YEAH!
HEYHEYHEY... LETS...DO THAT FREE LUNCH THING, MAN. I'M DOG HUNGRY.
CAN'T EAT. I'LL NEVER SHIT AGAIN, B.F. BOB
I LOVE THIS R.V., WE CAN JUST STAY HERE AN DRIIIINK!
NAH, FUCK THAT...C'MON, MAN...

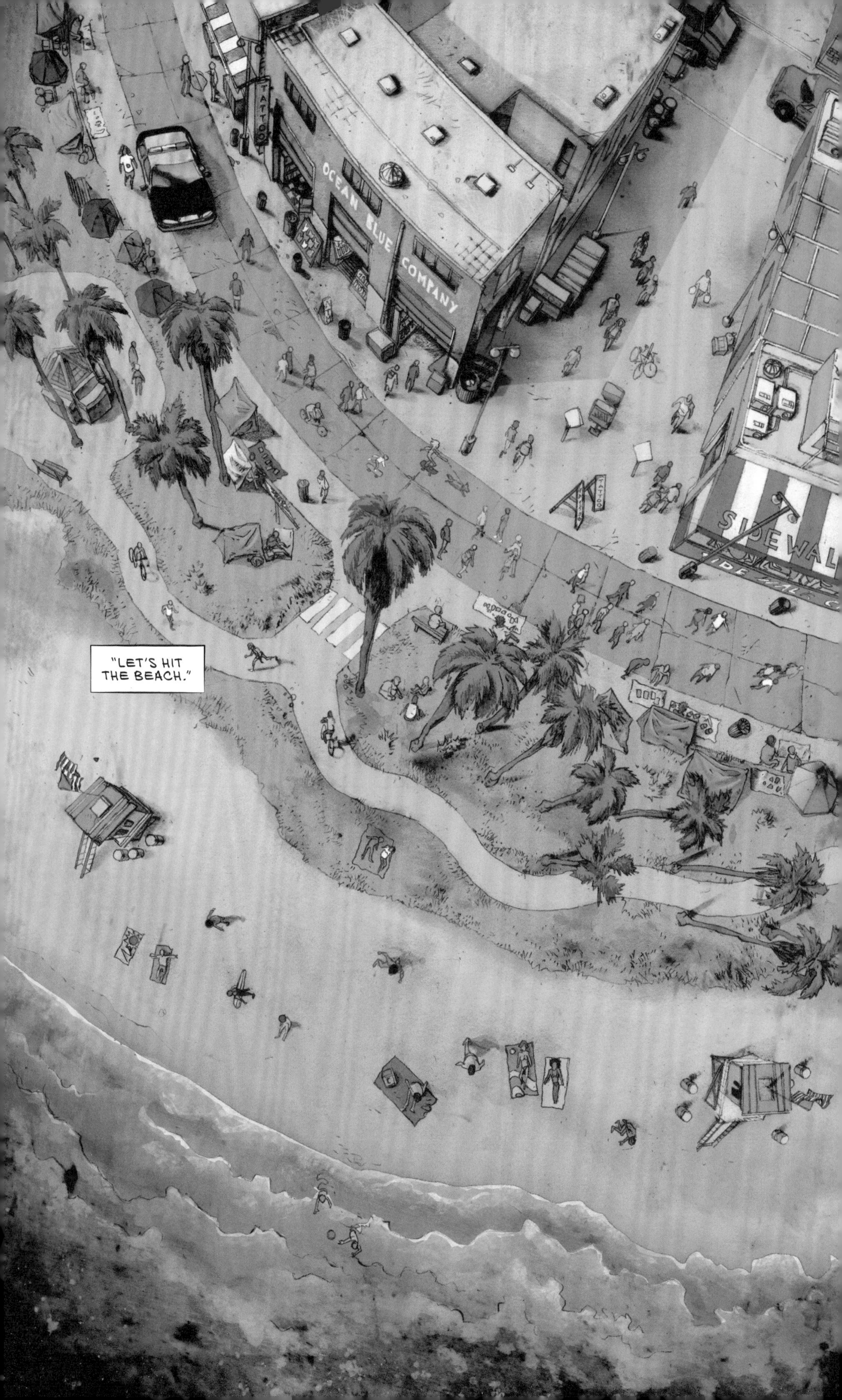
"LET'S HIT THE BEACH."
OCEAN BLUE COMPANY
TATTOO

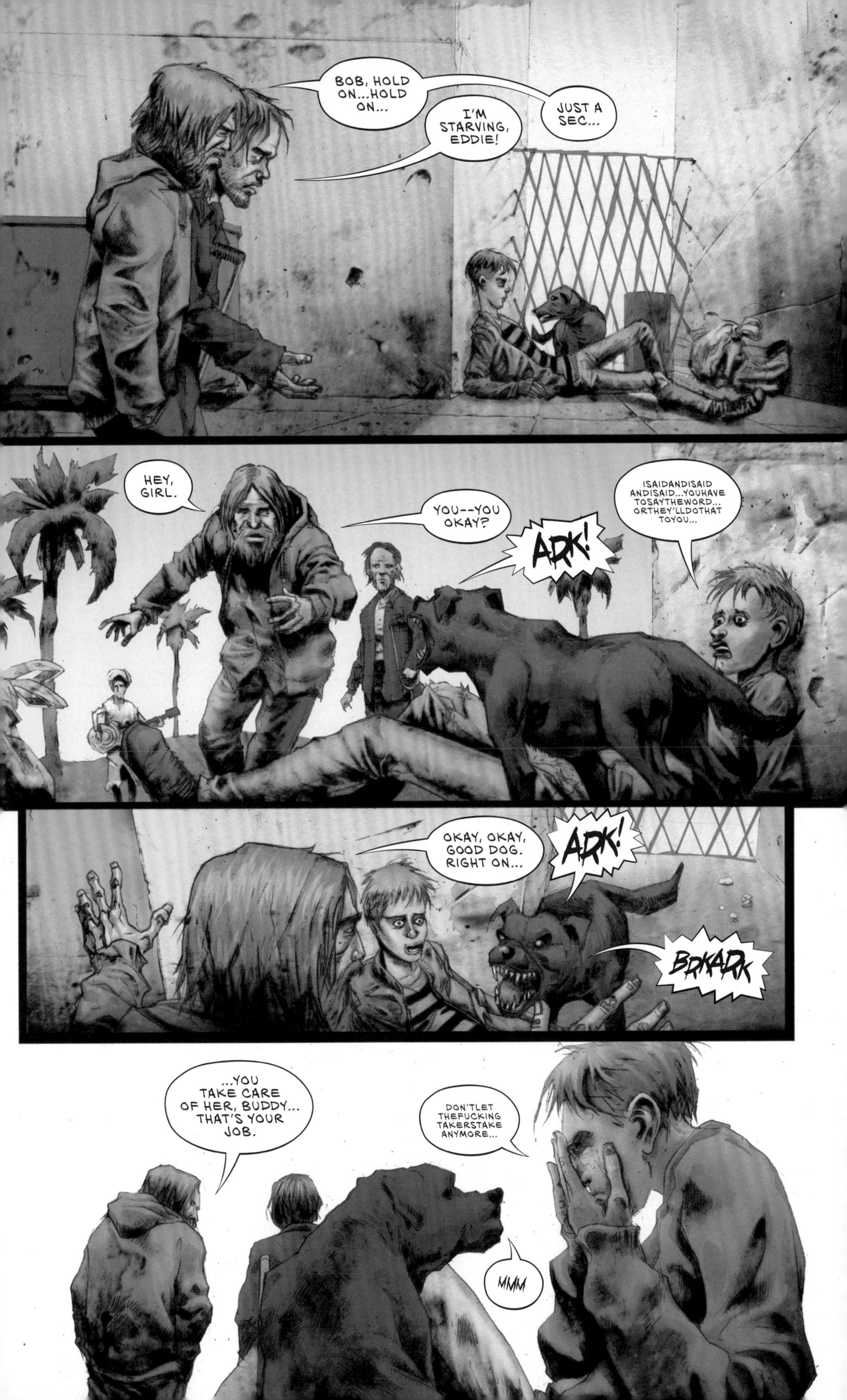
BOB, HOLD ON...HOLD ON...
JUST A SEC...
I'M STARVING, EDDIE!
HEY, GIRL.
YOU--YOU OKAY?
ARK!
ISAIDANDISAID ANDISAID...YOUHAVE TOSAYTHEWORD... ORTHEY'LLDOTHAT TOYOU...
OKAY, OKAY, GOOD DOG. RIGHT ON...
ARK!
BRKARK
...YOU TAKE CARE OF HER, BUDDY... THAT'S YOUR JOB.
DON'TLET THEFUCKING TAKERSTAKE ANYMORE...
MMM

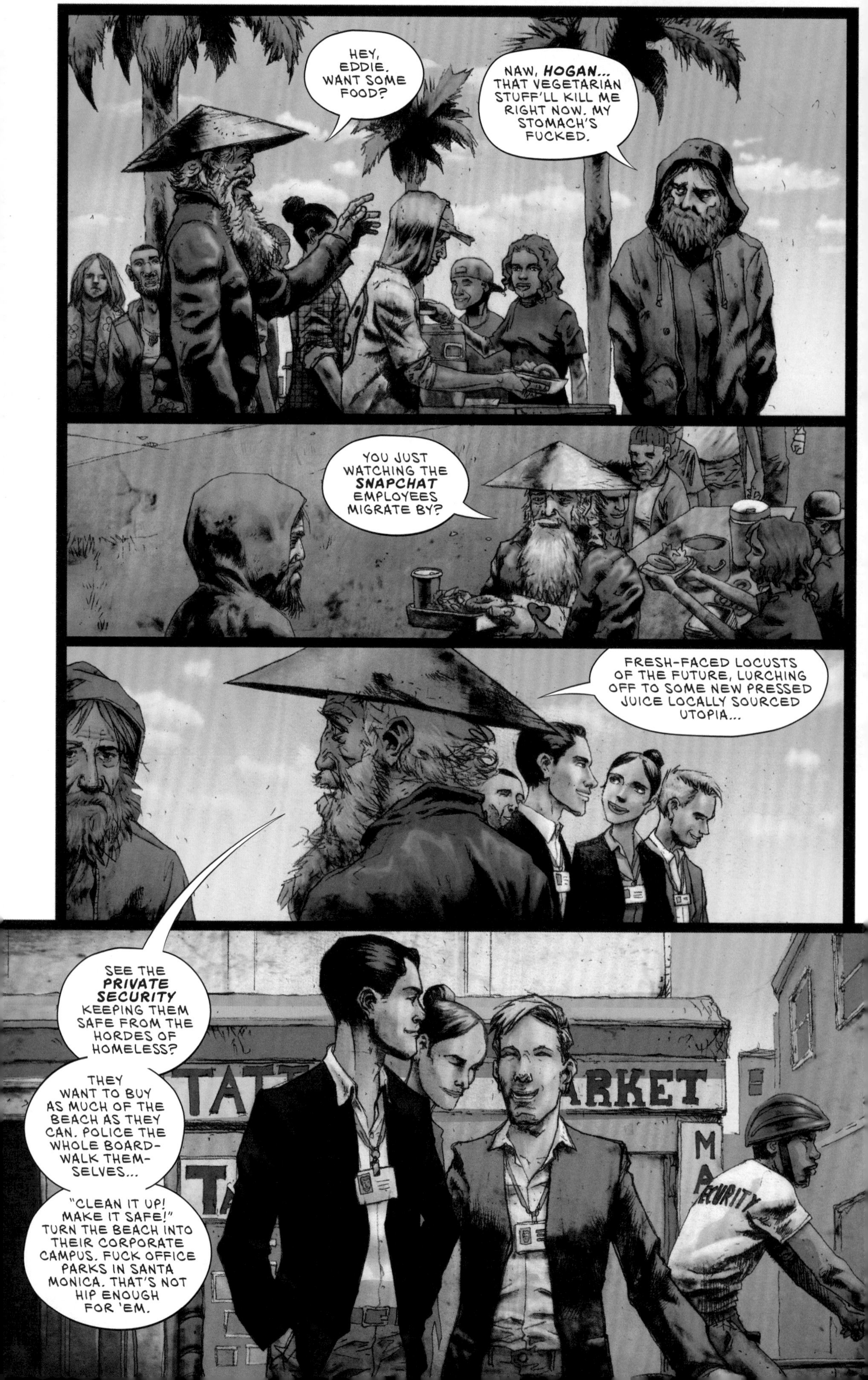
HEY, EDDIE. WANT SOME FOOD?
NAW, HOGAN... THAT VEGETARIAN STUFF'LL KILL ME RIGHT NOW. MY STOMACH'S FUCKED.
YOU JUST WATCHING THE SNAPCHAT EMPLOYEES MIGRATE BY?
FRESH-FACED LOCUSTS OF THE FUTURE, LURCHING OFF TO SOME NEW PRESSED JUICE LOCALLY SOURCED UTOPIA...
SEE THE PRIVATE SECURITY KEEPING THEM SAFE FROM THE HORDES OF HOMELESS?
THEY WANT TO BUY AS MUCH OF THE BEACH AS THEY CAN. POLICE THE WHOLE BOARD-WALK THEM-SELVES...
"CLEAN IT UP! MAKE IT SAFE!" TURN THE BEACH INTO THEIR CORPORATE CAMPUS. FUCK OFFICE PARKS IN SANTA MONICA. THAT'S NOT HIP ENOUGH FOR 'EM.
ARKET
SECURITY

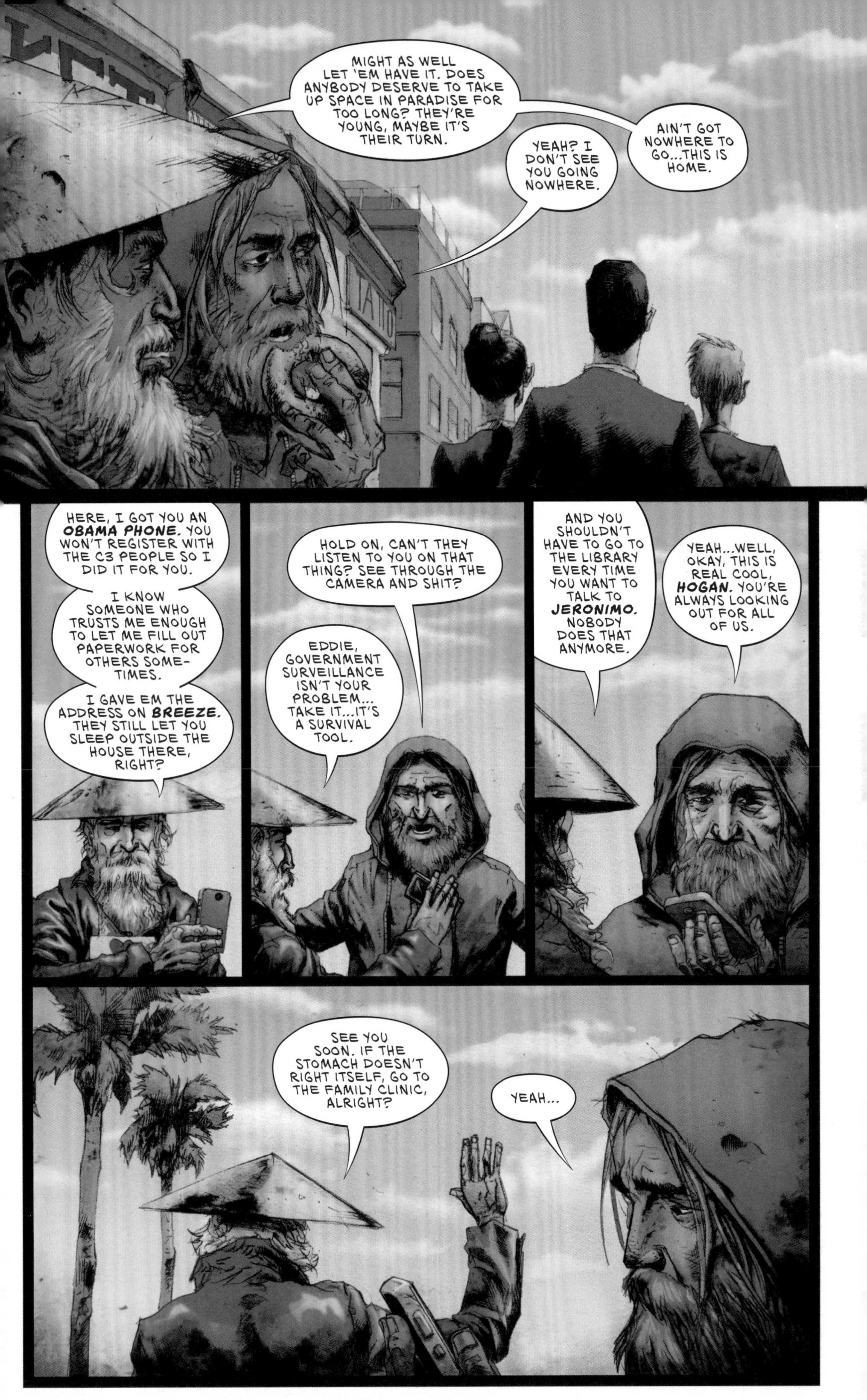
MIGHT AS WELL LET 'EM HAVE IT. DOES ANYBODY DESERVE TO TAKE UP SPACE IN PARADISE FOR TOO LONG? THEY'RE YOUNG, MAYBE IT'S THEIR TURN.
YEAH? I DON'T SEE YOU GOING NOWHERE.
AIN'T GOT NOWHERE TO GO...THIS IS HOME.
HERE, I GOT YOU AN **OBAMA PHONE.** YOU WON'T REGISTER WITH THE C3 PEOPLE SO I DID IT FOR YOU.
I KNOW SOMEONE WHO TRUSTS ME ENOUGH TO LET ME FILL OUT PAPERWORK FOR OTHERS SOME-TIMES.
I GAVE EM THE ADDRESS ON **BREEZE.** THEY STILL LET YOU SLEEP OUTSIDE THE HOUSE THERE, RIGHT?
HOLD ON, CAN'T THEY LISTEN TO YOU ON THAT THING? SEE THROUGH THE CAMERA AND SHIT?
EDDIE, GOVERNMENT SURVEILLANCE ISN'T YOUR PROBLEM... TAKE IT...IT'S A SURVIVAL TOOL.
AND YOU SHOULDN'T HAVE TO GO TO THE LIBRARY EVERY TIME YOU WANT TO TALK TO **JERONIMO.** NOBODY DOES THAT ANYMORE.
YEAH...WELL, OKAY, THIS IS REAL COOL, **HOGAN.** YOU'RE ALWAYS LOOKING OUT FOR ALL OF US.
SEE YOU SOON. IF THE STOMACH DOESN'T RIGHT ITSELF, GO TO THE FAMILY CLINIC, ALRIGHT?
YEAH...

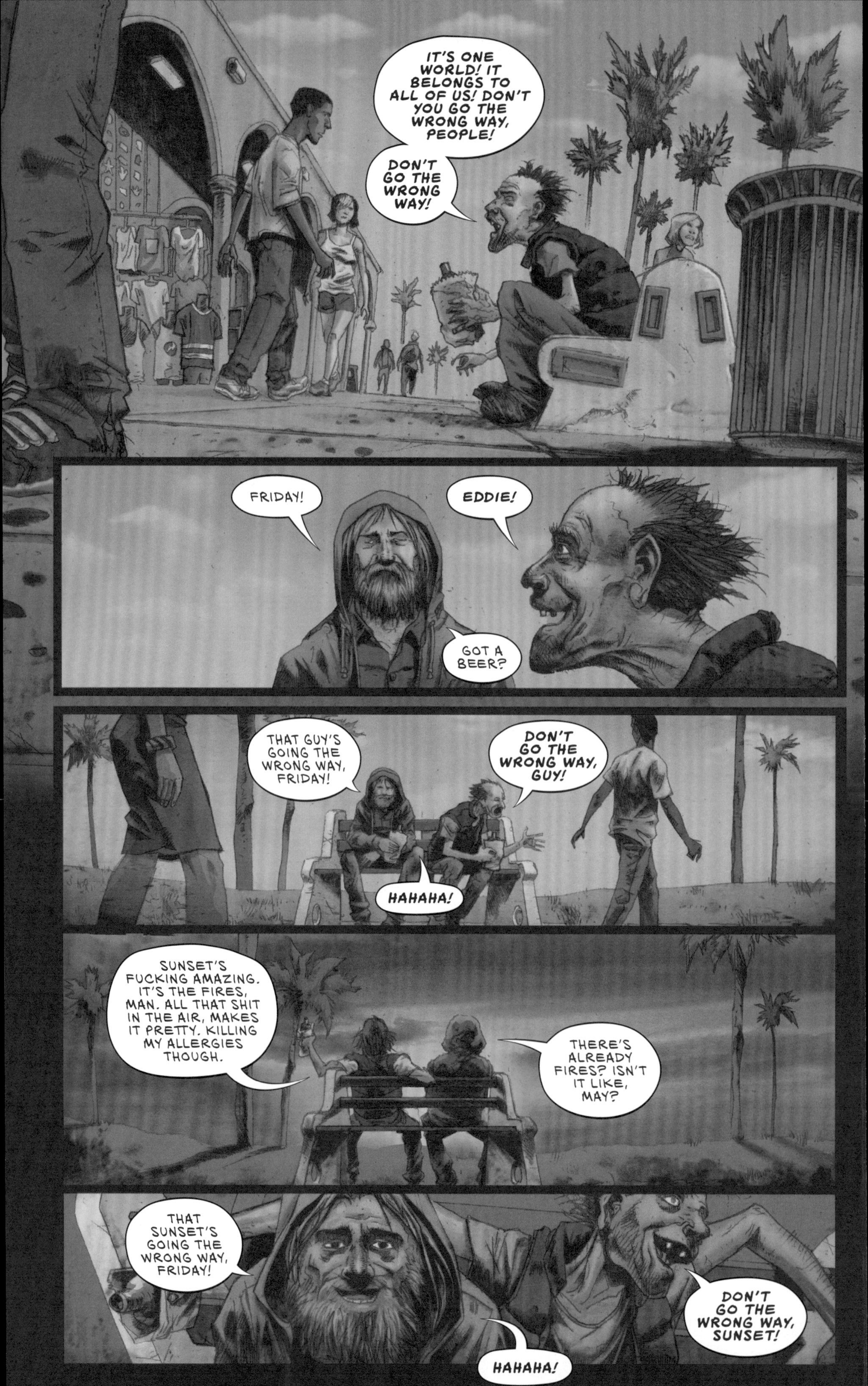
IT'S ONE WORLD! IT BELONGS TO ALL OF US! DON'T YOU GO THE WRONG WAY, PEOPLE!
DON'T GO THE WRONG WAY!
FRIDAY!
EDDIE!
GOT A BEER?
THAT GUY'S GOING THE WRONG WAY, FRIDAY!
DON'T GO THE WRONG WAY, GUY!
HAHAHA!
SUNSET'S FUCKING AMAZING. IT'S THE FIRES, MAN. ALL THAT SHIT IN THE AIR, MAKES IT PRETTY. KILLING MY ALLERGIES THOUGH.
THERE'S ALREADY FIRES? ISN'T IT LIKE, MAY?
THAT SUNSET'S GOING THE WRONG WAY, FRIDAY!
DON'T GO THE WRONG WAY, SUNSET!
HAHAHA!

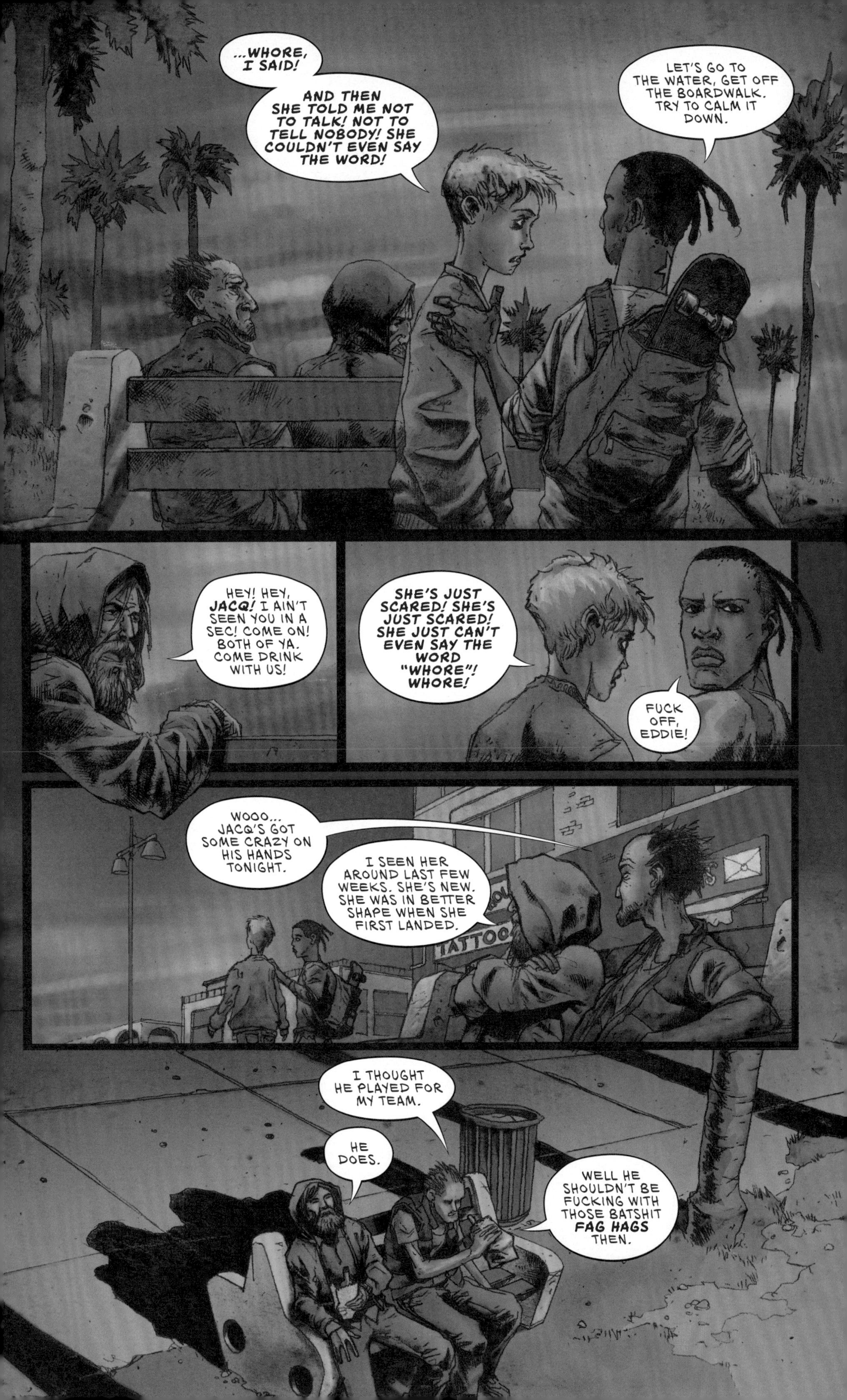
...WHORE, I SAID!
AND THEN SHE TOLD ME NOT TO TALK! NOT TO TELL NOBODY! SHE COULDN'T EVEN SAY THE WORD!
LET'S GO TO THE WATER, GET OFF THE BOARDWALK. TRY TO CALM IT DOWN.
HEY! HEY, JACQ! I AIN'T SEEN YOU IN A SEC! COME ON! BOTH OF YA. COME DRINK WITH US!
SHE'S JUST SCARED! SHE'S JUST SCARED! SHE JUST CAN'T EVEN SAY THE WORD "WHORE"! WHORE!
FUCK OFF, EDDIE!
WOOO... JACQ'S GOT SOME CRAZY ON HIS HANDS TONIGHT.
I SEEN HER AROUND LAST FEW WEEKS. SHE'S NEW. SHE WAS IN BETTER SHAPE WHEN SHE FIRST LANDED.
TATTOO
I THOUGHT HE PLAYED FOR MY TEAM.
HE DOES.
WELL HE SHOULDN'T BE FUCKING WITH THOSE BATSHIT FAG HAGS THEN.

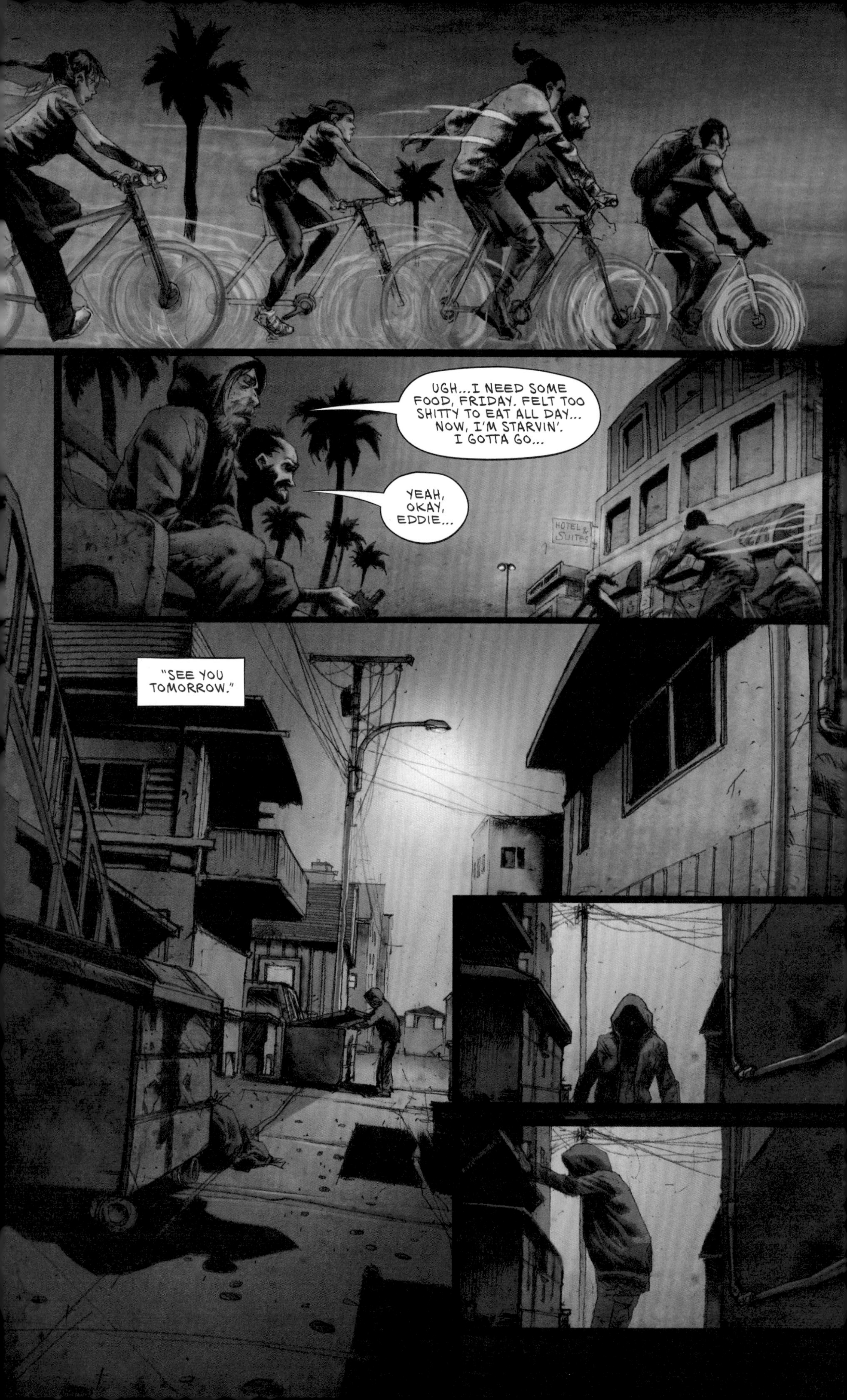
UGH...I NEED SOME FOOD, FRIDAY. FELT TOO SHITTY TO EAT ALL DAY... NOW, I'M STARVIN'. I GOTTA GO...
YEAH, OKAY, EDDIE...
HOTEL & SUITES
"SEE YOU TOMORROW."

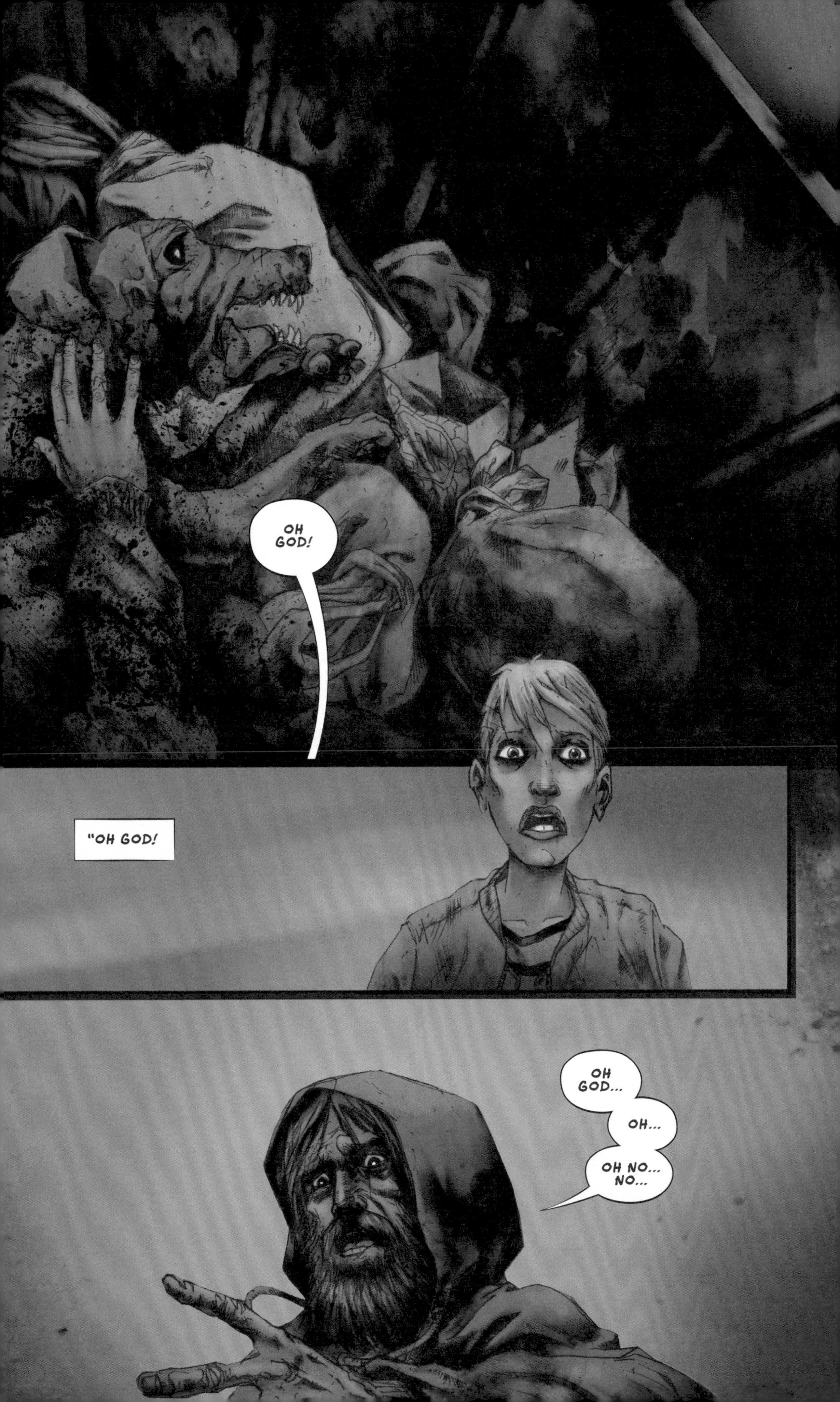
OH GOD!
"OH GOD!
OH GOD...
OH...
OH NO... NO...

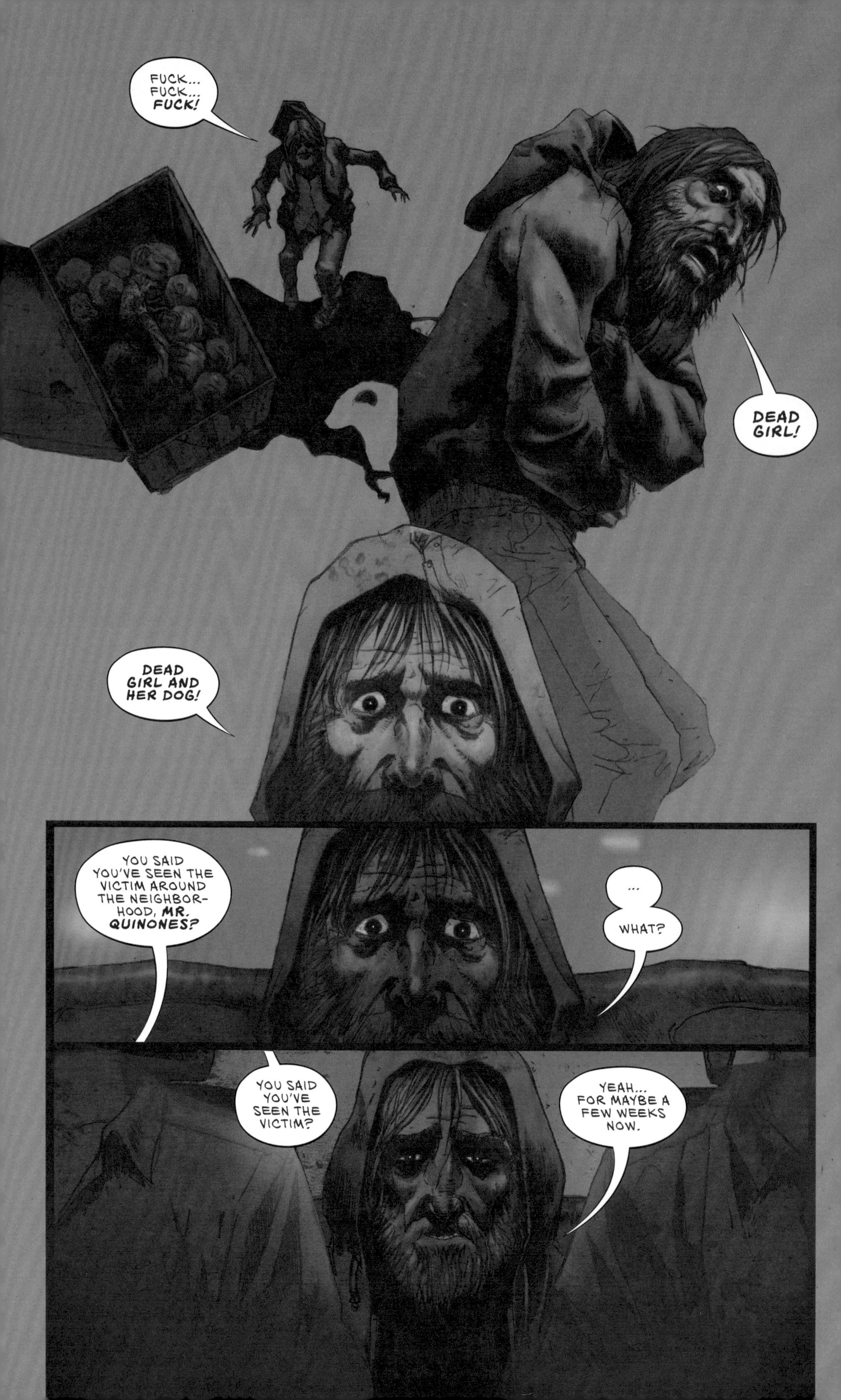
FUCK... FUCK... FUCK!
DEAD GIRL!
DEAD GIRL AND HER DOG!
YOU SAID YOU'VE SEEN THE VICTIM AROUND THE NEIGHBOR-HOOD, MR. QUINONES?
...
WHAT?
YOU SAID YOU'VE SEEN THE VICTIM?
YEAH... FOR MAYBE A FEW WEEKS NOW.

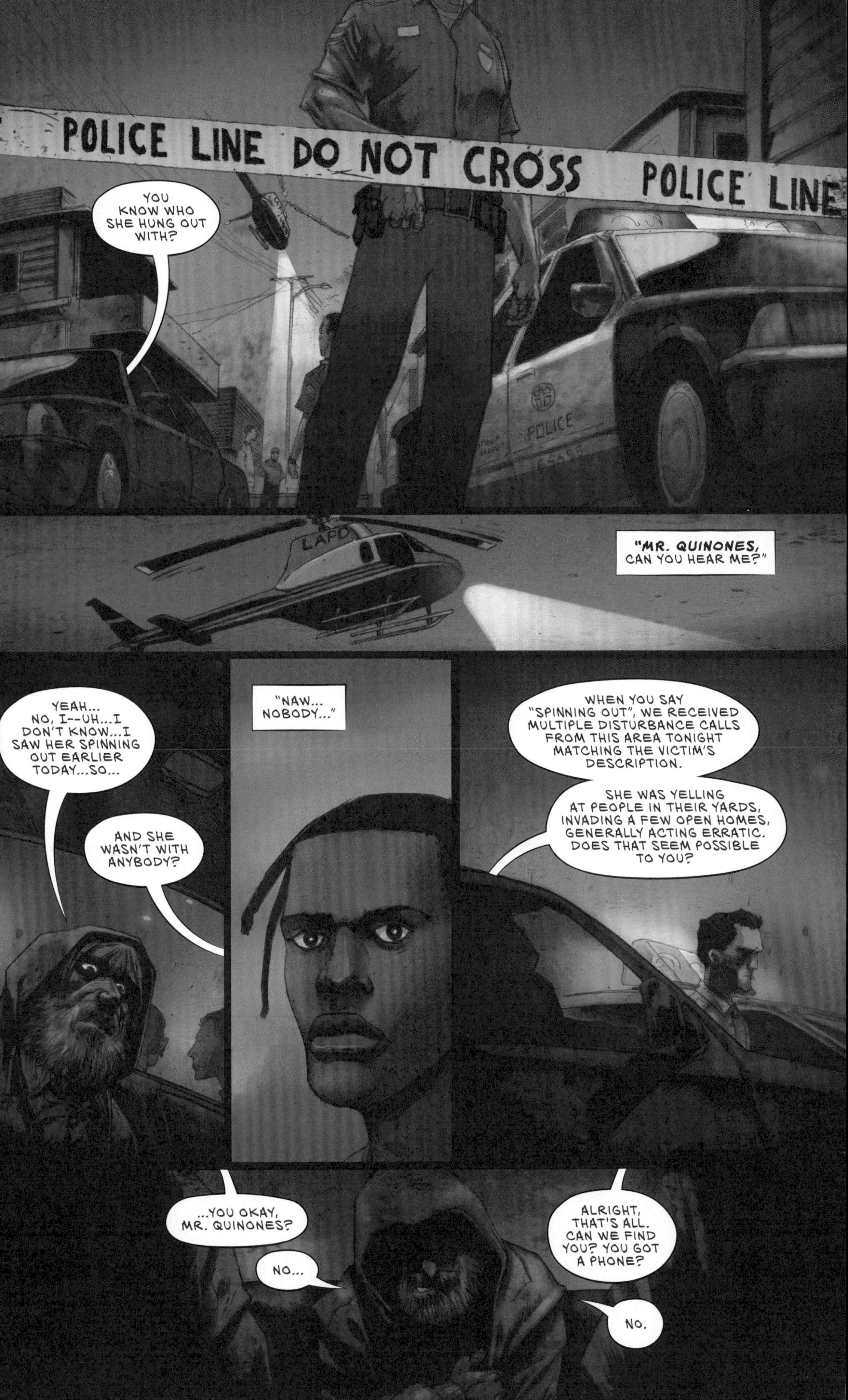
POLICE LINE DO NOT CROSS POLICE LINE
YOU KNOW WHO SHE HUNG OUT WITH?
POLICE
LAPD
"MR. QUINONES, CAN YOU HEAR ME?"
YEAH... NO, I--UH...I DON'T KNOW...I SAW HER SPINNING OUT EARLIER TODAY...SO...
AND SHE WASN'T WITH ANYBODY?
"NAW... NOBODY..."
WHEN YOU SAY "SPINNING OUT", WE RECEIVED MULTIPLE DISTURBANCE CALLS FROM THIS AREA TONIGHT MATCHING THE VICTIM'S DESCRIPTION.
SHE WAS YELLING AT PEOPLE IN THEIR YARDS, INVADING A FEW OPEN HOMES, GENERALLY ACTING ERRATIC. DOES THAT SEEM POSSIBLE TO YOU?
...YOU OKAY, MR. QUINONES?
NO...
ALRIGHT, THAT'S ALL. CAN WE FIND YOU? YOU GOT A PHONE?
NO.

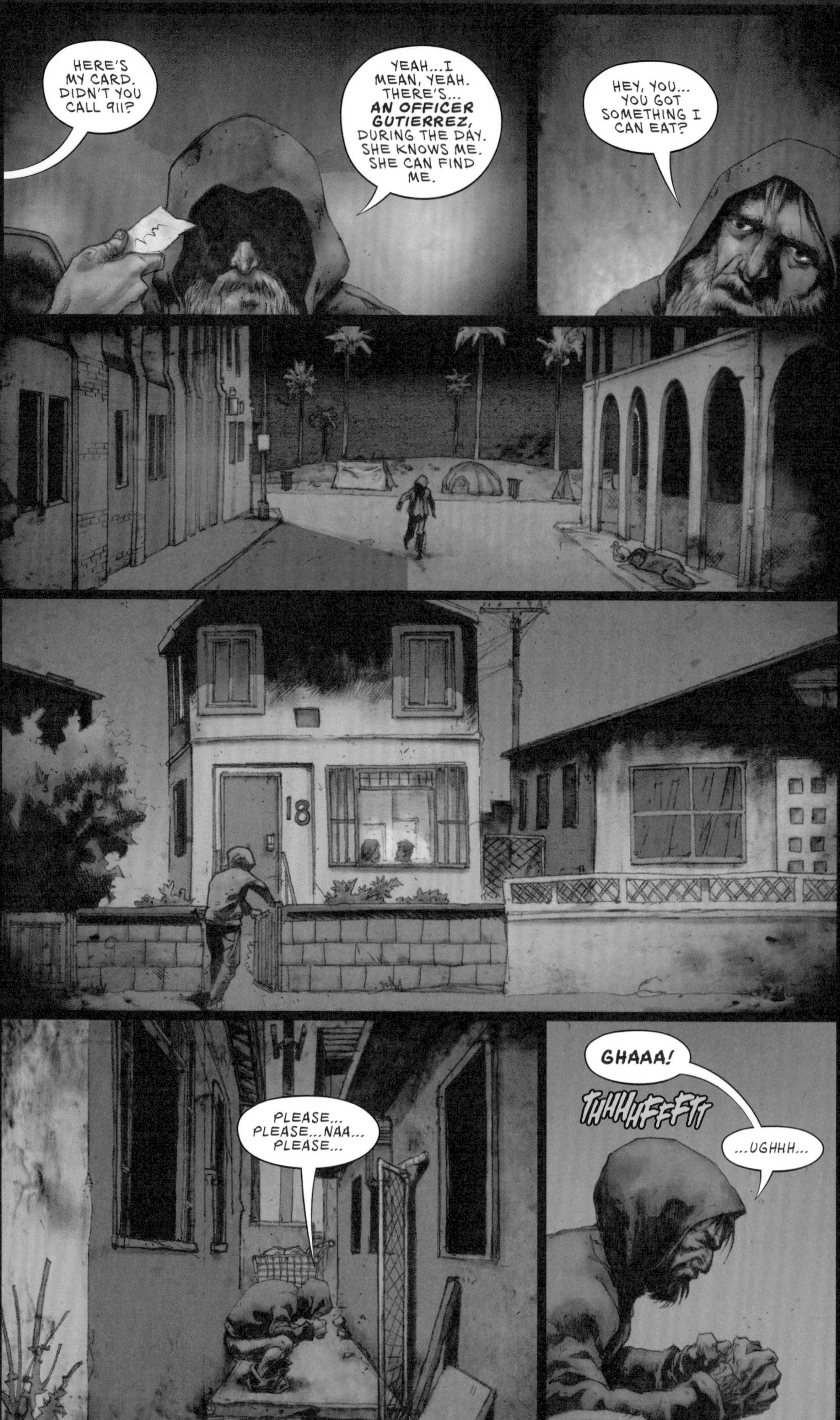
HERE'S MY CARD. DIDN'T YOU CALL 911?
YEAH... I MEAN, YEAH. THERE'S... AN OFFICER GUTIERREZ, DURING THE DAY. SHE KNOWS ME. SHE CAN FIND ME.
HEY, YOU... YOU GOT SOMETHING I CAN EAT?
18
PLEASE... PLEASE... NAA... PLEASE...
GHAAA!
THHHFFFTT
...UGHHH...

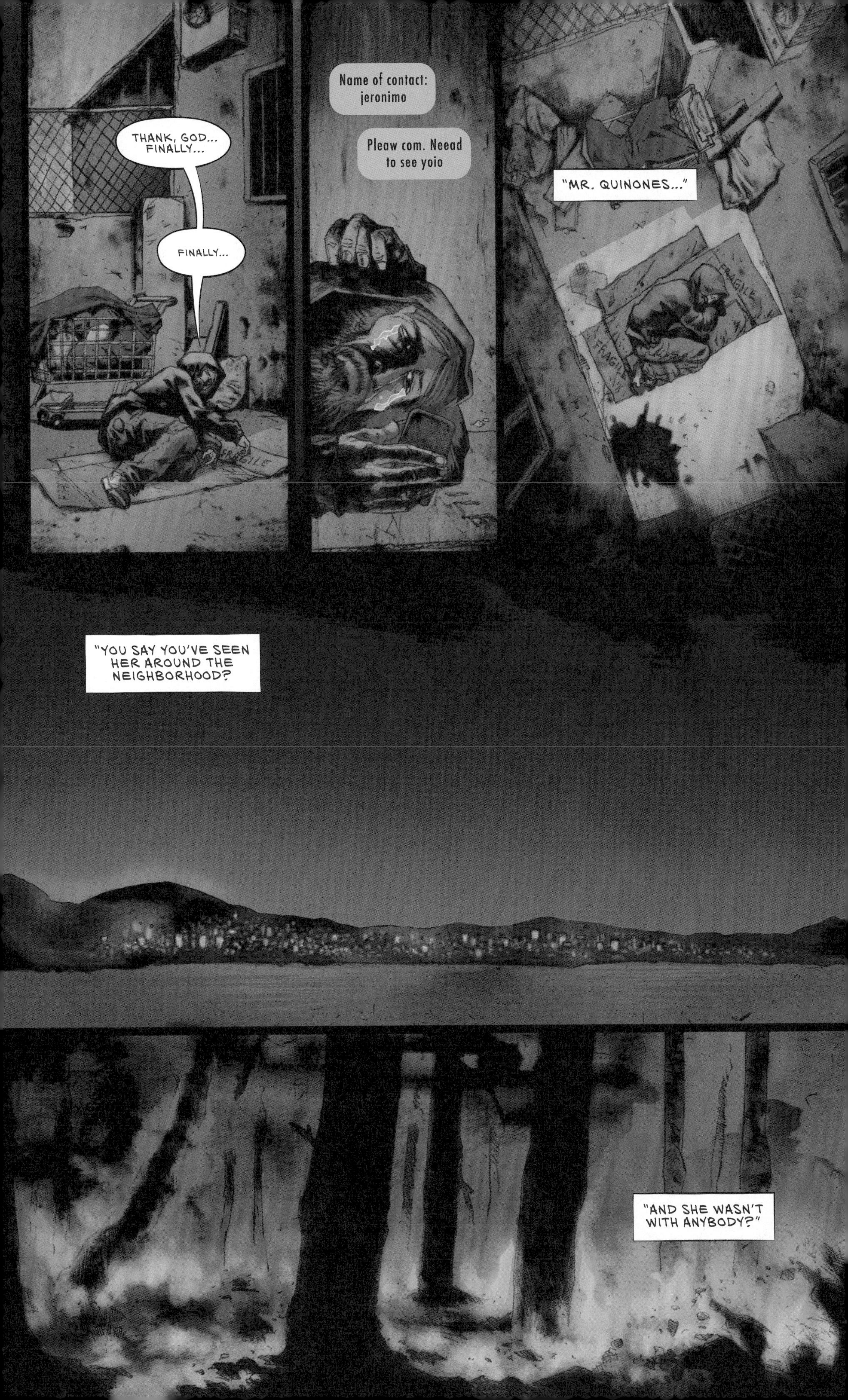
THANK, GOD... FINALLY...
FINALLY...
Name of contact: jeronimo
Pleaw com. Neead to see yoio
"MR. QUINONES..."
FRAGILE
"YOU SAY YOU'VE SEEN HER AROUND THE NEIGHBORHOOD?
"AND SHE WASN'T WITH ANYBODY?"

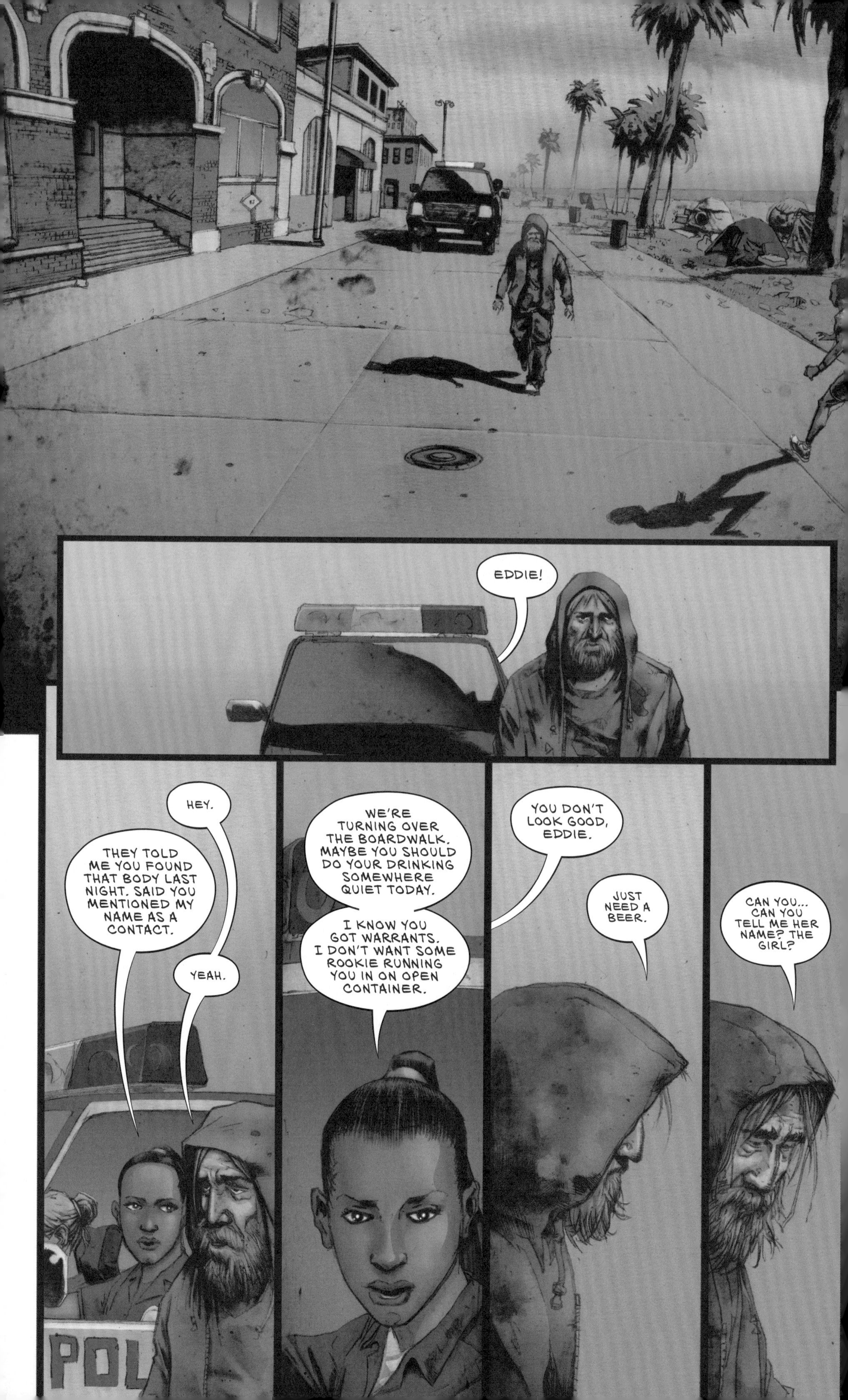
EDDIE!
HEY.
THEY TOLD ME YOU FOUND THAT BODY LAST NIGHT. SAID YOU MENTIONED MY NAME AS A CONTACT.
YEAH.
WE'RE TURNING OVER THE BOARDWALK. MAYBE YOU SHOULD DO YOUR DRINKING SOMEWHERE QUIET TODAY.
I KNOW YOU GOT WARRANTS. I DON'T WANT SOME ROOKIE RUNNING YOU IN ON OPEN CONTAINER.
YOU DON'T LOOK GOOD, EDDIE.
JUST NEED A BEER.
CAN YOU... CAN YOU TELL ME HER NAME? THE GIRL?
POL

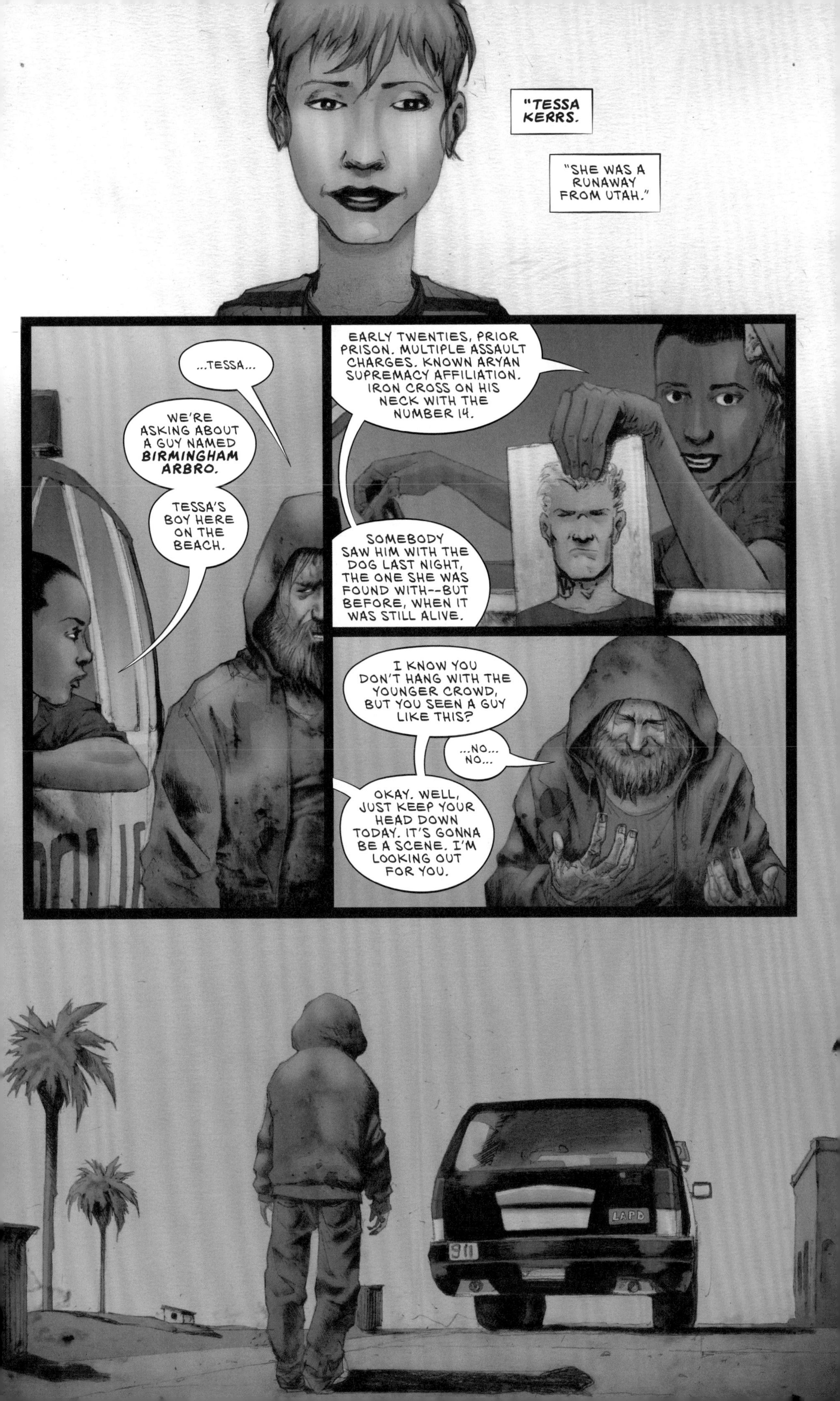
"TESSA KERRS.
"SHE WAS A RUNAWAY FROM UTAH."
...TESSA...
WE'RE ASKING ABOUT A GUY NAMED BIRMINGHAM ARBRO.
TESSA'S BOY HERE ON THE BEACH.
EARLY TWENTIES, PRIOR PRISON. MULTIPLE ASSAULT CHARGES. KNOWN ARYAN SUPREMACY AFFILIATION. IRON CROSS ON HIS NECK WITH THE NUMBER 14.
SOMEBODY SAW HIM WITH THE DOG LAST NIGHT, THE ONE SHE WAS FOUND WITH--BUT BEFORE, WHEN IT WAS STILL ALIVE.
I KNOW YOU DON'T HANG WITH THE YOUNGER CROWD, BUT YOU SEEN A GUY LIKE THIS?
...NO... NO...
OKAY. WELL, JUST KEEP YOUR HEAD DOWN TODAY. IT'S GONNA BE A SCENE. I'M LOOKING OUT FOR YOU.
LAPD
911

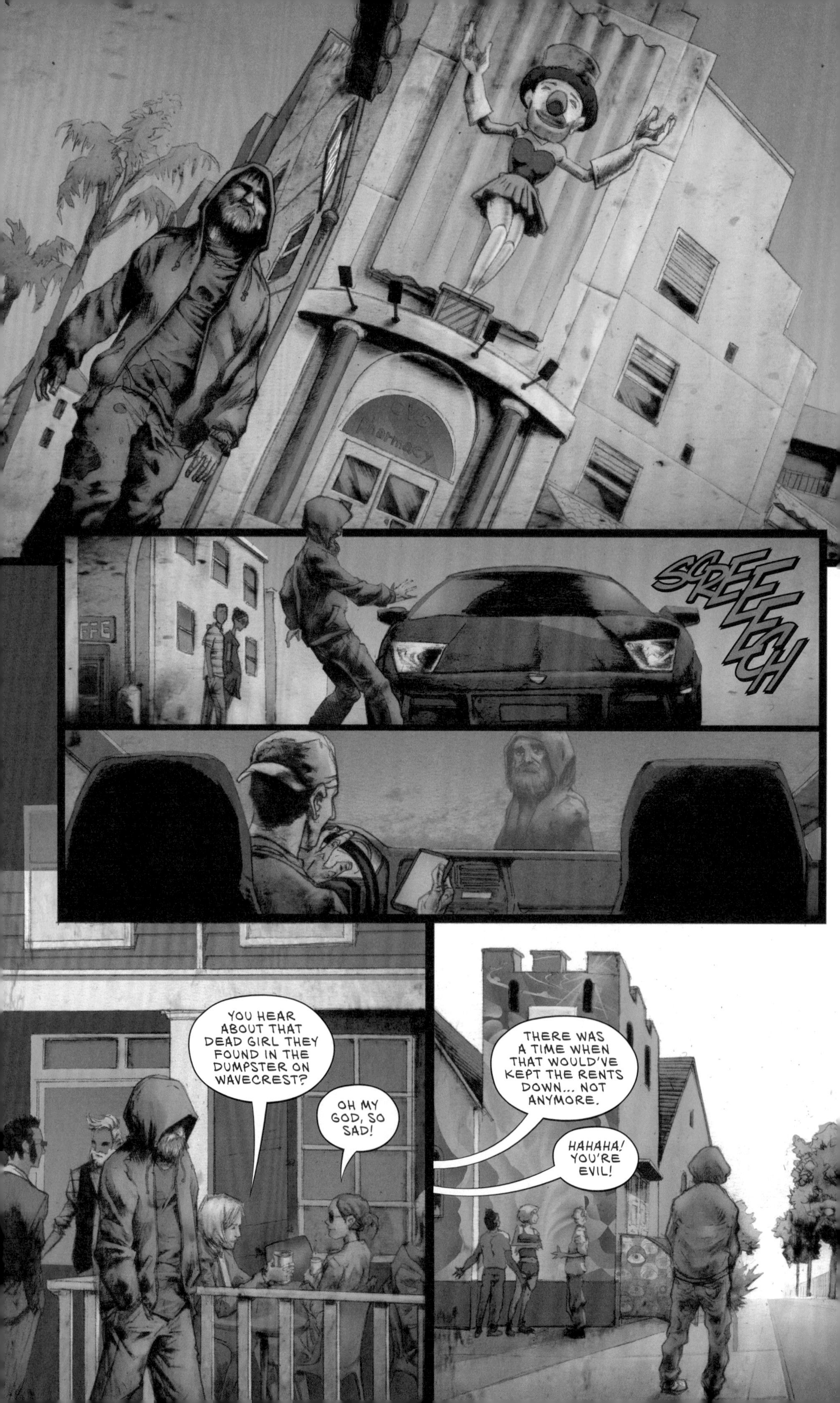

CVS Pharmacy
SCREEEECH
YOU HEAR ABOUT THAT DEAD GIRL THEY FOUND IN THE DUMPSTER ON WAVECREST?
OH MY GOD, SO SAD!
THERE WAS A TIME WHEN THAT WOULD'VE KEPT THE RENTS DOWN... NOT ANYMORE.
HAHAHA! YOU'RE EVIL!

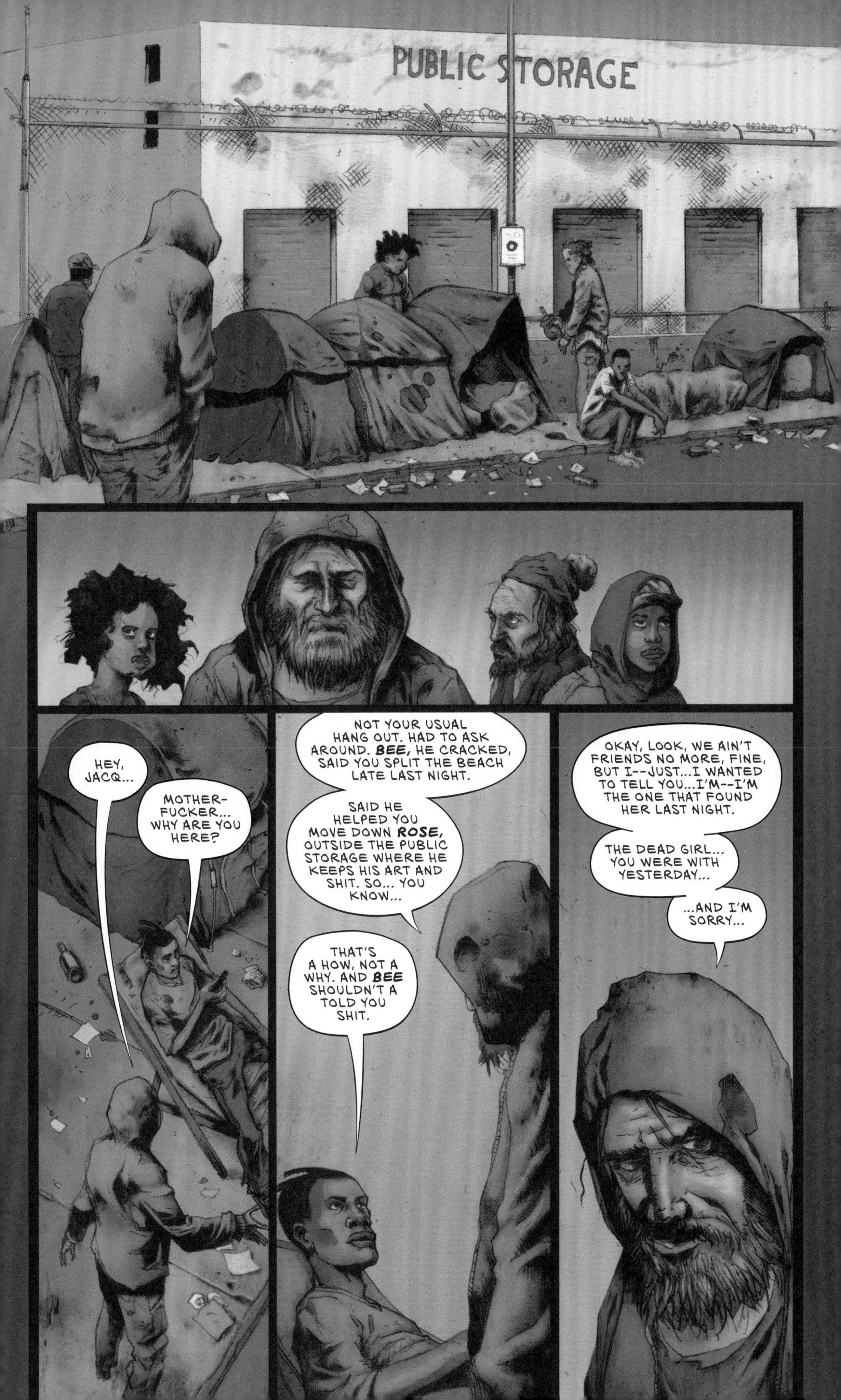
PUBLIC STORAGE
HEY, JACQ...
MOTHER-FUCKER... WHY ARE YOU HERE?
NOT YOUR USUAL HANG OUT. HAD TO ASK AROUND. BEE, HE CRACKED, SAID YOU SPLIT THE BEACH LATE LAST NIGHT.
SAID HE HELPED YOU MOVE DOWN ROSE, OUTSIDE THE PUBLIC STORAGE WHERE HE KEEPS HIS ART AND SHIT. SO... YOU KNOW...
THAT'S A HOW, NOT A WHY. AND BEE SHOULDN'T A TOLD YOU SHIT.
OKAY, LOOK, WE AIN'T FRIENDS NO MORE, FINE, BUT I--JUST...I WANTED TO TELL YOU...I'M--I'M THE ONE THAT FOUND HER LAST NIGHT.
THE DEAD GIRL... YOU WERE WITH YESTERDAY...
...AND I'M SORRY...

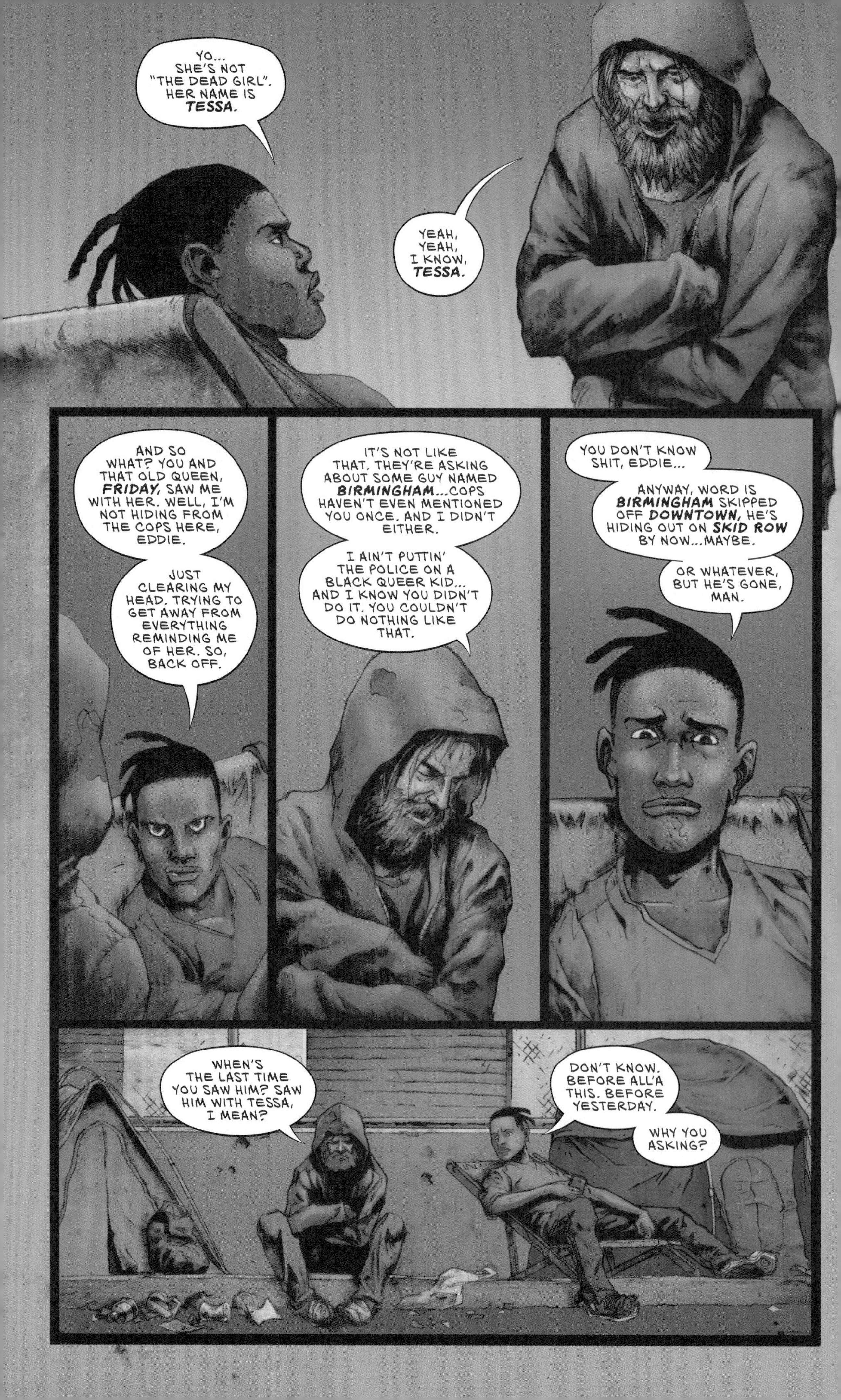

YO... SHE'S NOT "THE DEAD GIRL". HER NAME IS TESSA.
YEAH, YEAH, I KNOW, TESSA.
AND SO WHAT? YOU AND THAT OLD QUEEN, FRIDAY, SAW ME WITH HER. WELL, I'M NOT HIDING FROM THE COPS HERE, EDDIE.
JUST CLEARING MY HEAD. TRYING TO GET AWAY FROM EVERYTHING REMINDING ME OF HER. SO, BACK OFF.
IT'S NOT LIKE THAT. THEY'RE ASKING ABOUT SOME GUY NAMED BIRMINGHAM...COPS HAVEN'T EVEN MENTIONED YOU ONCE. AND I DIDN'T EITHER.
I AIN'T PUTTIN' THE POLICE ON A BLACK QUEER KID... AND I KNOW YOU DIDN'T DO IT. YOU COULDN'T DO NOTHING LIKE THAT.
YOU DON'T KNOW SHIT, EDDIE...
ANYWAY, WORD IS BIRMINGHAM SKIPPED OFF DOWNTOWN, HE'S HIDING OUT ON SKID ROW BY NOW...MAYBE.
OR WHATEVER, BUT HE'S GONE, MAN.
WHEN'S THE LAST TIME YOU SAW HIM? SAW HIM WITH TESSA, I MEAN?
DON'T KNOW. BEFORE ALL'A THIS. BEFORE YESTERDAY.
WHY YOU ASKING?

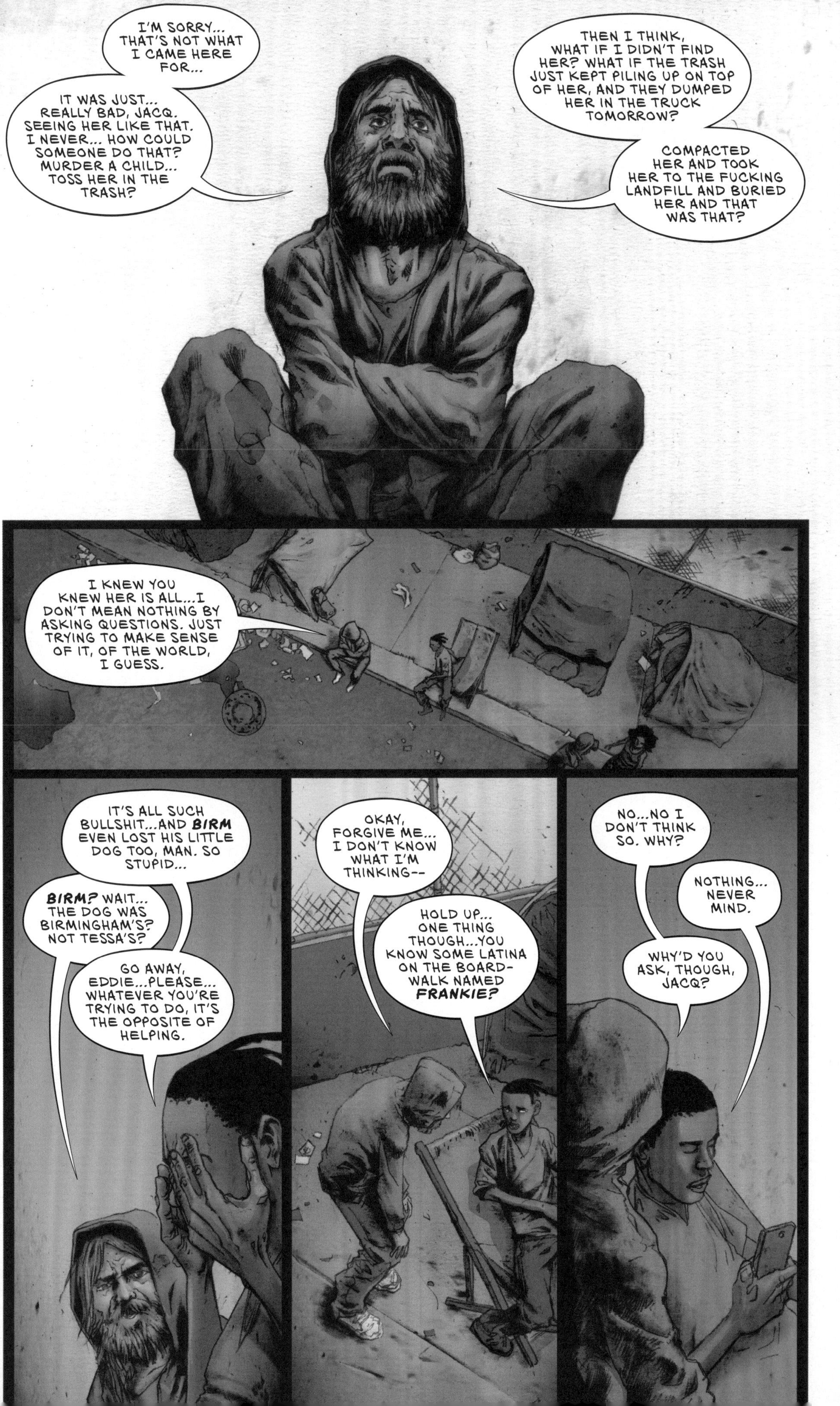
I'M SORRY... THAT'S NOT WHAT I CAME HERE FOR...
IT WAS JUST... REALLY BAD, JACQ. SEEING HER LIKE THAT. I NEVER... HOW COULD SOMEONE DO THAT? MURDER A CHILD... TOSS HER IN THE TRASH?
THEN I THINK, WHAT IF I DIDN'T FIND HER? WHAT IF THE TRASH JUST KEPT PILING UP ON TOP OF HER, AND THEY DUMPED HER IN THE TRUCK TOMORROW?
COMPACTED HER AND TOOK HER TO THE FUCKING LANDFILL AND BURIED HER AND THAT WAS THAT?
I KNEW YOU KNEW HER IS ALL...I DON'T MEAN NOTHING BY ASKING QUESTIONS. JUST TRYING TO MAKE SENSE OF IT, OF THE WORLD, I GUESS.
IT'S ALL SUCH BULLSHIT...AND **BIRM** EVEN LOST HIS LITTLE DOG TOO, MAN. SO STUPID...
BIRM? WAIT... THE DOG WAS BIRMINGHAM'S? NOT TESSA'S?
GO AWAY, EDDIE...PLEASE... WHATEVER YOU'RE TRYING TO DO, IT'S THE OPPOSITE OF HELPING.
OKAY, FORGIVE ME... I DON'T KNOW WHAT I'M THINKING--
HOLD UP... ONE THING THOUGH...YOU KNOW SOME LATINA ON THE BOARD-WALK NAMED **FRANKIE?**
NO...NO I DON'T THINK SO. WHY?
NOTHING... NEVER MIND.
WHY'D YOU ASK, THOUGH, JACQ?

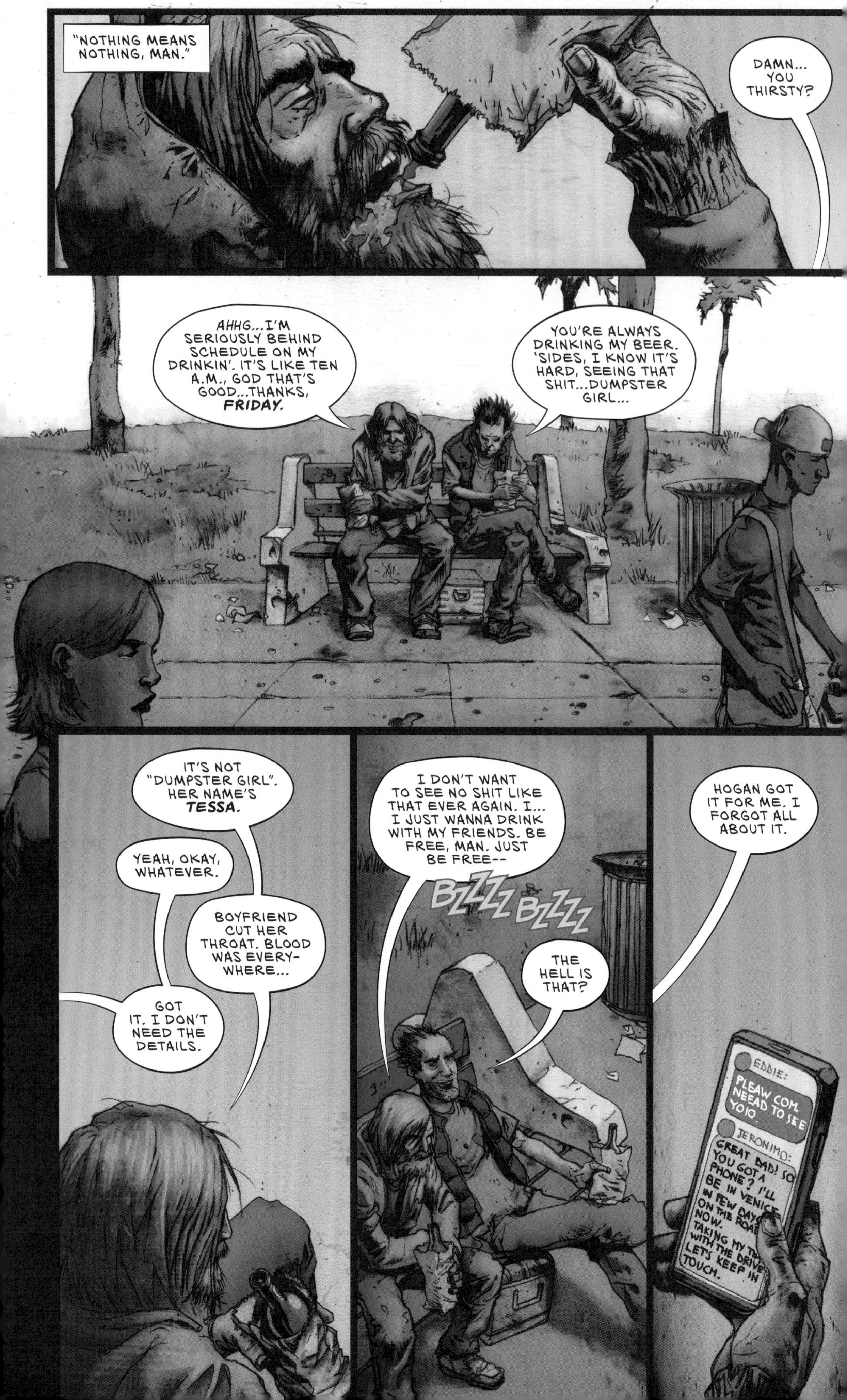
"NOTHING MEANS NOTHING, MAN."
DAMN... YOU THIRSTY?
AHHG...I'M SERIOUSLY BEHIND SCHEDULE ON MY DRINKIN'. IT'S LIKE TEN A.M., GOD THAT'S GOOD...THANKS, FRIDAY.
YOU'RE ALWAYS DRINKING MY BEER. 'SIDES, I KNOW IT'S HARD, SEEING THAT SHIT...DUMPSTER GIRL...
IT'S NOT "DUMPSTER GIRL". HER NAME'S TESSA.
YEAH, OKAY, WHATEVER.
BOYFRIEND CUT HER THROAT. BLOOD WAS EVERY-WHERE...
GOT IT. I DON'T NEED THE DETAILS.
I DON'T WANT TO SEE NO SHIT LIKE THAT EVER AGAIN. I... I JUST WANNA DRINK WITH MY FRIENDS. BE FREE, MAN. JUST BE FREE--
BZZZZ BZZZZ
THE HELL IS THAT?
HOGAN GOT IT FOR ME. I FORGOT ALL ABOUT IT.
EDDIE:
PLEAW COM. NEEAD TO SEE YOIO.
JERONIMO:
GREAT DAD! SO YOU GOT A PHONE? I'LL BE IN VENICE IN FEW DAYS ON THE ROAD NOW.
TAKING MY TI WITH THE DRIVE LET'S KEEP IN TOUCH.

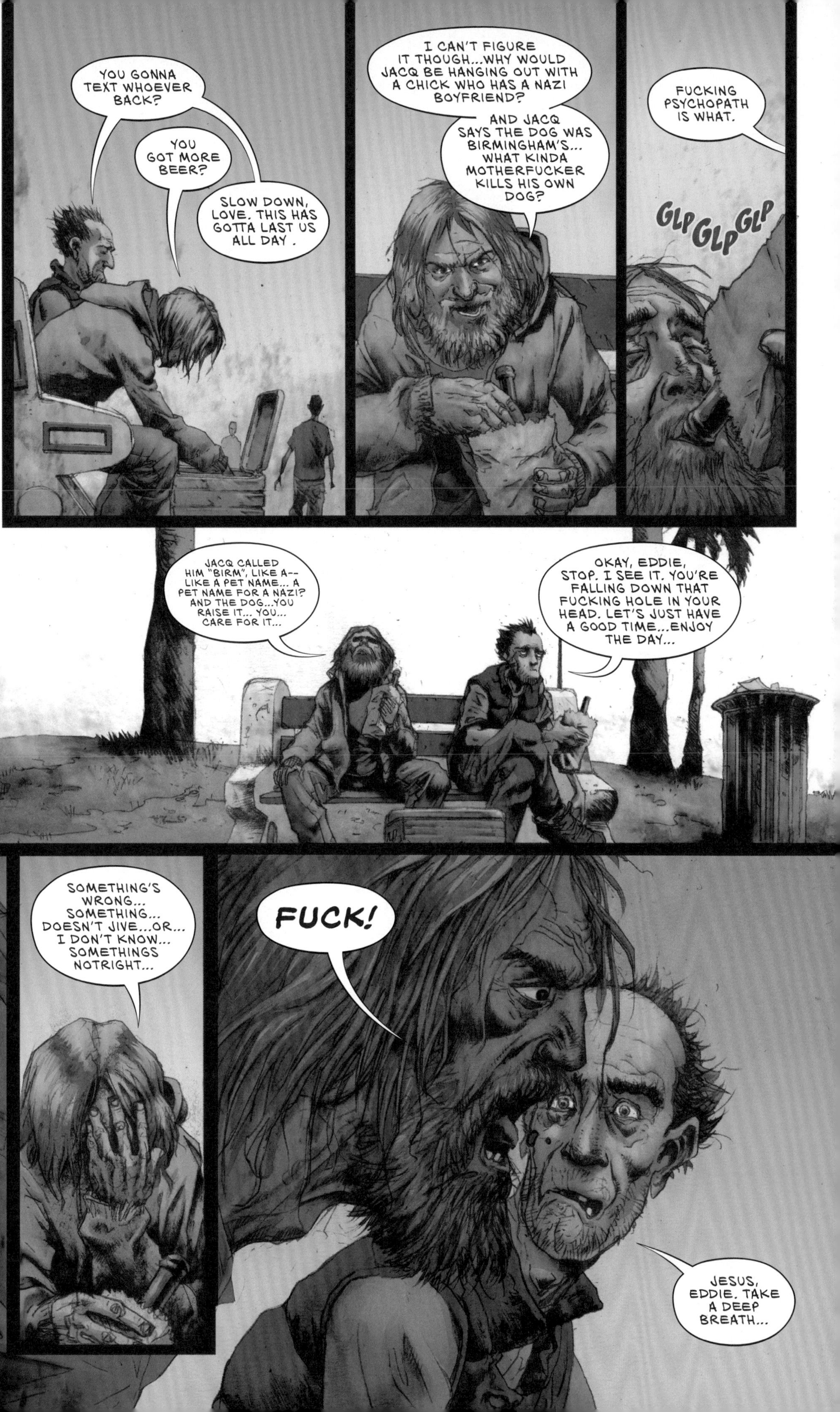
YOU GONNA TEXT WHOEVER BACK?
YOU GOT MORE BEER?
SLOW DOWN, LOVE. THIS HAS GOTTA LAST US ALL DAY .
I CAN'T FIGURE IT THOUGH...WHY WOULD JACQ BE HANGING OUT WITH A CHICK WHO HAS A NAZI BOYFRIEND?
AND JACQ SAYS THE DOG WAS BIRMINGHAM'S... WHAT KINDA MOTHERFUCKER KILLS HIS OWN DOG?
FUCKING PSYCHOPATH IS WHAT.
GLP GLP GLP
JACQ CALLED HIM "BIRM", LIKE A-- LIKE A PET NAME... A PET NAME FOR A NAZI? AND THE DOG...YOU RAISE IT... YOU... CARE FOR IT...
OKAY, EDDIE, STOP. I SEE IT. YOU'RE FALLING DOWN THAT FUCKING HOLE IN YOUR HEAD. LET'S JUST HAVE A GOOD TIME...ENJOY THE DAY...
SOMETHING'S WRONG... SOMETHING... DOESN'T JIVE...OR... I DON'T KNOW... SOMETHINGS NOTRIGHT...
FUCK!
JESUS, EDDIE. TAKE A DEEP BREATH...

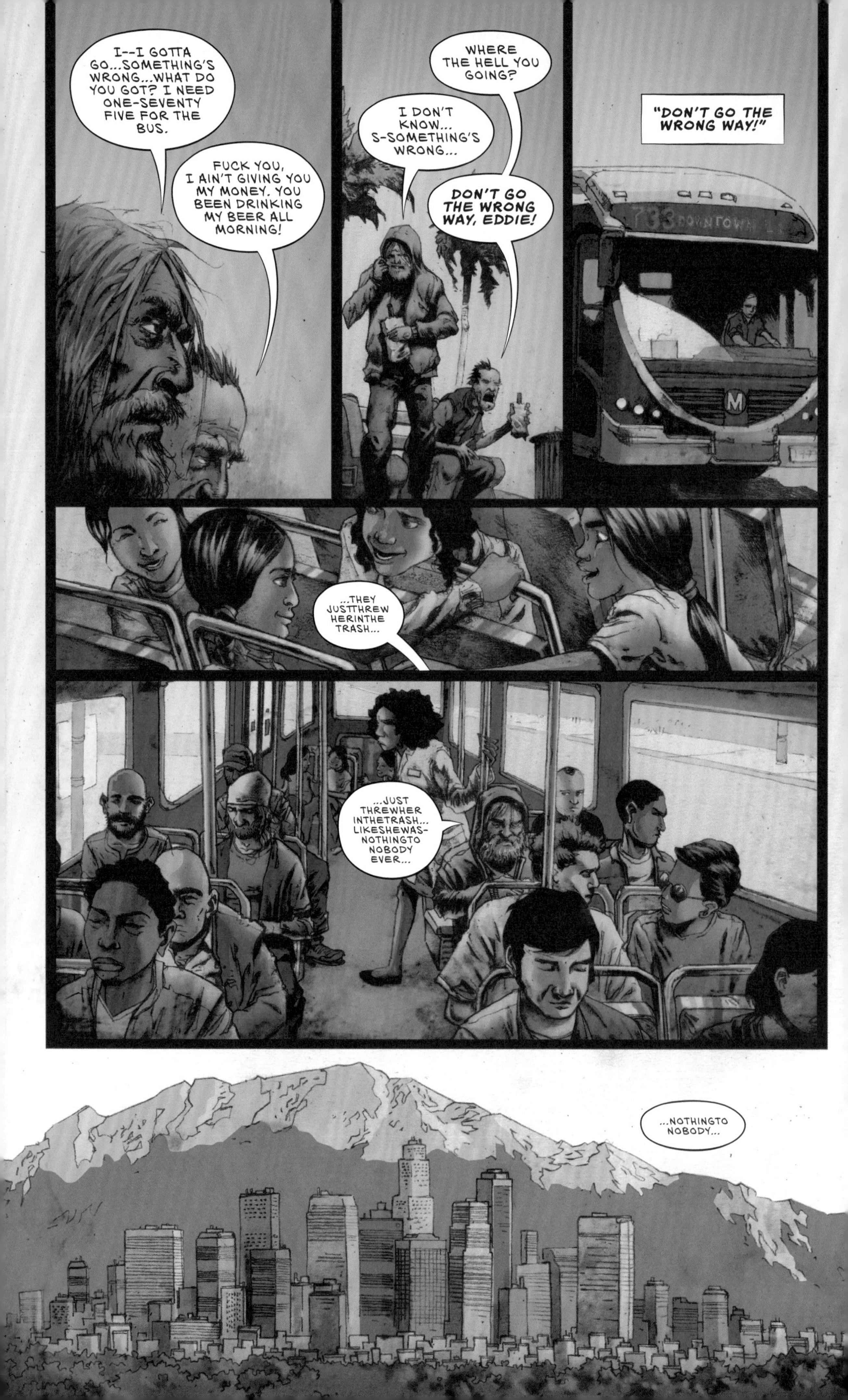
I--I GOTTA GO...SOMETHING'S WRONG...WHAT DO YOU GOT? I NEED ONE-SEVENTY FIVE FOR THE BUS.
FUCK YOU, I AIN'T GIVING YOU MY MONEY. YOU BEEN DRINKING MY BEER ALL MORNING!
WHERE THE HELL YOU GOING?
I DON'T KNOW... S-SOMETHING'S WRONG...
DON'T GO THE WRONG WAY, EDDIE!
"DON'T GO THE WRONG WAY!"
...THEY JUSTTHREW HERINTHE TRASH...
...JUST THREWHER INTHETRASH... LIKESHEWAS-NOTHINGTO NOBODY EVER...
...NOTHINGTO NOBODY...

CHAPTER 2

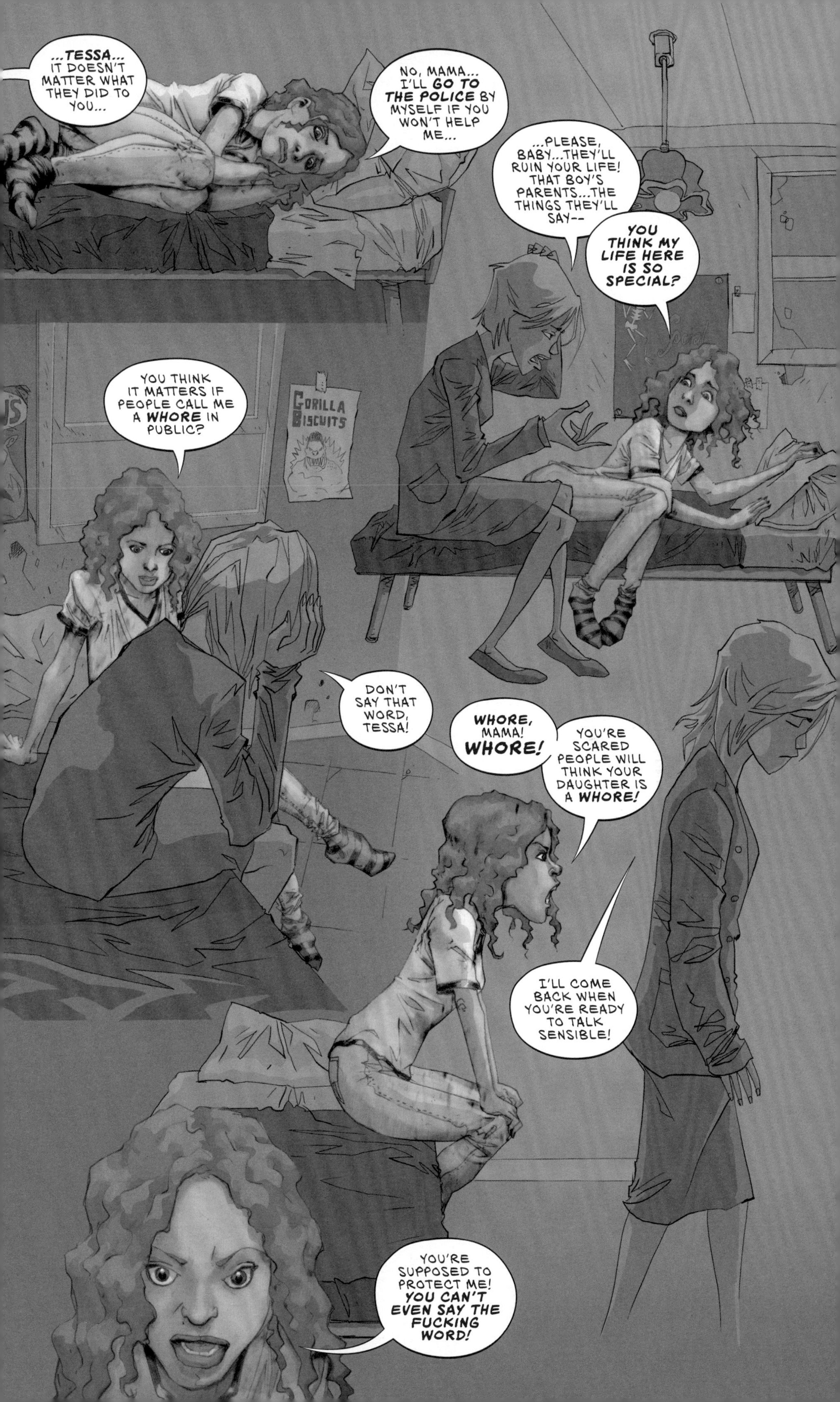

...TESSA... IT DOESN'T MATTER WHAT THEY DID TO YOU...
NO, MAMA... I'LL GO TO THE POLICE BY MYSELF IF YOU WON'T HELP ME...
...PLEASE, BABY...THEY'LL RUIN YOUR LIFE! THAT BOY'S PARENTS...THE THINGS THEY'LL SAY--
YOU THINK MY LIFE HERE IS SO SPECIAL?
GORILLA BISCUITS
YOU THINK IT MATTERS IF PEOPLE CALL ME A WHORE IN PUBLIC?
DON'T SAY THAT WORD, TESSA!
WHORE, MAMA! WHORE!
YOU'RE SCARED PEOPLE WILL THINK YOUR DAUGHTER IS A WHORE!
I'LL COME BACK WHEN YOU'RE READY TO TALK SENSIBLE!
YOU'RE SUPPOSED TO PROTECT ME! YOU CAN'T EVEN SAY THE FUCKING WORD!

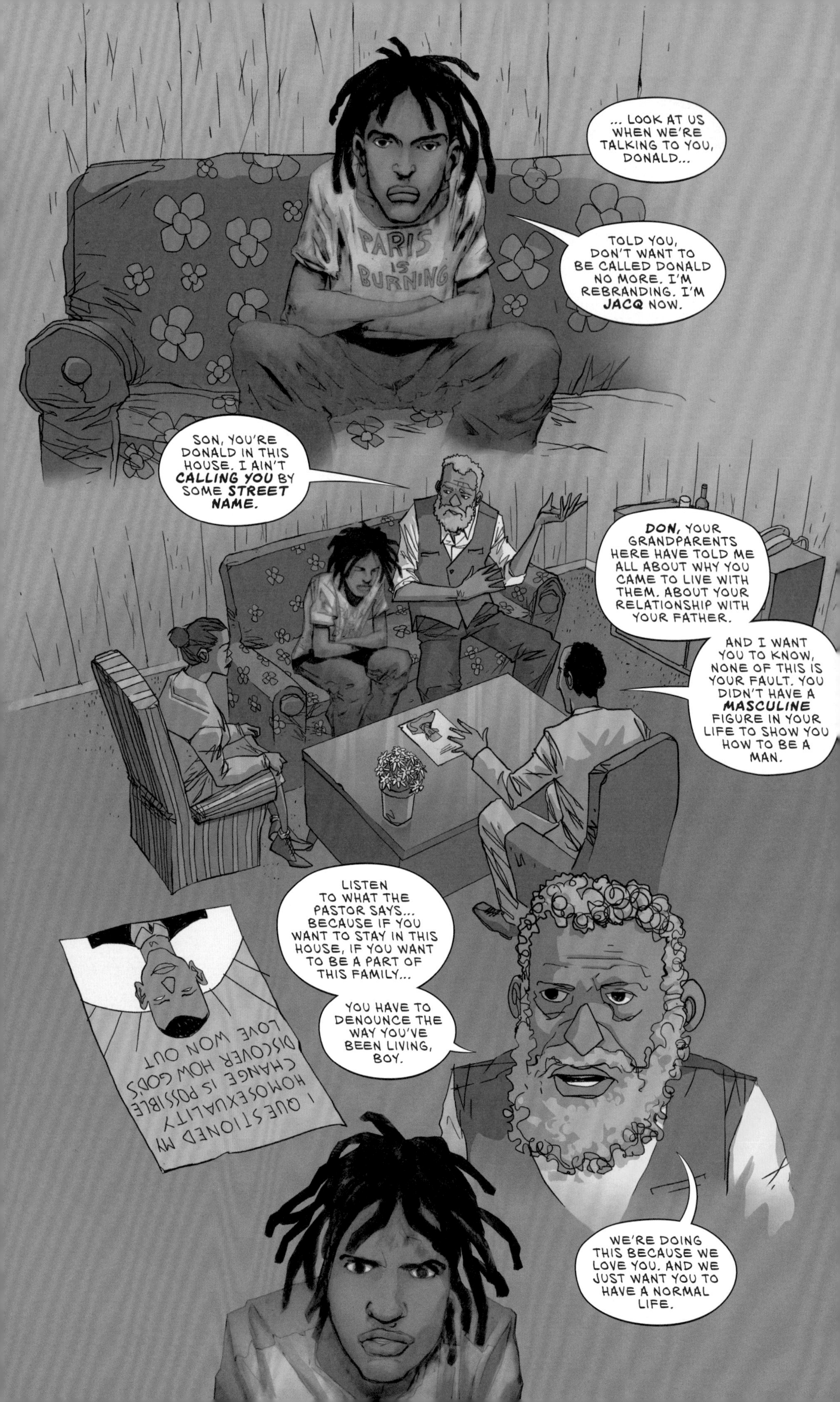

... LOOK AT US WHEN WE'RE TALKING TO YOU, DONALD...
PARIS IS BURNING
TOLD YOU, DON'T WANT TO BE CALLED DONALD NO MORE. I'M REBRANDING. I'M **JACQ** NOW.
SON, YOU'RE DONALD IN THIS HOUSE. I AIN'T ***CALLING YOU*** BY SOME ***STREET NAME.***
DON, YOUR GRANDPARENTS HERE HAVE TOLD ME ALL ABOUT WHY YOU CAME TO LIVE WITH THEM. ABOUT YOUR RELATIONSHIP WITH YOUR FATHER.
AND I WANT YOU TO KNOW, NONE OF THIS IS YOUR FAULT. YOU DIDN'T HAVE A ***MASCULINE*** FIGURE IN YOUR LIFE TO SHOW YOU HOW TO BE A MAN.
LISTEN TO WHAT THE PASTOR SAYS... BECAUSE IF YOU WANT TO STAY IN THIS HOUSE, IF YOU WANT TO BE A PART OF THIS FAMILY...
YOU HAVE TO DENOUNCE THE WAY YOU'VE BEEN LIVING, BOY.
I QUESTIONED MY HOMOSEXUALITY
CHANGE IS POSSIBLE
DISCOVER HOW GOD'S LOVE WON OUT
WE'RE DOING THIS BECAUSE WE LOVE YOU. AND WE JUST WANT YOU TO HAVE A NORMAL LIFE.

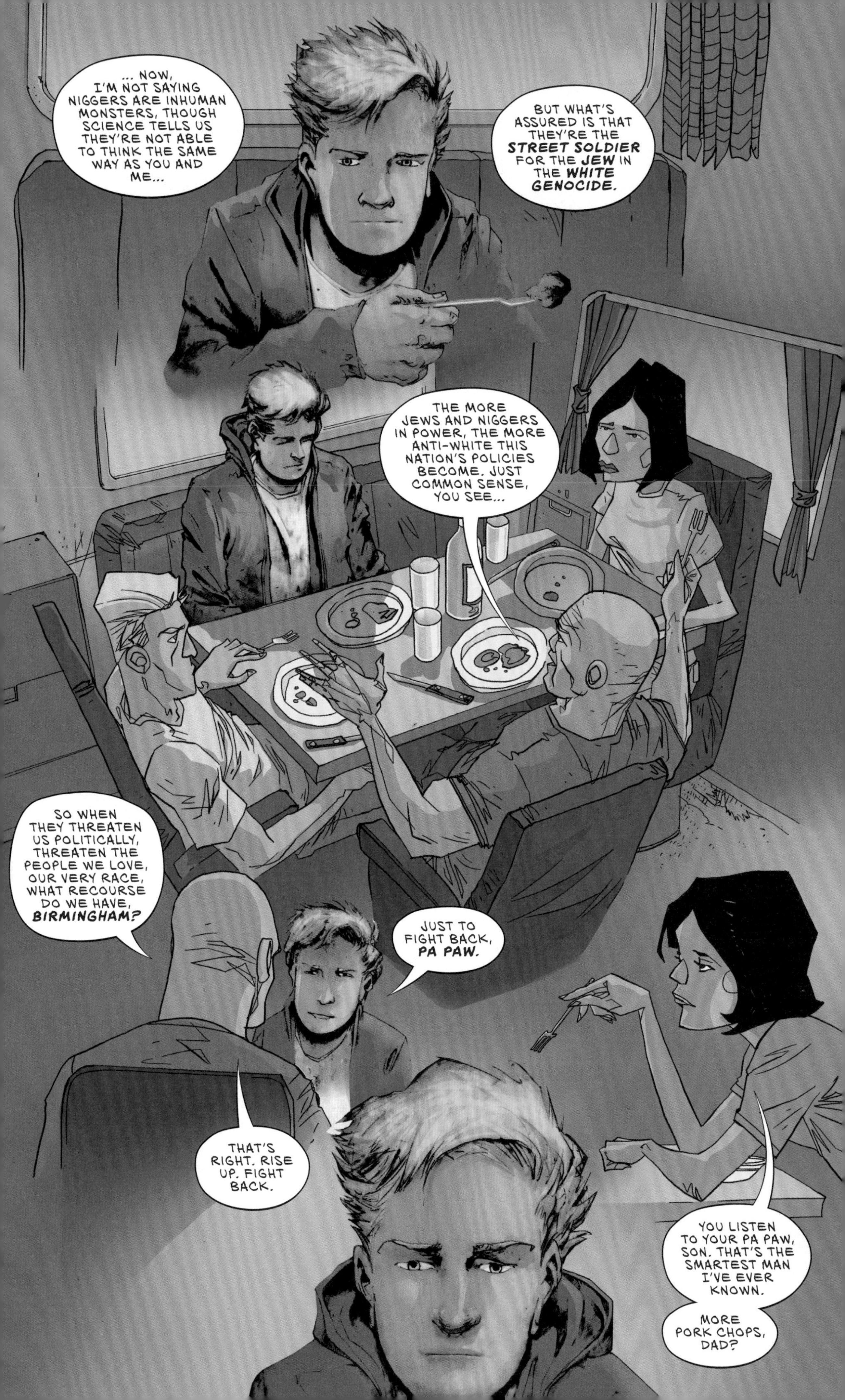
... NOW, I'M NOT SAYING NIGGERS ARE INHUMAN MONSTERS, THOUGH SCIENCE TELLS US THEY'RE NOT ABLE TO THINK THE SAME WAY AS YOU AND ME...
BUT WHAT'S ASSURED IS THAT THEY'RE THE **STREET SOLDIER** FOR THE **JEW** IN THE **WHITE GENOCIDE.**
THE MORE JEWS AND NIGGERS IN POWER, THE MORE ANTI-WHITE THIS NATION'S POLICIES BECOME. JUST COMMON SENSE, YOU SEE...
SO WHEN THEY THREATEN US POLITICALLY, THREATEN THE PEOPLE WE LOVE, OUR VERY RACE, WHAT RECOURSE DO WE HAVE, **BIRMINGHAM?**
JUST TO FIGHT BACK, **PA PAW.**
THAT'S RIGHT. RISE UP. FIGHT BACK.
YOU LISTEN TO YOUR PA PAW, SON. THAT'S THE SMARTEST MAN I'VE EVER KNOWN.
MORE PORK CHOPS, DAD?

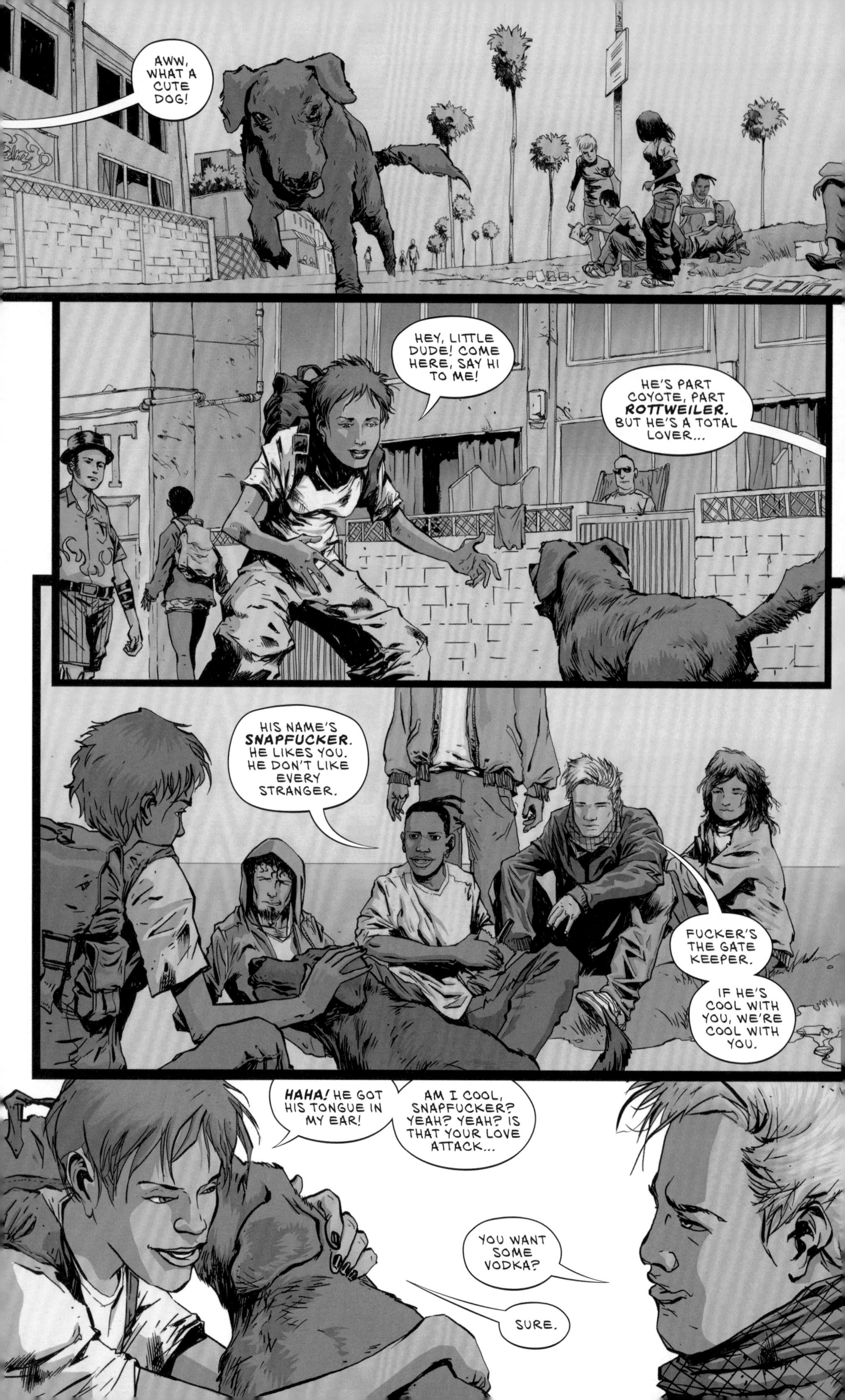
AWW, WHAT A CUTE DOG!
HEY, LITTLE DUDE! COME HERE, SAY HI TO ME!
HE'S PART COYOTE, PART **ROTTWEILER.** BUT HE'S A TOTAL LOVER...
HIS NAME'S ***SNAPFUCKER.*** HE LIKES YOU. HE DON'T LIKE EVERY STRANGER.
FUCKER'S THE GATE KEEPER.
IF HE'S COOL WITH YOU, WE'RE COOL WITH YOU.
HAHA! HE GOT HIS TONGUE IN MY EAR!
AM I COOL, SNAPFUCKER? YEAH? YEAH? IS THAT YOUR LOVE ATTACK...
YOU WANT SOME VODKA?
SURE.

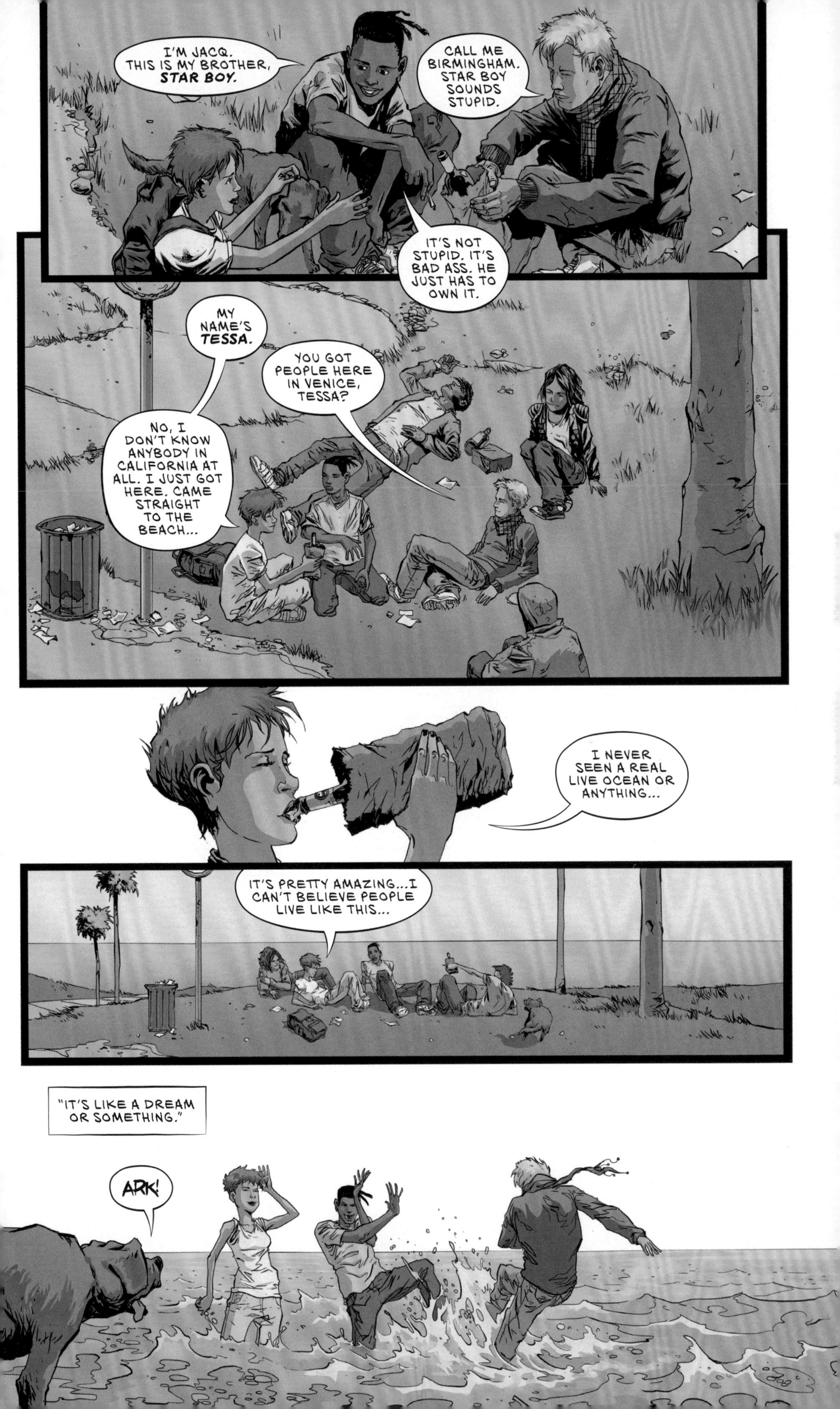

I'M JACQ. THIS IS MY BROTHER, STAR BOY.
CALL ME BIRMINGHAM. STAR BOY SOUNDS STUPID.
IT'S NOT STUPID. IT'S BAD ASS. HE JUST HAS TO OWN IT.
MY NAME'S TESSA.
YOU GOT PEOPLE HERE IN VENICE, TESSA?
NO, I DON'T KNOW ANYBODY IN CALIFORNIA AT ALL. I JUST GOT HERE. CAME STRAIGHT TO THE BEACH...
I NEVER SEEN A REAL LIVE OCEAN OR ANYTHING...
IT'S PRETTY AMAZING...I CAN'T BELIEVE PEOPLE LIVE LIKE THIS...
"IT'S LIKE A DREAM OR SOMETHING."
ARK!

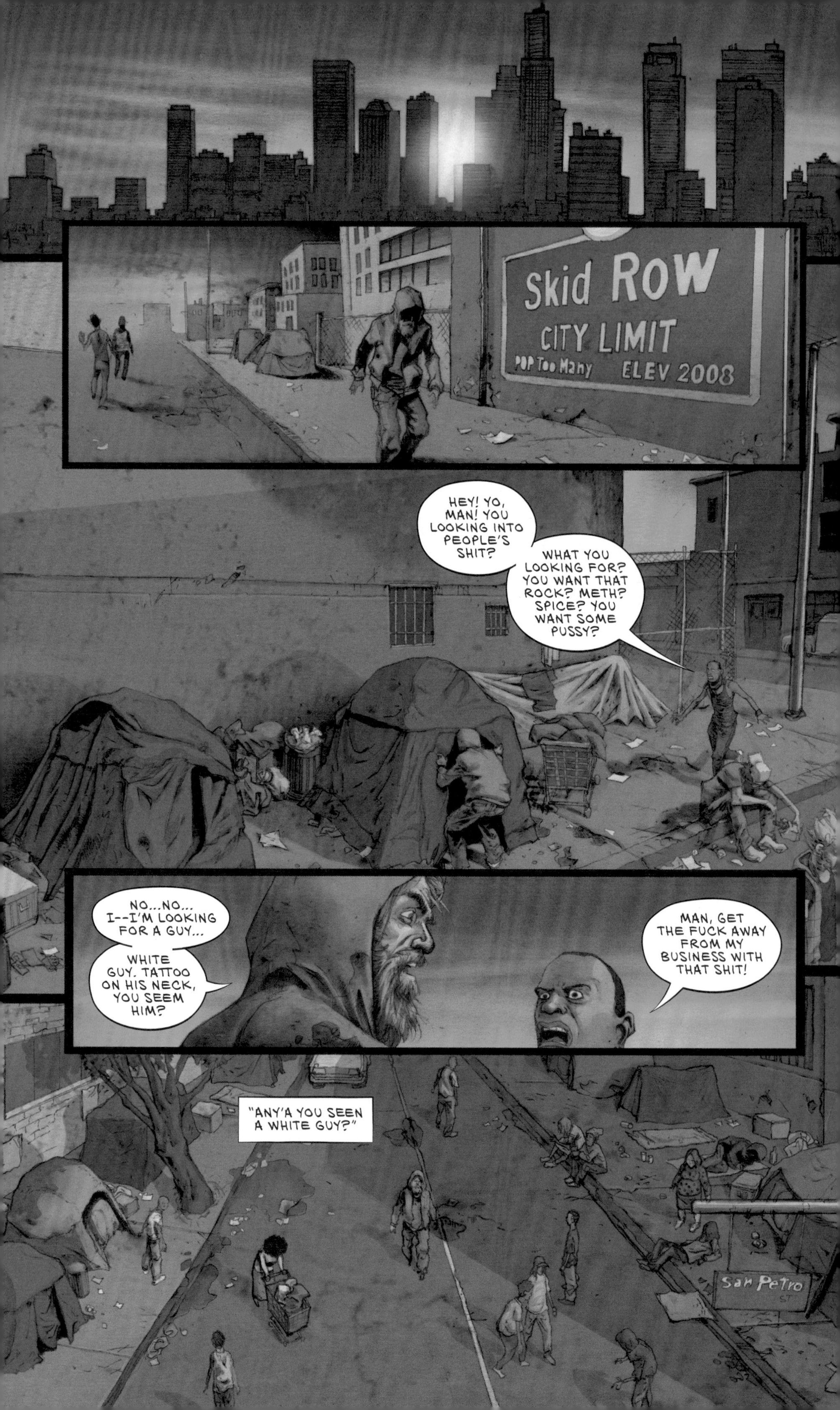
Skid ROW
CITY LIMIT
POP Too Many
ELEV 2008
HEY! YO, MAN! YOU LOOKING INTO PEOPLE'S SHIT?
WHAT YOU LOOKING FOR? YOU WANT THAT ROCK? METH? SPICE? YOU WANT SOME PUSSY?
NO...NO... I--I'M LOOKING FOR A GUY...
WHITE GUY. TATTOO ON HIS NECK, YOU SEEM HIM?
MAN, GET THE FUCK AWAY FROM MY BUSINESS WITH THAT SHIT!
"ANY'A YOU SEEN A WHITE GUY?"
San Petro ST

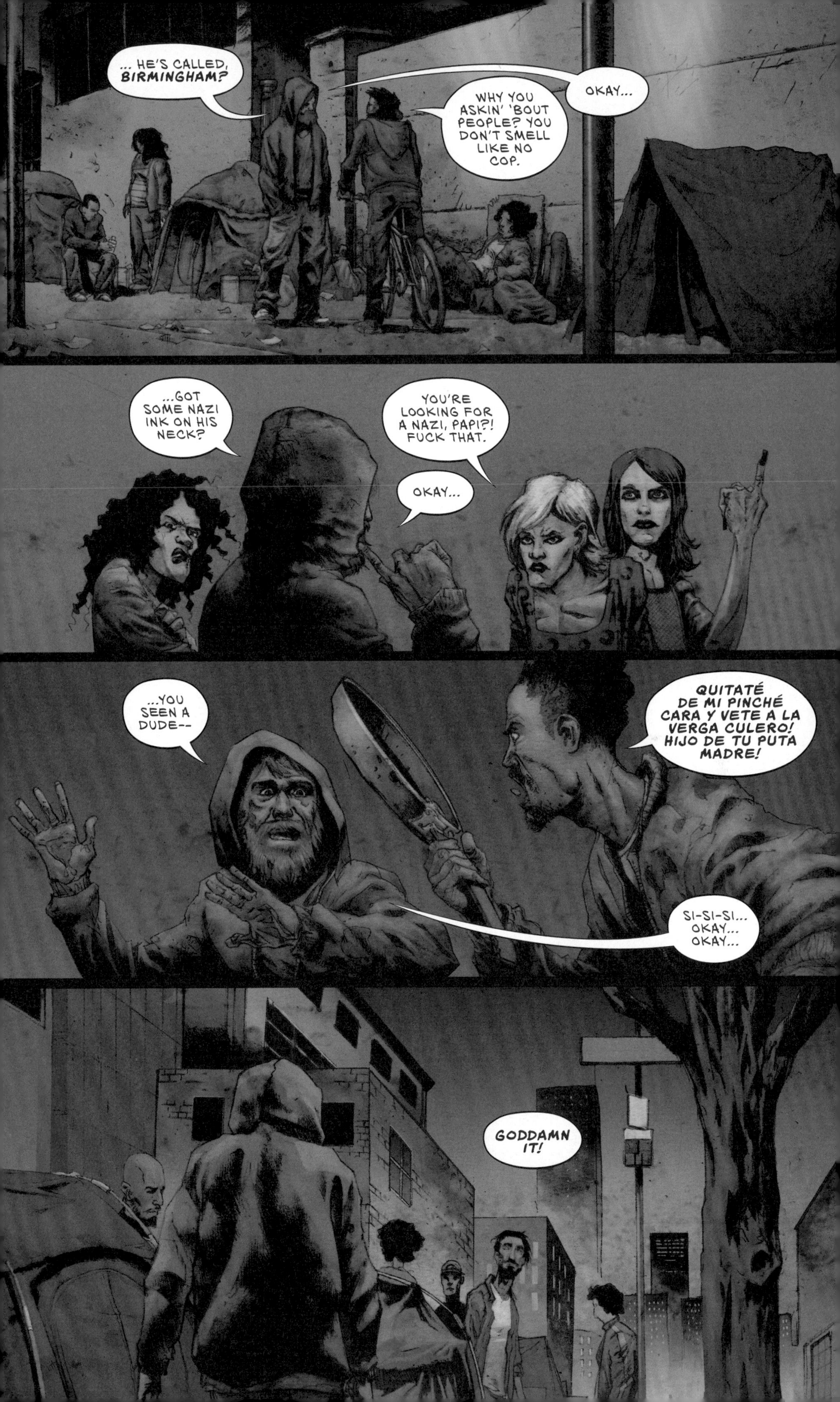
... HE'S CALLED, BIRMINGHAM?
OKAY...
WHY YOU ASKIN' 'BOUT PEOPLE? YOU DON'T SMELL LIKE NO COP.
...GOT SOME NAZI INK ON HIS NECK?
YOU'RE LOOKING FOR A NAZI, PAPI?! FUCK THAT.
OKAY...
...YOU SEEN A DUDE--
QUITATÉ DE MI PINCHÉ CARA Y VETE A LA VERGA CULERO! HIJO DE TU PUTA MADRE!
SI-SI-SI... OKAY... OKAY...
GODDAMN IT!

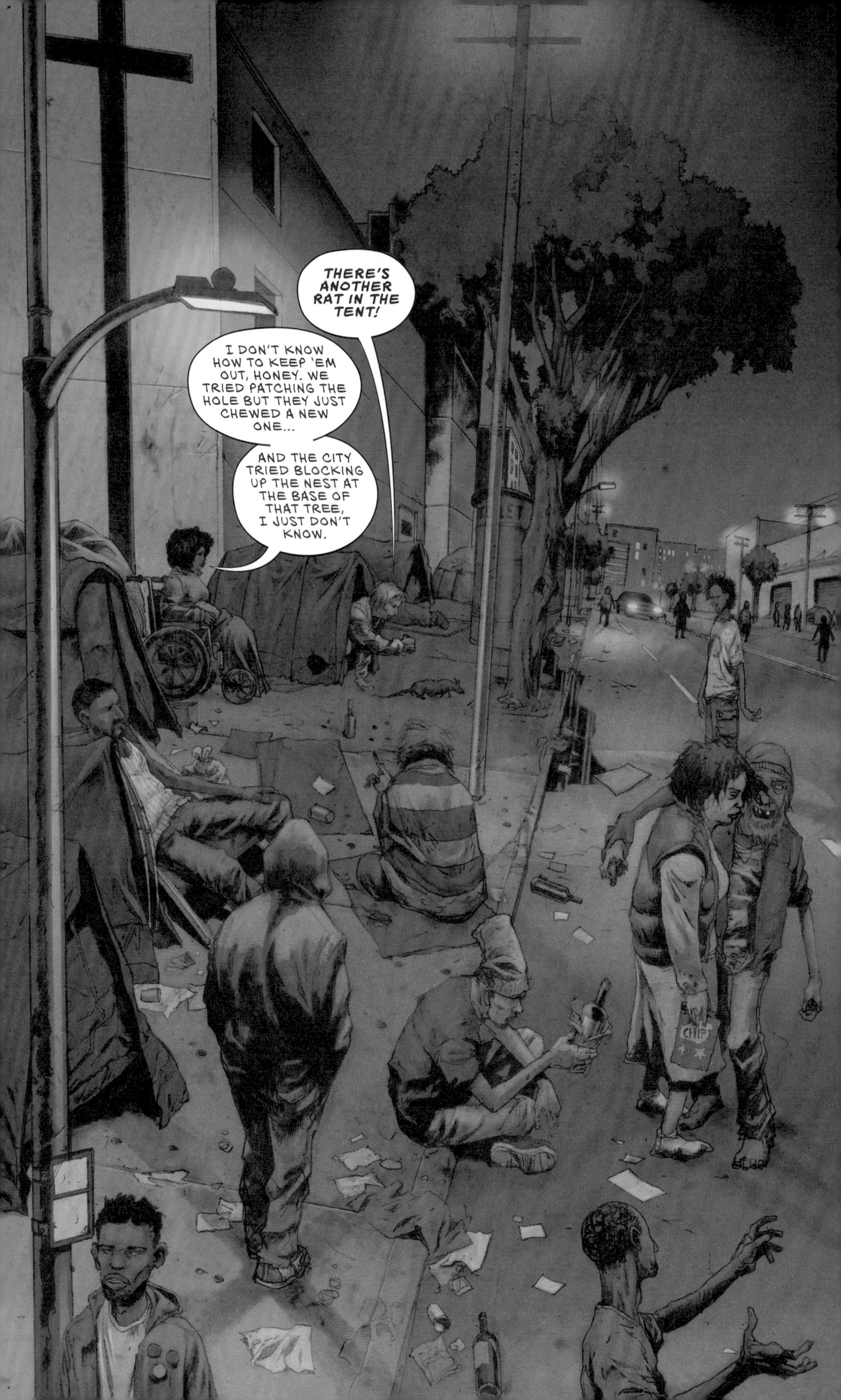
THERE'S ANOTHER RAT IN THE TENT!
I DON'T KNOW HOW TO KEEP 'EM OUT, HONEY. WE TRIED PATCHING THE HOLE BUT THEY JUST CHEWED A NEW ONE...
AND THE CITY TRIED BLOCKING UP THE NEST AT THE BASE OF THAT TREE, I JUST DON'T KNOW.
CHIPS

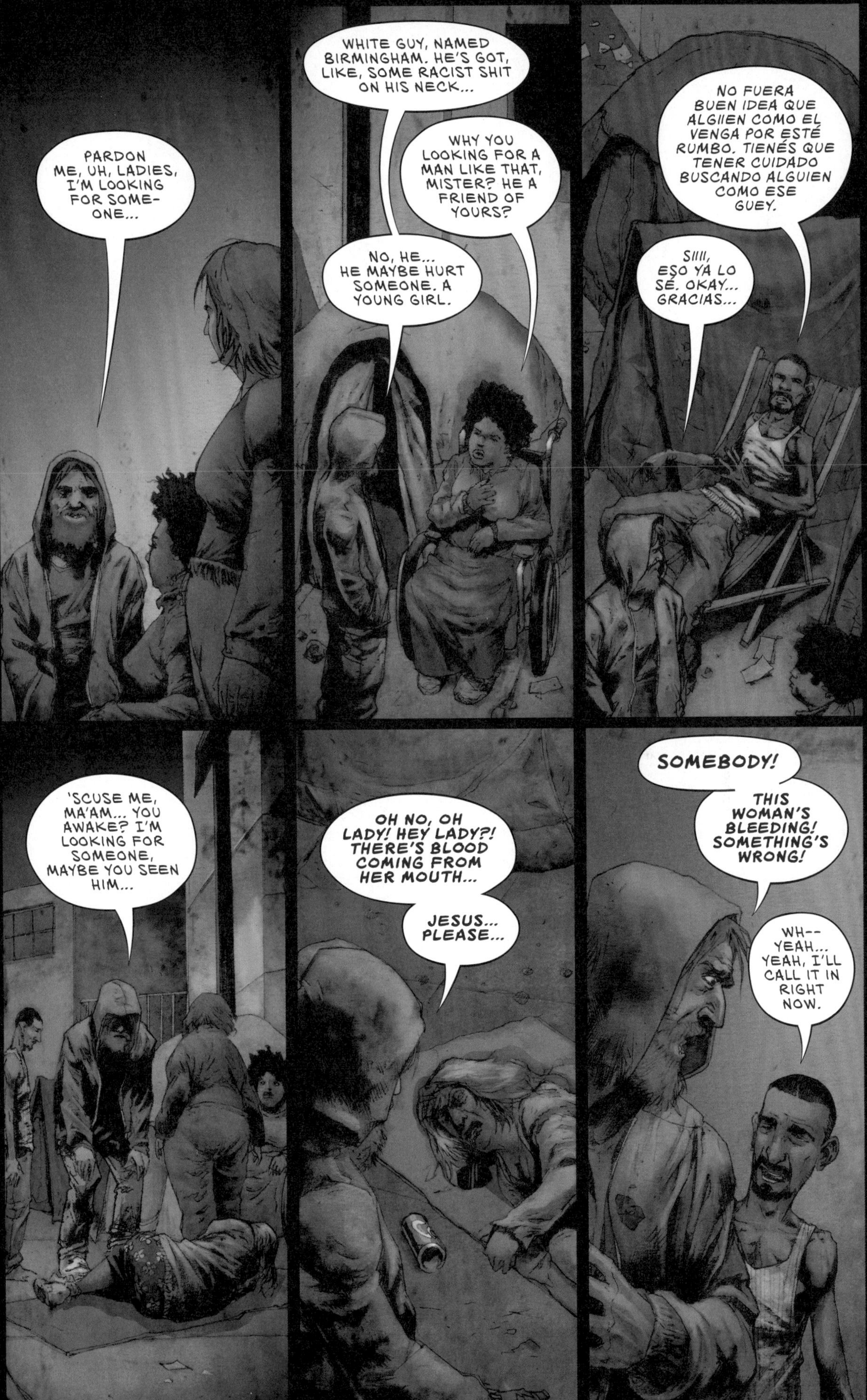
PARDON ME, UH, LADIES, I'M LOOKING FOR SOME-ONE...
WHITE GUY, NAMED BIRMINGHAM. HE'S GOT, LIKE, SOME RACIST SHIT ON HIS NECK...
WHY YOU LOOKING FOR A MAN LIKE THAT, MISTER? HE A FRIEND OF YOURS?
NO, HE... HE MAYBE HURT SOMEONE. A YOUNG GIRL.
NO FUERA BUEN IDEA QUE ALGIIEN COMO EL VENGA POR ESTÉ RUMBO. TIENÉS QUE TENER CUIDADO BUSCANDO ALGUIEN COMO ESE GUEY.
SIIII, ESO YA LO SÉ. OKAY... GRACIAS...
'SCUSE ME, MA'AM... YOU AWAKE? I'M LOOKING FOR SOMEONE, MAYBE YOU SEEN HIM...
OH NO, OH LADY! HEY LADY?! THERE'S BLOOD COMING FROM HER MOUTH...
JESUS... PLEASE...
SOMEBODY!
THIS WOMAN'S BLEEDING! SOMETHING'S WRONG!
WH-- YEAH... YEAH, I'LL CALL IT IN RIGHT NOW.

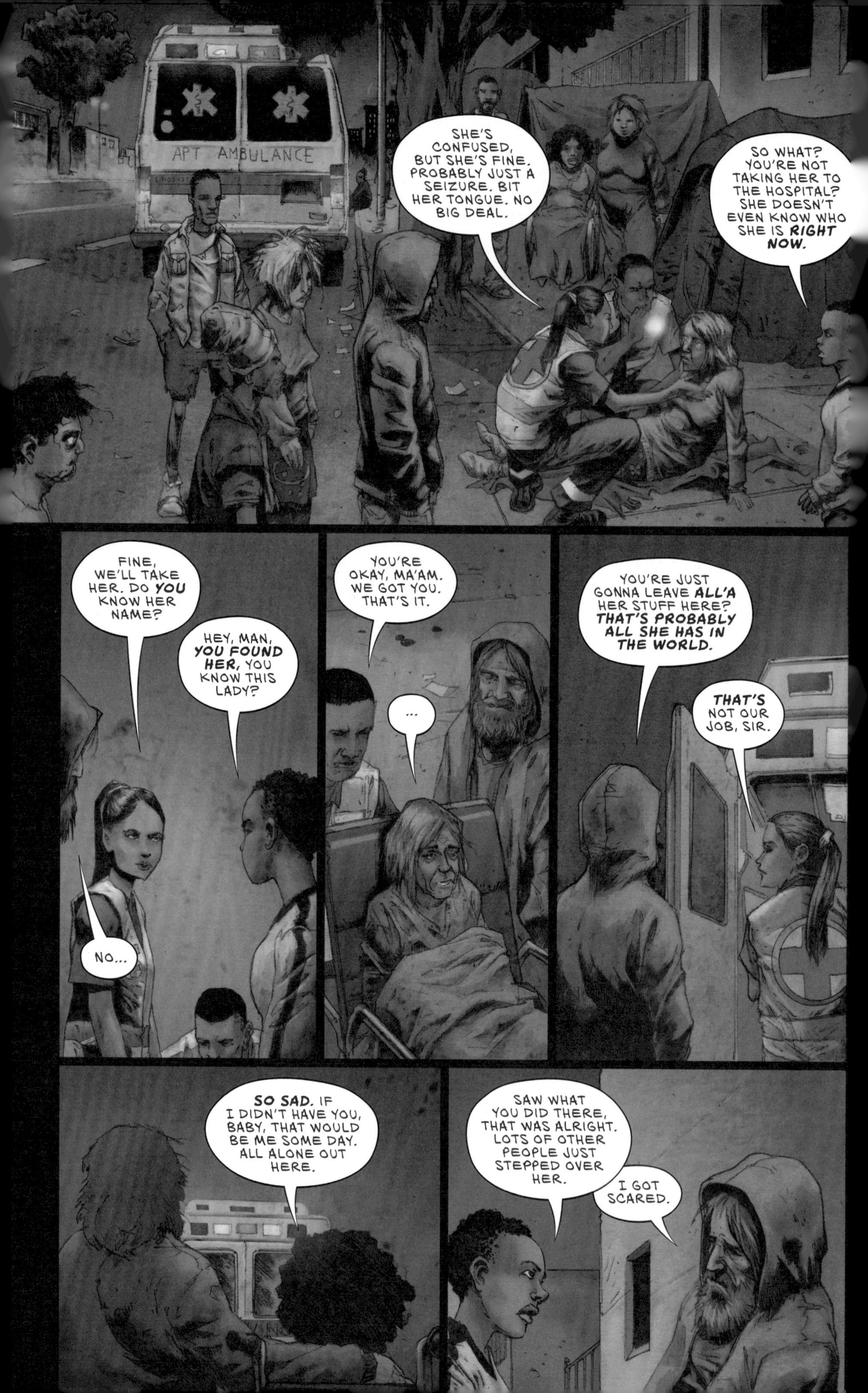
APT AMBULANCE
SHE'S CONFUSED, BUT SHE'S FINE. PROBABLY JUST A SEIZURE. BIT HER TONGUE. NO BIG DEAL.
SO WHAT? YOU'RE NOT TAKING HER TO THE HOSPITAL? SHE DOESN'T EVEN KNOW WHO SHE IS **RIGHT NOW.**
FINE, WE'LL TAKE HER. DO **YOU** KNOW HER NAME?
HEY, MAN, **YOU FOUND HER,** YOU KNOW THIS LADY?
NO...
YOU'RE OKAY, MA'AM. WE GOT YOU. THAT'S IT.
...
YOU'RE JUST GONNA LEAVE **ALL'A** HER STUFF HERE? **THAT'S PROBABLY ALL SHE HAS IN THE WORLD.**
THAT'S NOT OUR JOB, SIR.
SO SAD. IF I DIDN'T HAVE YOU, BABY, THAT WOULD BE ME SOME DAY. ALL ALONE OUT HERE.
SAW WHAT YOU DID THERE, THAT WAS ALRIGHT. LOTS OF OTHER PEOPLE JUST STEPPED OVER HER.
I GOT SCARED.

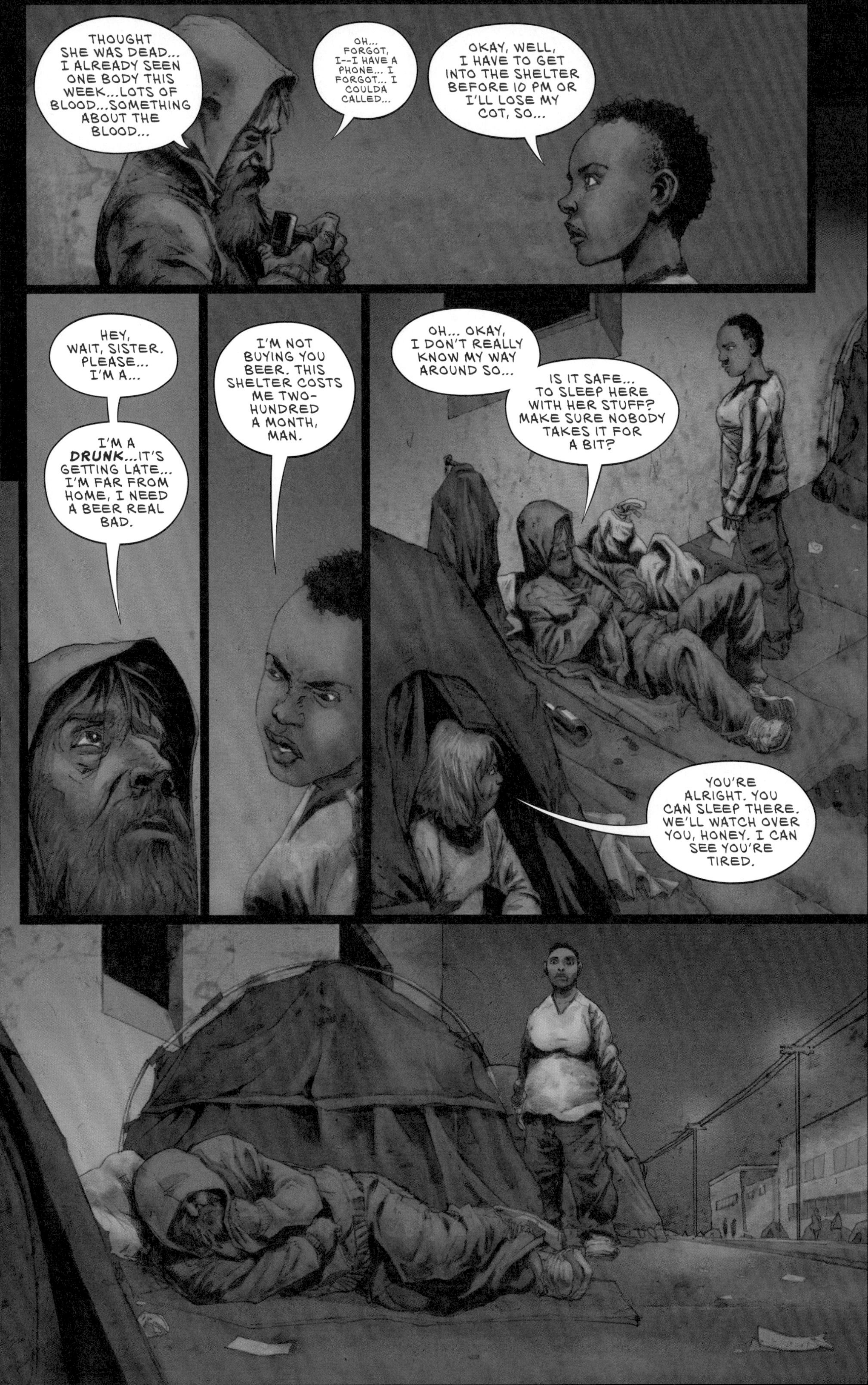
THOUGHT SHE WAS DEAD... I ALREADY SEEN ONE BODY THIS WEEK...LOTS OF BLOOD...SOMETHING ABOUT THE BLOOD...
OH... FORGOT, I--I HAVE A PHONE... I FORGOT... I COULDA CALLED...
OKAY, WELL, I HAVE TO GET INTO THE SHELTER BEFORE 10 PM OR I'LL LOSE MY COT, SO...
HEY, WAIT, SISTER. PLEASE... I'M A...
I'M A DRUNK...IT'S GETTING LATE... I'M FAR FROM HOME, I NEED A BEER REAL BAD.
I'M NOT BUYING YOU BEER. THIS SHELTER COSTS ME TWO-HUNDRED A MONTH, MAN.
OH... OKAY, I DON'T REALLY KNOW MY WAY AROUND SO...
IS IT SAFE... TO SLEEP HERE WITH HER STUFF? MAKE SURE NOBODY TAKES IT FOR A BIT?
YOU'RE ALRIGHT. YOU CAN SLEEP THERE. WE'LL WATCH OVER YOU, HONEY. I CAN SEE YOU'RE TIRED.

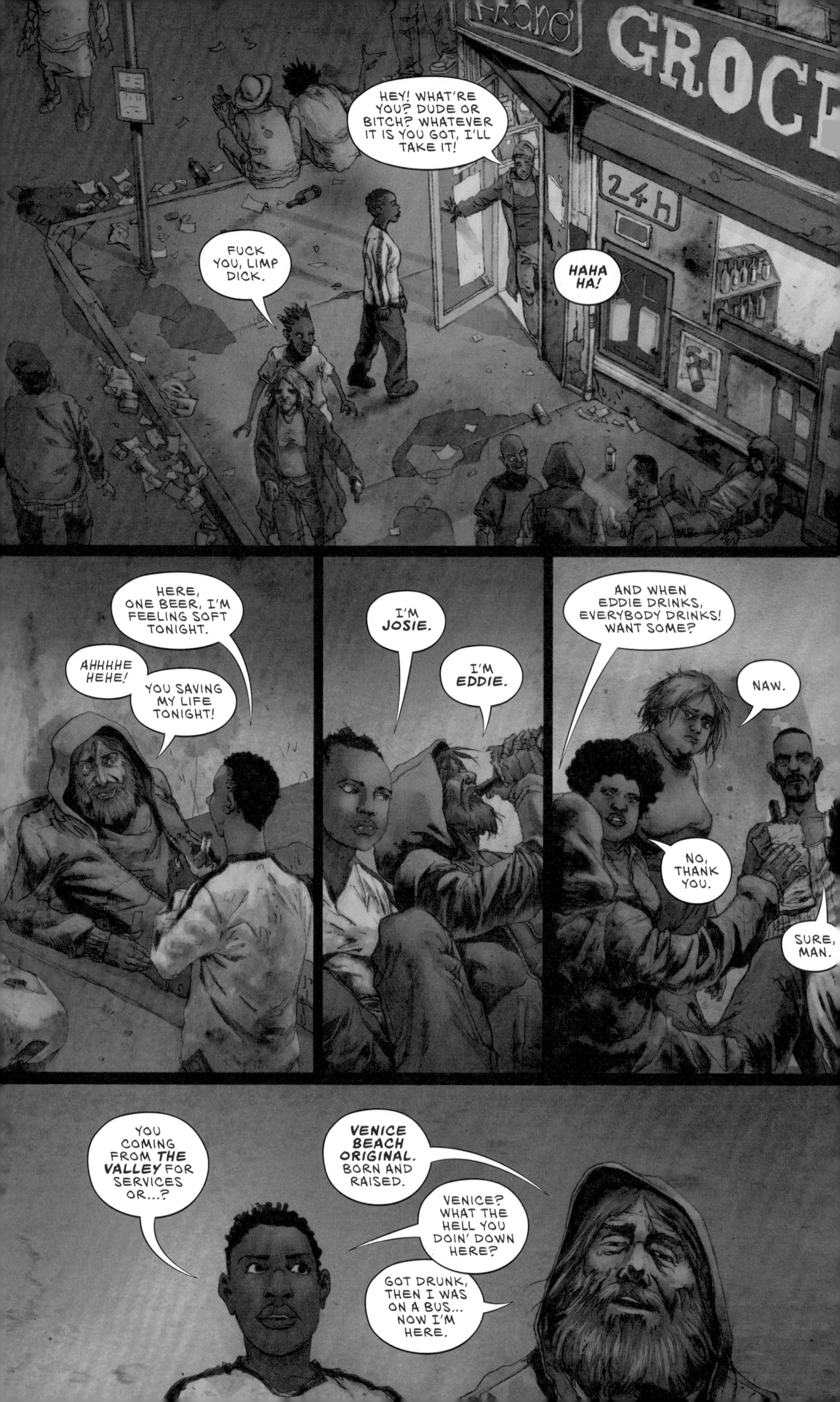
GROCE
24h
HEY! WHAT'RE YOU? DUDE OR BITCH? WHATEVER IT IS YOU GOT, I'LL TAKE IT!
FUCK YOU, LIMP DICK.
HAHA HA!
HERE, ONE BEER, I'M FEELING SOFT TONIGHT.
AHHHHE HEHE!
YOU SAVING MY LIFE TONIGHT!
I'M JOSIE.
I'M EDDIE.
AND WHEN EDDIE DRINKS, EVERYBODY DRINKS! WANT SOME?
NAW.
NO, THANK YOU.
SURE, MAN.
YOU COMING FROM THE VALLEY FOR SERVICES OR...?
VENICE BEACH ORIGINAL. BORN AND RAISED.
VENICE? WHAT THE HELL YOU DOIN' DOWN HERE?
GOT DRUNK, THEN I WAS ON A BUS... NOW I'M HERE.

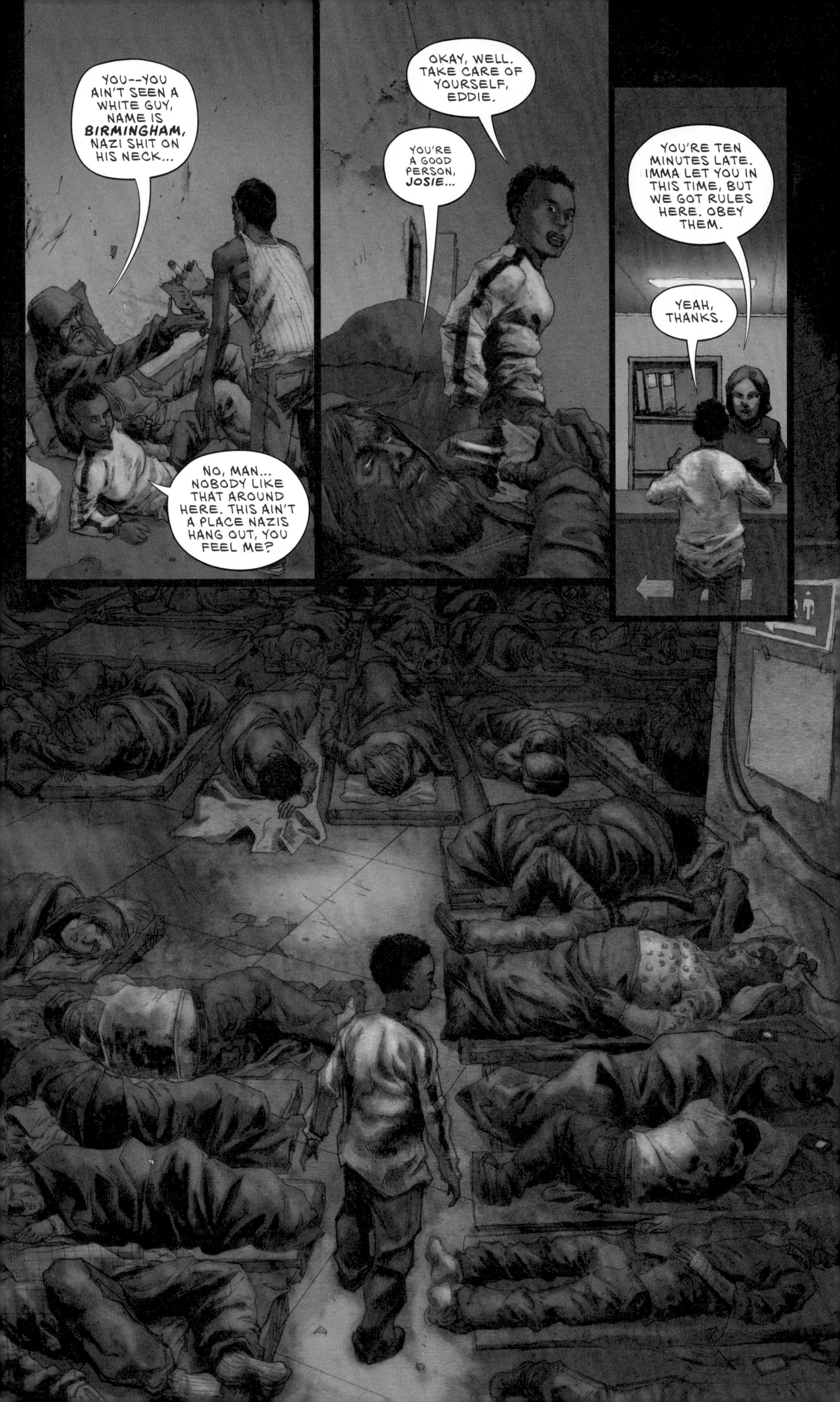

YOU--YOU AIN'T SEEN A WHITE GUY, NAME IS BIRMINGHAM, NAZI SHIT ON HIS NECK...
NO, MAN... NOBODY LIKE THAT AROUND HERE. THIS AIN'T A PLACE NAZIS HANG OUT, YOU FEEL ME?
OKAY, WELL. TAKE CARE OF YOURSELF, EDDIE.
YOU'RE A GOOD PERSON, JOSIE...
YOU'RE TEN MINUTES LATE. IMMA LET YOU IN THIS TIME, BUT WE GOT RULES HERE. OBEY THEM.
YEAH, THANKS.

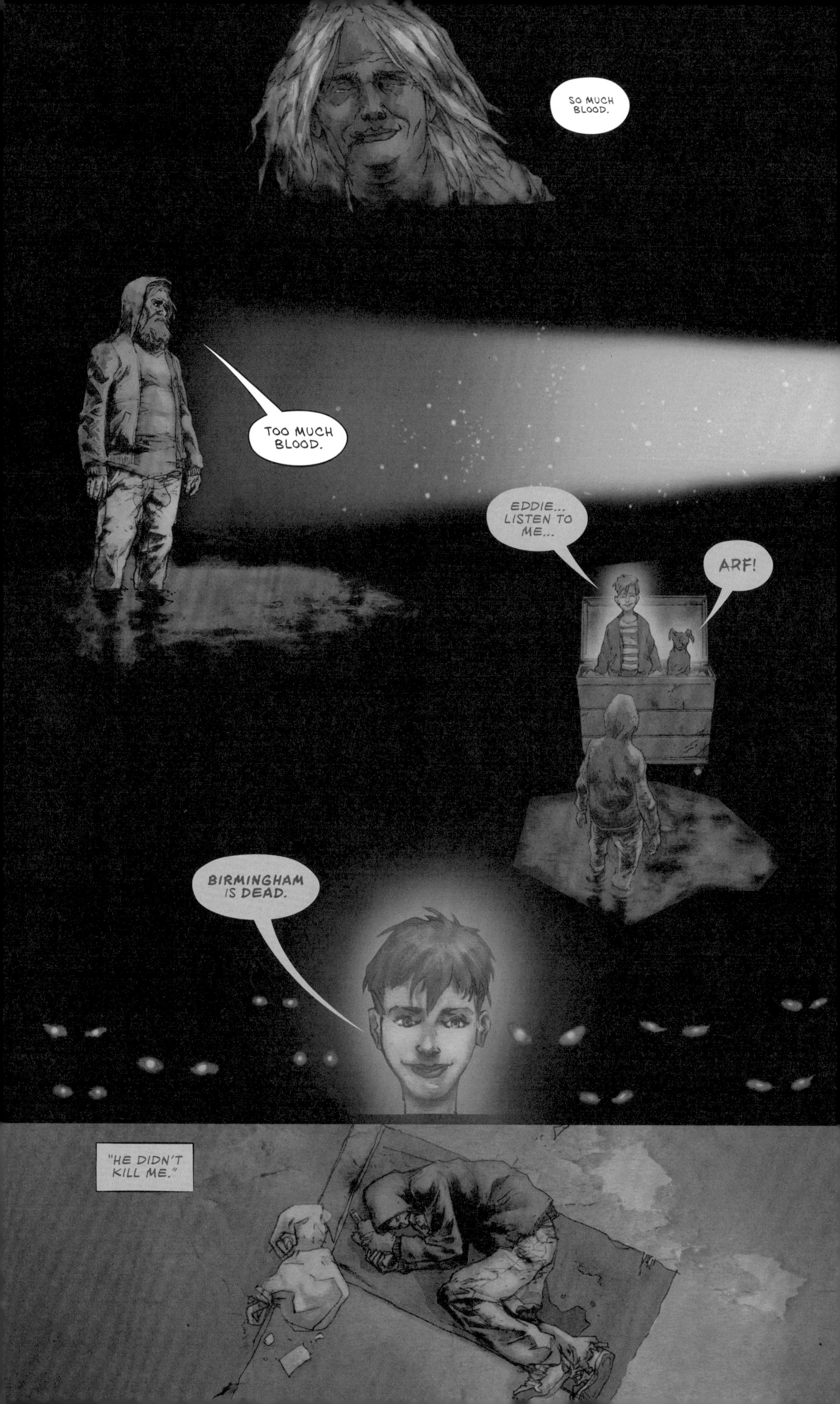
SO MUCH BLOOD.
TOO MUCH BLOOD.
EDDIE... LISTEN TO ME...
ARF!
BIRMINGHAM IS DEAD.
"HE DIDN'T KILL ME."

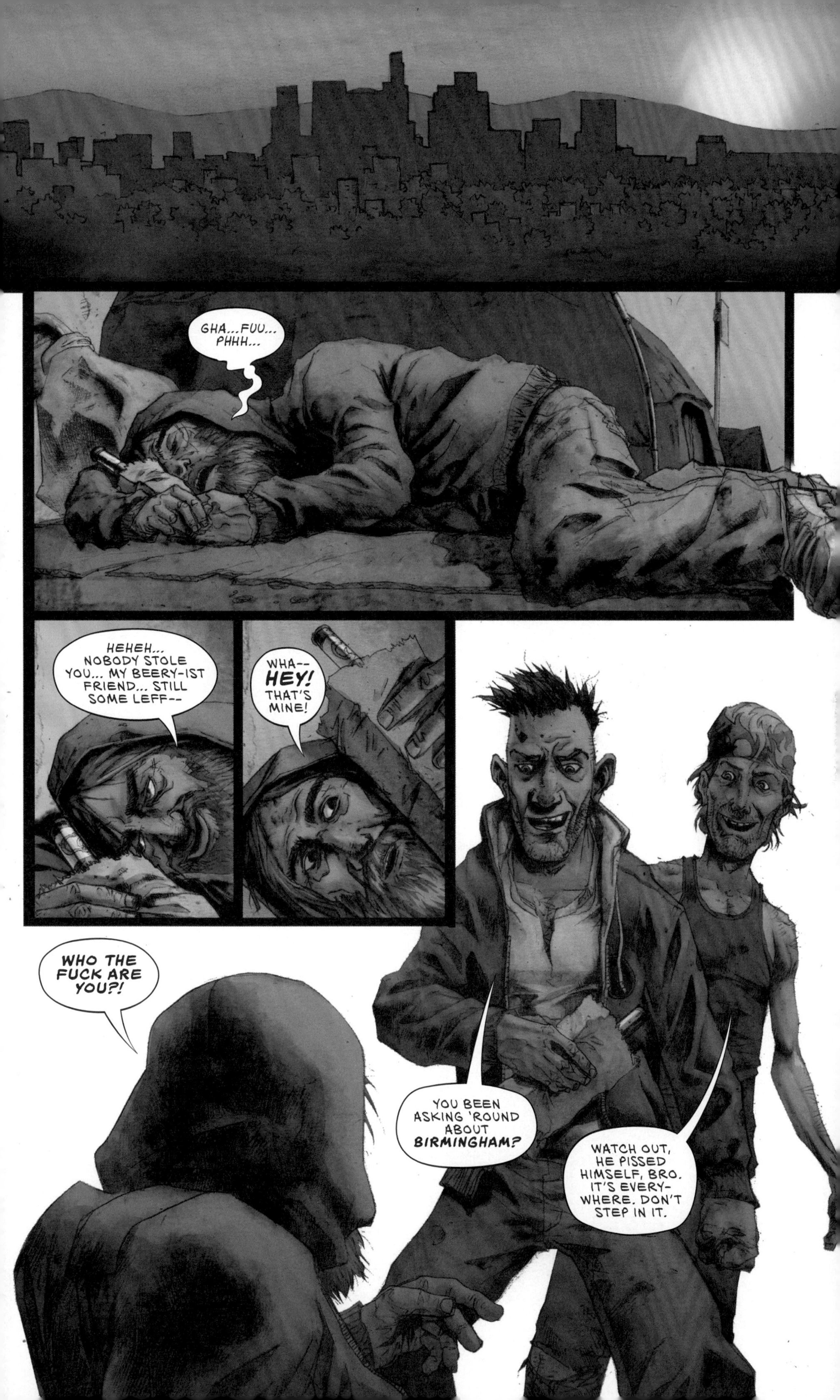
GHA... FUU... PHHH...
HEHEH... NOBODY STOLE YOU... MY BEERY-IST FRIEND... STILL SOME LEFF--
WHA-- HEY! THAT'S MINE!
WHO THE FUCK ARE YOU?!
YOU BEEN ASKING 'ROUND ABOUT BIRMINGHAM?
WATCH OUT, HE PISSED HIMSELF, BRO. IT'S EVERY-WHERE. DON'T STEP IN IT.

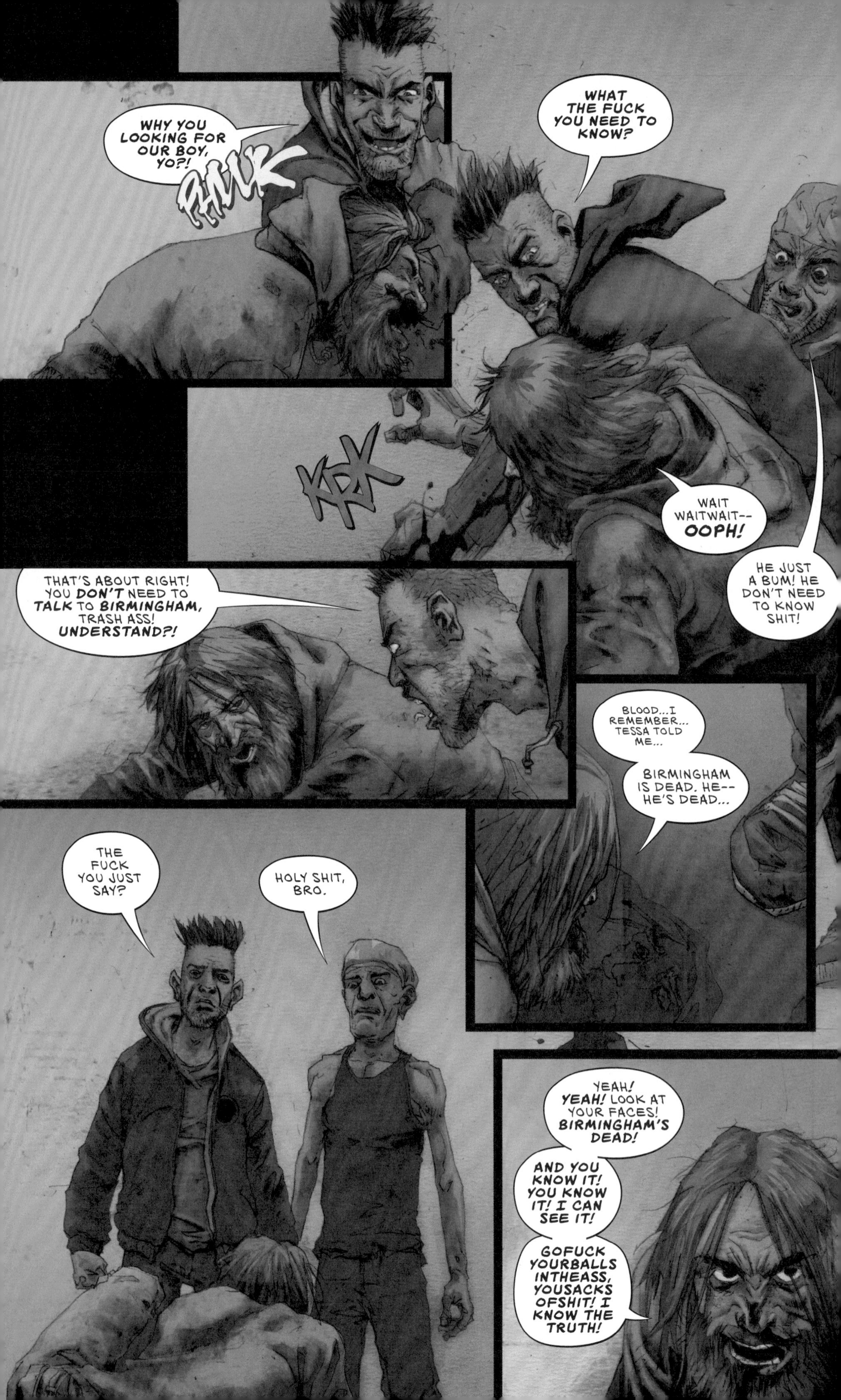

WHY YOU LOOKING FOR OUR BOY, YO?!
PHUK
WHAT THE FUCK YOU NEED TO KNOW?
KDK
WAIT WAITWAIT-- OOPH!
HE JUST A BUM! HE DON'T NEED TO KNOW SHIT!
THAT'S ABOUT RIGHT! YOU DON'T NEED TO TALK TO BIRMINGHAM, TRASH ASS! UNDERSTAND?!
BLOOD...I REMEMBER... TESSA TOLD ME...
BIRMINGHAM IS DEAD. HE-- HE'S DEAD...
THE FUCK YOU JUST SAY?
HOLY SHIT, BRO.
YEAH! YEAH! LOOK AT YOUR FACES! BIRMINGHAM'S DEAD!
AND YOU KNOW IT! YOU KNOW IT! I CAN SEE IT!
GOFUCK YOURBALLS INTHEASS, YOUSACKS OFSHIT! I KNOW THE TRUTH!

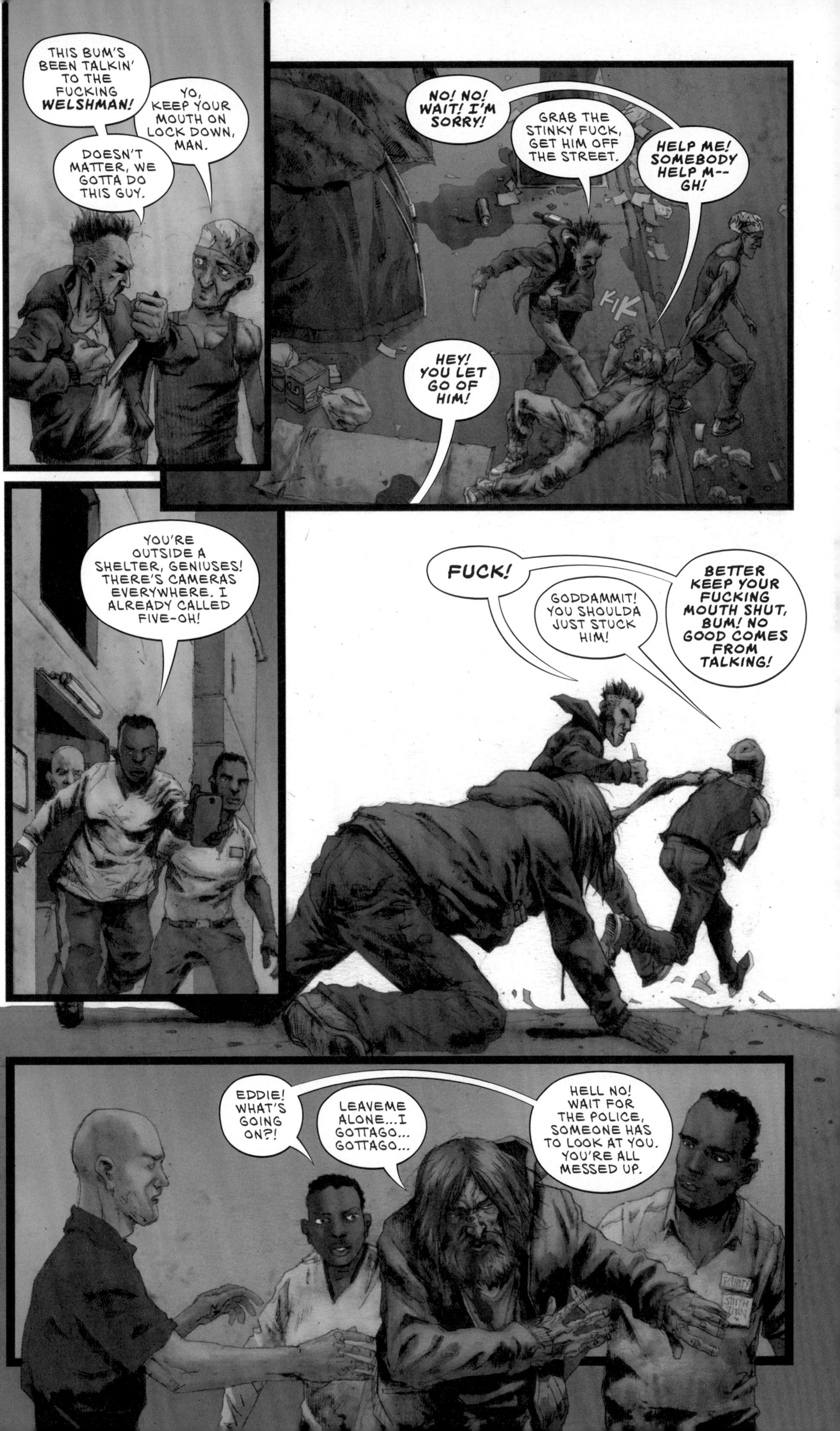
THIS BUM'S BEEN TALKIN' TO THE FUCKING WELSHMAN!
YO, KEEP YOUR MOUTH ON LOCK DOWN, MAN.
DOESN'T MATTER, WE GOTTA DO THIS GUY.
NO! NO! WAIT! I'M SORRY!
GRAB THE STINKY FUCK, GET HIM OFF THE STREET.
HELP ME! SOMEBODY HELP M--GH!
KIK
HEY! YOU LET GO OF HIM!
YOU'RE OUTSIDE A SHELTER, GENIUSES! THERE'S CAMERAS EVERYWHERE. I ALREADY CALLED FIVE-OH!
FUCK!
GODDAMMIT! YOU SHOULDA JUST STUCK HIM!
BETTER KEEP YOUR FUCKING MOUTH SHUT, BUM! NO GOOD COMES FROM TALKING!
EDDIE! WHAT'S GOING ON?!
LEAVEME ALONE...I GOTTAGO... GOTTAGO...
HELL NO! WAIT FOR THE POLICE, SOMEONE HAS TO LOOK AT YOU. YOU'RE ALL MESSED UP.

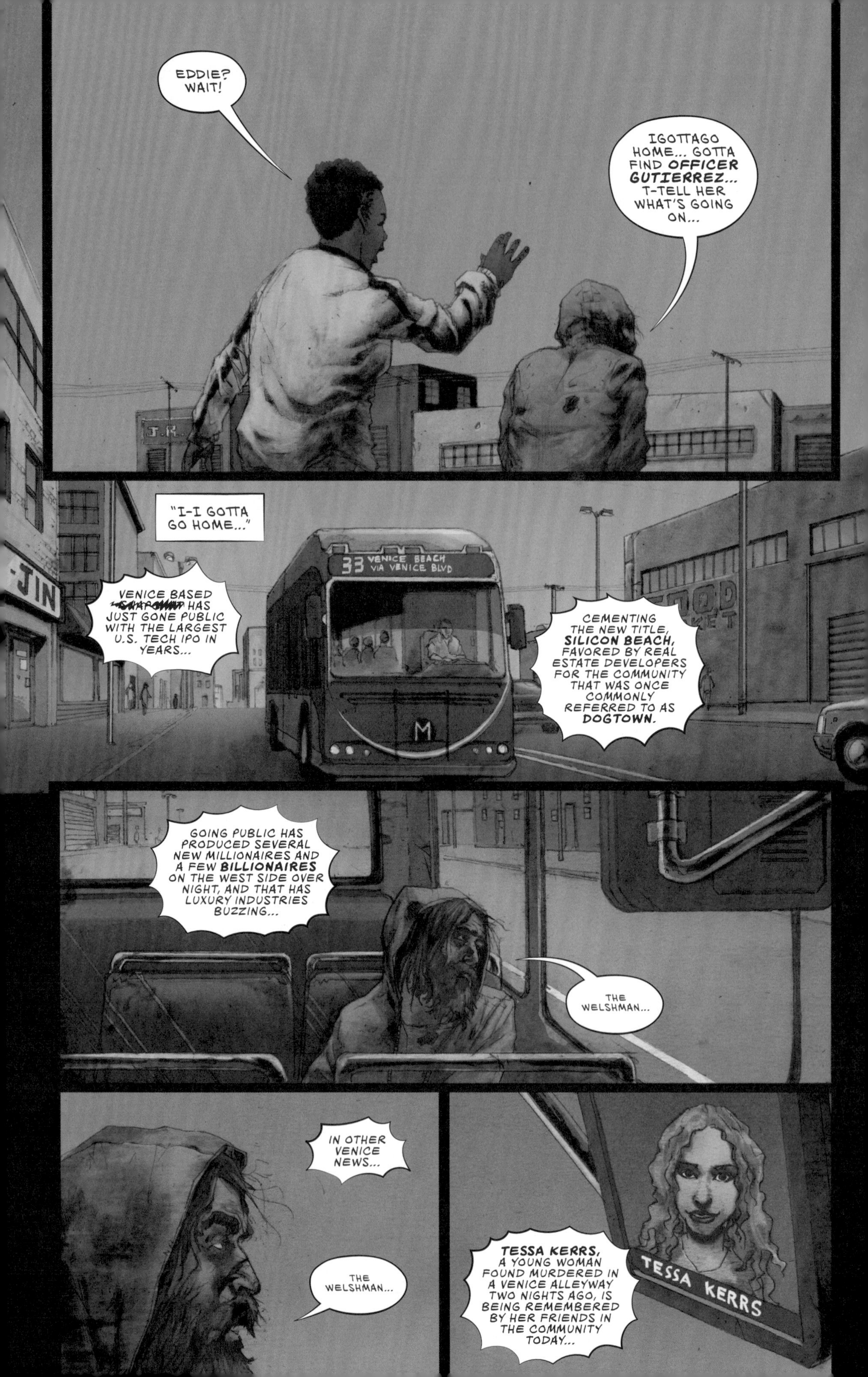
EDDIE? WAIT!
IGOTTAGO HOME... GOTTA FIND **OFFICER GUTIERREZ...** T-TELL HER WHAT'S GOING ON...
J.R.
"I-I GOTTA GO HOME..."
33 VENICE BEACH VIA VENICE BLVD
-JIN
VENICE BASED [redacted] HAS JUST GONE PUBLIC WITH THE LARGEST U.S. TECH IPO IN YEARS...
CEMENTING THE NEW TITLE, **SILICON BEACH,** FAVORED BY REAL ESTATE DEVELOPERS FOR THE COMMUNITY THAT WAS ONCE COMMONLY REFERRED TO AS **DOGTOWN.**
M
GOING PUBLIC HAS PRODUCED SEVERAL NEW MILLIONAIRES AND A FEW **BILLIONAIRES** ON THE WEST SIDE OVER NIGHT, AND THAT HAS LUXURY INDUSTRIES BUZZING...
THE WELSHMAN...
IN OTHER VENICE NEWS...
THE WELSHMAN...
TESSA KERRS
TESSA KERRS, A YOUNG WOMAN FOUND MURDERED IN A VENICE ALLEYWAY TWO NIGHTS AGO, IS BEING REMEMBERED BY HER FRIENDS IN THE COMMUNITY TODAY...

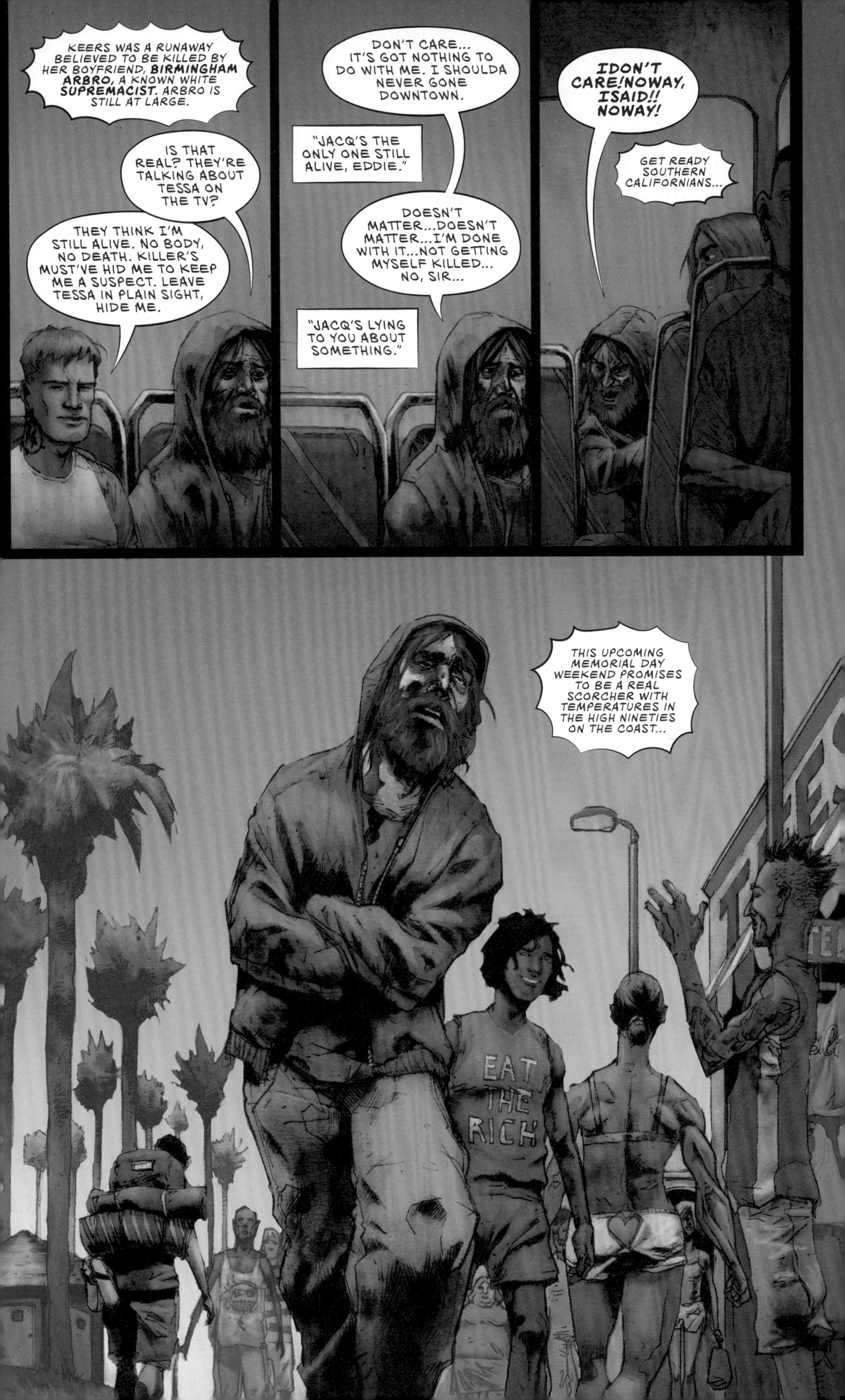
KEERS WAS A RUNAWAY BELIEVED TO BE KILLED BY HER BOYFRIEND, BIRMINGHAM ARBRO, A KNOWN WHITE SUPREMACIST. ARBRO IS STILL AT LARGE.
IS THAT REAL? THEY'RE TALKING ABOUT TESSA ON THE TV?
THEY THINK I'M STILL ALIVE. NO BODY, NO DEATH. KILLER'S MUST'VE HID ME TO KEEP ME A SUSPECT. LEAVE TESSA IN PLAIN SIGHT, HIDE ME.
DON'T CARE... IT'S GOT NOTHING TO DO WITH ME. I SHOULDA NEVER GONE DOWNTOWN.
"JACQ'S THE ONLY ONE STILL ALIVE, EDDIE."
DOESN'T MATTER...DOESN'T MATTER...I'M DONE WITH IT...NOT GETTING MYSELF KILLED... NO, SIR...
"JACQ'S LYING TO YOU ABOUT SOMETHING."
IDON'T CARE!NOWAY, ISAID!! NOWAY!
GET READY SOUTHERN CALIFORNIANS...
THIS UPCOMING MEMORIAL DAY WEEKEND PROMISES TO BE A REAL SCORCHER WITH TEMPERATURES IN THE HIGH NINETIES ON THE COAST...
EAT THE RICH

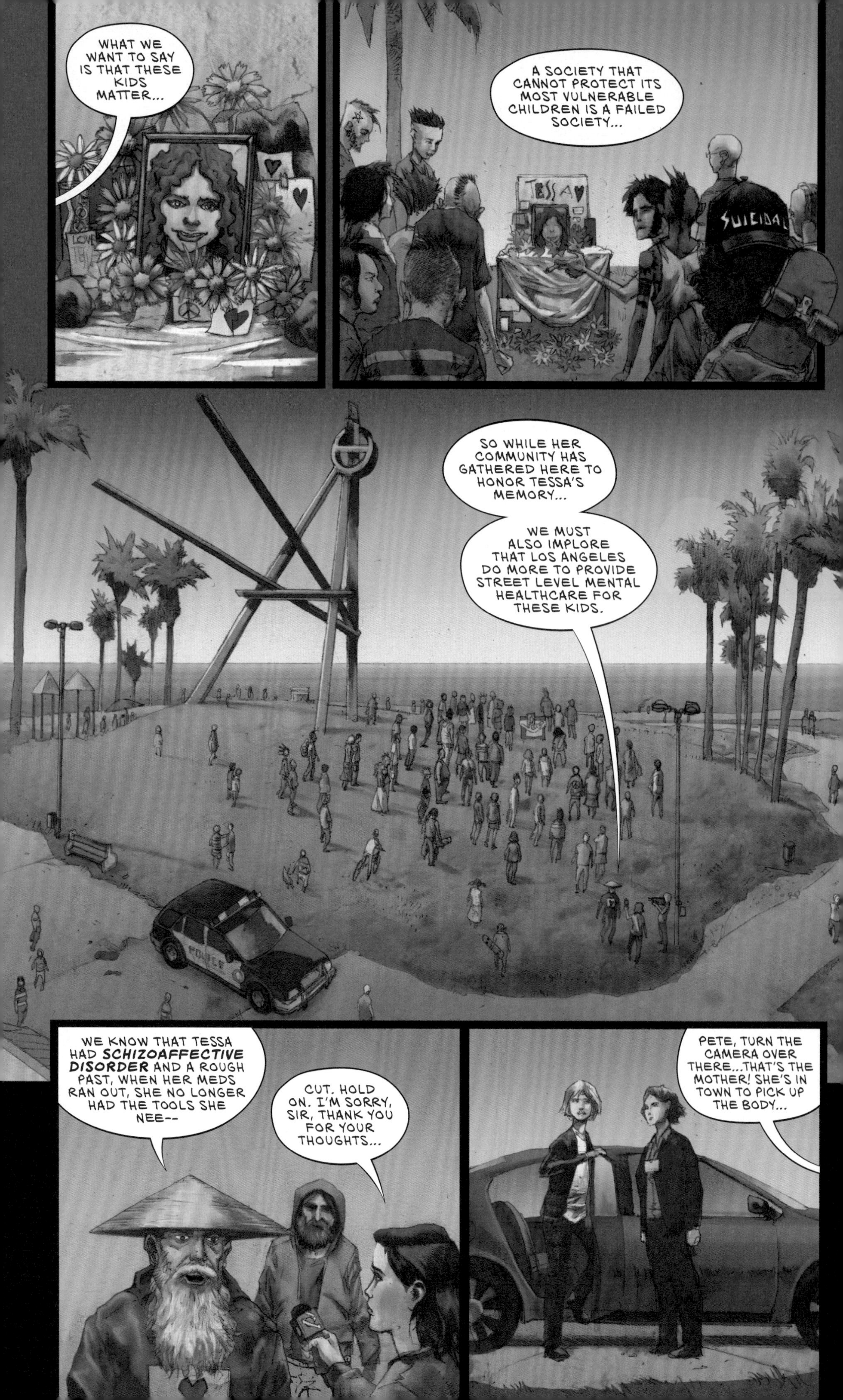
WHAT WE WANT TO SAY IS THAT THESE KIDS MATTER...
A SOCIETY THAT CANNOT PROTECT ITS MOST VULNERABLE CHILDREN IS A FAILED SOCIETY...
TESSA
SUICIDAL
SO WHILE HER COMMUNITY HAS GATHERED HERE TO HONOR TESSA'S MEMORY...
WE MUST ALSO IMPLORE THAT LOS ANGELES DO MORE TO PROVIDE STREET LEVEL MENTAL HEALTHCARE FOR THESE KIDS.
POLICE
WE KNOW THAT TESSA HAD **SCHIZOAFFECTIVE DISORDER** AND A ROUGH PAST, WHEN HER MEDS RAN OUT, SHE NO LONGER HAD THE TOOLS SHE NEE--
CUT. HOLD ON. I'M SORRY, SIR, THANK YOU FOR YOUR THOUGHTS...
PETE, TURN THE CAMERA OVER THERE...THAT'S THE MOTHER! SHE'S IN TOWN TO PICK UP THE BODY...

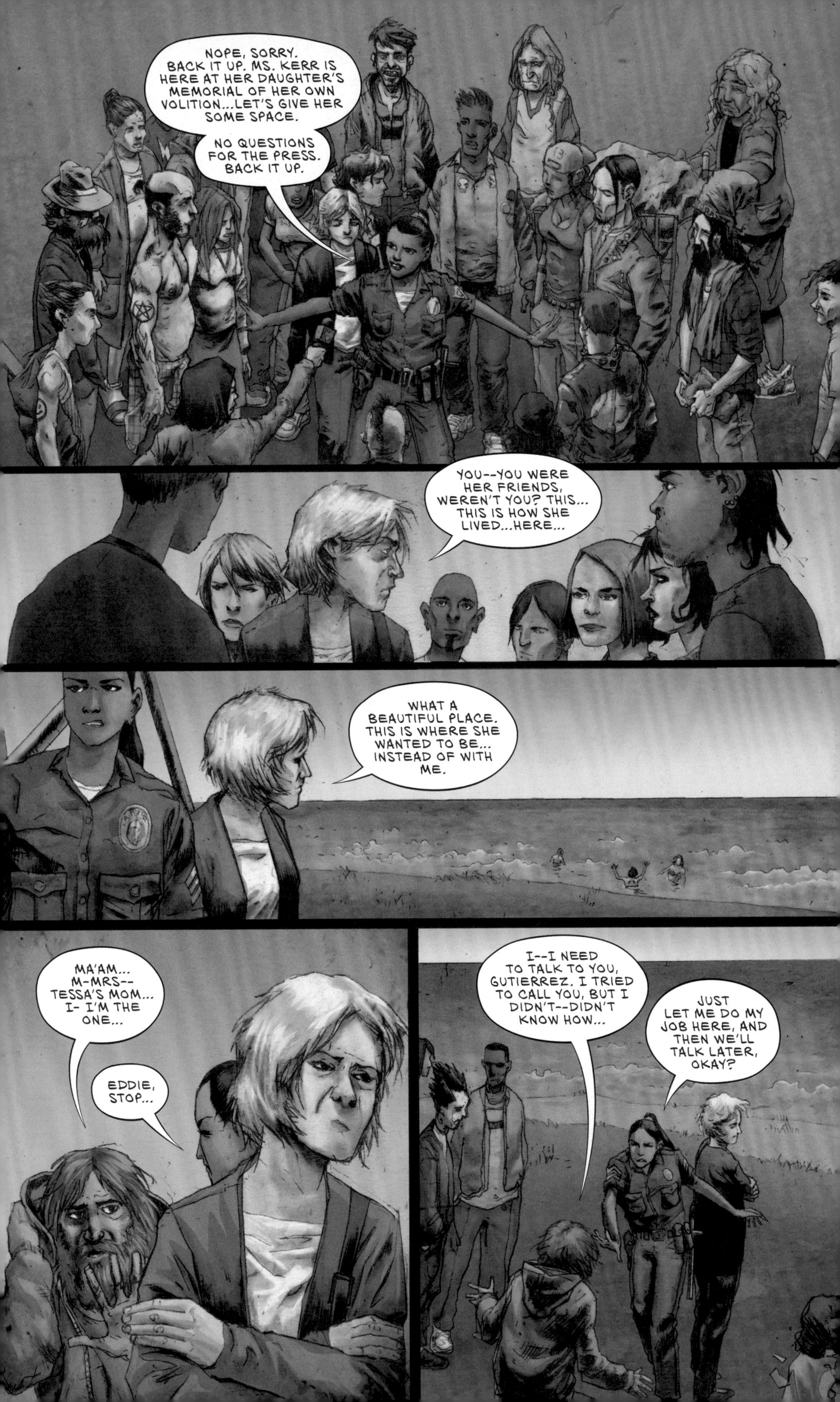
NOPE, SORRY. BACK IT UP. MS. KERR IS HERE AT HER DAUGHTER'S MEMORIAL OF HER OWN VOLITION...LET'S GIVE HER SOME SPACE.
NO QUESTIONS FOR THE PRESS. BACK IT UP.
YOU--YOU WERE HER FRIENDS, WEREN'T YOU? THIS... THIS IS HOW SHE LIVED...HERE...
WHAT A BEAUTIFUL PLACE. THIS IS WHERE SHE WANTED TO BE... INSTEAD OF WITH ME.
MA'AM... M-MRS-- TESSA'S MOM... I- I'M THE ONE...
EDDIE, STOP...
I--I NEED TO TALK TO YOU, GUTIERREZ. I TRIED TO CALL YOU, BUT I DIDN'T--DIDN'T KNOW HOW...
JUST LET ME DO MY JOB HERE, AND THEN WE'LL TALK LATER, OKAY?

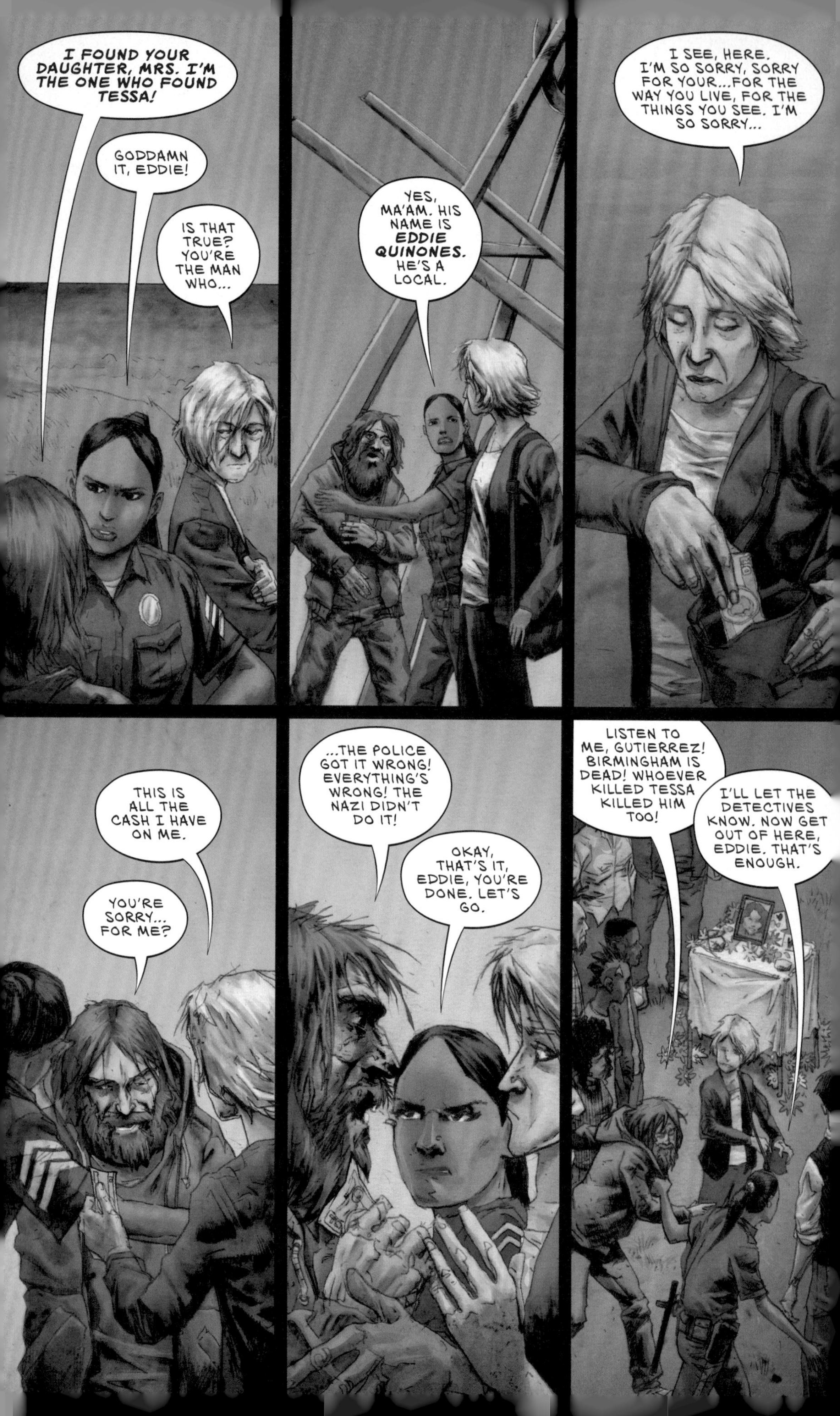
I FOUND YOUR DAUGHTER, MRS. I'M THE ONE WHO FOUND TESSA!
GODDAMN IT, EDDIE!
IS THAT TRUE? YOU'RE THE MAN WHO...
YES, MA'AM. HIS NAME IS EDDIE QUINONES. HE'S A LOCAL.
I SEE, HERE. I'M SO SORRY, SORRY FOR YOUR...FOR THE WAY YOU LIVE, FOR THE THINGS YOU SEE. I'M SO SORRY...
THIS IS ALL THE CASH I HAVE ON ME.
YOU'RE SORRY... FOR ME?
...THE POLICE GOT IT WRONG! EVERYTHING'S WRONG! THE NAZI DIDN'T DO IT!
OKAY, THAT'S IT, EDDIE, YOU'RE DONE. LET'S GO.
LISTEN TO ME, GUTIERREZ! BIRMINGHAM IS DEAD! WHOEVER KILLED TESSA KILLED HIM TOO!
I'LL LET THE DETECTIVES KNOW. NOW GET OUT OF HERE, EDDIE. THAT'S ENOUGH.

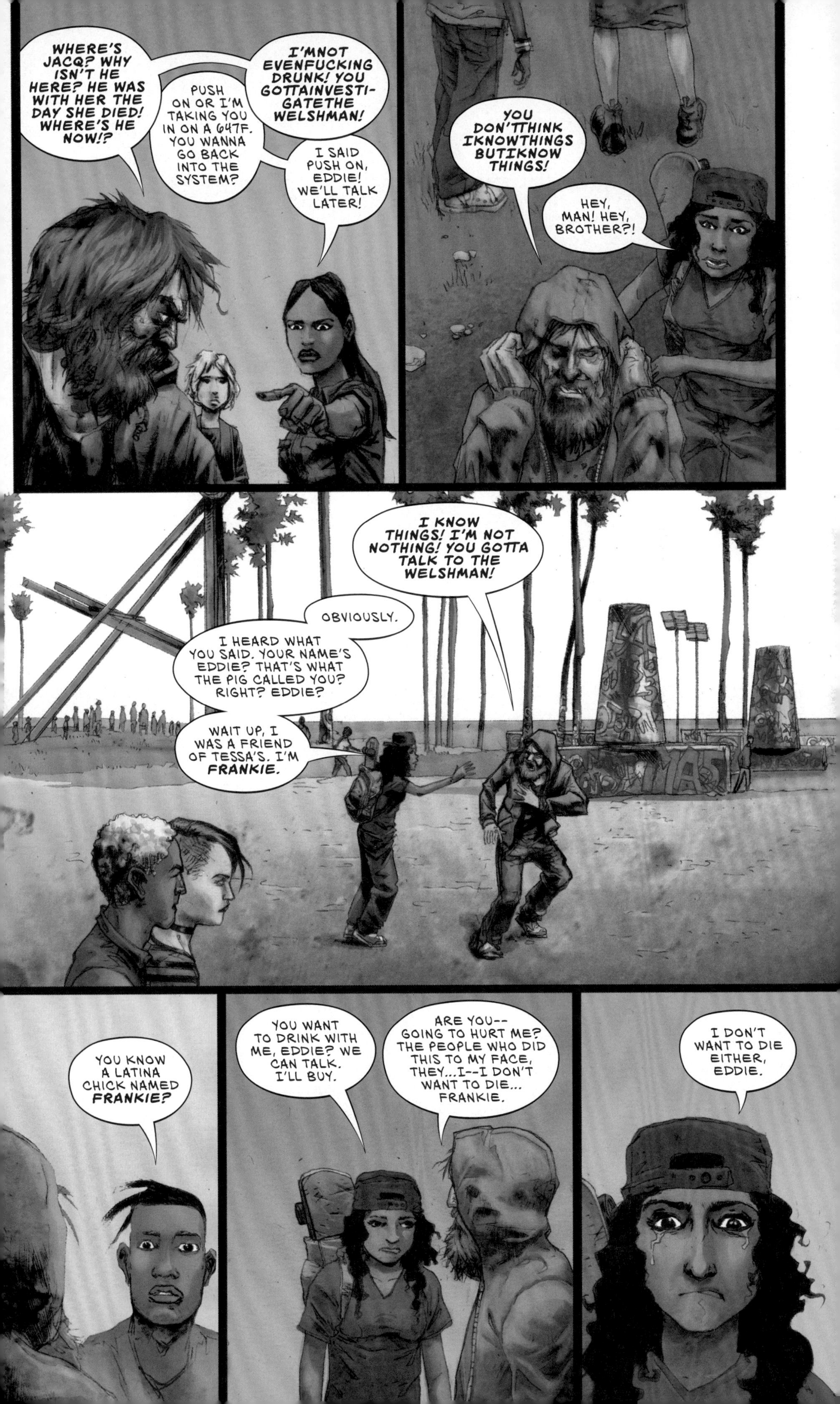
WHERE'S JACQ? WHY ISN'T HE HERE? HE WAS WITH HER THE DAY SHE DIED! WHERE'S HE NOW!?
I'MNOT EVENFUCKING DRUNK! YOU GOTTAINVESTI-GATETHE WELSHMAN!
PUSH ON OR I'M TAKING YOU IN ON A 647F. YOU WANNA GO BACK INTO THE SYSTEM?
I SAID PUSH ON, EDDIE! WE'LL TALK LATER!
YOU DON'TTHINK IKNOWTHINGS BUTIKNOW THINGS!
HEY, MAN! HEY, BROTHER?!
I KNOW THINGS! I'M NOT NOTHING! YOU GOTTA TALK TO THE WELSHMAN!
OBVIOUSLY.
I HEARD WHAT YOU SAID. YOUR NAME'S EDDIE? THAT'S WHAT THE PIG CALLED YOU? RIGHT? EDDIE?
WAIT UP, I WAS A FRIEND OF TESSA'S. I'M FRANKIE.
YOU KNOW A LATINA CHICK NAMED FRANKIE?
YOU WANT TO DRINK WITH ME, EDDIE? WE CAN TALK. I'LL BUY.
ARE YOU-- GOING TO HURT ME? THE PEOPLE WHO DID THIS TO MY FACE, THEY...I--I DON'T WANT TO DIE... FRANKIE.
I DON'T WANT TO DIE EITHER, EDDIE.

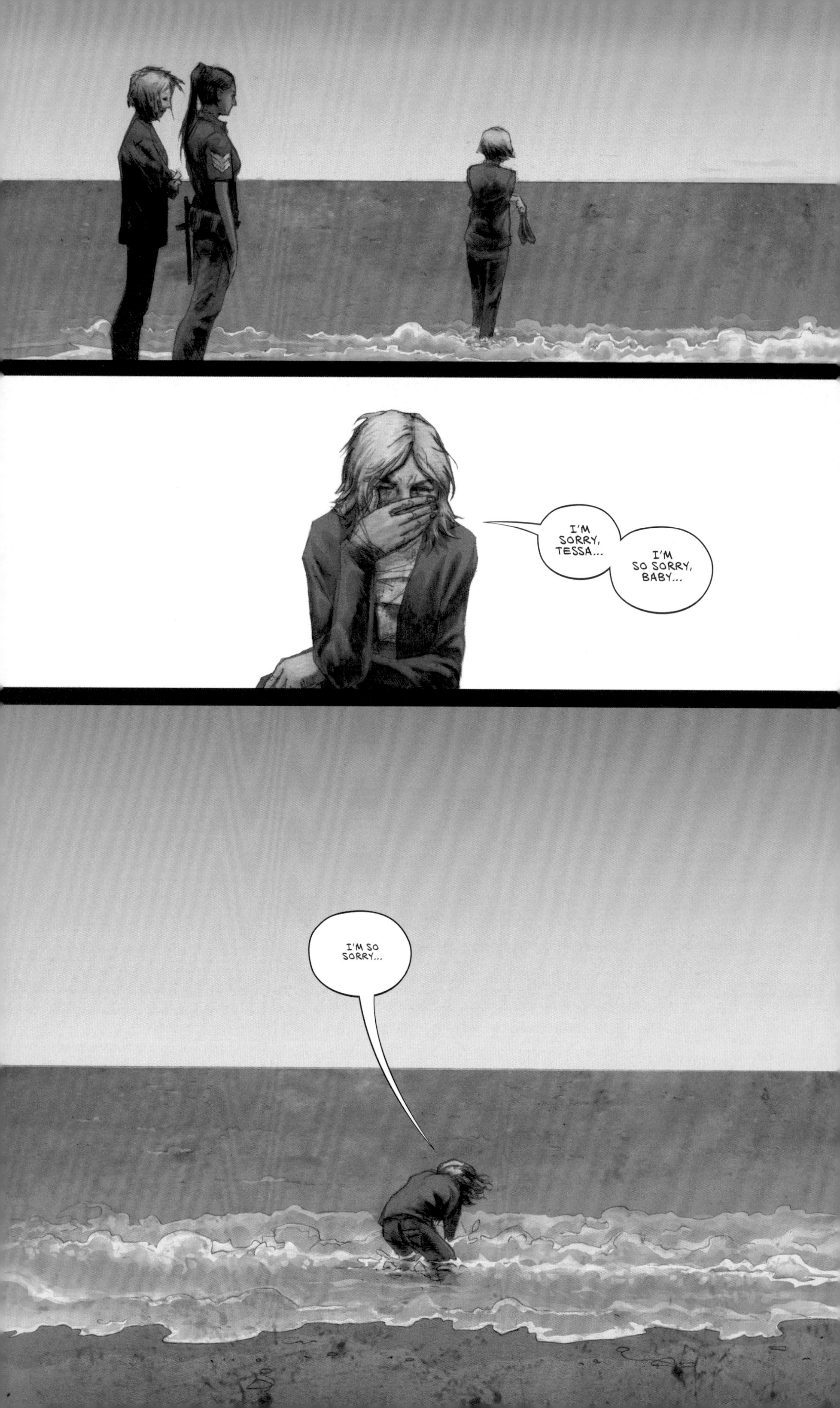
I'M SORRY, TESSA...
I'M SO SORRY, BABY...
I'M SO SORRY...

CHAPTER 3

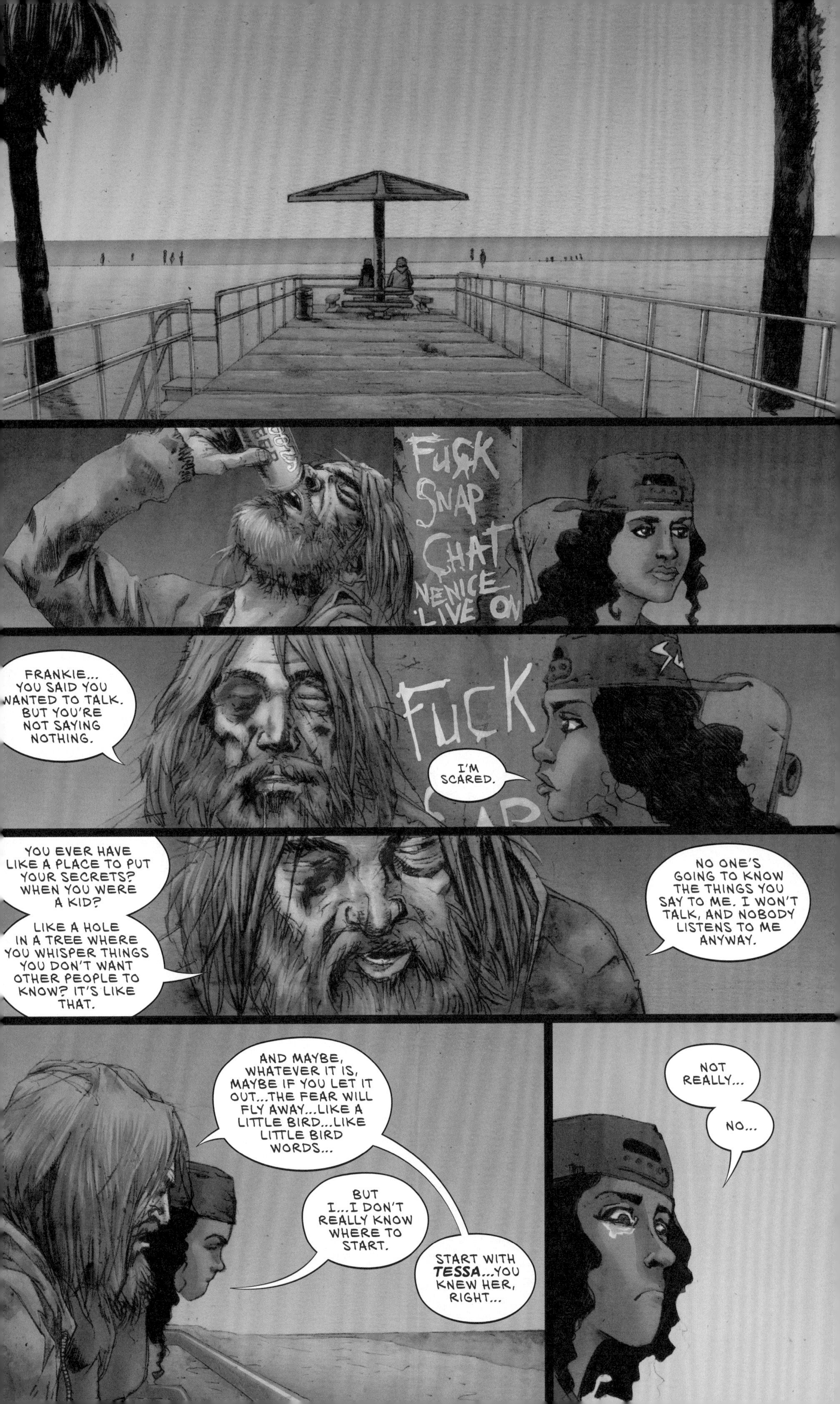
FUCK SNAP CHAT VENICE LIVE ON
FRANKIE... YOU SAID YOU WANTED TO TALK. BUT YOU'RE NOT SAYING NOTHING.
FUCK
I'M SCARED.
YOU EVER HAVE LIKE A PLACE TO PUT YOUR SECRETS? WHEN YOU WERE A KID?
LIKE A HOLE IN A TREE WHERE YOU WHISPER THINGS YOU DON'T WANT OTHER PEOPLE TO KNOW? IT'S LIKE THAT.
NO ONE'S GOING TO KNOW THE THINGS YOU SAY TO ME. I WON'T TALK, AND NOBODY LISTENS TO ME ANYWAY.
AND MAYBE, WHATEVER IT IS, MAYBE IF YOU LET IT OUT...THE FEAR WILL FLY AWAY...LIKE A LITTLE BIRD...LIKE LITTLE BIRD WORDS...
BUT I...I DON'T REALLY KNOW WHERE TO START.
START WITH ***TESSA***...YOU KNEW HER, RIGHT...
NOT REALLY...
NO...

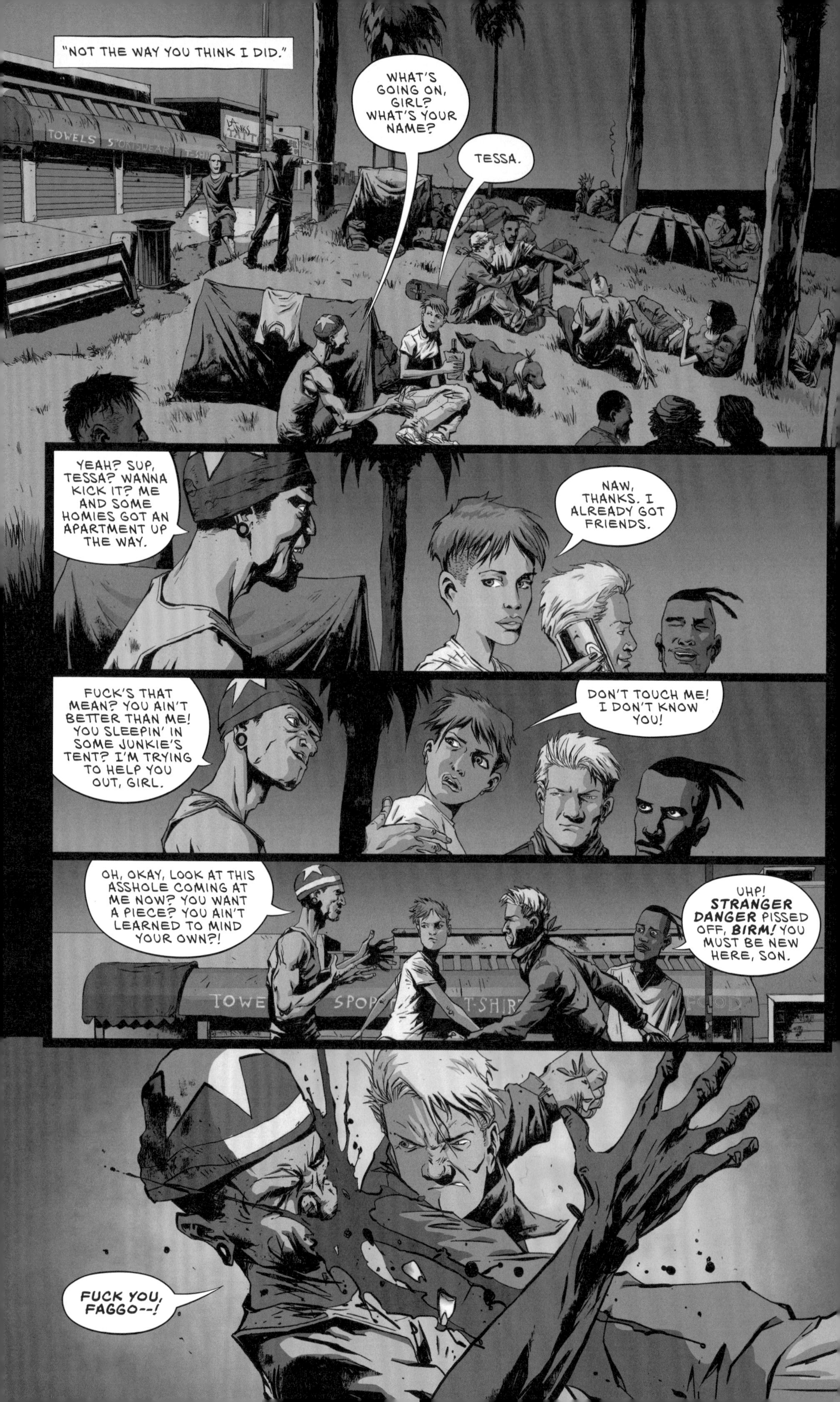

"NOT THE WAY YOU THINK I DID."
TOWELS SPORTSWEAR T-SHIRTS
WHAT'S GOING ON, GIRL? WHAT'S YOUR NAME?
TESSA.
YEAH? SUP, TESSA? WANNA KICK IT? ME AND SOME HOMIES GOT AN APARTMENT UP THE WAY.
NAW, THANKS. I ALREADY GOT FRIENDS.
FUCK'S THAT MEAN? YOU AIN'T BETTER THAN ME! YOU SLEEPIN' IN SOME JUNKIE'S TENT? I'M TRYING TO HELP YOU OUT, GIRL.
DON'T TOUCH ME! I DON'T KNOW YOU!
OH, OKAY, LOOK AT THIS ASSHOLE COMING AT ME NOW? YOU WANT A PIECE? YOU AIN'T LEARNED TO MIND YOUR OWN?!
UHP! STRANGER DANGER PISSED OFF, BIRM! YOU MUST BE NEW HERE, SON.
FUCK YOU, FAGGO--!

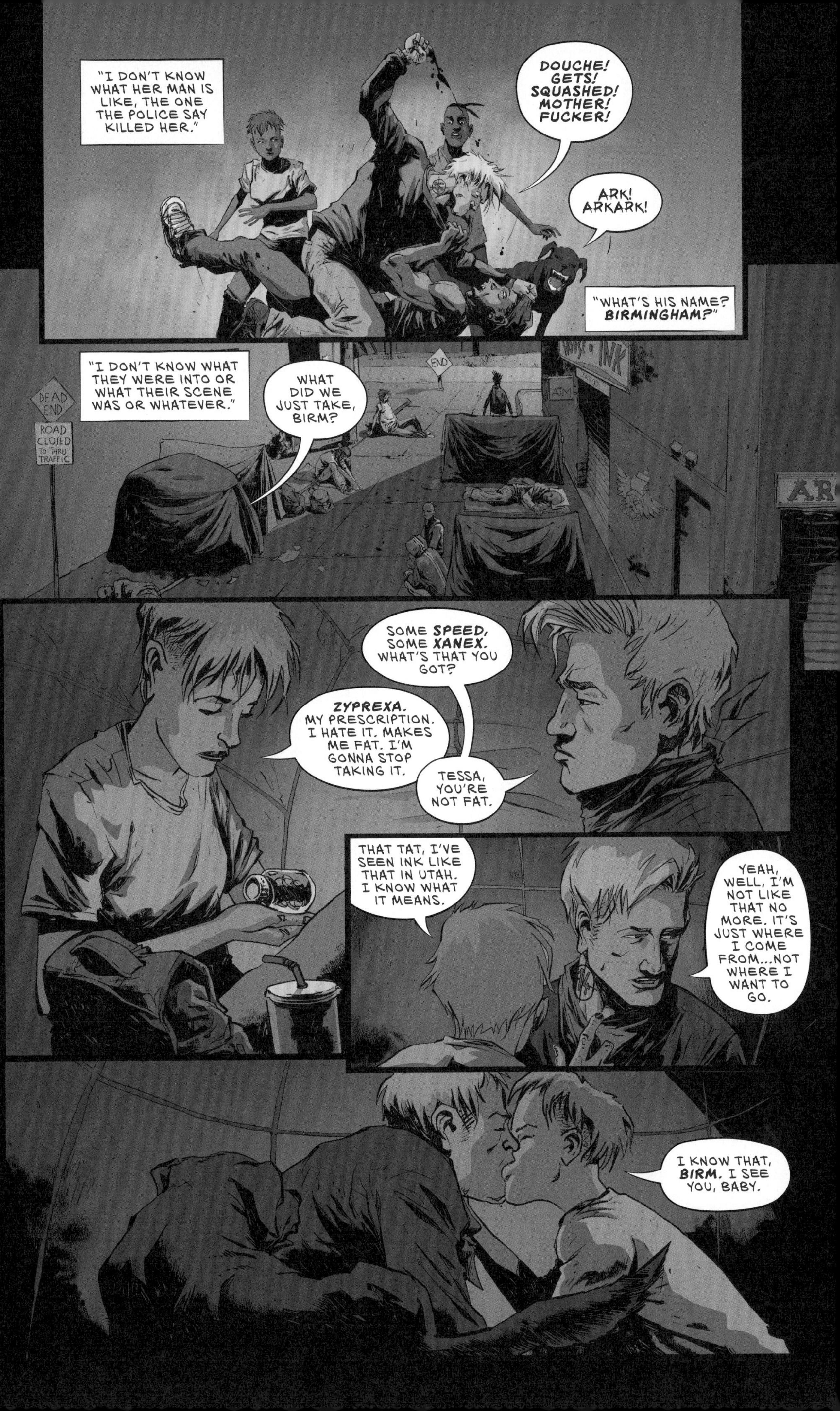
"I DON'T KNOW WHAT HER MAN IS LIKE, THE ONE THE POLICE SAY KILLED HER."
DOUCHE! GETS! SQUASHED! MOTHER! FUCKER!
ARK! ARKARK!
"WHAT'S HIS NAME? BIRMINGHAM?"
DEAD END
ROAD CLOSED TO THRU TRAFFIC
END
HOUSE OF INK
ATM
"I DON'T KNOW WHAT THEY WERE INTO OR WHAT THEIR SCENE WAS OR WHATEVER."
WHAT DID WE JUST TAKE, BIRM?
SOME SPEED, SOME XANEX. WHAT'S THAT YOU GOT?
ZYPREXA. MY PRESCRIPTION. I HATE IT. MAKES ME FAT. I'M GONNA STOP TAKING IT.
TESSA, YOU'RE NOT FAT.
THAT TAT, I'VE SEEN INK LIKE THAT IN UTAH. I KNOW WHAT IT MEANS.
YEAH, WELL, I'M NOT LIKE THAT NO MORE. IT'S JUST WHERE I COME FROM...NOT WHERE I WANT TO GO.
I KNOW THAT, BIRM. I SEE YOU, BABY.

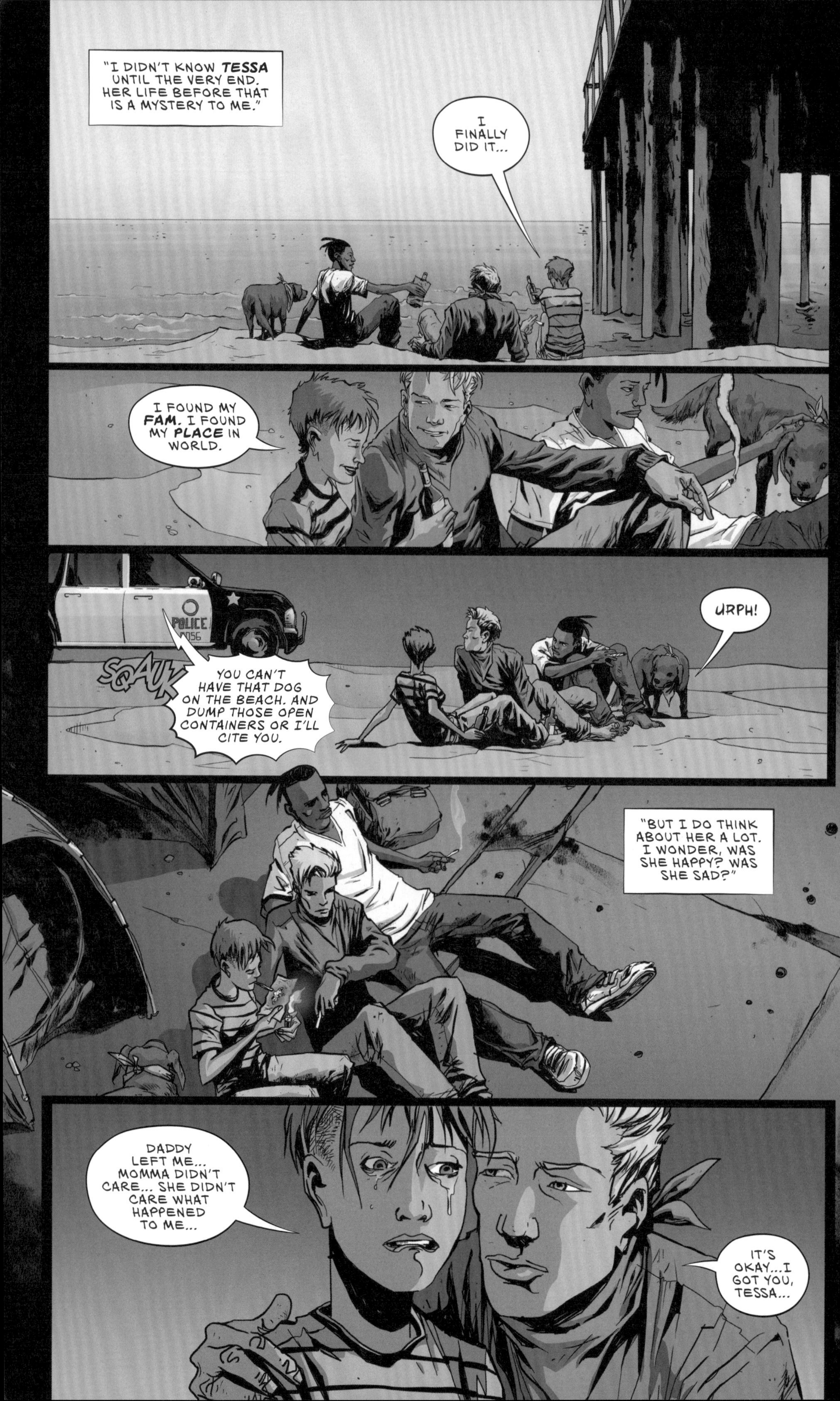
"I DIDN'T KNOW TESSA UNTIL THE VERY END. HER LIFE BEFORE THAT IS A MYSTERY TO ME."
I FINALLY DID IT...
I FOUND MY FAM. I FOUND MY PLACE IN WORLD.
POLICE
SQAUK
YOU CAN'T HAVE THAT DOG ON THE BEACH. AND DUMP THOSE OPEN CONTAINERS OR I'LL CITE YOU.
URPH!
"BUT I DO THINK ABOUT HER A LOT. I WONDER, WAS SHE HAPPY? WAS SHE SAD?"
DADDY LEFT ME... MOMMA DIDN'T CARE... SHE DIDN'T CARE WHAT HAPPENED TO ME...
IT'S OKAY...I GOT YOU, TESSA...

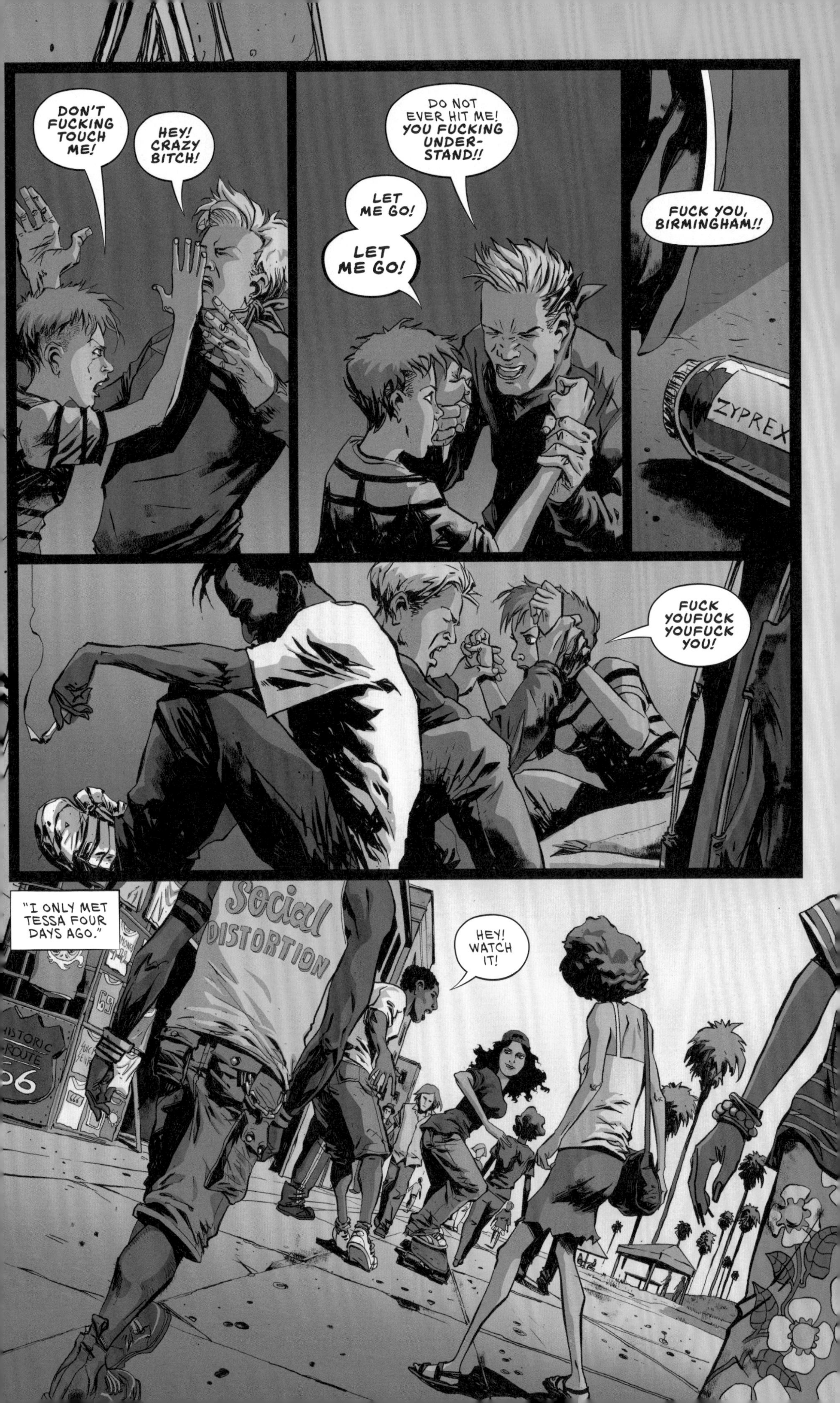
DON'T FUCKING TOUCH ME!
HEY! CRAZY BITCH!
DO NOT EVER HIT ME! YOU FUCKING UNDER-STAND!!
LET ME GO!
LET ME GO!
FUCK YOU, BIRMINGHAM!!
ZYPREX
FUCK YOUFUCK YOUFUCK YOU!
"I ONLY MET TESSA FOUR DAYS AGO."
Social DISTORTION
HEY! WATCH IT!
HISTORIC ROUTE 66

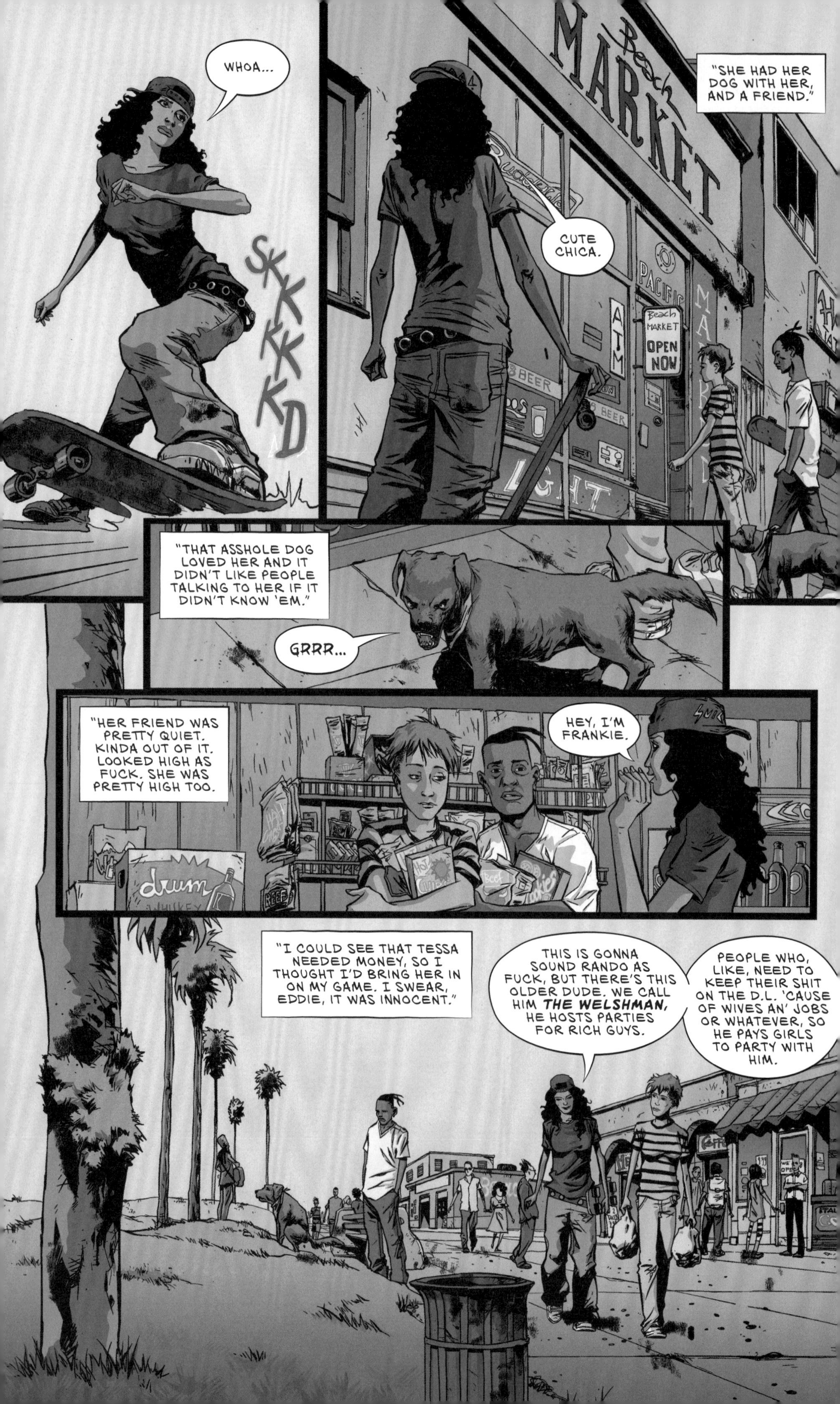
WHOA...
SKKKKD
"SHE HAD HER DOG WITH HER, AND A FRIEND."
CUTE CHICA.
Beach MARKET
OPEN NOW
"THAT ASSHOLE DOG LOVED HER AND IT DIDN'T LIKE PEOPLE TALKING TO HER IF IT DIDN'T KNOW 'EM."
GRRR...
"HER FRIEND WAS PRETTY QUIET. KINDA OUT OF IT. LOOKED HIGH AS FUCK. SHE WAS PRETTY HIGH TOO.
HEY, I'M FRANKIE.
"I COULD SEE THAT TESSA NEEDED MONEY, SO I THOUGHT I'D BRING HER IN ON MY GAME. I SWEAR, EDDIE, IT WAS INNOCENT."
THIS IS GONNA SOUND RANDO AS FUCK, BUT THERE'S THIS OLDER DUDE. WE CALL HIM ***THE WELSHMAN,*** HE HOSTS PARTIES FOR RICH GUYS.
PEOPLE WHO, LIKE, NEED TO KEEP THEIR SHIT ON THE D.L. 'CAUSE OF WIVES AN' JOBS OR WHATEVER, SO HE PAYS GIRLS TO PARTY WITH HIM.

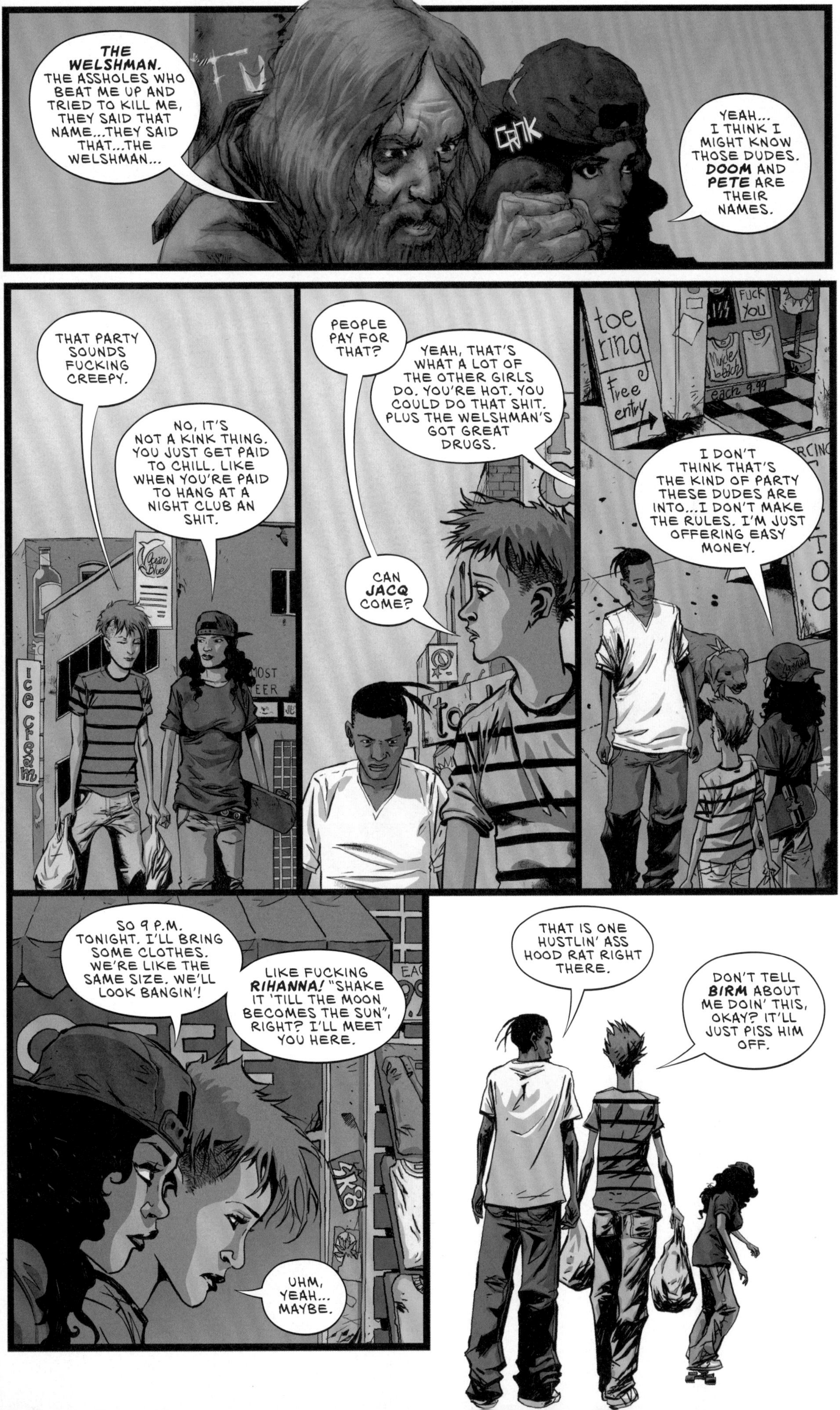
THE WELSHMAN. THE ASSHOLES WHO BEAT ME UP AND TRIED TO KILL ME, THEY SAID THAT NAME...THEY SAID THAT...THE WELSHMAN...
YEAH... I THINK I MIGHT KNOW THOSE DUDES. DOOM AND PETE ARE THEIR NAMES.
THAT PARTY SOUNDS FUCKING CREEPY.
NO, IT'S NOT A KINK THING. YOU JUST GET PAID TO CHILL. LIKE WHEN YOU'RE PAID TO HANG AT A NIGHT CLUB AN SHIT.
PEOPLE PAY FOR THAT?
YEAH, THAT'S WHAT A LOT OF THE OTHER GIRLS DO. YOU'RE HOT. YOU COULD DO THAT SHIT. PLUS THE WELSHMAN'S GOT GREAT DRUGS.
CAN JACQ COME?
toe ring
Free entry
FUCK YOU
I DON'T THINK THAT'S THE KIND OF PARTY THESE DUDES ARE INTO...I DON'T MAKE THE RULES. I'M JUST OFFERING EASY MONEY.
SO 9 P.M. TONIGHT. I'LL BRING SOME CLOTHES. WE'RE LIKE THE SAME SIZE. WE'LL LOOK BANGIN'!
LIKE FUCKING RIHANNA! "SHAKE IT 'TILL THE MOON BECOMES THE SUN", RIGHT? I'LL MEET YOU HERE.
UHM, YEAH... MAYBE.
THAT IS ONE HUSTLIN' ASS HOOD RAT RIGHT THERE.
DON'T TELL BIRM ABOUT ME DOIN' THIS, OKAY? IT'LL JUST PISS HIM OFF.

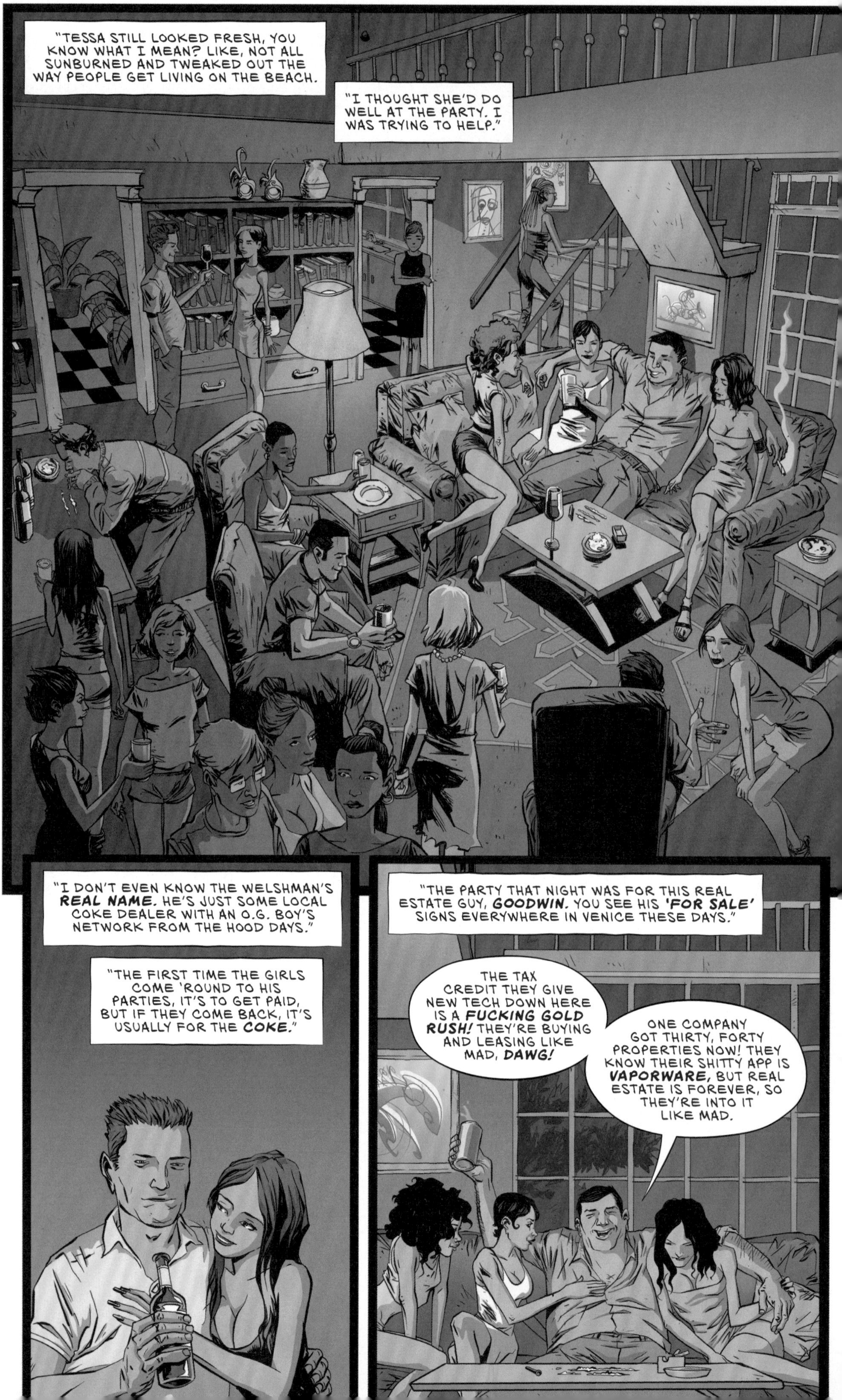
"TESSA STILL LOOKED FRESH, YOU KNOW WHAT I MEAN? LIKE, NOT ALL SUNBURNED AND TWEAKED OUT THE WAY PEOPLE GET LIVING ON THE BEACH.
"I THOUGHT SHE'D DO WELL AT THE PARTY. I WAS TRYING TO HELP."
"I DON'T EVEN KNOW THE WELSHMAN'S **REAL NAME.** HE'S JUST SOME LOCAL COKE DEALER WITH AN O.G. BOY'S NETWORK FROM THE HOOD DAYS."
"THE FIRST TIME THE GIRLS COME 'ROUND TO HIS PARTIES, IT'S TO GET PAID, BUT IF THEY COME BACK, IT'S USUALLY FOR THE **COKE.**"
"THE PARTY THAT NIGHT WAS FOR THIS REAL ESTATE GUY, **GOODWIN.** YOU SEE HIS **'FOR SALE'** SIGNS EVERYWHERE IN VENICE THESE DAYS."
THE TAX CREDIT THEY GIVE NEW TECH DOWN HERE IS A ***FUCKING GOLD RUSH!*** THEY'RE BUYING AND LEASING LIKE MAD, ***DAWG!***
ONE COMPANY GOT THIRTY, FORTY PROPERTIES NOW! THEY KNOW THEIR SHITTY APP IS ***VAPORWARE,*** BUT REAL ESTATE IS FOREVER, SO THEY'RE INTO IT LIKE MAD.

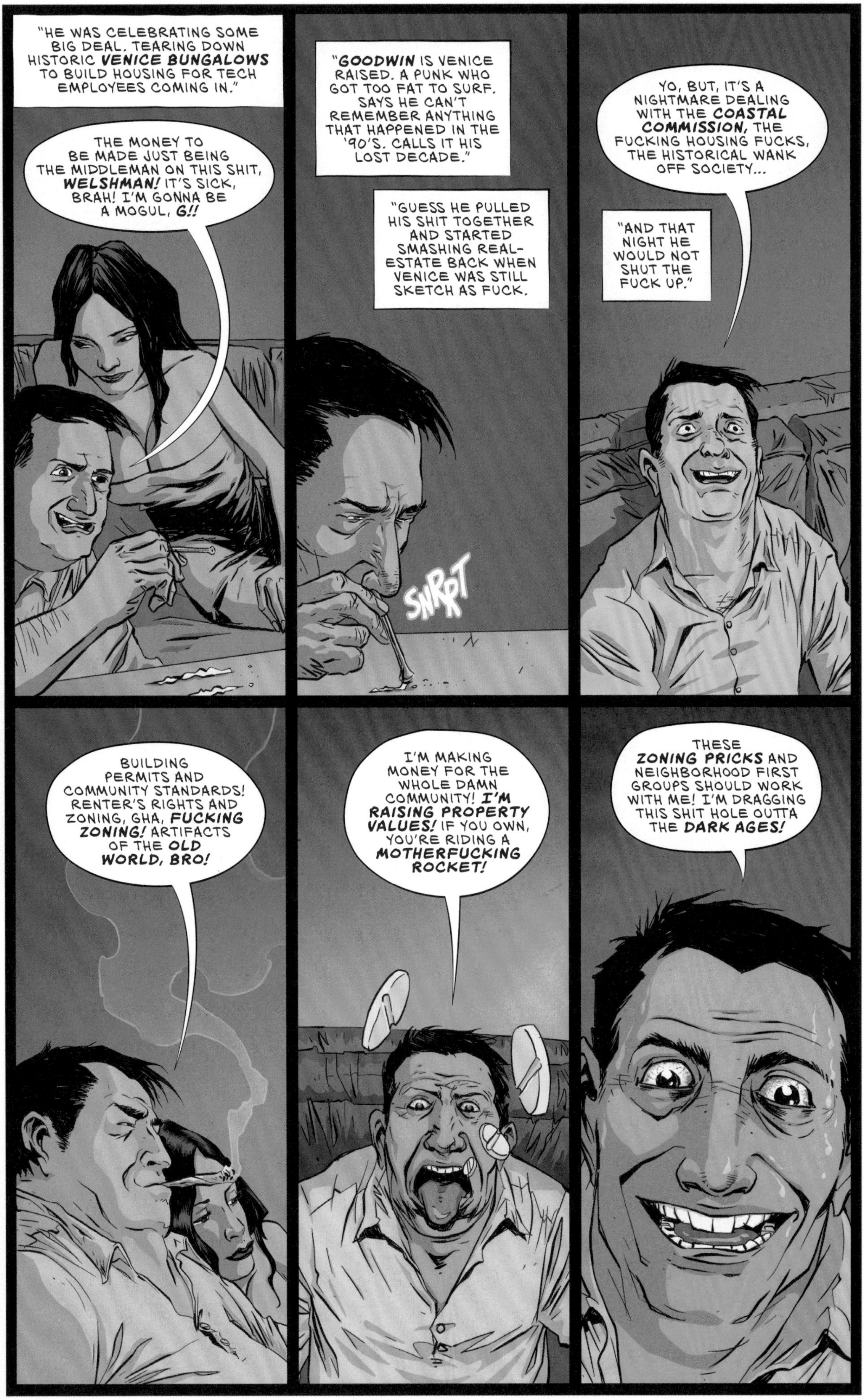
"HE WAS CELEBRATING SOME BIG DEAL. TEARING DOWN HISTORIC VENICE BUNGALOWS TO BUILD HOUSING FOR TECH EMPLOYEES COMING IN."
THE MONEY TO BE MADE JUST BEING THE MIDDLEMAN ON THIS SHIT, WELSHMAN! IT'S SICK, BRAH! I'M GONNA BE A MOGUL, G!!
"GOODWIN IS VENICE RAISED. A PUNK WHO GOT TOO FAT TO SURF. SAYS HE CAN'T REMEMBER ANYTHING THAT HAPPENED IN THE '90'S. CALLS IT HIS LOST DECADE."
"GUESS HE PULLED HIS SHIT TOGETHER AND STARTED SMASHING REAL-ESTATE BACK WHEN VENICE WAS STILL SKETCH AS FUCK.
SNRRT
YO, BUT, IT'S A NIGHTMARE DEALING WITH THE COASTAL COMMISSION, THE FUCKING HOUSING FUCKS, THE HISTORICAL WANK OFF SOCIETY...
"AND THAT NIGHT HE WOULD NOT SHUT THE FUCK UP."
BUILDING PERMITS AND COMMUNITY STANDARDS! RENTER'S RIGHTS AND ZONING, GHA, FUCKING ZONING! ARTIFACTS OF THE OLD WORLD, BRO!
I'M MAKING MONEY FOR THE WHOLE DAMN COMMUNITY! I'M RAISING PROPERTY VALUES! IF YOU OWN, YOU'RE RIDING A MOTHERFUCKING ROCKET!
THESE ZONING PRICKS AND NEIGHBORHOOD FIRST GROUPS SHOULD WORK WITH ME! I'M DRAGGING THIS SHIT HOLE OUTTA THE DARK AGES!

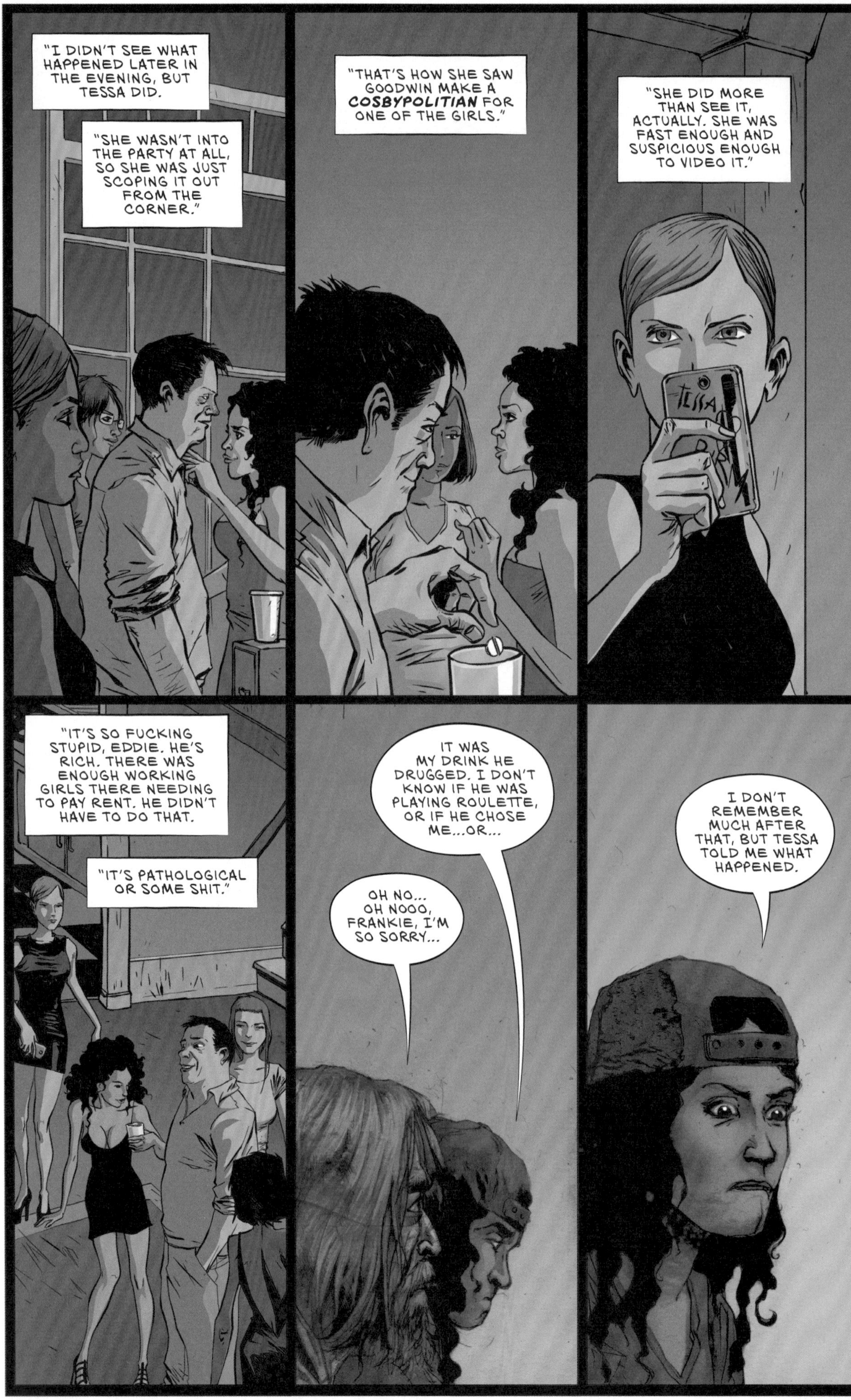
"I DIDN'T SEE WHAT HAPPENED LATER IN THE EVENING, BUT TESSA DID.
"SHE WASN'T INTO THE PARTY AT ALL, SO SHE WAS JUST SCOPING IT OUT FROM THE CORNER."
"THAT'S HOW SHE SAW GOODWIN MAKE A **COSBYPOLITIAN** FOR ONE OF THE GIRLS."
"SHE DID MORE THAN SEE IT, ACTUALLY. SHE WAS FAST ENOUGH AND SUSPICIOUS ENOUGH TO VIDEO IT."
TESSA
"IT'S SO FUCKING STUPID, EDDIE. HE'S RICH. THERE WAS ENOUGH WORKING GIRLS THERE NEEDING TO PAY RENT. HE DIDN'T HAVE TO DO THAT.
"IT'S PATHOLOGICAL OR SOME SHIT."
IT WAS MY DRINK HE DRUGGED. I DON'T KNOW IF HE WAS PLAYING ROULETTE, OR IF HE CHOSE ME...OR...
OH NO... OH NOOO, FRANKIE, I'M SO SORRY...
I DON'T REMEMBER MUCH AFTER THAT, BUT TESSA TOLD ME WHAT HAPPENED.

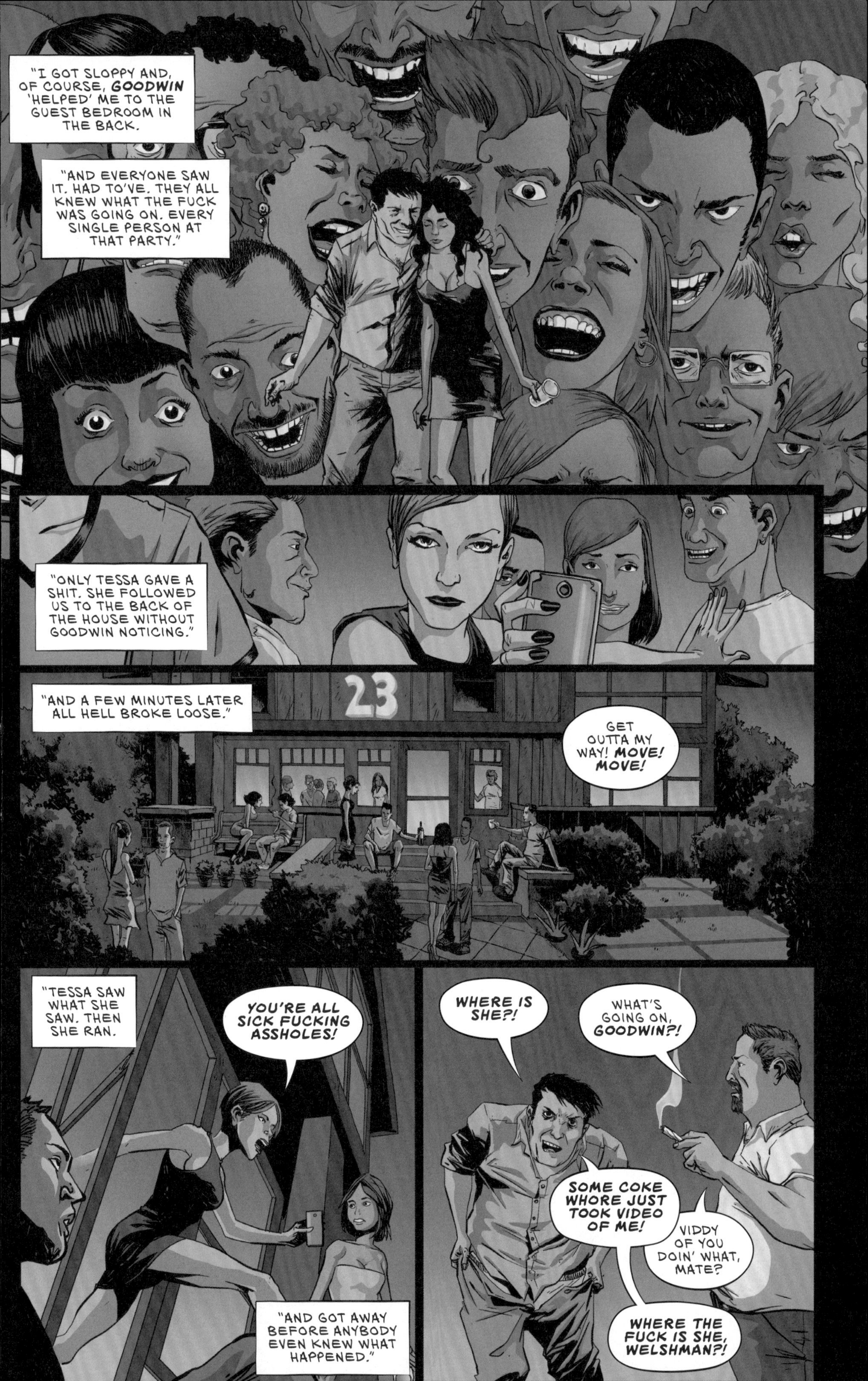
"I GOT SLOPPY AND, OF COURSE, GOODWIN 'HELPED' ME TO THE GUEST BEDROOM IN THE BACK.
"AND EVERYONE SAW IT. HAD TO'VE. THEY ALL KNEW WHAT THE FUCK WAS GOING ON. EVERY SINGLE PERSON AT THAT PARTY."
"ONLY TESSA GAVE A SHIT. SHE FOLLOWED US TO THE BACK OF THE HOUSE WITHOUT GOODWIN NOTICING."
"AND A FEW MINUTES LATER ALL HELL BROKE LOOSE."
23
GET OUTTA MY WAY! MOVE! MOVE!
"TESSA SAW WHAT SHE SAW. THEN SHE RAN.
YOU'RE ALL SICK FUCKING ASSHOLES!
"AND GOT AWAY BEFORE ANYBODY EVEN KNEW WHAT HAPPENED."
WHERE IS SHE?!
WHAT'S GOING ON, GOODWIN?!
SOME COKE WHORE JUST TOOK VIDEO OF ME!
VIDDY OF YOU DOIN' WHAT, MATE?
WHERE THE FUCK IS SHE, WELSHMAN?!

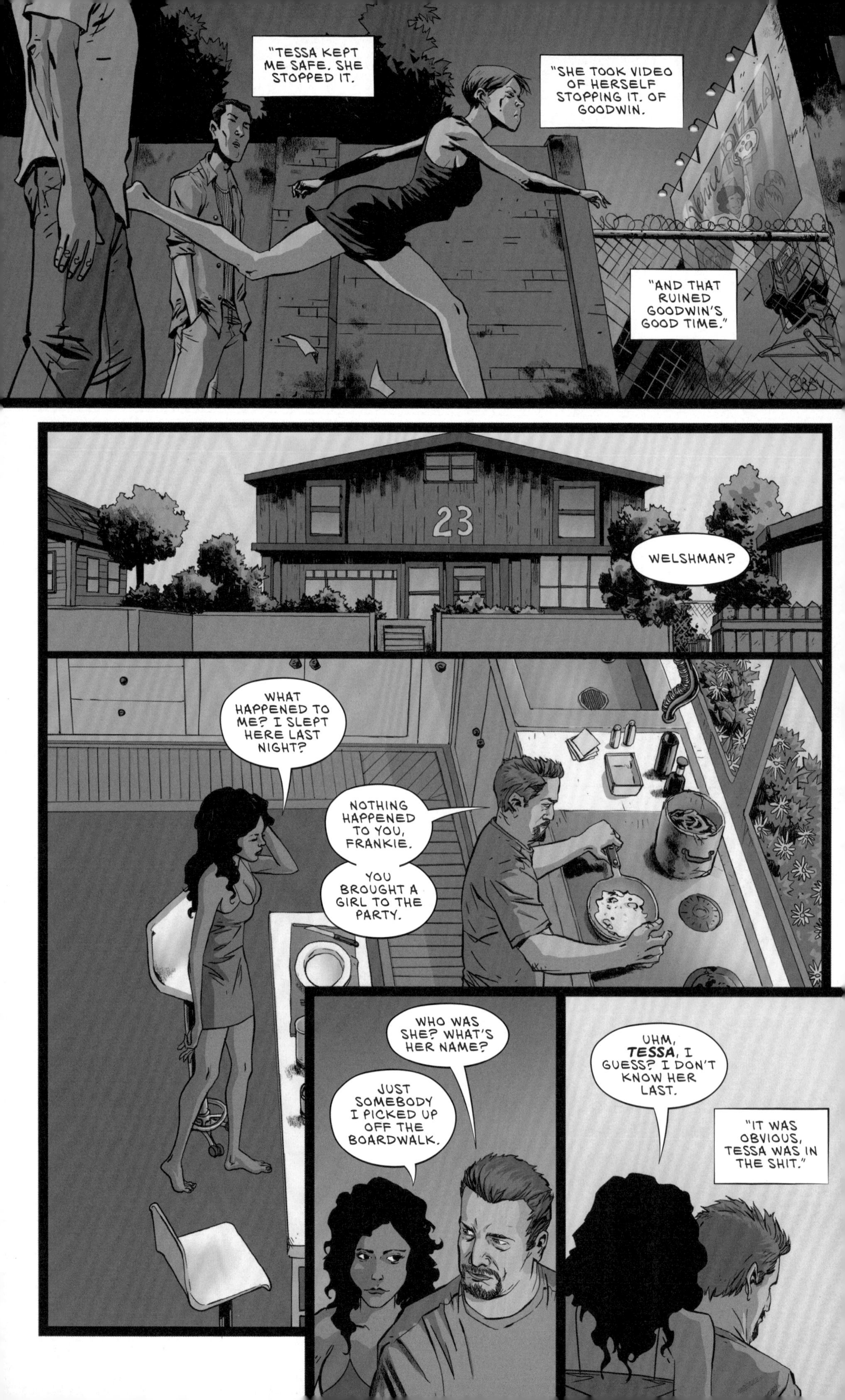
"TESSA KEPT ME SAFE. SHE STOPPED IT.
"SHE TOOK VIDEO OF HERSELF STOPPING IT. OF GOODWIN.
"AND THAT RUINED GOODWIN'S GOOD TIME."
23
WELSHMAN?
WHAT HAPPENED TO ME? I SLEPT HERE LAST NIGHT?
NOTHING HAPPENED TO YOU, FRANKIE.
YOU BROUGHT A GIRL TO THE PARTY.
WHO WAS SHE? WHAT'S HER NAME?
JUST SOMEBODY I PICKED UP OFF THE BOARDWALK.
UHM, **TESSA**, I GUESS? I DON'T KNOW HER LAST.
"IT WAS OBVIOUS, TESSA WAS IN THE SHIT."

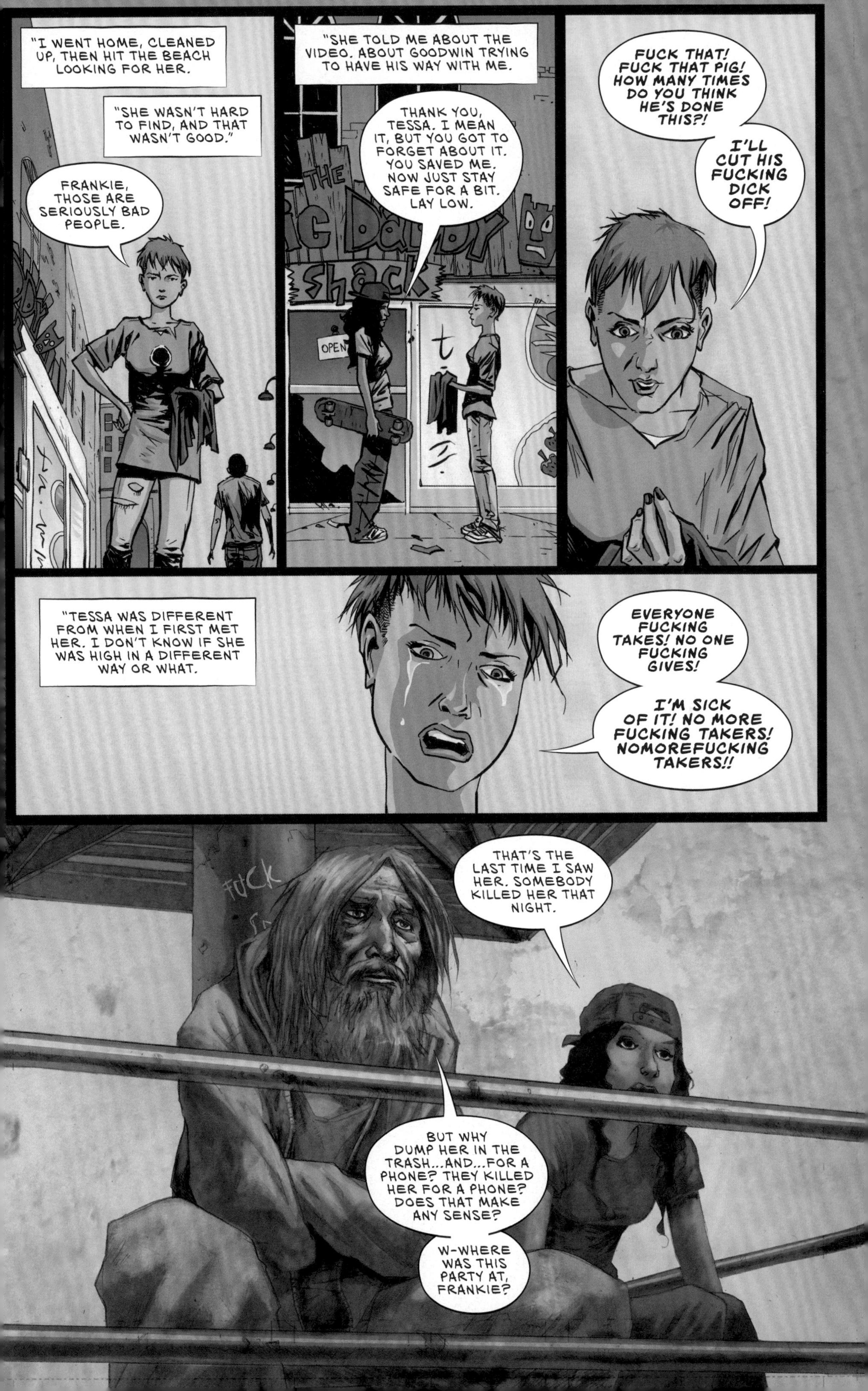
"I WENT HOME, CLEANED UP, THEN HIT THE BEACH LOOKING FOR HER.
"SHE WASN'T HARD TO FIND, AND THAT WASN'T GOOD."
FRANKIE, THOSE ARE SERIOUSLY BAD PEOPLE.
"SHE TOLD ME ABOUT THE VIDEO. ABOUT GOODWIN TRYING TO HAVE HIS WAY WITH ME.
THANK YOU, TESSA. I MEAN IT, BUT YOU GOT TO FORGET ABOUT IT. YOU SAVED ME. NOW JUST STAY SAFE FOR A BIT. LAY LOW.
OPEN
FUCK THAT! FUCK THAT PIG! HOW MANY TIMES DO YOU THINK HE'S DONE THIS?!
I'LL CUT HIS FUCKING DICK OFF!
"TESSA WAS DIFFERENT FROM WHEN I FIRST MET HER. I DON'T KNOW IF SHE WAS HIGH IN A DIFFERENT WAY OR WHAT.
EVERYONE FUCKING TAKES! NO ONE FUCKING GIVES!
I'M SICK OF IT! NO MORE FUCKING TAKERS! NOMOREFUCKING TAKERS!!
FUCK
THAT'S THE LAST TIME I SAW HER. SOMEBODY KILLED HER THAT NIGHT.
BUT WHY DUMP HER IN THE TRASH...AND...FOR A PHONE? THEY KILLED HER FOR A PHONE? DOES THAT MAKE ANY SENSE?
W-WHERE WAS THIS PARTY AT, FRANKIE?

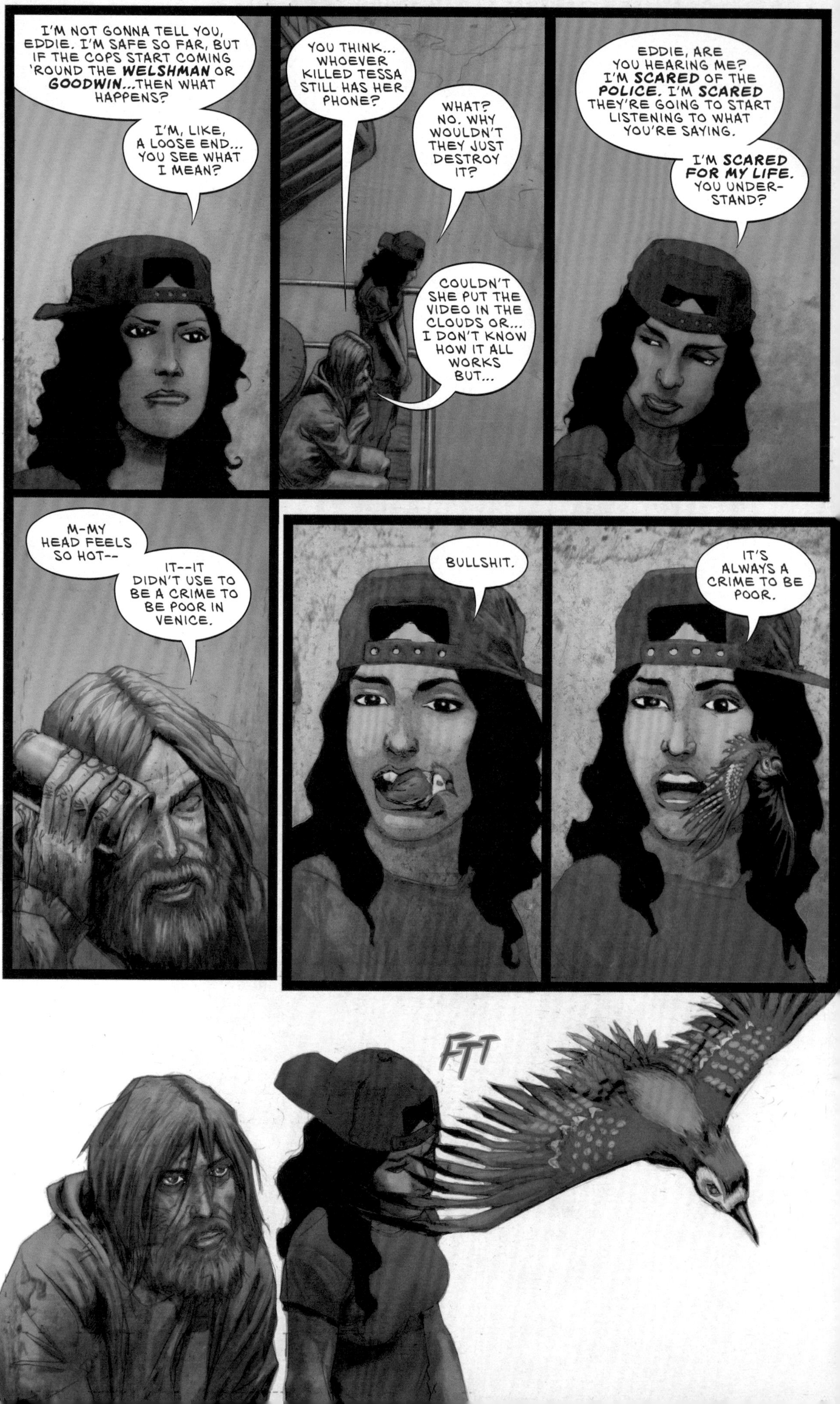
I'M NOT GONNA TELL YOU, EDDIE. I'M SAFE SO FAR, BUT IF THE COPS START COMING 'ROUND THE **WELSHMAN** OR **GOODWIN**...THEN WHAT HAPPENS?
I'M, LIKE, A LOOSE END... YOU SEE WHAT I MEAN?
YOU THINK... WHOEVER KILLED TESSA STILL HAS HER PHONE?
WHAT? NO. WHY WOULDN'T THEY JUST DESTROY IT?
COULDN'T SHE PUT THE VIDEO IN THE CLOUDS OR... I DON'T KNOW HOW IT ALL WORKS BUT...
EDDIE, ARE YOU HEARING ME? I'M **SCARED** OF THE **POLICE.** I'M **SCARED** THEY'RE GOING TO START LISTENING TO WHAT YOU'RE SAYING.
I'M **SCARED FOR MY LIFE.** YOU UNDER-STAND?
M-MY HEAD FEELS SO HOT--
IT--IT DIDN'T USE TO BE A CRIME TO BE POOR IN VENICE.
BULLSHIT.
IT'S ALWAYS A CRIME TO BE POOR.
FTT

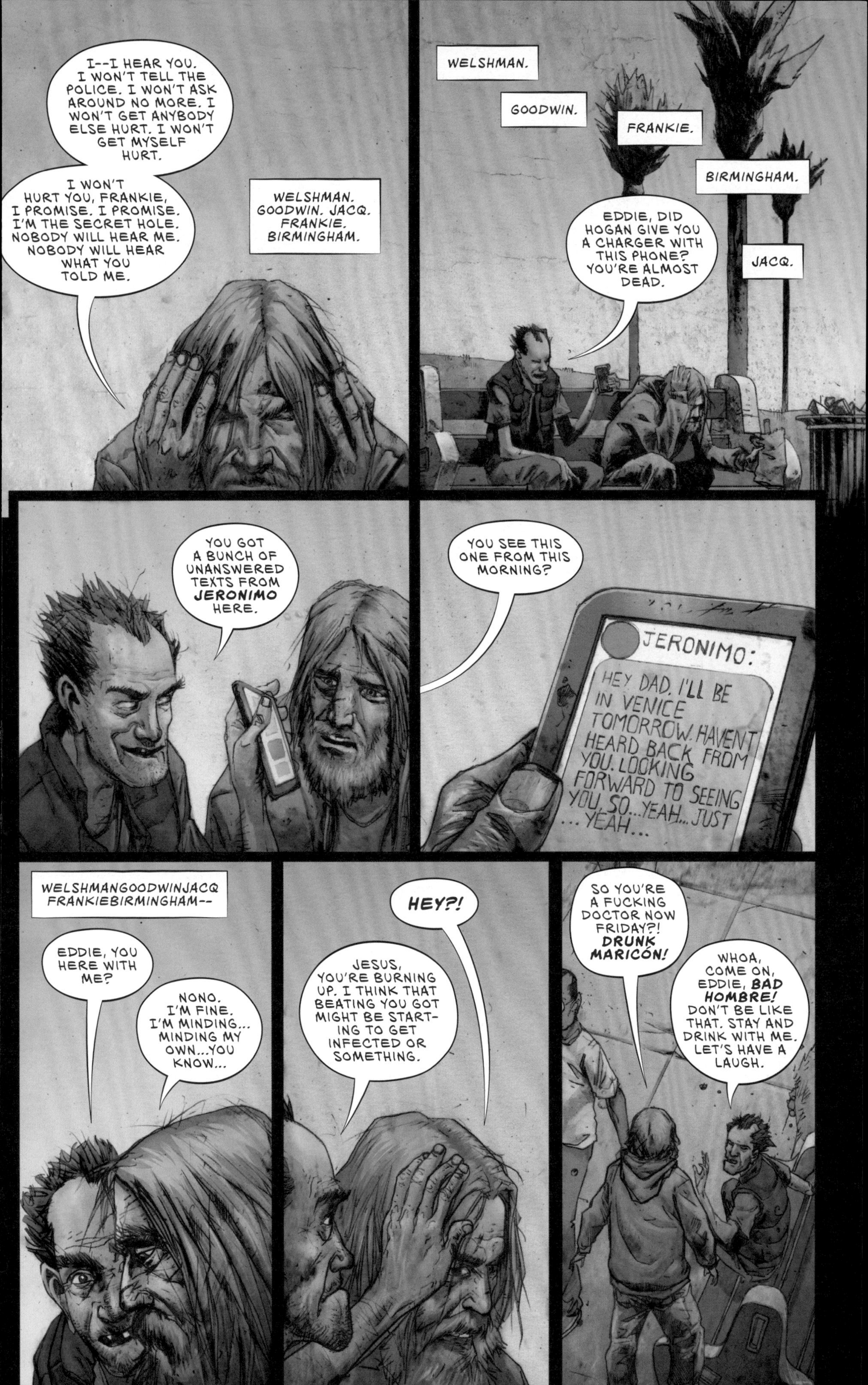
I--I HEAR YOU. I WON'T TELL THE POLICE. I WON'T ASK AROUND NO MORE. I WON'T GET ANYBODY ELSE HURT. I WON'T GET MYSELF HURT.
I WON'T HURT YOU, FRANKIE, I PROMISE. I PROMISE. I'M THE SECRET HOLE. NOBODY WILL HEAR ME. NOBODY WILL HEAR WHAT YOU TOLD ME.
WELSHMAN. GOODWIN. JACQ. FRANKIE. BIRMINGHAM.
WELSHMAN.
GOODWIN.
FRANKIE.
BIRMINGHAM.
EDDIE, DID HOGAN GIVE YOU A CHARGER WITH THIS PHONE? YOU'RE ALMOST DEAD.
JACQ.
YOU GOT A BUNCH OF UNANSWERED TEXTS FROM **JERONIMO** HERE.
YOU SEE THIS ONE FROM THIS MORNING?
JERONIMO:
HEY DAD. I'LL BE IN VENICE TOMORROW. HAVENT HEARD BACK FROM YOU. LOOKING FORWARD TO SEEING YOU, SO... YEAH... JUST ... YEAH...
WELSHMANGOODWINJACQ FRANKIEBIRMINGHAM--
EDDIE, YOU HERE WITH ME?
NONO. I'M FINE. I'M MINDING... MINDING MY OWN... YOU KNOW...
HEY?!
JESUS, YOU'RE BURNING UP. I THINK THAT BEATING YOU GOT MIGHT BE STARTING TO GET INFECTED OR SOMETHING.
SO YOU'RE A FUCKING DOCTOR NOW FRIDAY?! **DRUNK MARICÓN!**
WHOA, COME ON, EDDIE, **BAD HOMBRE!** DON'T BE LIKE THAT. STAY AND DRINK WITH ME. LET'S HAVE A LAUGH.

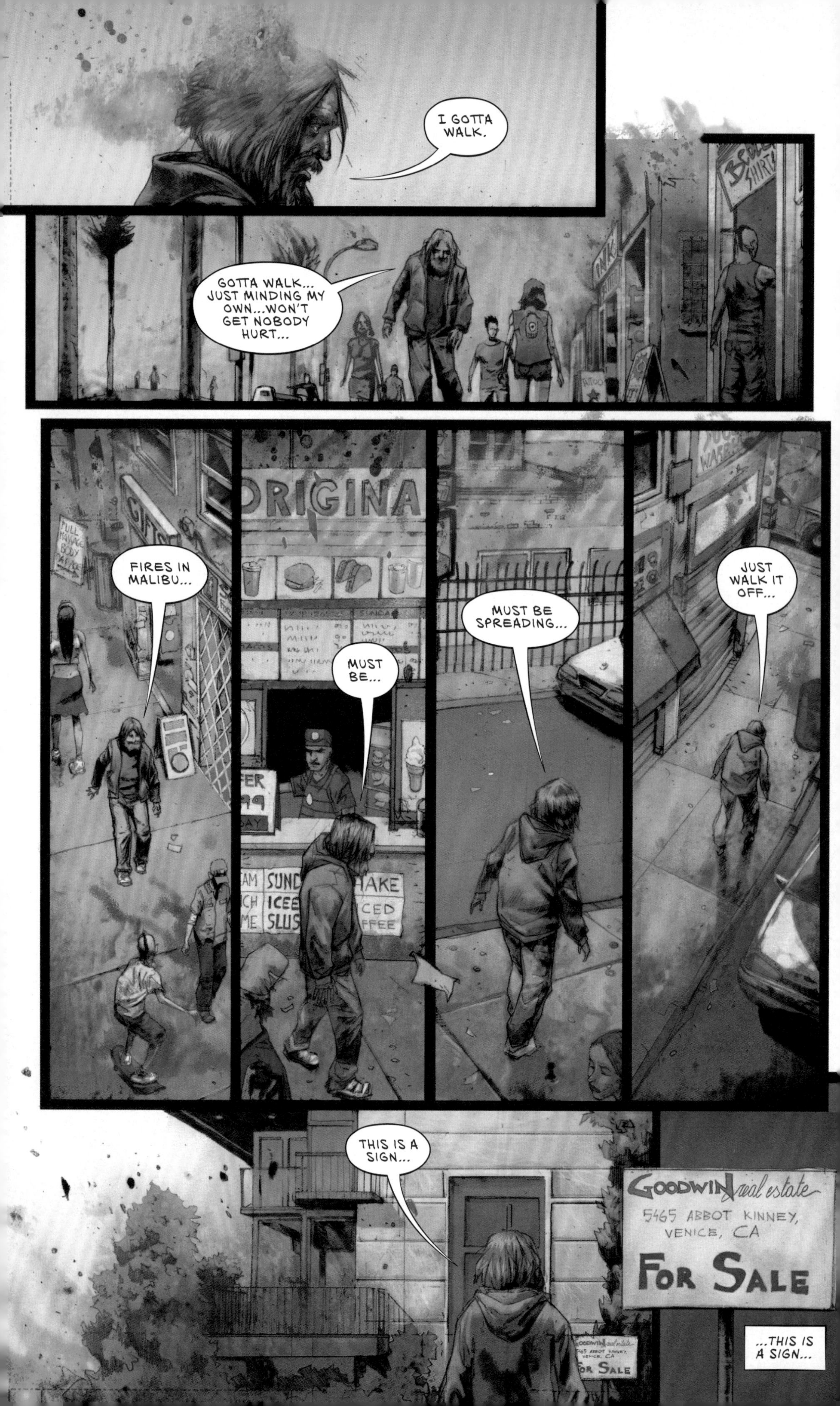

I GOTTA WALK.
GOTTA WALK... JUST MINDING MY OWN...WON'T GET NOBODY HURT...
ORIGINA
FIRES IN MALIBU...
MUST BE...
MUST BE SPREADING...
JUST WALK IT OFF...
THIS IS A SIGN...
GOODWIN real estate
5465 ABBOT KINNEY, VENICE, CA
FOR SALE
...THIS IS A SIGN...

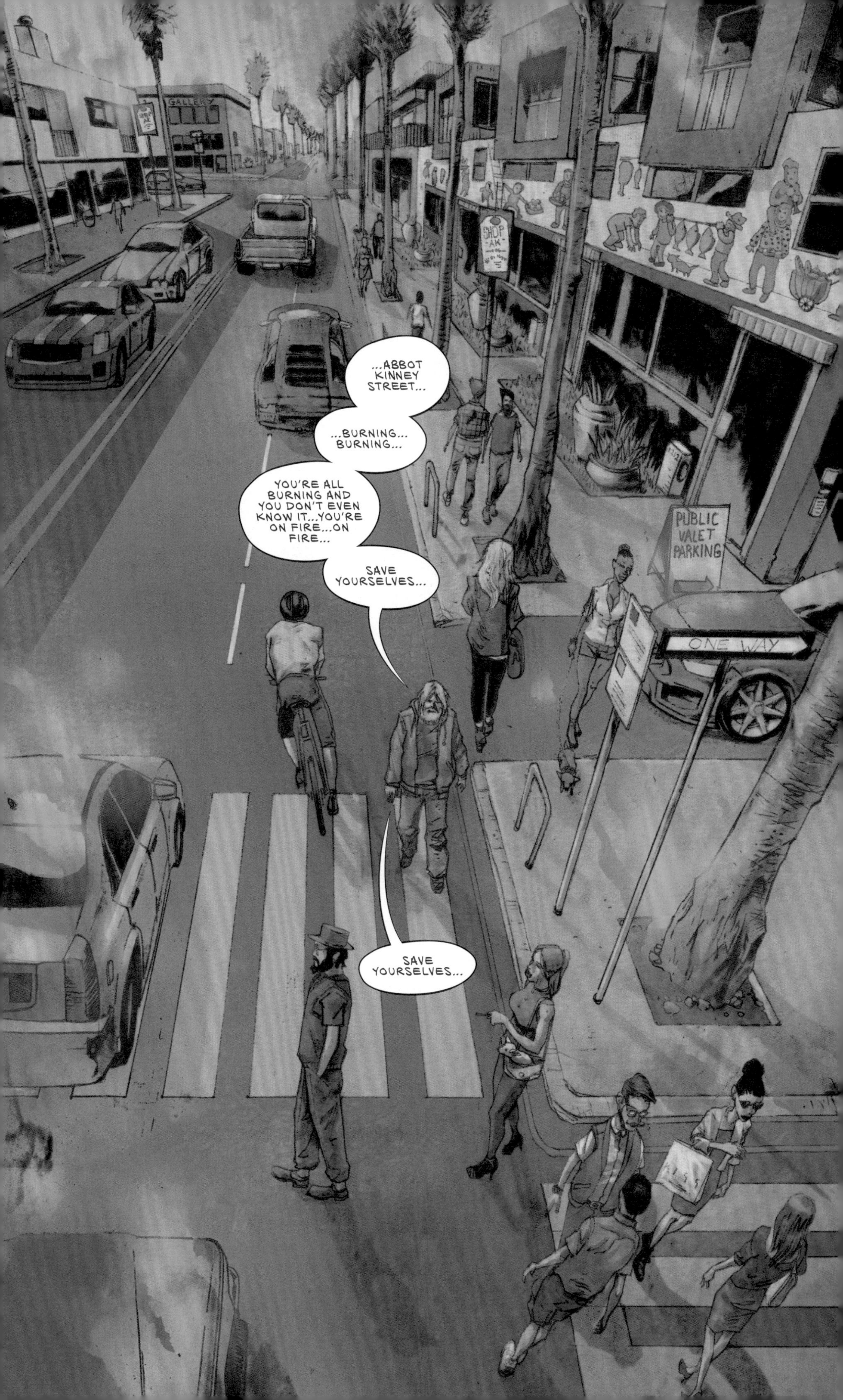

GALLERY
SHOP AK
...ABBOT KINNEY STREET...
...BURNING... BURNING...
YOU'RE ALL BURNING AND YOU DON'T EVEN KNOW IT...YOU'RE ON FIRE...ON FIRE...
SAVE YOURSELVES...
PUBLIC VALET PARKING
ONE WAY
SAVE YOURSELVES...

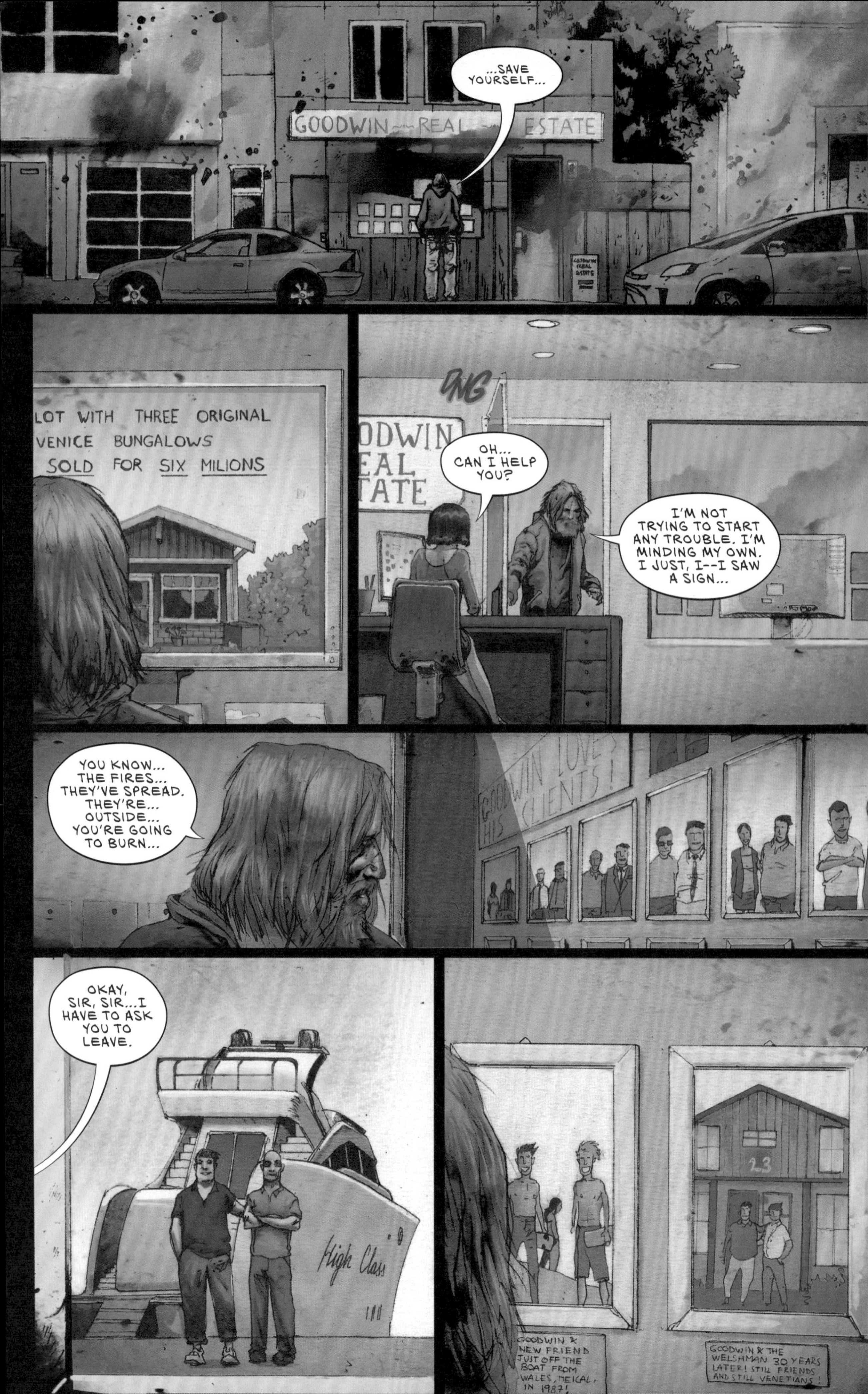
...SAVE YOURSELF...
GOODWIN REAL ESTATE
LOT WITH THREE ORIGINAL VENICE BUNGALOWS SOLD FOR SIX MILIONS
DING
GOODWIN REAL ESTATE
OH... CAN I HELP YOU?
I'M NOT TRYING TO START ANY TROUBLE. I'M MINDING MY OWN. I JUST, I--I SAW A SIGN...
YOU KNOW... THE FIRES... THEY'VE SPREAD. THEY'RE... OUTSIDE... YOU'RE GOING TO BURN...
GOODWIN LOVES HIS CLIENTS!
OKAY, SIR, SIR...I HAVE TO ASK YOU TO LEAVE.
High Class
23
GOODWIN & NEW FRIEND JUST OFF THE BOAT FROM WALES, MEICAL, IN 1987!
GOODWIN & THE WELSHMAN 30 YEARS LATER! STILL FRIENDS AND STILL VENETIANS!

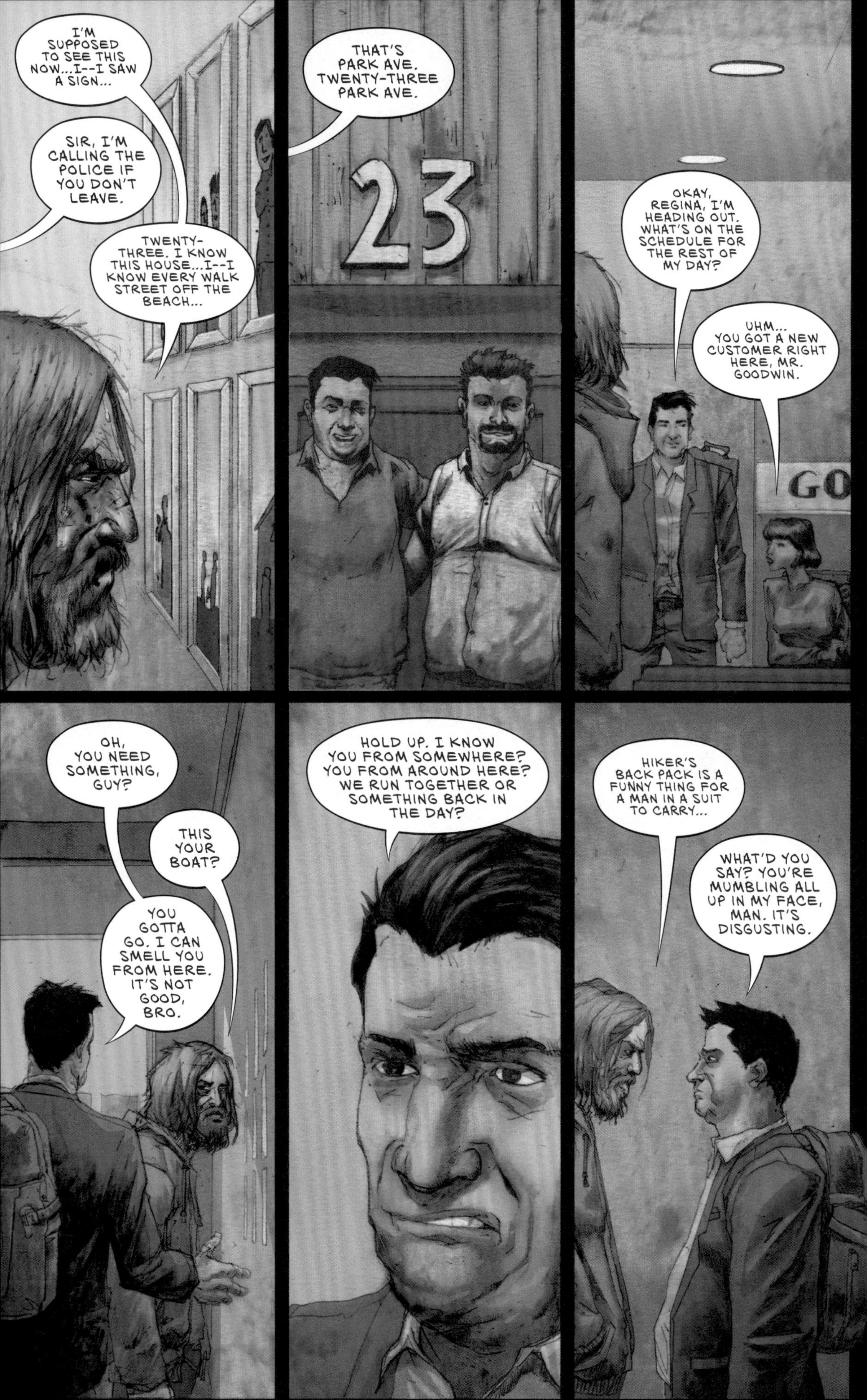
I'M SUPPOSED TO SEE THIS NOW...I--I SAW A SIGN...
SIR, I'M CALLING THE POLICE IF YOU DON'T LEAVE.
TWENTY-THREE. I KNOW THIS HOUSE...I--I KNOW EVERY WALK STREET OFF THE BEACH...
THAT'S PARK AVE. TWENTY-THREE PARK AVE.
23
OKAY, REGINA, I'M HEADING OUT. WHAT'S ON THE SCHEDULE FOR THE REST OF MY DAY?
UHM... YOU GOT A NEW CUSTOMER RIGHT HERE, MR. GOODWIN.
GO
OH, YOU NEED SOMETHING, GUY?
THIS YOUR BOAT?
YOU GOTTA GO. I CAN SMELL YOU FROM HERE. IT'S NOT GOOD, BRO.
HOLD UP. I KNOW YOU FROM SOMEWHERE? YOU FROM AROUND HERE? WE RUN TOGETHER OR SOMETHING BACK IN THE DAY?
HIKER'S BACK PACK IS A FUNNY THING FOR A MAN IN A SUIT TO CARRY...
WHAT'D YOU SAY? YOU'RE MUMBLING ALL UP IN MY FACE, MAN. IT'S DISGUSTING.

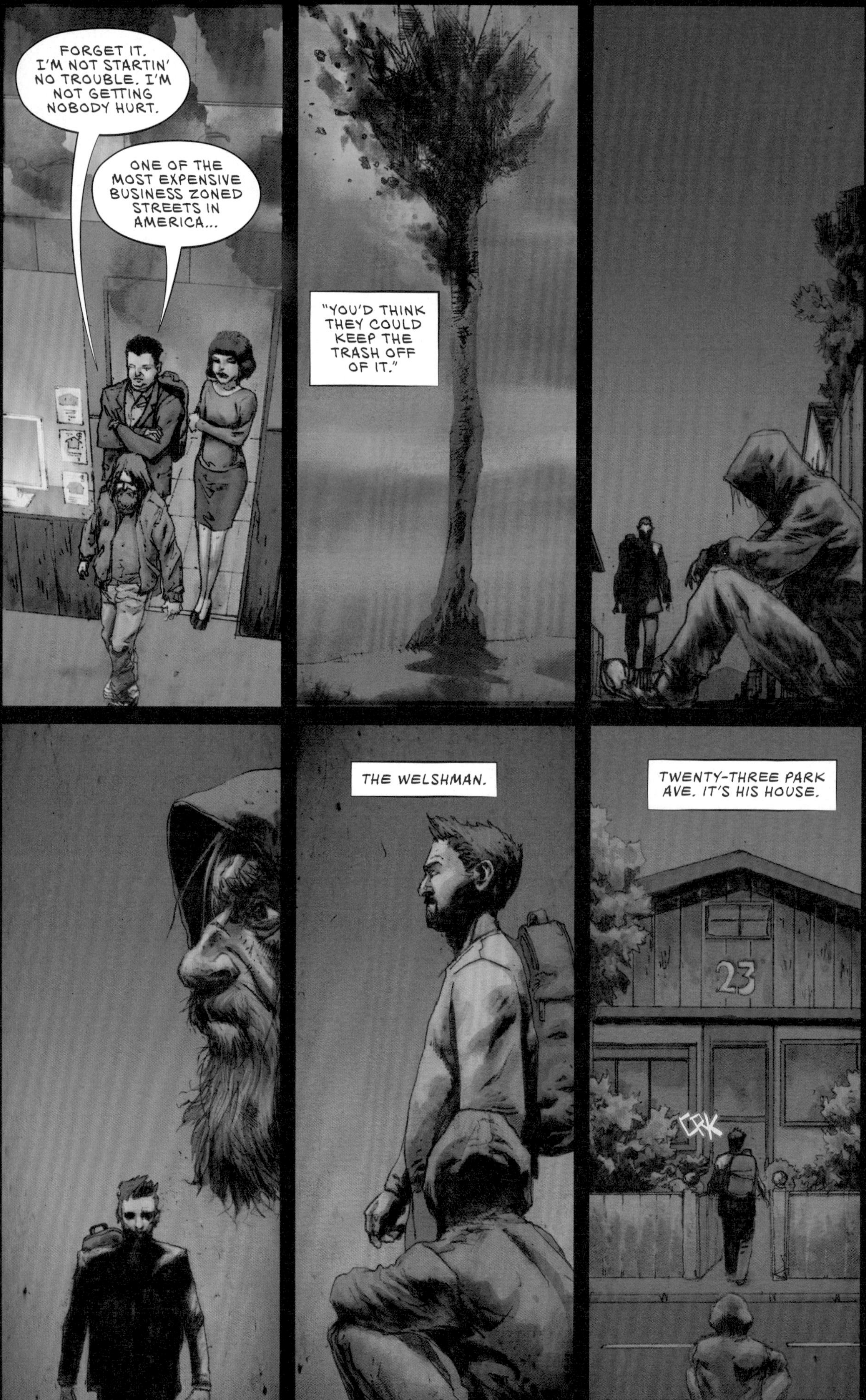
FORGET IT. I'M NOT STARTIN' NO TROUBLE. I'M NOT GETTING NOBODY HURT.
ONE OF THE MOST EXPENSIVE BUSINESS ZONED STREETS IN AMERICA...
"YOU'D THINK THEY COULD KEEP THE TRASH OFF OF IT."
THE WELSHMAN.
TWENTY-THREE PARK AVE. IT'S HIS HOUSE.
23
CRK

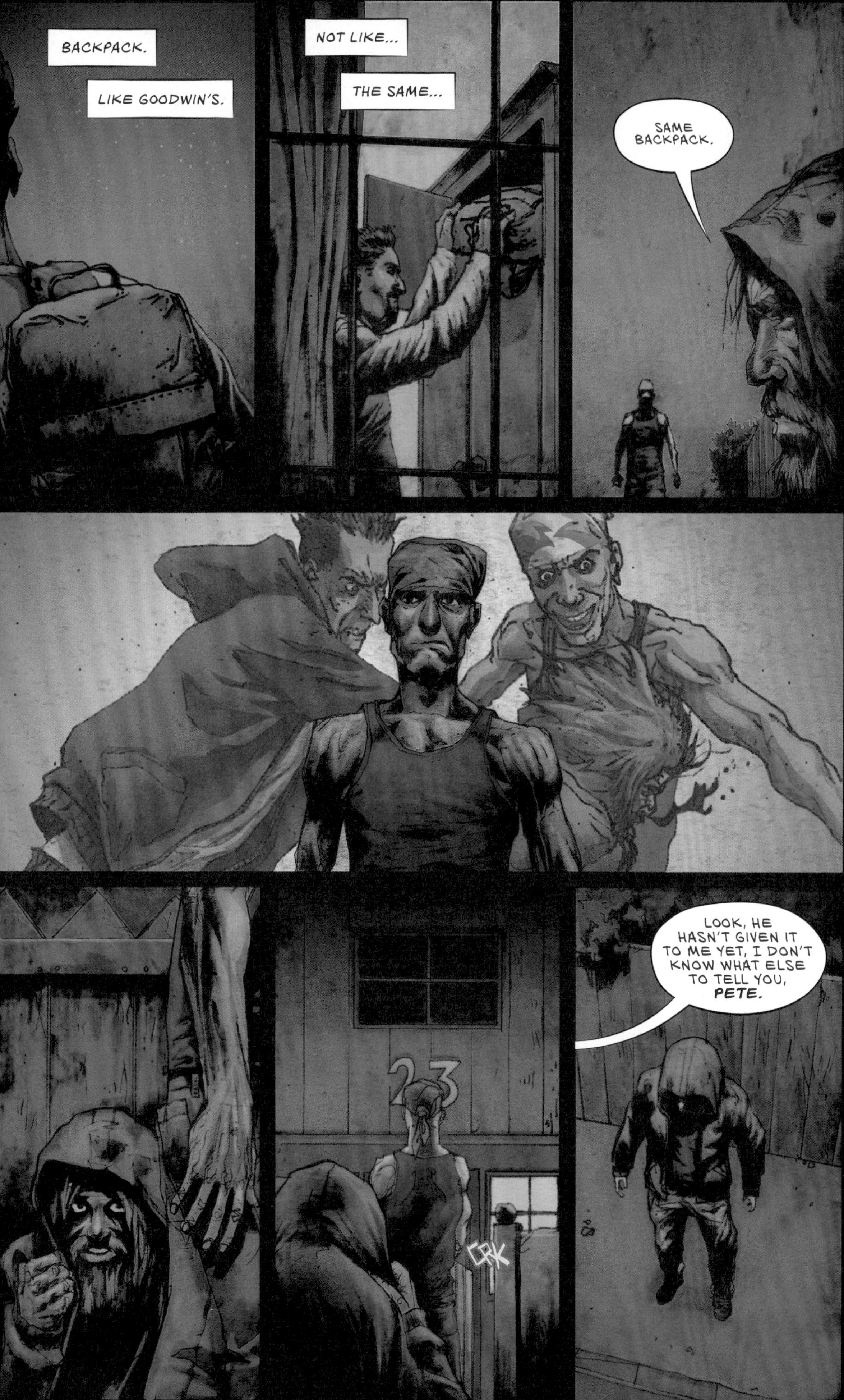
BACKPACK.
LIKE GOODWIN'S.
NOT LIKE...
THE SAME...
SAME BACKPACK.
CRK
LOOK, HE HASN'T GIVEN IT TO ME YET, I DON'T KNOW WHAT ELSE TO TELL YOU, **PETE.**

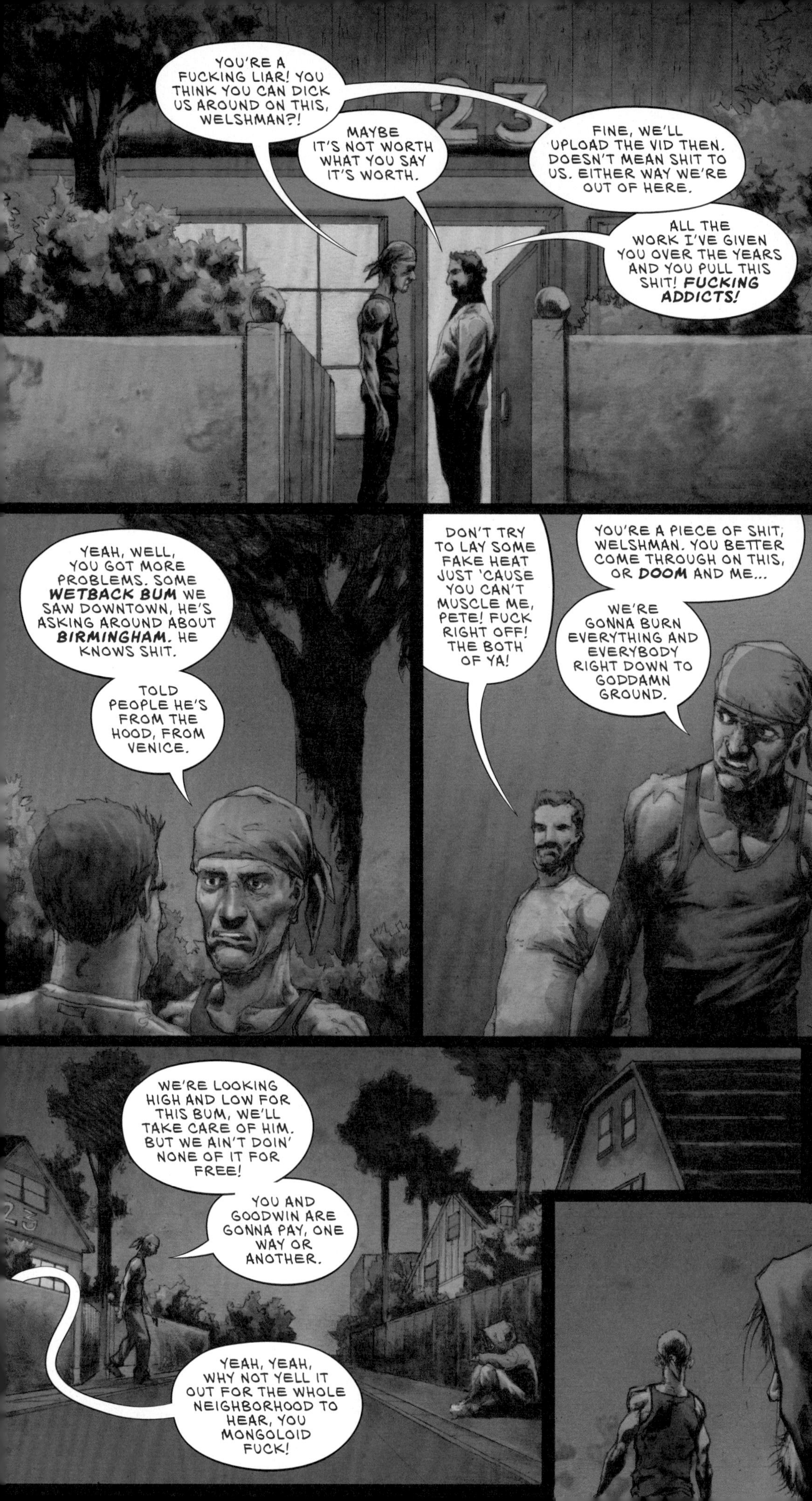

YOU'RE A FUCKING LIAR! YOU THINK YOU CAN DICK US AROUND ON THIS, WELSHMAN?!
MAYBE IT'S NOT WORTH WHAT YOU SAY IT'S WORTH.
FINE, WE'LL UPLOAD THE VID THEN. DOESN'T MEAN SHIT TO US. EITHER WAY WE'RE OUT OF HERE.
ALL THE WORK I'VE GIVEN YOU OVER THE YEARS AND YOU PULL THIS SHIT! FUCKING ADDICTS!
YEAH, WELL, YOU GOT MORE PROBLEMS. SOME WETBACK BUM WE SAW DOWNTOWN, HE'S ASKING AROUND ABOUT BIRMINGHAM. HE KNOWS SHIT.
TOLD PEOPLE HE'S FROM THE HOOD, FROM VENICE.
DON'T TRY TO LAY SOME FAKE HEAT JUST 'CAUSE YOU CAN'T MUSCLE ME, PETE! FUCK RIGHT OFF! THE BOTH OF YA!
YOU'RE A PIECE OF SHIT, WELSHMAN. YOU BETTER COME THROUGH ON THIS, OR DOOM AND ME...
WE'RE GONNA BURN EVERYTHING AND EVERYBODY RIGHT DOWN TO GODDAMN GROUND.
WE'RE LOOKING HIGH AND LOW FOR THIS BUM, WE'LL TAKE CARE OF HIM. BUT WE AIN'T DOIN' NONE OF IT FOR FREE!
YOU AND GOODWIN ARE GONNA PAY, ONE WAY OR ANOTHER.
YEAH, YEAH, WHY NOT YELL IT OUT FOR THE WHOLE NEIGHBORHOOD TO HEAR, YOU MONGOLOID FUCK!

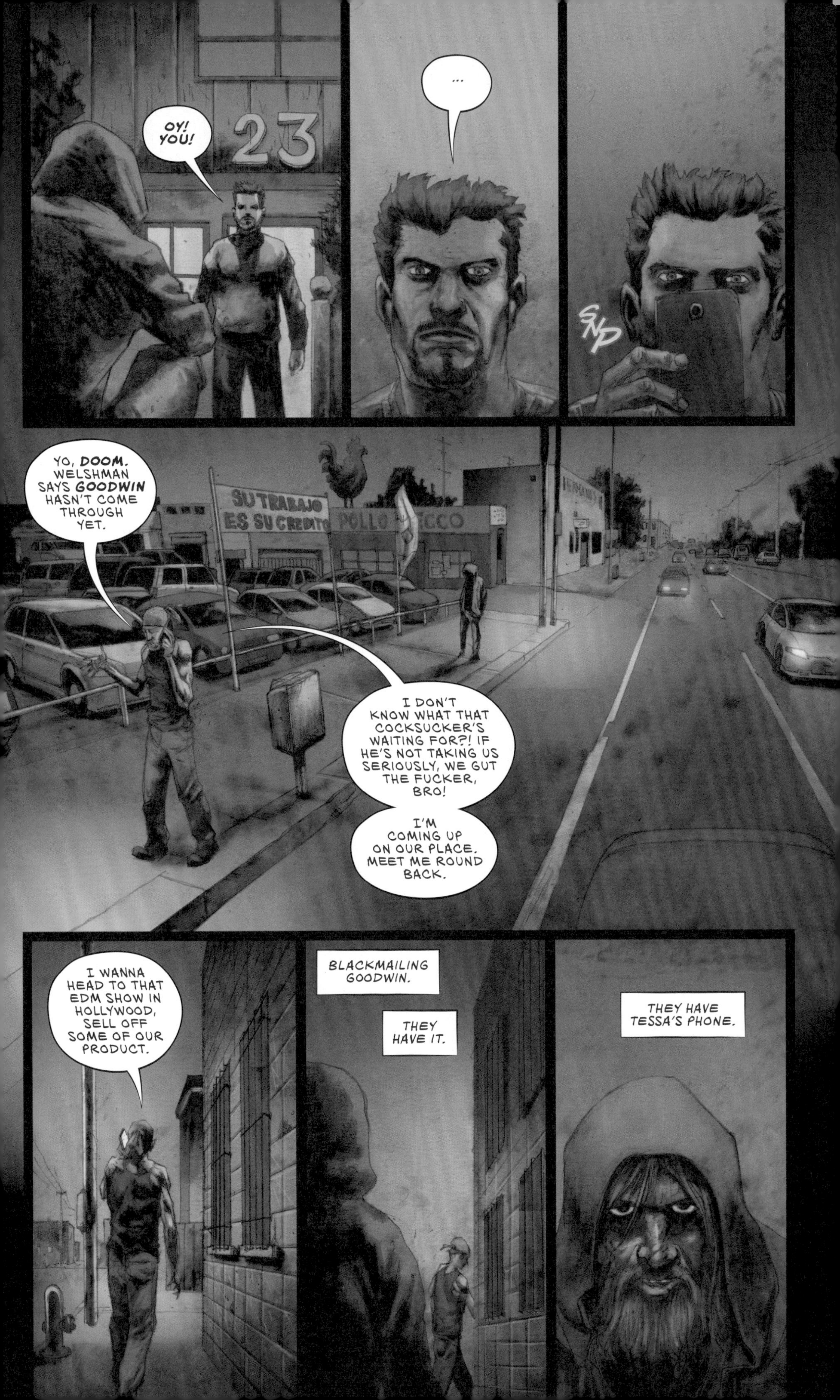

OY! YOU!
23
...
SNP
YO, DOOM. WELSHMAN SAYS GOODWIN HASN'T COME THROUGH YET.
SU TRABAJO ES SU CREDITO
I DON'T KNOW WHAT THAT COCKSUCKER'S WAITING FOR?! IF HE'S NOT TAKING US SERIOUSLY, WE GUT THE FUCKER, BRO!
I'M COMING UP ON OUR PLACE. MEET ME ROUND BACK.
I WANNA HEAD TO THAT EDM SHOW IN HOLLYWOOD, SELL OFF SOME OF OUR PRODUCT.
BLACKMAILING GOODWIN.
THEY HAVE IT.
THEY HAVE TESSA'S PHONE.

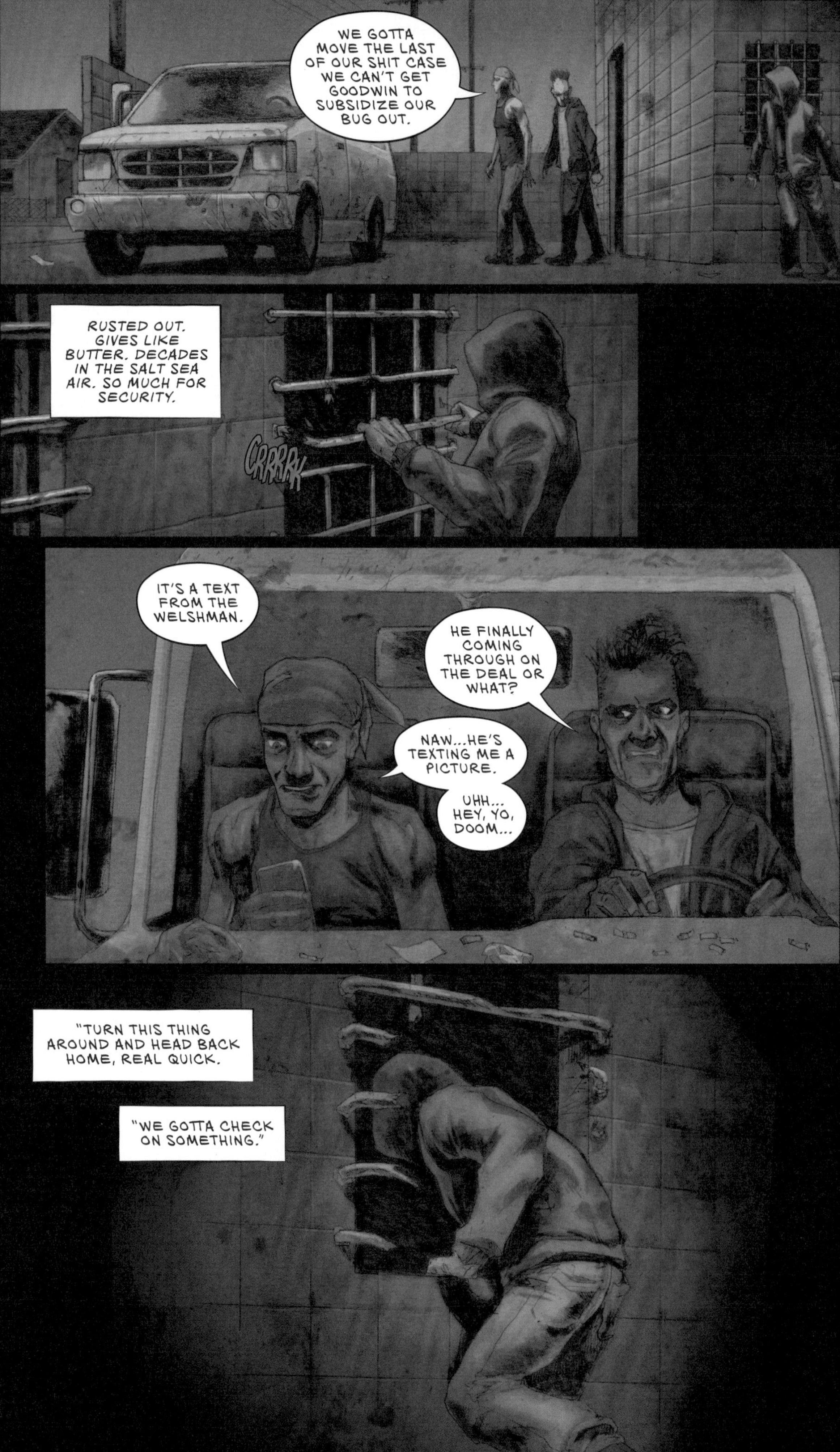
WE GOTTA MOVE THE LAST OF OUR SHIT CASE WE CAN'T GET GOODWIN TO SUBSIDIZE OUR BUG OUT.
RUSTED OUT. GIVES LIKE BUTTER. DECADES IN THE SALT SEA AIR. SO MUCH FOR SECURITY.
CRRRRK
IT'S A TEXT FROM THE WELSHMAN.
HE FINALLY COMING THROUGH ON THE DEAL OR WHAT?
NAW...HE'S TEXTING ME A PICTURE.
UHH... HEY, YO, DOOM...
"TURN THIS THING AROUND AND HEAD BACK HOME, REAL QUICK.
"WE GOTTA CHECK ON SOMETHING."

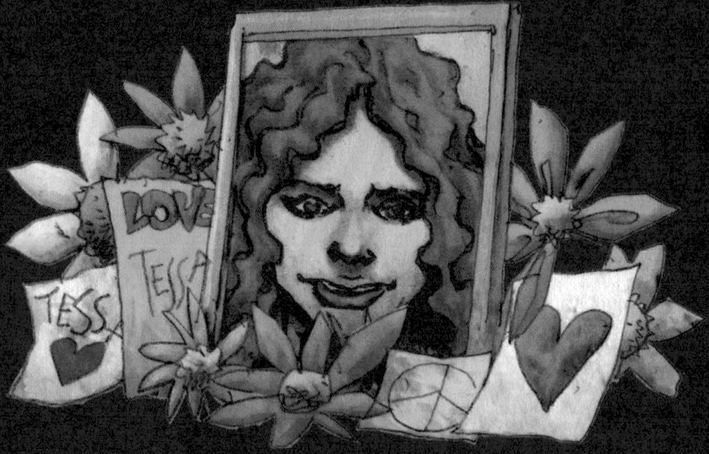
LOVE
TESSA
TESSA

CHAPTER 4

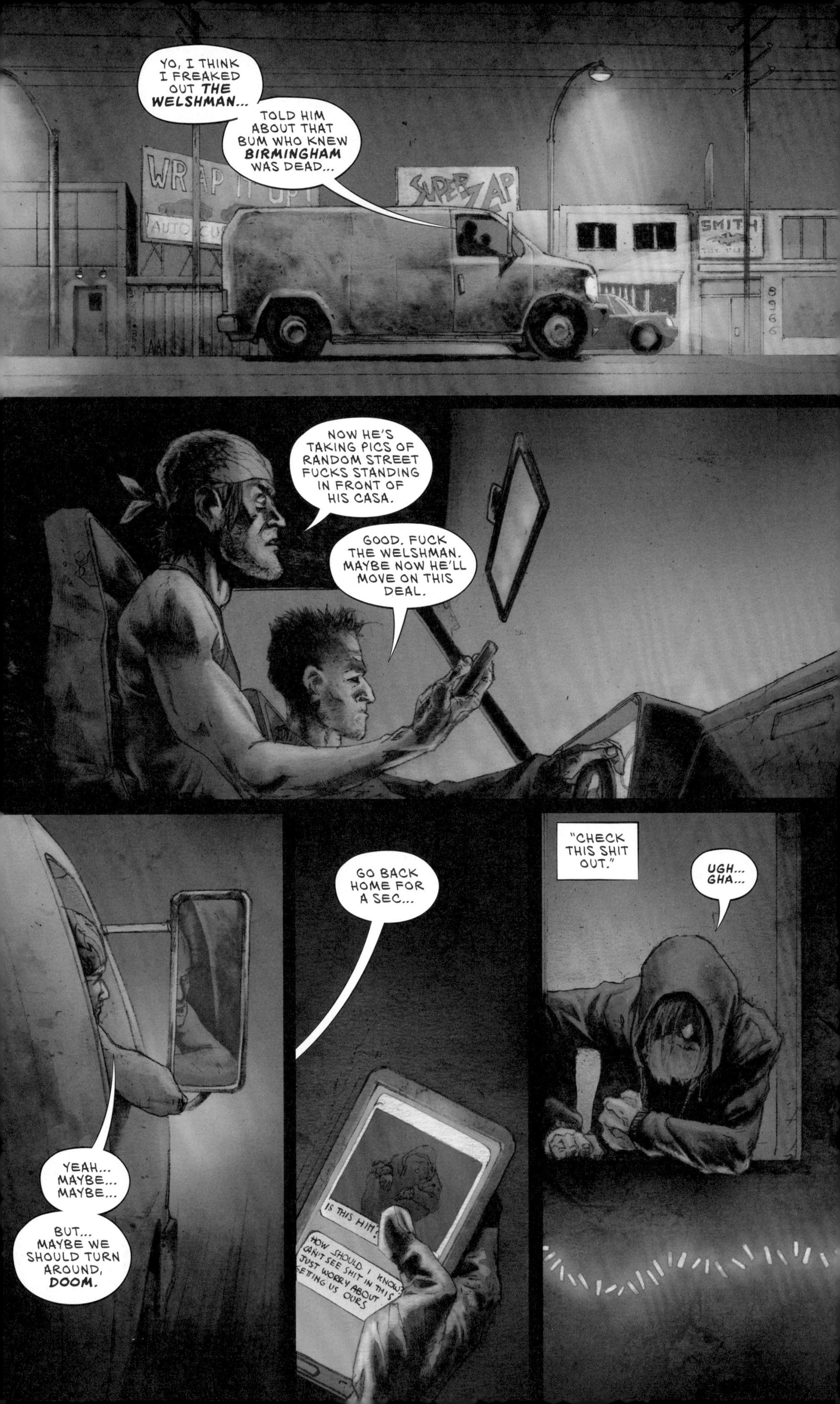
YO, I THINK I FREAKED OUT THE WELSHMAN...
TOLD HIM ABOUT THAT BUM WHO KNEW BIRMINGHAM WAS DEAD...
WRAP IT UP!
AUTO
SUPER ZAP
SMITH
8966
NOW HE'S TAKING PICS OF RANDOM STREET FUCKS STANDING IN FRONT OF HIS CASA.
GOOD. FUCK THE WELSHMAN. MAYBE NOW HE'LL MOVE ON THIS DEAL.
YEAH... MAYBE... MAYBE...
BUT... MAYBE WE SHOULD TURN AROUND, DOOM.
GO BACK HOME FOR A SEC...
IS THIS HIM?
HOW SHOULD I KNOW? CAN'T SEE SHIT IN THIS JUST WORRY ABOUT GETTING US OURS
"CHECK THIS SHIT OUT."
UGH... GHA...

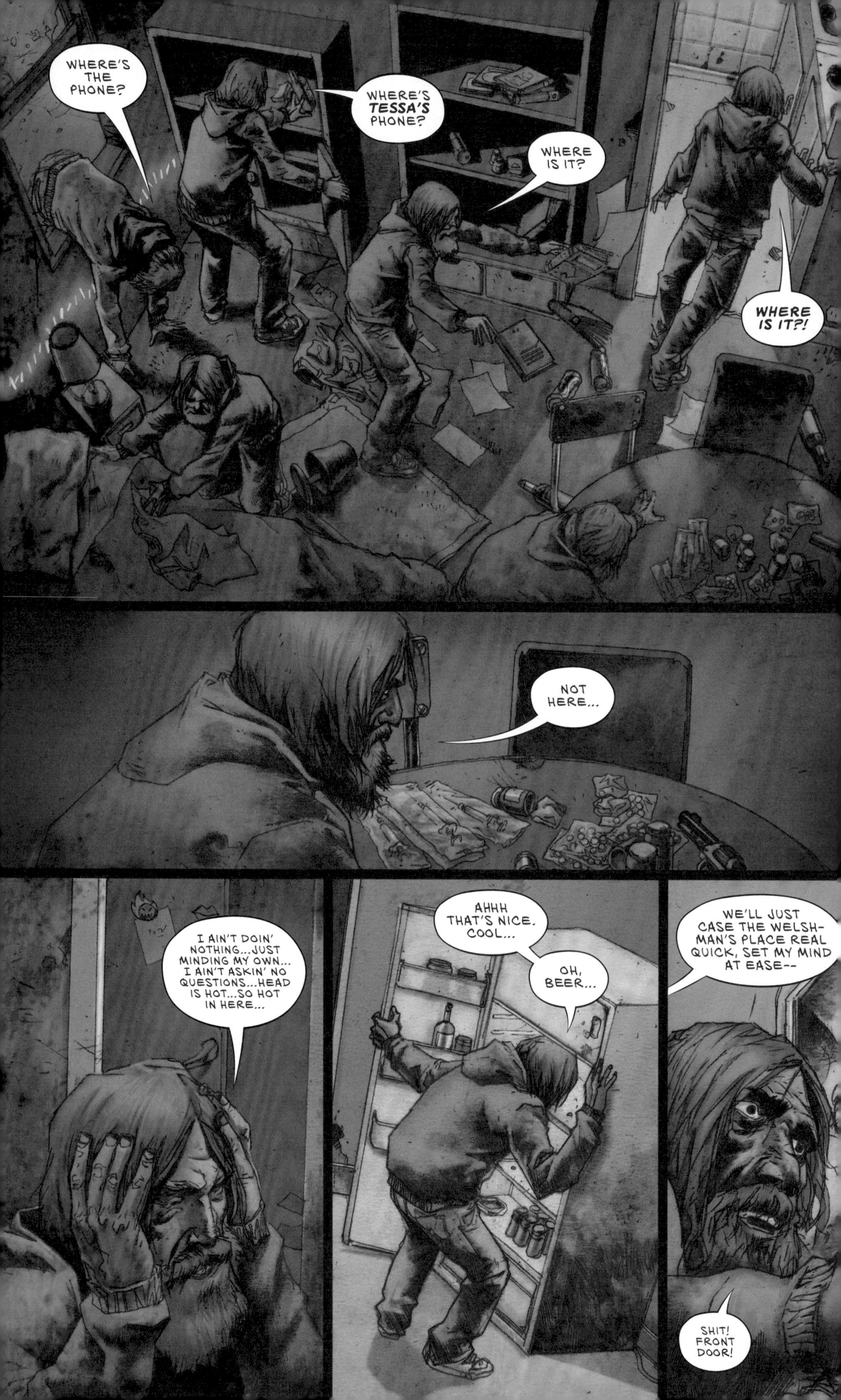
WHERE'S THE PHONE?
WHERE'S TESSA'S PHONE?
WHERE IS IT?
WHERE IS IT?!
NOT HERE...
I AIN'T DOIN' NOTHING...JUST MINDING MY OWN... I AIN'T ASKIN' NO QUESTIONS...HEAD IS HOT...SO HOT IN HERE...
AHHH THAT'S NICE. COOL...
OH, BEER...
WE'LL JUST CASE THE WELSH-MAN'S PLACE REAL QUICK, SET MY MIND AT EASE--
SHIT! FRONT DOOR!

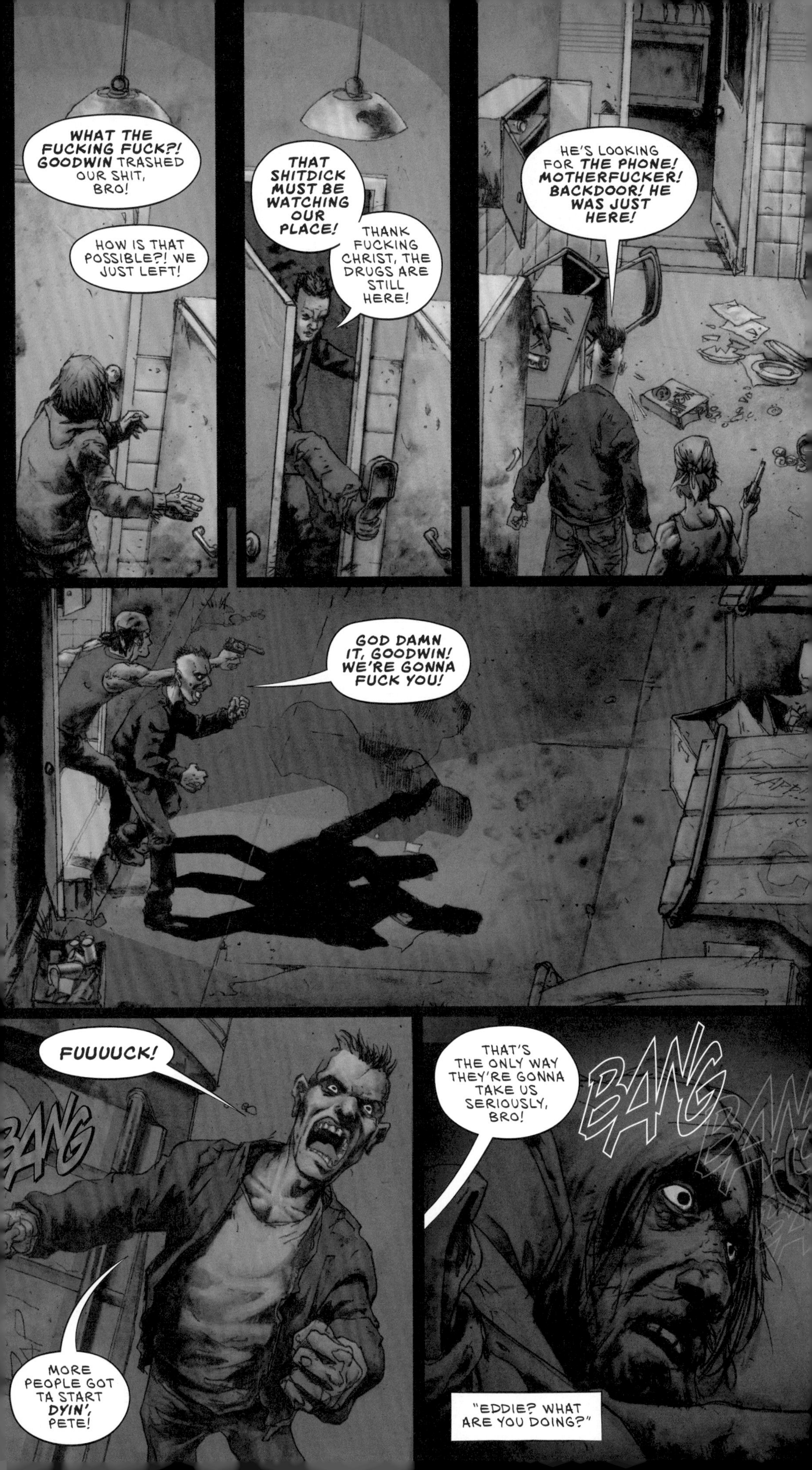
WHAT THE FUCKING FUCK?! GOODWIN TRASHED OUR SHIT, BRO!
HOW IS THAT POSSIBLE?! WE JUST LEFT!
THAT SHITDICK MUST BE WATCHING OUR PLACE!
THANK FUCKING CHRIST, THE DRUGS ARE STILL HERE!
HE'S LOOKING FOR THE PHONE! MOTHERFUCKER! BACKDOOR! HE WAS JUST HERE!
GOD DAMN IT, GOODWIN! WE'RE GONNA FUCK YOU!
FUUUUCK!
MORE PEOPLE GOT TA START DYIN', PETE!
THAT'S THE ONLY WAY THEY'RE GONNA TAKE US SERIOUSLY, BRO!
BANG
"EDDIE? WHAT ARE YOU DOING?"

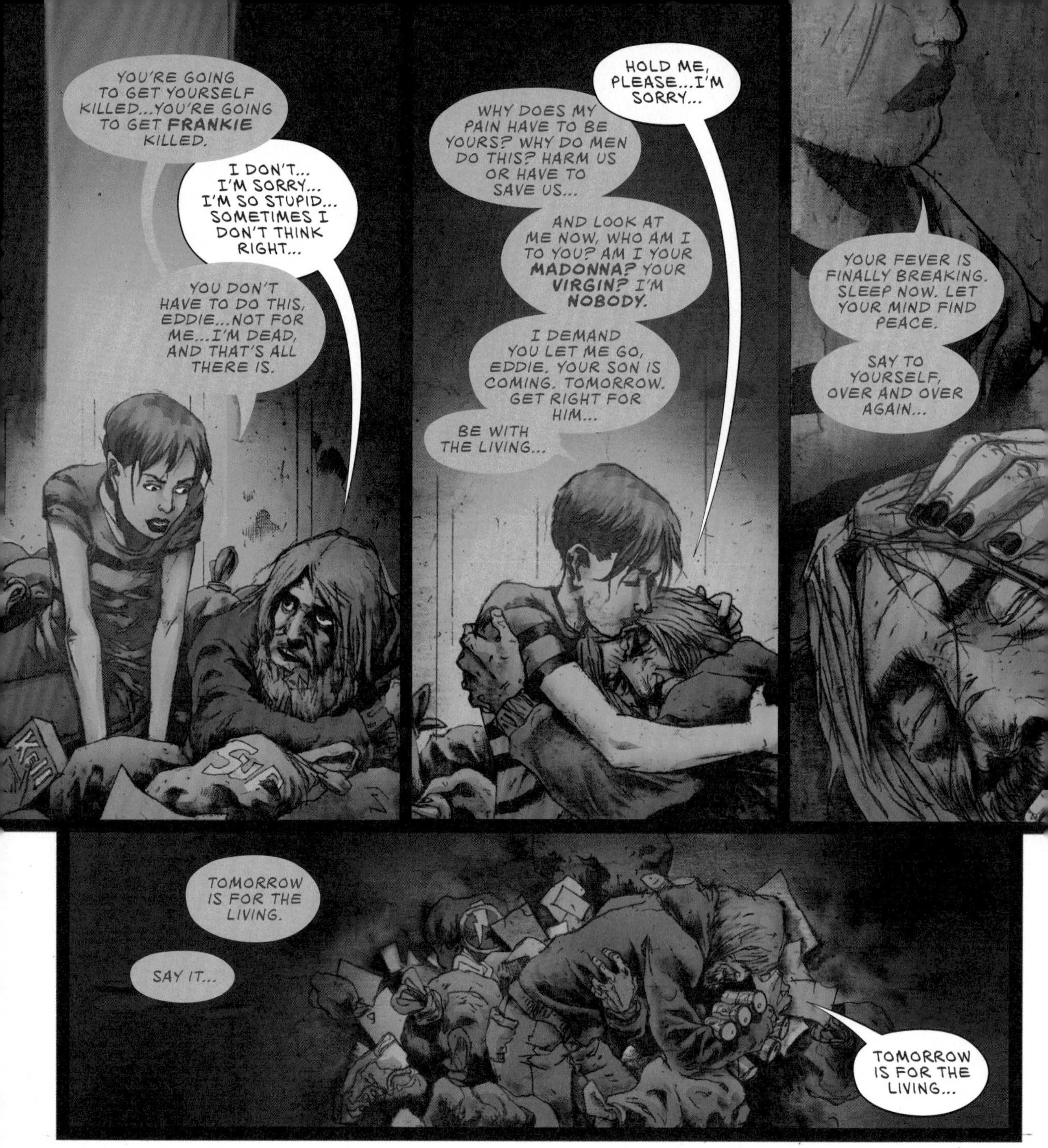
YOU'RE GOING TO GET YOURSELF KILLED...YOU'RE GOING TO GET **FRANKIE** KILLED.
I DON'T... I'M SORRY... I'M SO STUPID... SOMETIMES I DON'T THINK RIGHT...
YOU DON'T HAVE TO DO THIS, EDDIE...NOT FOR ME...I'M DEAD, AND THAT'S ALL THERE IS.
HOLD ME, PLEASE...I'M SORRY...
WHY DOES MY PAIN HAVE TO BE YOURS? WHY DO MEN DO THIS? HARM US OR HAVE TO SAVE US...
AND LOOK AT ME NOW, WHO AM I TO YOU? AM I YOUR **MADONNA?** YOUR **VIRGIN?** I'M **NOBODY.**
I DEMAND YOU LET ME GO, EDDIE. YOUR SON IS COMING. TOMORROW. GET RIGHT FOR HIM...
BE WITH THE LIVING...
YOUR FEVER IS FINALLY BREAKING. SLEEP NOW. LET YOUR MIND FIND PEACE.
SAY TO YOURSELF, OVER AND OVER AGAIN...
TOMORROW IS FOR THE LIVING.
SAY IT...
TOMORROW IS FOR THE LIVING...

"TOMORROW IS FOR THE LIVING."

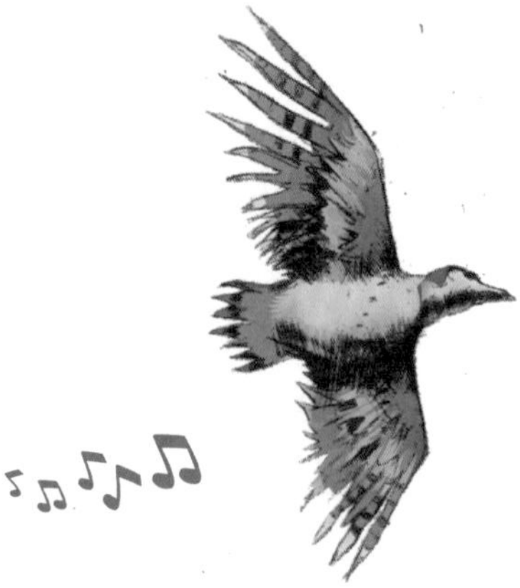

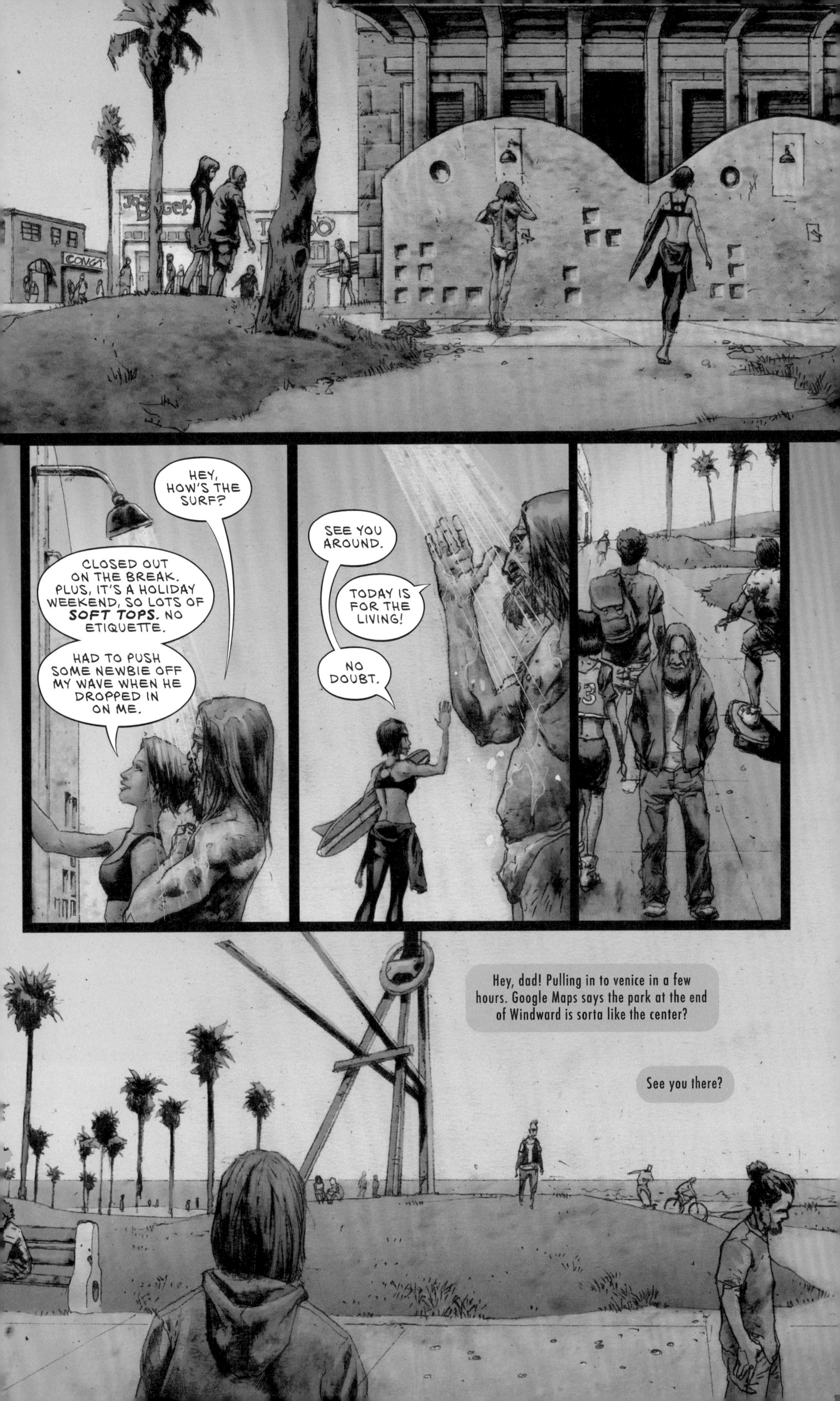
CONGA
HEY, HOW'S THE SURF?
CLOSED OUT ON THE BREAK. PLUS, IT'S A HOLIDAY WEEKEND, SO LOTS OF **SOFT TOPS.** NO ETIQUETTE.
HAD TO PUSH SOME NEWBIE OFF MY WAVE WHEN HE DROPPED IN ON ME.
SEE YOU AROUND.
TODAY IS FOR THE LIVING!
NO DOUBT.
Hey, dad! Pulling in to venice in a few hours. Google Maps says the park at the end of Windward is sorta like the center?
See you there?

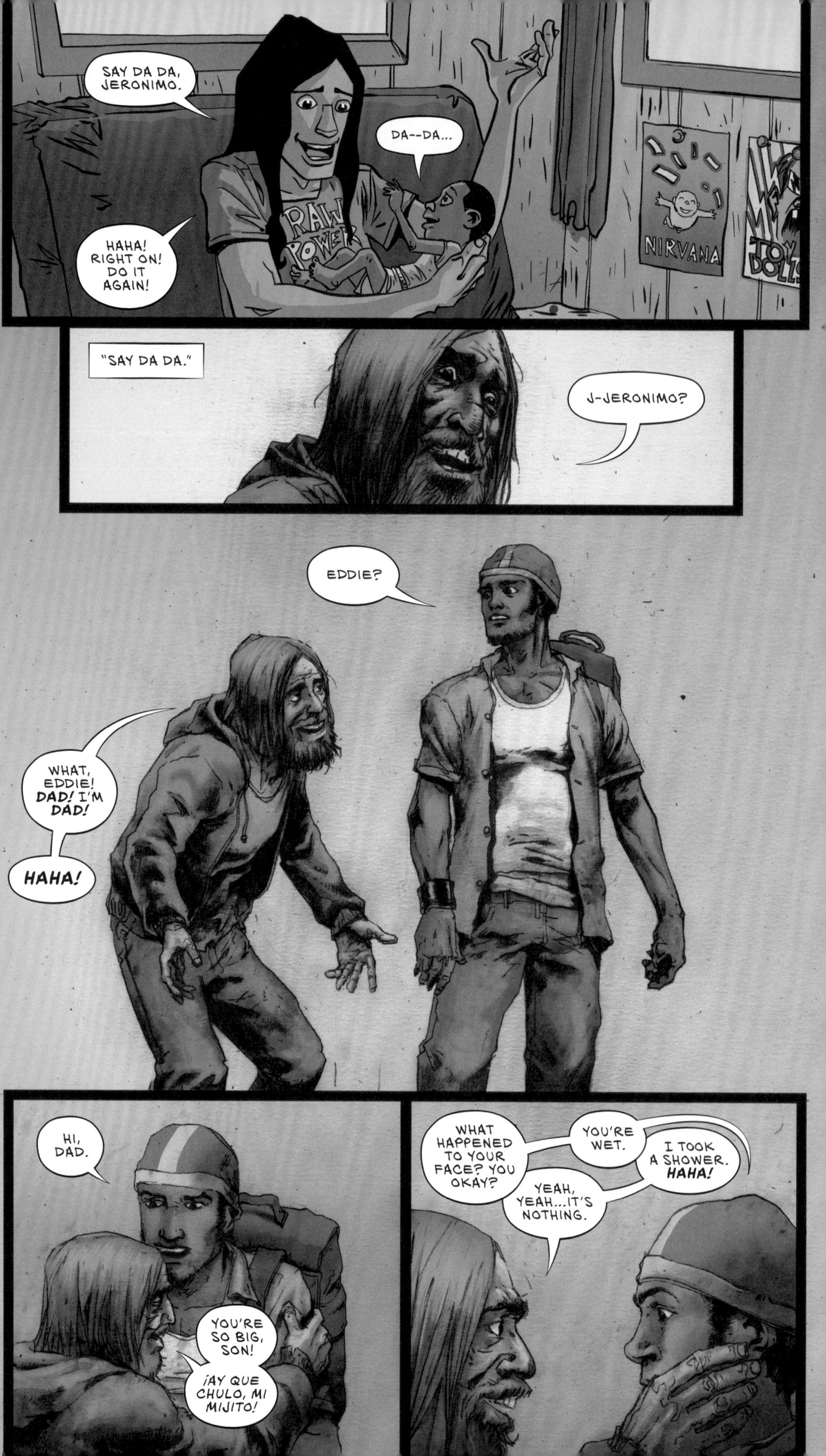
SAY DA DA, JERONIMO.
DA--DA...
HAHA! RIGHT ON! DO IT AGAIN!
RAW POWER
NIRVANA
TOY DOLLS
"SAY DA DA."
J-JERONIMO?
EDDIE?
WHAT, EDDIE! DAD! I'M DAD!
HAHA!
HI, DAD.
YOU'RE SO BIG, SON!
¡AY QUE CHULO, MI MIJITO!
WHAT HAPPENED TO YOUR FACE? YOU OKAY?
YEAH, YEAH...IT'S NOTHING.
YOU'RE WET.
I TOOK A SHOWER. HAHA!

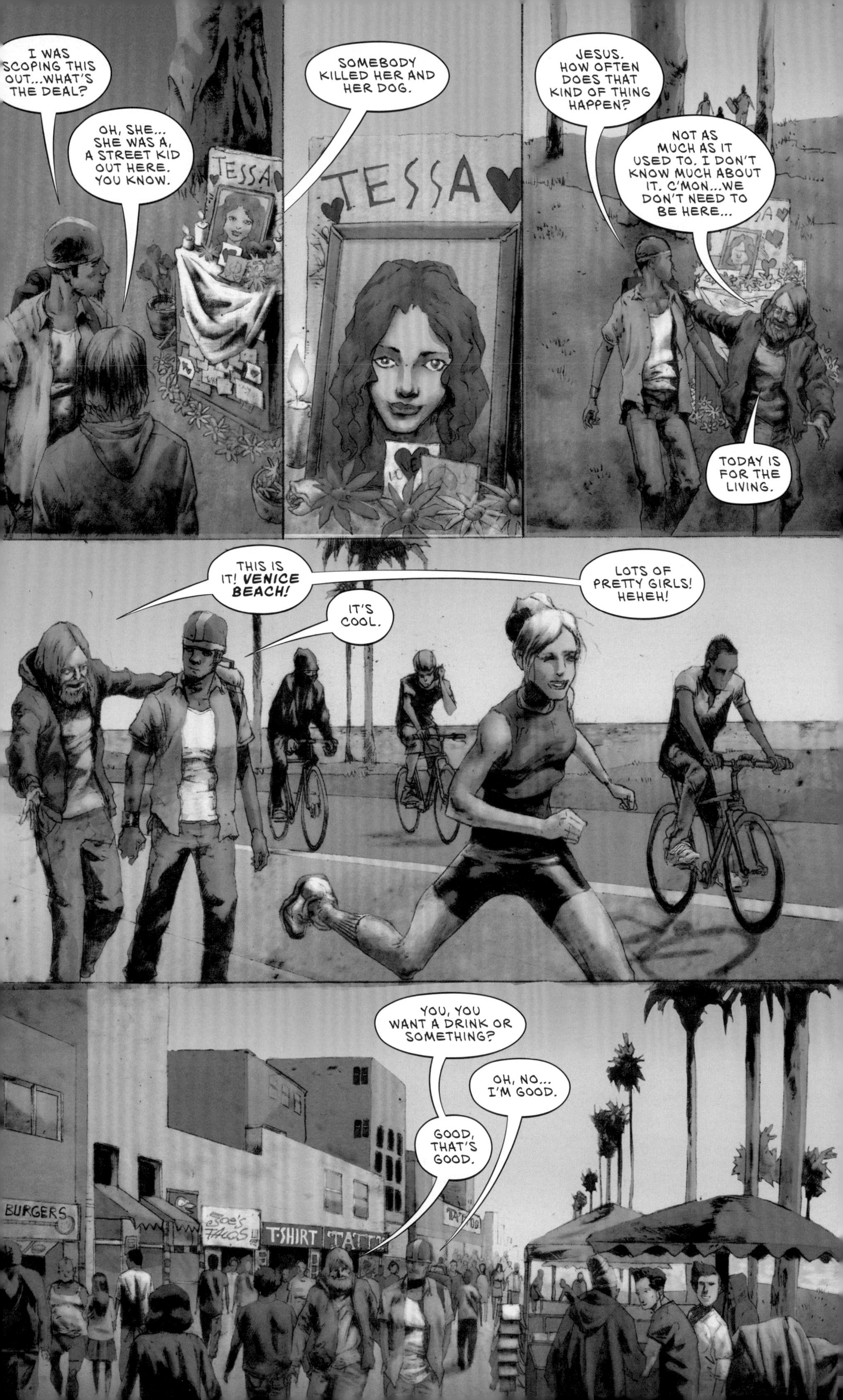

I WAS SCOPING THIS OUT...WHAT'S THE DEAL?
OH, SHE... SHE WAS A, A STREET KID OUT HERE. YOU KNOW.
TESSA
SOMEBODY KILLED HER AND HER DOG.
TESSA
JESUS. HOW OFTEN DOES THAT KIND OF THING HAPPEN?
NOT AS MUCH AS IT USED TO. I DON'T KNOW MUCH ABOUT IT. C'MON...WE DON'T NEED TO BE HERE...
TODAY IS FOR THE LIVING.
THIS IS IT! **VENICE BEACH!**
IT'S COOL.
LOTS OF PRETTY GIRLS! HEHEH!
YOU, YOU WANT A DRINK OR SOMETHING?
OH, NO... I'M GOOD.
GOOD, THAT'S GOOD.
BURGERS
Joe's TACOS
T-SHIRT
TATT

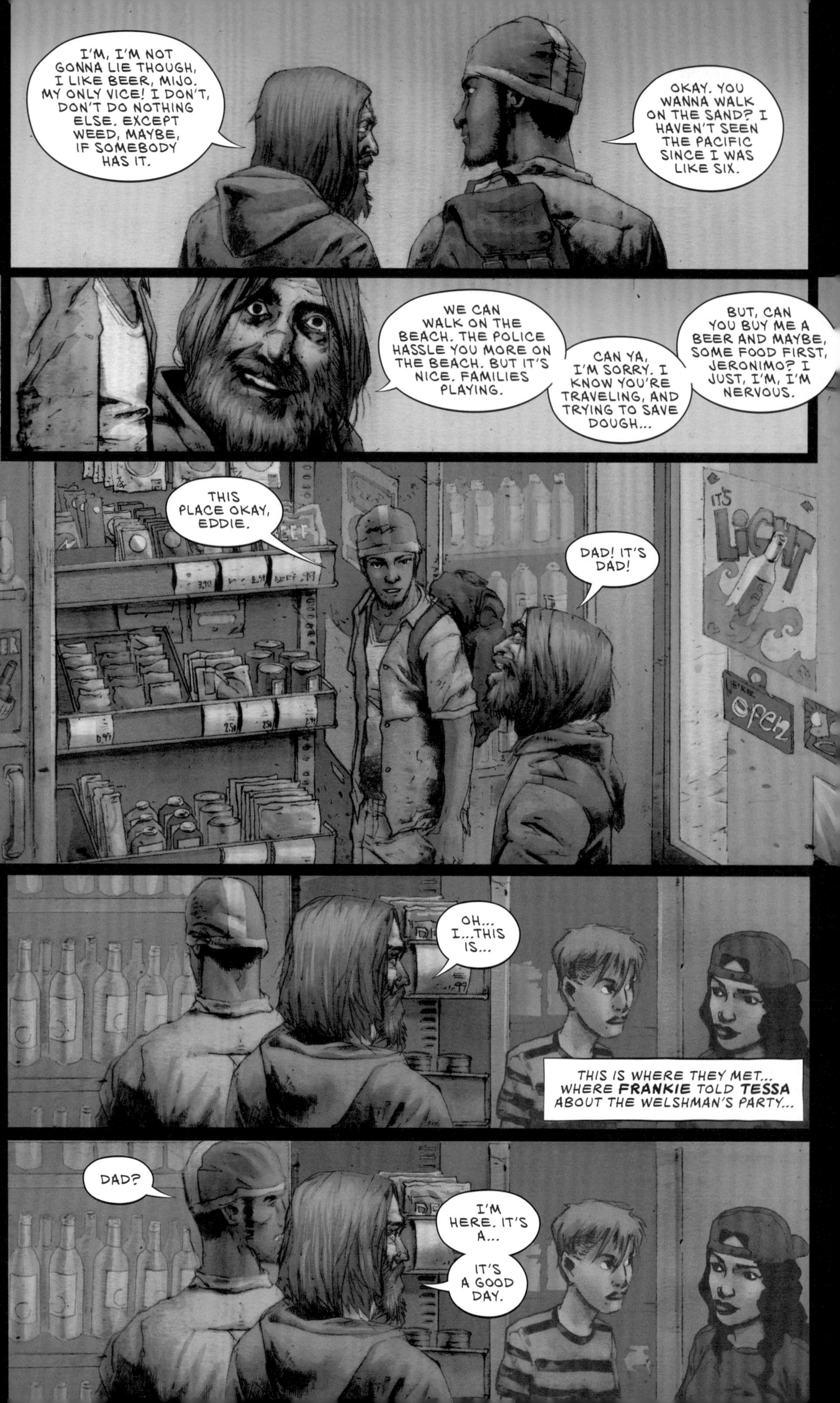
I'M, I'M NOT GONNA LIE THOUGH, I LIKE BEER, MIJO. MY ONLY VICE! I DON'T, DON'T DO NOTHING ELSE. EXCEPT WEED, MAYBE, IF SOMEBODY HAS IT.
OKAY. YOU WANNA WALK ON THE SAND? I HAVEN'T SEEN THE PACIFIC SINCE I WAS LIKE SIX.
WE CAN WALK ON THE BEACH. THE POLICE HASSLE YOU MORE ON THE BEACH. BUT IT'S NICE. FAMILIES PLAYING.
CAN YA, I'M SORRY. I KNOW YOU'RE TRAVELING, AND TRYING TO SAVE DOUGH...
BUT, CAN YOU BUY ME A BEER AND MAYBE, SOME FOOD FIRST, JERONIMO? I JUST, I'M, I'M NERVOUS.
THIS PLACE OKAY, EDDIE.
DAD! IT'S DAD!
IT'S LIGHT
BEER
OPEN
OH... I...THIS IS...
THIS IS WHERE THEY MET... WHERE FRANKIE TOLD TESSA ABOUT THE WELSHMAN'S PARTY...
DAD?
I'M HERE. IT'S A...
IT'S A GOOD DAY.

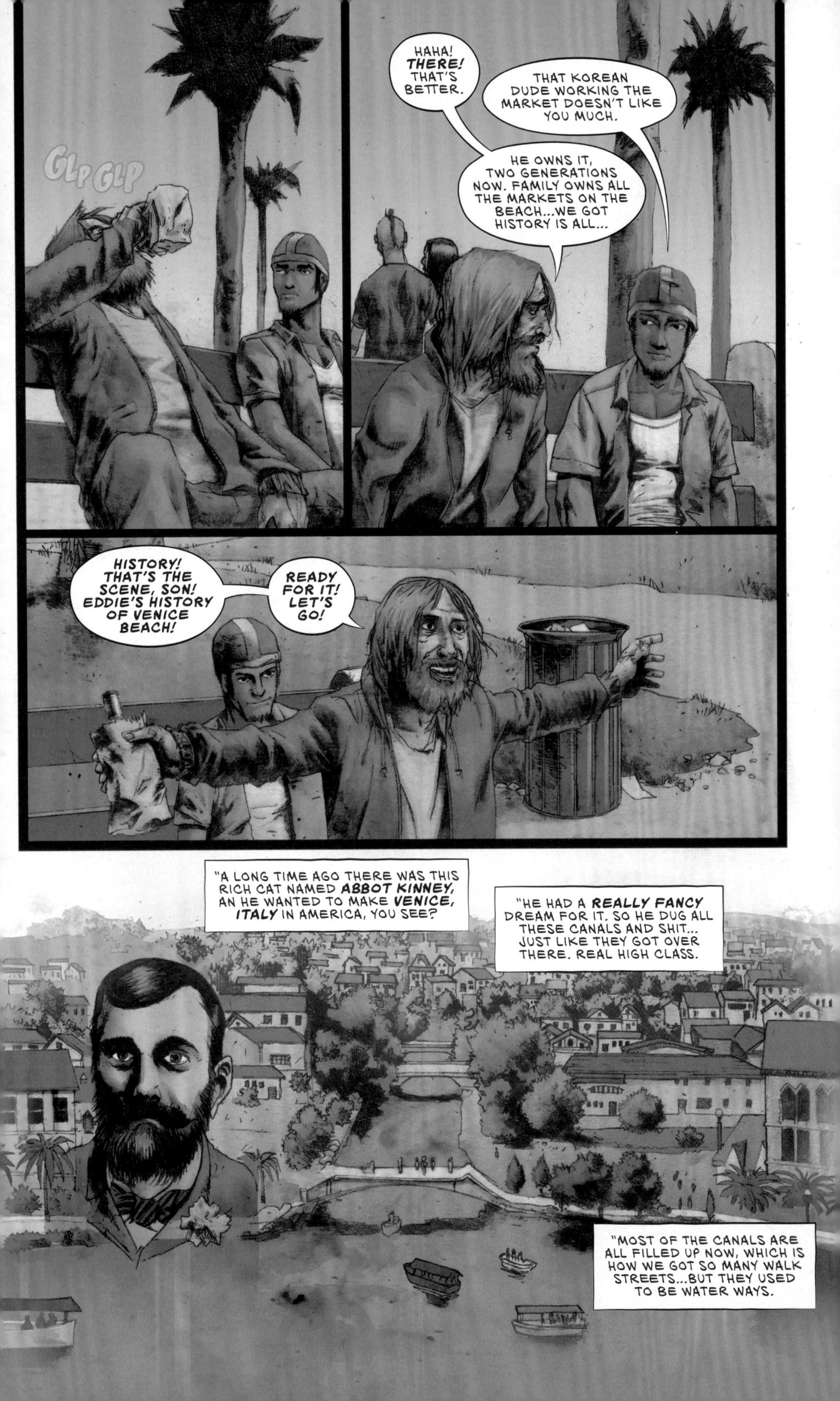
GLP GLP
HAHA! THERE! THAT'S BETTER.
THAT KOREAN DUDE WORKING THE MARKET DOESN'T LIKE YOU MUCH.
HE OWNS IT, TWO GENERATIONS NOW. FAMILY OWNS ALL THE MARKETS ON THE BEACH...WE GOT HISTORY IS ALL...
HISTORY! THAT'S THE SCENE, SON! EDDIE'S HISTORY OF VENICE BEACH!
READY FOR IT! LET'S GO!
"A LONG TIME AGO THERE WAS THIS RICH CAT NAMED ABBOT KINNEY, AN HE WANTED TO MAKE VENICE, ITALY IN AMERICA, YOU SEE?
"HE HAD A REALLY FANCY DREAM FOR IT. SO HE DUG ALL THESE CANALS AND SHIT... JUST LIKE THEY GOT OVER THERE. REAL HIGH CLASS.
"MOST OF THE CANALS ARE ALL FILLED UP NOW, WHICH IS HOW WE GOT SO MANY WALK STREETS...BUT THEY USED TO BE WATER WAYS.

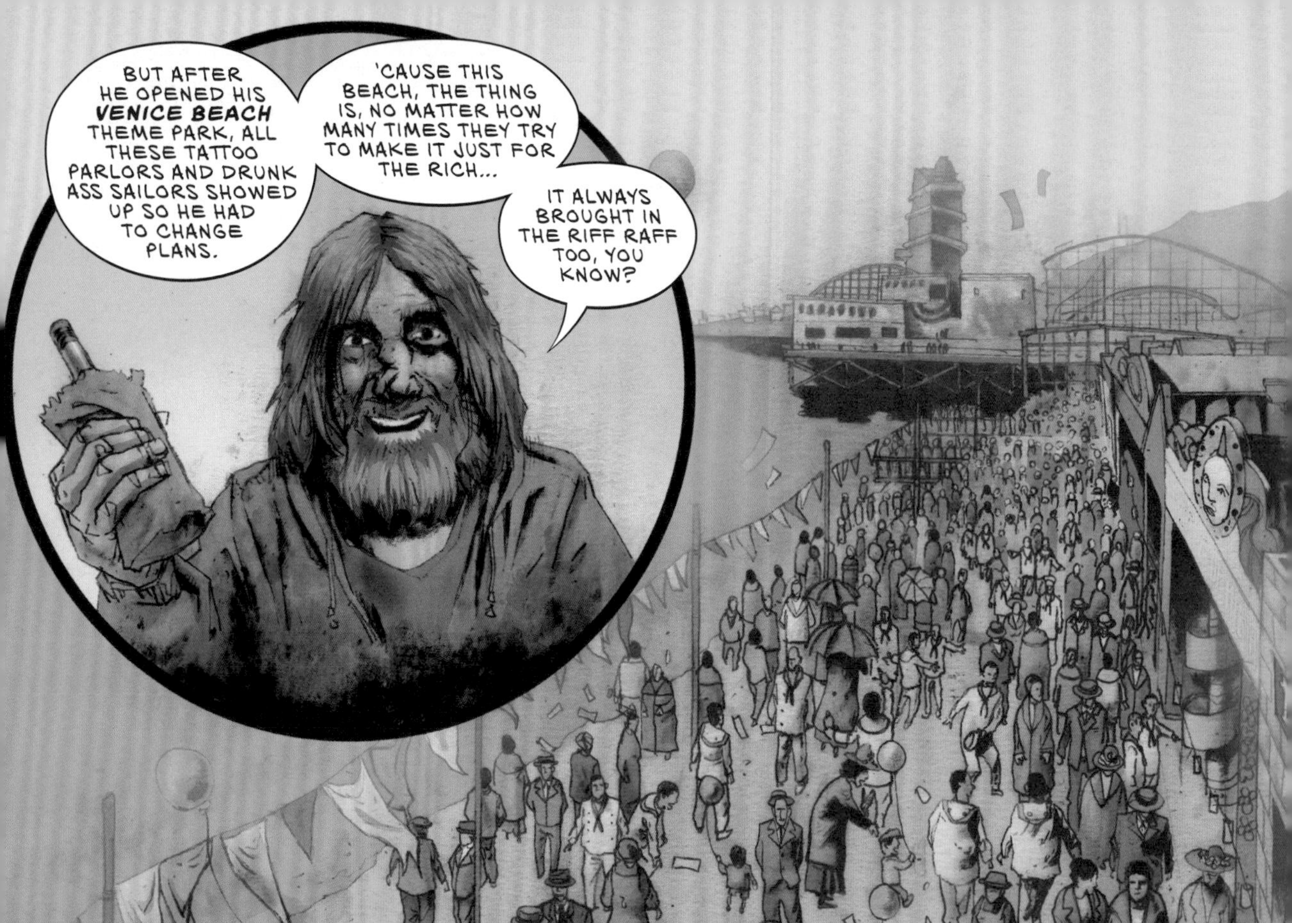
BUT AFTER HE OPENED HIS **VENICE BEACH** THEME PARK, ALL THESE TATTOO PARLORS AND DRUNK ASS SAILORS SHOWED UP SO HE HAD TO CHANGE PLANS.
'CAUSE THIS BEACH, THE THING IS, NO MATTER HOW MANY TIMES THEY TRY TO MAKE IT JUST FOR THE RICH...
IT ALWAYS BROUGHT IN THE RIFF RAFF TOO, YOU KNOW?

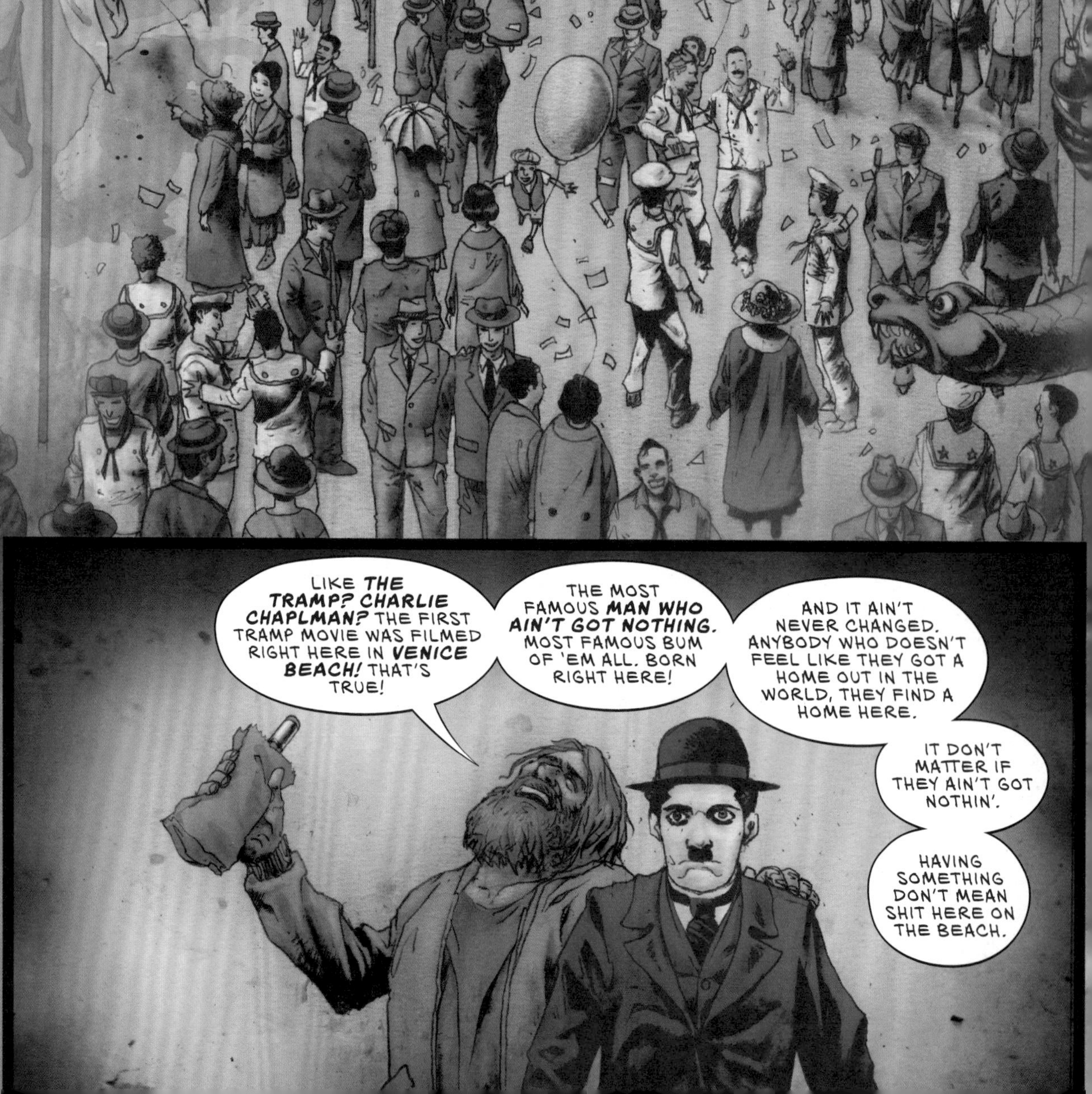
LIKE **THE TRAMP? CHARLIE CHAPLMAN?** THE FIRST TRAMP MOVIE WAS FILMED RIGHT HERE IN **VENICE BEACH!** THAT'S TRUE!
THE MOST FAMOUS **MAN WHO AIN'T GOT NOTHING.** MOST FAMOUS BUM OF 'EM ALL. BORN RIGHT HERE!
AND IT AIN'T NEVER CHANGED. ANYBODY WHO DOESN'T FEEL LIKE THEY GOT A HOME OUT IN THE WORLD, THEY FIND A HOME HERE.
IT DON'T MATTER IF THEY AIN'T GOT NOTHIN'.
HAVING SOMETHING DON'T MEAN SHIT HERE ON THE BEACH.

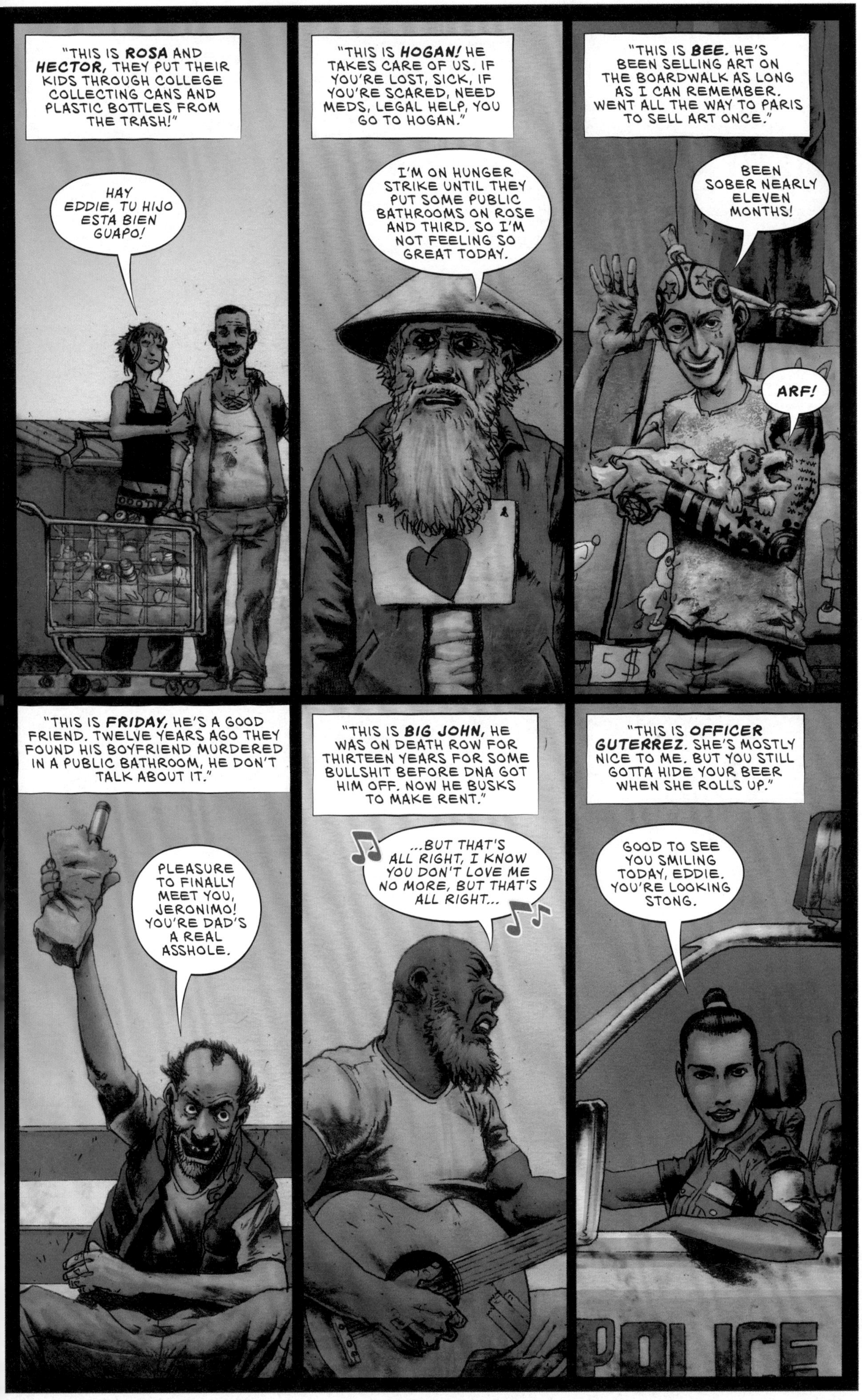
"THIS IS ROSA AND HECTOR, THEY PUT THEIR KIDS THROUGH COLLEGE COLLECTING CANS AND PLASTIC BOTTLES FROM THE TRASH!"
HAY EDDIE, TU HIJO ESTA BIEN GUAPO!
"THIS IS HOGAN! HE TAKES CARE OF US. IF YOU'RE LOST, SICK, IF YOU'RE SCARED, NEED MEDS, LEGAL HELP, YOU GO TO HOGAN."
I'M ON HUNGER STRIKE UNTIL THEY PUT SOME PUBLIC BATHROOMS ON ROSE AND THIRD. SO I'M NOT FEELING SO GREAT TODAY.
"THIS IS BEE. HE'S BEEN SELLING ART ON THE BOARDWALK AS LONG AS I CAN REMEMBER. WENT ALL THE WAY TO PARIS TO SELL ART ONCE."
BEEN SOBER NEARLY ELEVEN MONTHS!
ARF!
5$
"THIS IS FRIDAY, HE'S A GOOD FRIEND. TWELVE YEARS AGO THEY FOUND HIS BOYFRIEND MURDERED IN A PUBLIC BATHROOM, HE DON'T TALK ABOUT IT."
PLEASURE TO FINALLY MEET YOU, JERONIMO! YOU'RE DAD'S A REAL ASSHOLE.
"THIS IS BIG JOHN, HE WAS ON DEATH ROW FOR THIRTEEN YEARS FOR SOME BULLSHIT BEFORE DNA GOT HIM OFF. NOW HE BUSKS TO MAKE RENT."
...BUT THAT'S ALL RIGHT, I KNOW YOU DON'T LOVE ME NO MORE, BUT THAT'S ALL RIGHT...
"THIS IS OFFICER GUTERREZ. SHE'S MOSTLY NICE TO ME. BUT YOU STILL GOTTA HIDE YOUR BEER WHEN SHE ROLLS UP."
GOOD TO SEE YOU SMILING TODAY, EDDIE. YOU'RE LOOKING STONG.
POLICE

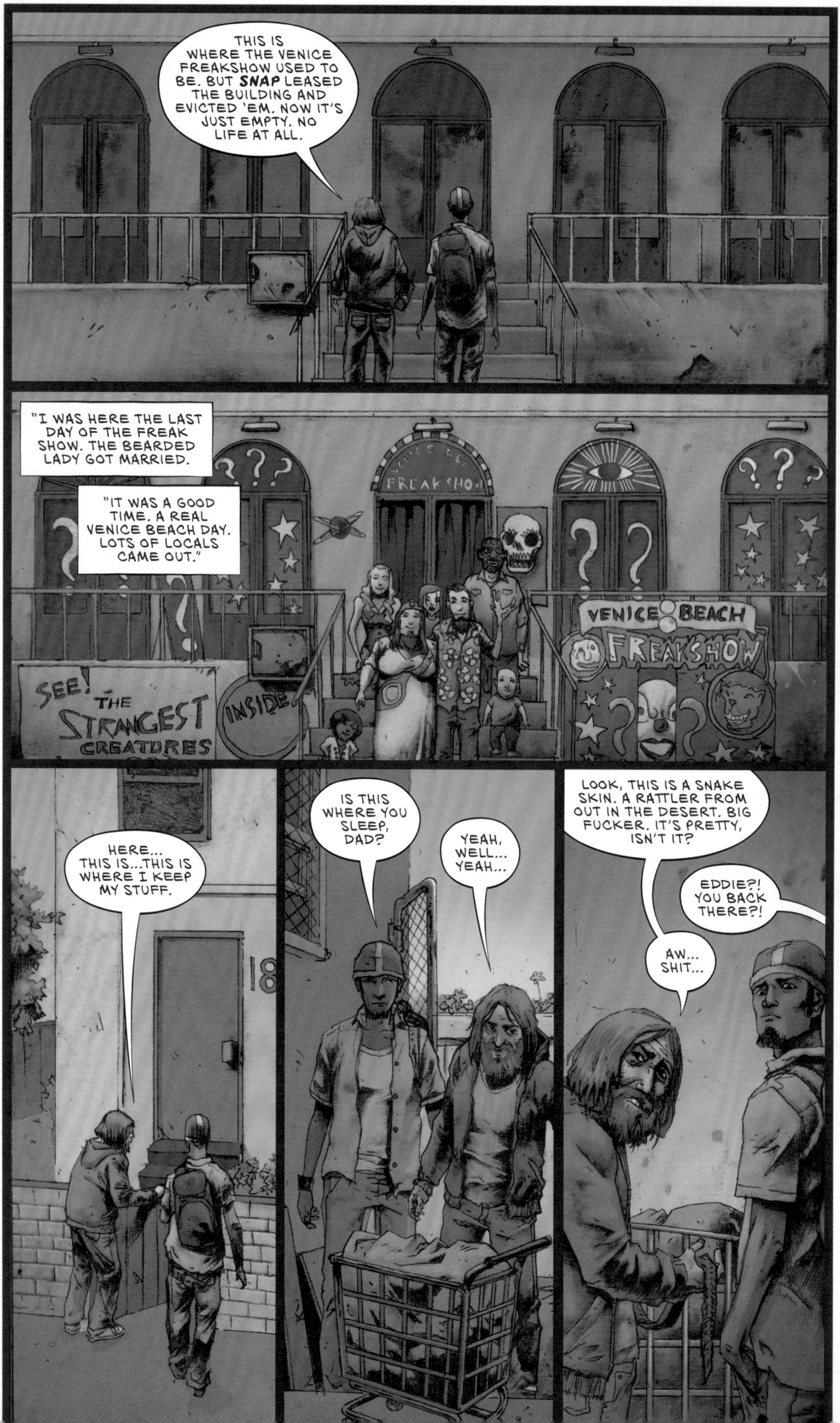
THIS IS WHERE THE VENICE FREAKSHOW USED TO BE. BUT SNAP LEASED THE BUILDING AND EVICTED 'EM. NOW IT'S JUST EMPTY. NO LIFE AT ALL.
"I WAS HERE THE LAST DAY OF THE FREAK SHOW. THE BEARDED LADY GOT MARRIED.
"IT WAS A GOOD TIME. A REAL VENICE BEACH DAY. LOTS OF LOCALS CAME OUT."
FREAKSHOW
VENICE BEACH
FREAKSHOW
SEE! THE STRANGEST CREATURES
INSIDE
HERE... THIS IS...THIS IS WHERE I KEEP MY STUFF.
18
IS THIS WHERE YOU SLEEP, DAD?
YEAH, WELL... YEAH...
LOOK, THIS IS A SNAKE SKIN. A RATTLER FROM OUT IN THE DESERT. BIG FUCKER. IT'S PRETTY, ISN'T IT?
EDDIE?! YOU BACK THERE?!
AW... SHIT...

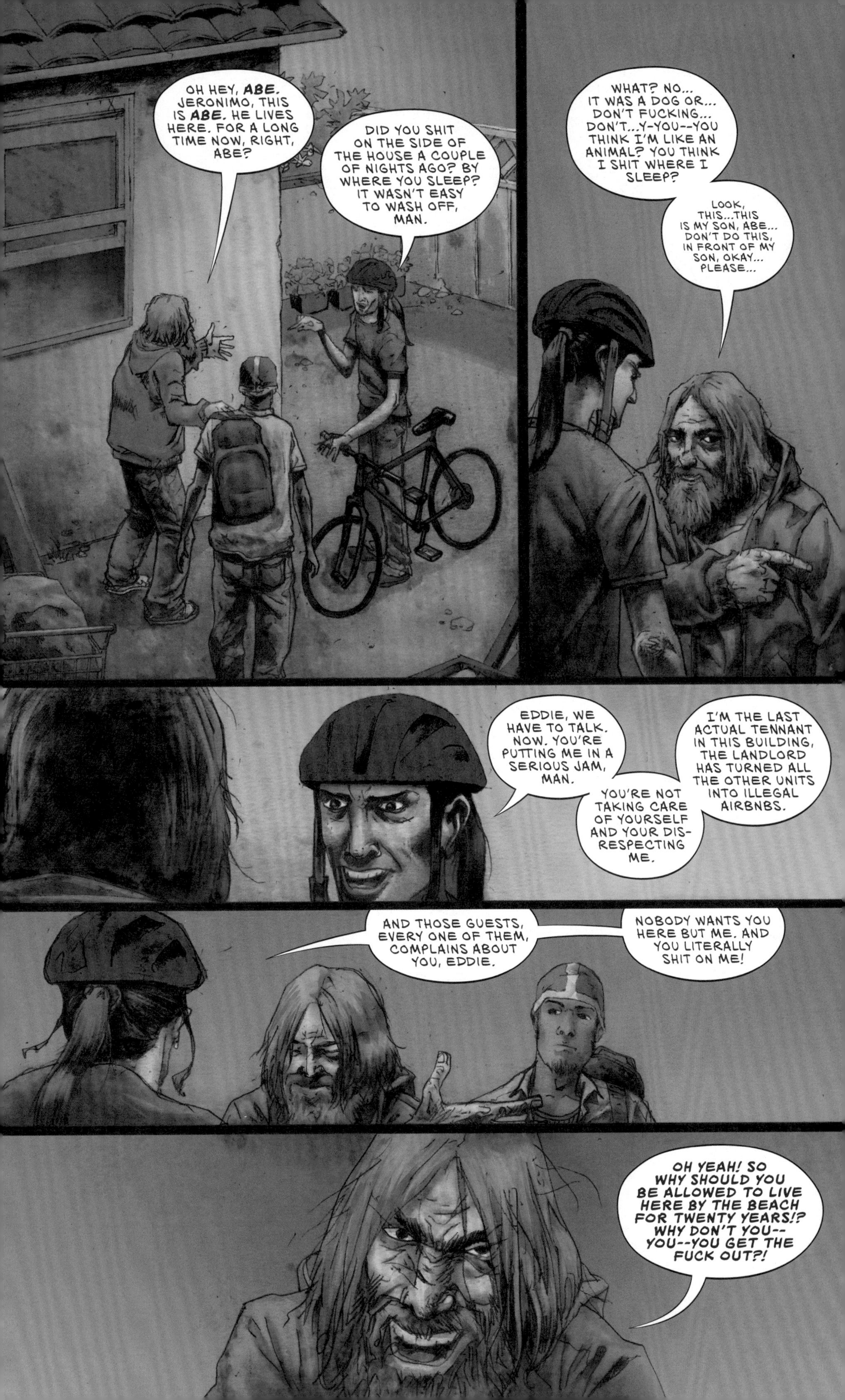
OH HEY, ABE. JERONIMO, THIS IS ABE. HE LIVES HERE. FOR A LONG TIME NOW, RIGHT, ABE?
DID YOU SHIT ON THE SIDE OF THE HOUSE A COUPLE OF NIGHTS AGO? BY WHERE YOU SLEEP? IT WASN'T EASY TO WASH OFF, MAN.
WHAT? NO... IT WAS A DOG OR... DON'T FUCKING... DON'T...Y-YOU--YOU THINK I'M LIKE AN ANIMAL? YOU THINK I SHIT WHERE I SLEEP?
LOOK, THIS...THIS IS MY SON, ABE... DON'T DO THIS, IN FRONT OF MY SON, OKAY... PLEASE...
EDDIE, WE HAVE TO TALK. NOW. YOU'RE PUTTING ME IN A SERIOUS JAM, MAN.
I'M THE LAST ACTUAL TENNANT IN THIS BUILDING, THE LANDLORD HAS TURNED ALL THE OTHER UNITS INTO ILLEGAL AIRBNBS.
YOU'RE NOT TAKING CARE OF YOURSELF AND YOUR DIS-RESPECTING ME.
AND THOSE GUESTS, EVERY ONE OF THEM, COMPLAINS ABOUT YOU, EDDIE.
NOBODY WANTS YOU HERE BUT ME. AND YOU LITERALLY SHIT ON ME!
OH YEAH! SO WHY SHOULD YOU BE ALLOWED TO LIVE HERE BY THE BEACH FOR TWENTY YEARS!? WHY DON'T YOU-- YOU--YOU GET THE FUCK OUT?!

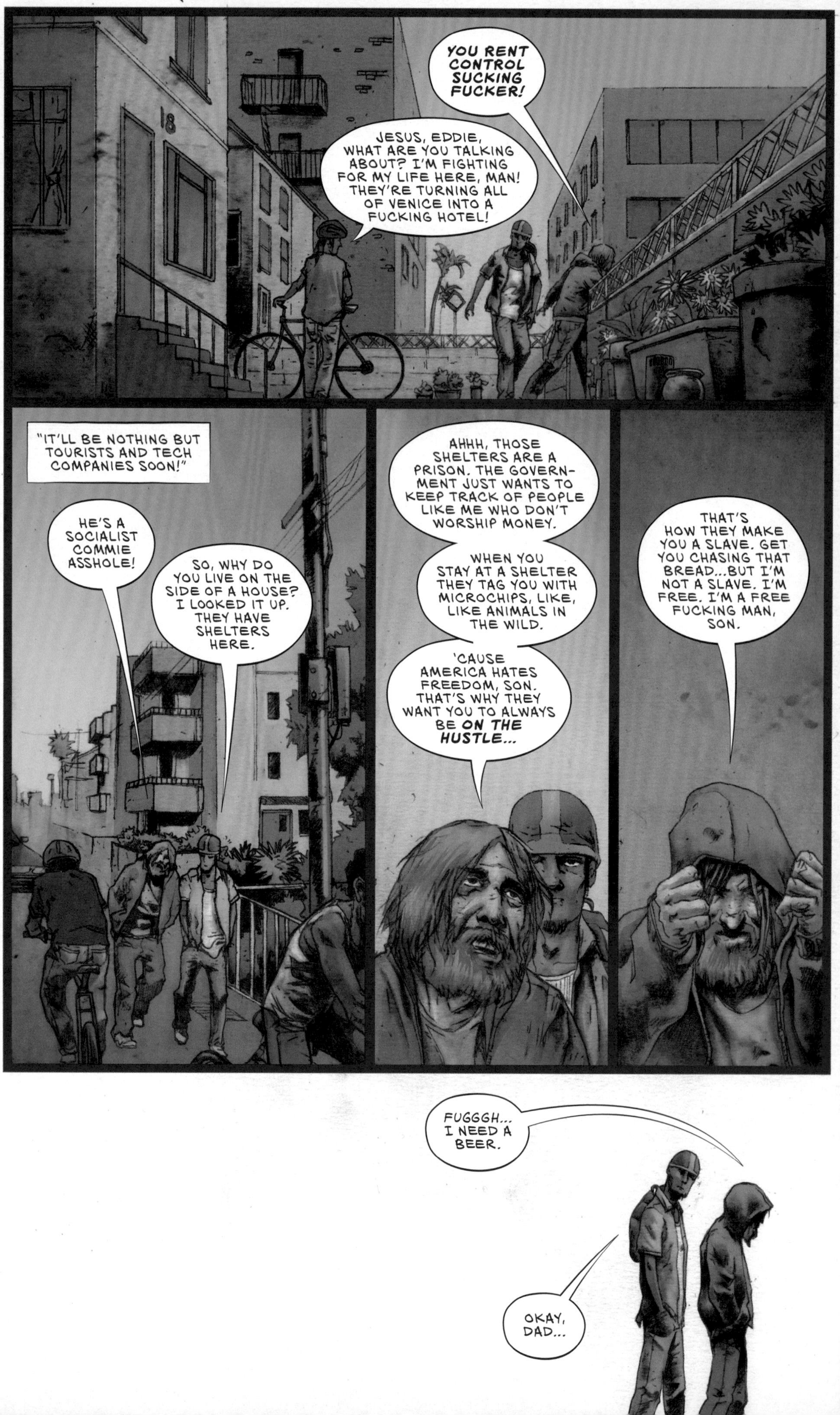
YOU RENT CONTROL SUCKING FUCKER!
JESUS, EDDIE, WHAT ARE YOU TALKING ABOUT? I'M FIGHTING FOR MY LIFE HERE, MAN! THEY'RE TURNING ALL OF VENICE INTO A FUCKING HOTEL!
"IT'LL BE NOTHING BUT TOURISTS AND TECH COMPANIES SOON!"
HE'S A SOCIALIST COMMIE ASSHOLE!
SO, WHY DO YOU LIVE ON THE SIDE OF A HOUSE? I LOOKED IT UP. THEY HAVE SHELTERS HERE.
AHHH, THOSE SHELTERS ARE A PRISON. THE GOVERNMENT JUST WANTS TO KEEP TRACK OF PEOPLE LIKE ME WHO DON'T WORSHIP MONEY.
WHEN YOU STAY AT A SHELTER THEY TAG YOU WITH MICROCHIPS, LIKE, LIKE ANIMALS IN THE WILD.
'CAUSE AMERICA HATES FREEDOM, SON. THAT'S WHY THEY WANT YOU TO ALWAYS BE ON THE HUSTLE...
THAT'S HOW THEY MAKE YOU A SLAVE. GET YOU CHASING THAT BREAD...BUT I'M NOT A SLAVE. I'M FREE. I'M A FREE FUCKING MAN, SON.
FUGGGH... I NEED A BEER.
OKAY, DAD...

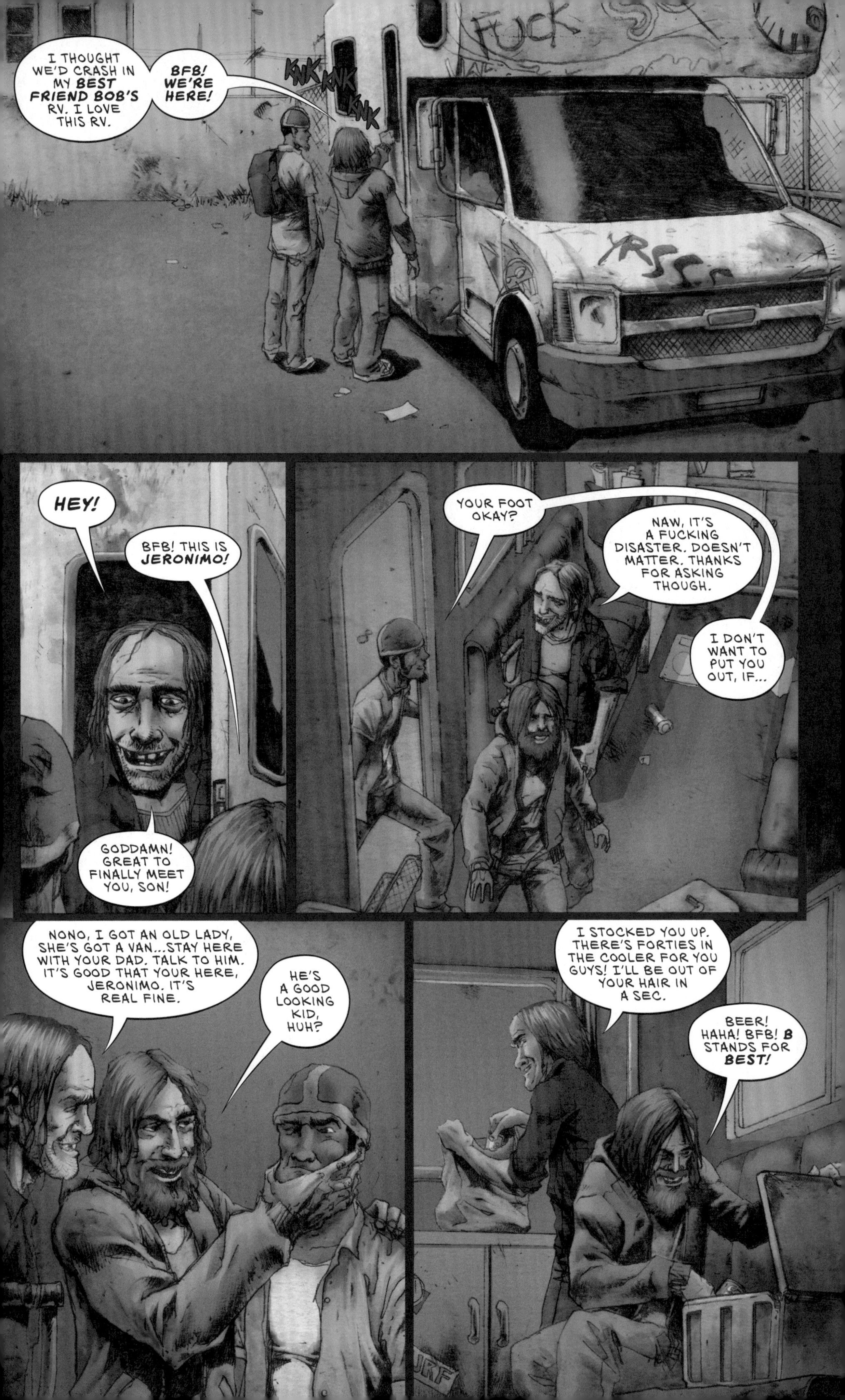

I THOUGHT WE'D CRASH IN MY **BEST FRIEND BOB'S** RV. I LOVE THIS RV.
BFB! WE'RE HERE!
KNK KNK KNK
HEY!
BFB! THIS IS **JERONIMO!**
GODDAMN! GREAT TO FINALLY MEET YOU, SON!
YOUR FOOT OKAY?
NAW, IT'S A FUCKING DISASTER. DOESN'T MATTER. THANKS FOR ASKING THOUGH.
I DON'T WANT TO PUT YOU OUT, IF...
NONO, I GOT AN OLD LADY, SHE'S GOT A VAN...STAY HERE WITH YOUR DAD. TALK TO HIM. IT'S GOOD THAT YOUR HERE, JERONIMO. IT'S REAL FINE.
HE'S A GOOD LOOKING KID, HUH?
I STOCKED YOU UP. THERE'S FORTIES IN THE COOLER FOR YOU GUYS! I'LL BE OUT OF YOUR HAIR IN A SEC.
BEER! HAHA! BFB! **B** STANDS FOR **BEST!**

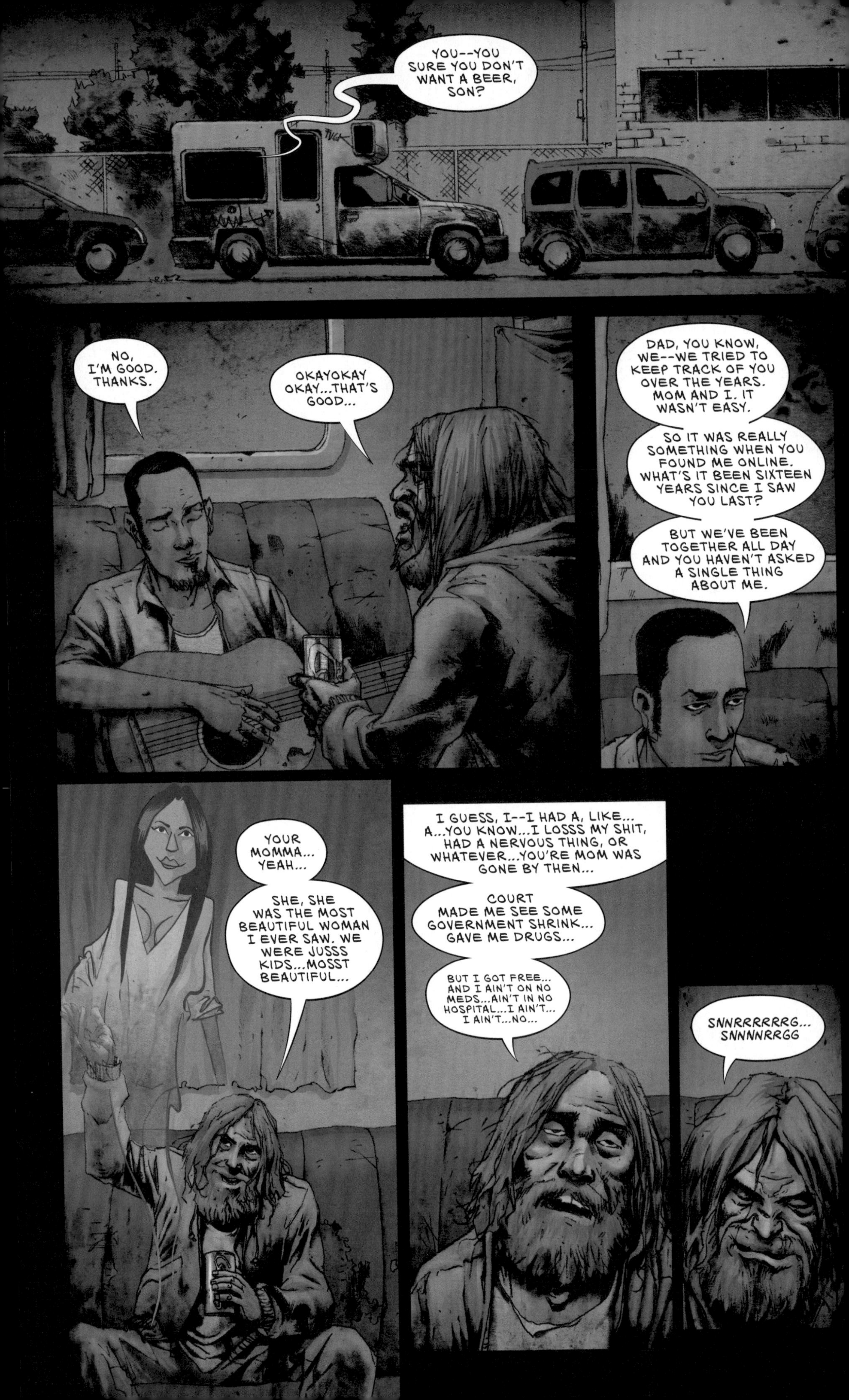
YOU--YOU SURE YOU DON'T WANT A BEER, SON?
NO, I'M GOOD. THANKS.
OKAYOKAY OKAY...THAT'S GOOD...
DAD, YOU KNOW, WE--WE TRIED TO KEEP TRACK OF YOU OVER THE YEARS. MOM AND I. IT WASN'T EASY.
SO IT WAS REALLY SOMETHING WHEN YOU FOUND ME ONLINE. WHAT'S IT BEEN SIXTEEN YEARS SINCE I SAW YOU LAST?
BUT WE'VE BEEN TOGETHER ALL DAY AND YOU HAVEN'T ASKED A SINGLE THING ABOUT ME.
YOUR MOMMA... YEAH...
SHE, SHE WAS THE MOST BEAUTIFUL WOMAN I EVER SAW. WE WERE JUSSS KIDS...MOSST BEAUTIFUL...
I GUESS, I--I HAD A, LIKE... A...YOU KNOW...I LOSSS MY SHIT, HAD A NERVOUS THING, OR WHATEVER...YOU'RE MOM WAS GONE BY THEN...
COURT MADE ME SEE SOME GOVERNMENT SHRINK... GAVE ME DRUGS...
BUT I GOT FREE... AND I AIN'T ON NO MEDS...AIN'T IN NO HOSPITAL...I AIN'T... I AIN'T...NO...
SNNRRRRRRG... SNNNNRRGG

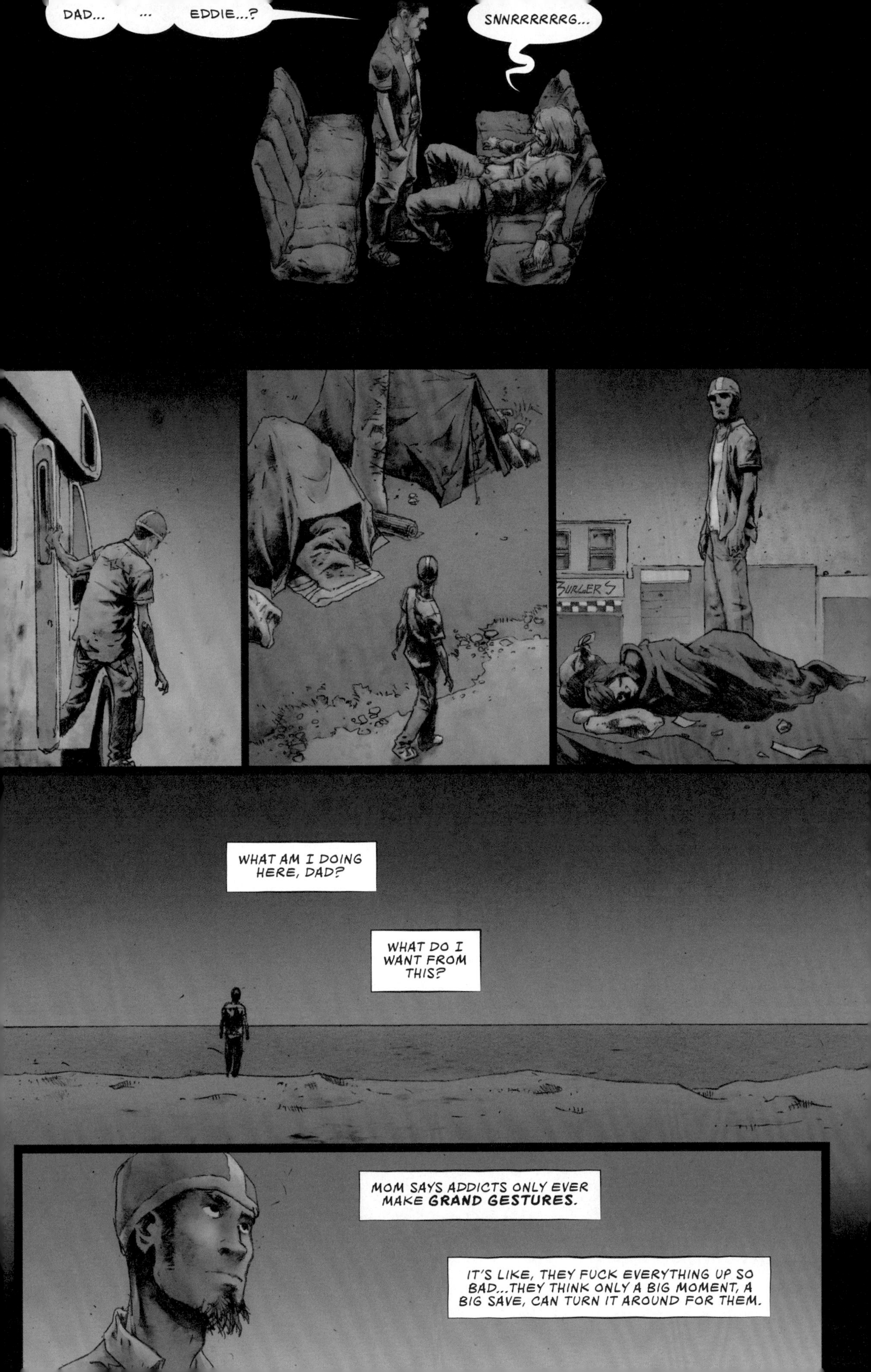
DAD... ... EDDIE...?
SNNRRRRRRG...
BURGERS
WHAT AM I DOING HERE, DAD?
WHAT DO I WANT FROM THIS?
MOM SAYS ADDICTS ONLY EVER MAKE GRAND GESTURES.
IT'S LIKE, THEY FUCK EVERYTHING UP SO BAD...THEY THINK ONLY A BIG MOMENT, A BIG SAVE, CAN TURN IT AROUND FOR THEM.

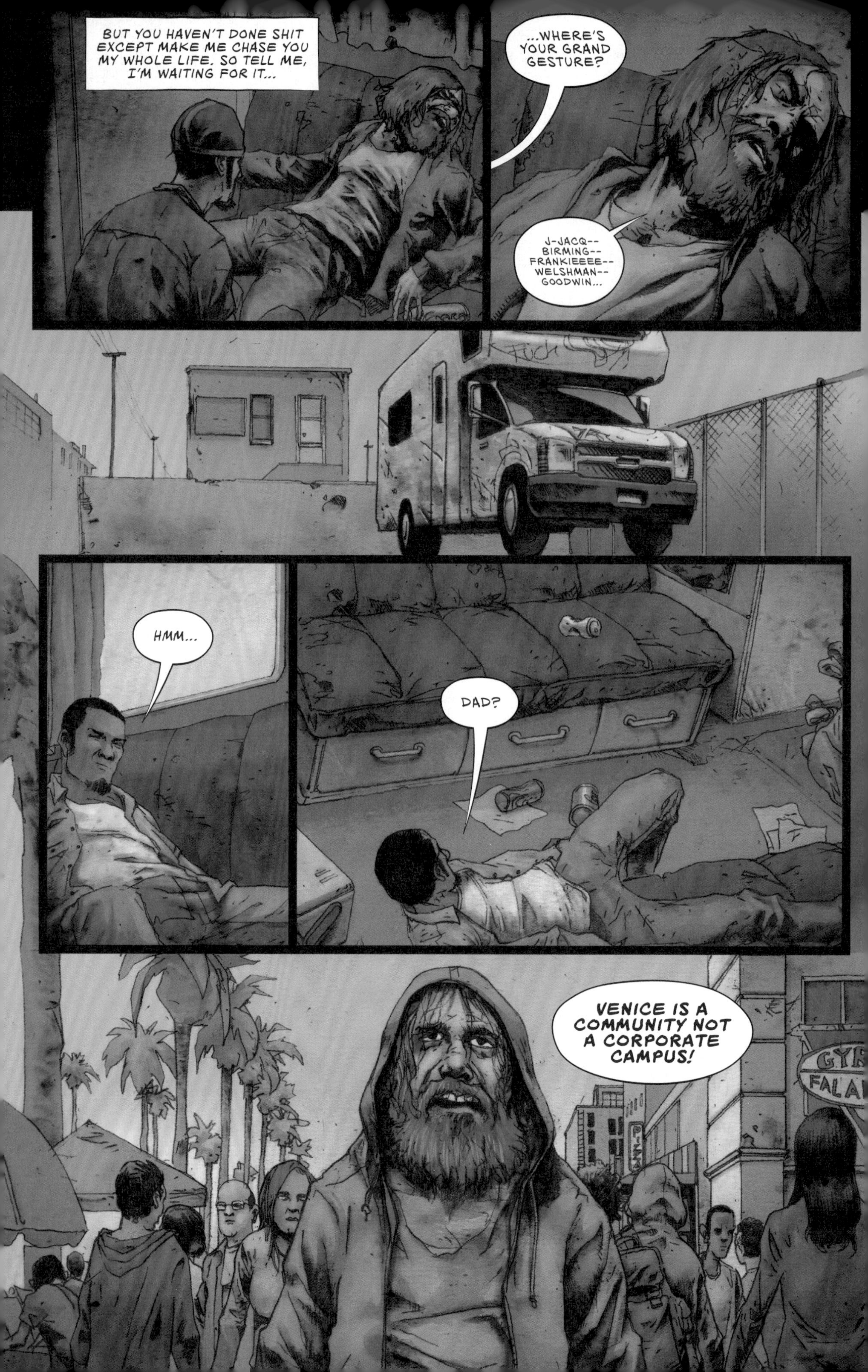
BUT YOU HAVEN'T DONE SHIT EXCEPT MAKE ME CHASE YOU MY WHOLE LIFE. SO TELL ME, I'M WAITING FOR IT...
...WHERE'S YOUR GRAND GESTURE?
J-JACQ-- BIRMING-- FRANKIEEEE-- WELSHMAN-- GOODWIN...
HMM...
DAD?
VENICE IS A COMMUNITY NOT A CORPORATE CAMPUS!

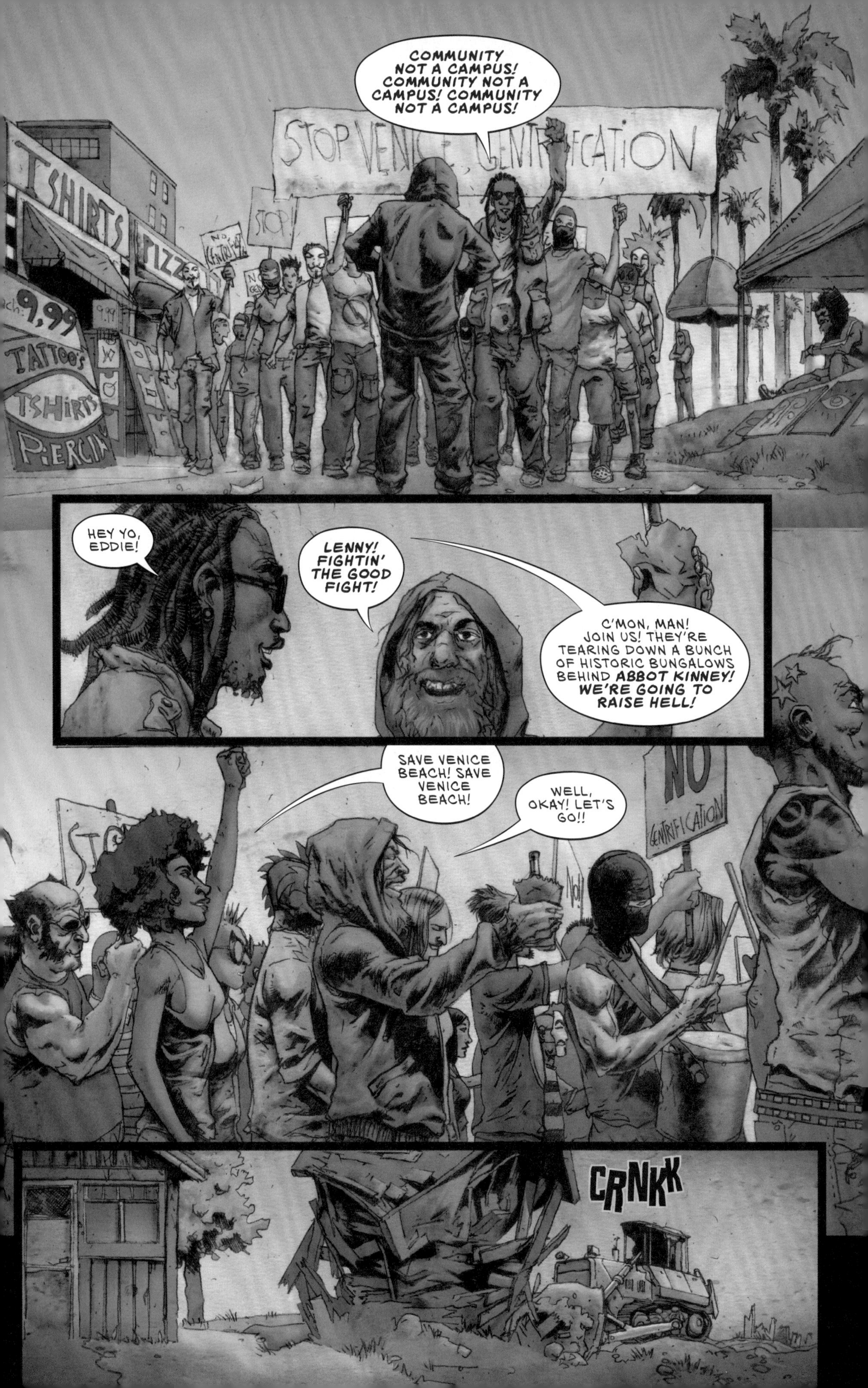
COMMUNITY NOT A CAMPUS! COMMUNITY NOT A CAMPUS! COMMUNITY NOT A CAMPUS!
STOP VENICE GENTRIFICATION
STOP!
NO GENTRIFICATION
T SHIRTS
PIZZ
9.99
TATTOO'S
TSHIRTS
PiERCIN
HEY YO, EDDIE!
LENNY! FIGHTIN' THE GOOD FIGHT!
C'MON, MAN! JOIN US! THEY'RE TEARING DOWN A BUNCH OF HISTORIC BUNGALOWS BEHIND ABBOT KINNEY! WE'RE GOING TO RAISE HELL!
SAVE VENICE BEACH! SAVE VENICE BEACH!
WELL, OKAY! LET'S GO!!
NO GENTRIFICATION
CRNKK

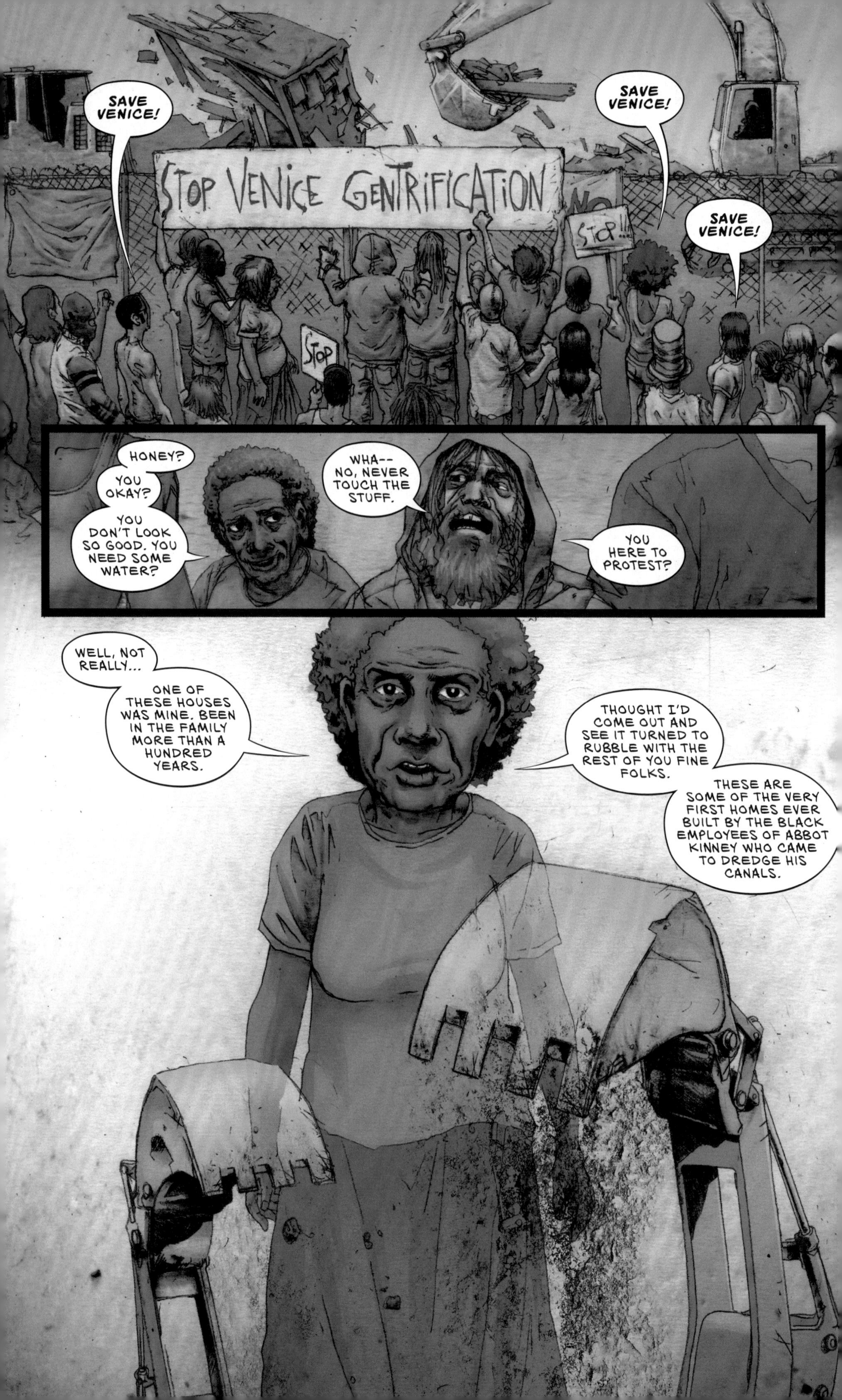
SAVE VENICE!
STOP VENICE GENTRIFICATION
NO
STOP!!
STOP
SAVE VENICE!
SAVE VENICE!
HONEY?
YOU OKAY?
YOU DON'T LOOK SO GOOD. YOU NEED SOME WATER?
WHA-- NO, NEVER TOUCH THE STUFF.
YOU HERE TO PROTEST?
WELL, NOT REALLY...
ONE OF THESE HOUSES WAS MINE. BEEN IN THE FAMILY MORE THAN A HUNDRED YEARS.
THOUGHT I'D COME OUT AND SEE IT TURNED TO RUBBLE WITH THE REST OF YOU FINE FOLKS.
THESE ARE SOME OF THE VERY FIRST HOMES EVER BUILT BY THE BLACK EMPLOYEES OF ABBOT KINNEY WHO CAME TO DREDGE HIS CANALS.

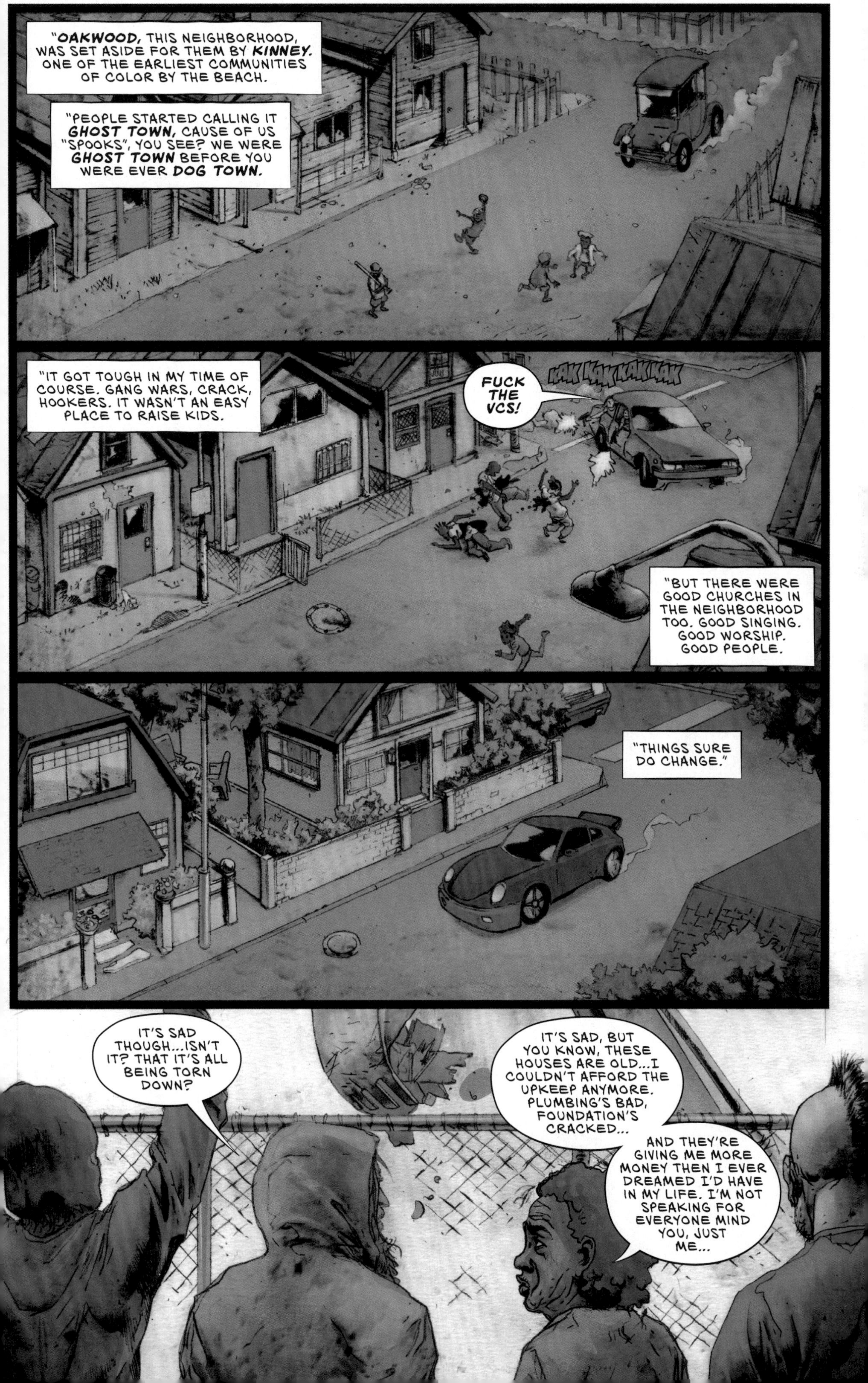
"OAKWOOD, THIS NEIGHBORHOOD, WAS SET ASIDE FOR THEM BY KINNEY. ONE OF THE EARLIEST COMMUNITIES OF COLOR BY THE BEACH.
"PEOPLE STARTED CALLING IT GHOST TOWN, CAUSE OF US "SPOOKS", YOU SEE? WE WERE GHOST TOWN BEFORE YOU WERE EVER DOG TOWN.
"IT GOT TOUGH IN MY TIME OF COURSE. GANG WARS, CRACK, HOOKERS. IT WASN'T AN EASY PLACE TO RAISE KIDS.
FUCK THE VCS!
KAK KAK KAK KAK
"BUT THERE WERE GOOD CHURCHES IN THE NEIGHBORHOOD TOO. GOOD SINGING. GOOD WORSHIP. GOOD PEOPLE.
"THINGS SURE DO CHANGE."
IT'S SAD THOUGH...ISN'T IT? THAT IT'S ALL BEING TORN DOWN?
IT'S SAD, BUT YOU KNOW, THESE HOUSES ARE OLD...I COULDN'T AFFORD THE UPKEEP ANYMORE. PLUMBING'S BAD, FOUNDATION'S CRACKED...
AND THEY'RE GIVING ME MORE MONEY THEN I EVER DREAMED I'D HAVE IN MY LIFE. I'M NOT SPEAKING FOR EVERYONE MIND YOU, JUST ME...

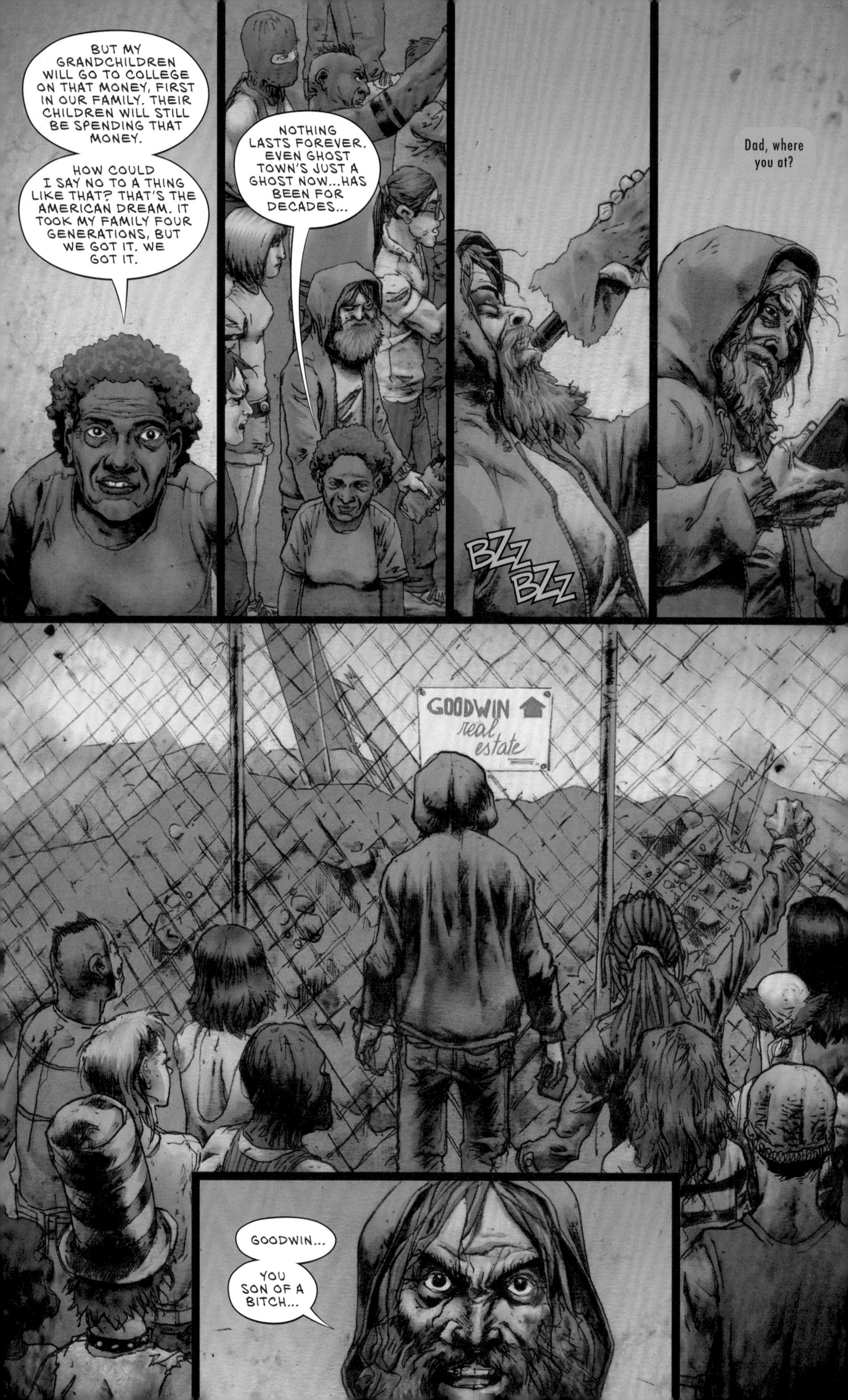
BUT MY GRANDCHILDREN WILL GO TO COLLEGE ON THAT MONEY, FIRST IN OUR FAMILY. THEIR CHILDREN WILL STILL BE SPENDING THAT MONEY.
HOW COULD I SAY NO TO A THING LIKE THAT? THAT'S THE AMERICAN DREAM. IT TOOK MY FAMILY FOUR GENERATIONS, BUT WE GOT IT. WE GOT IT.
NOTHING LASTS FOREVER. EVEN GHOST TOWN'S JUST A GHOST NOW...HAS BEEN FOR DECADES...
BZZ BZZ
Dad, where you at?
GOODWIN real estate
GOODWIN...
YOU SON OF A BITCH...

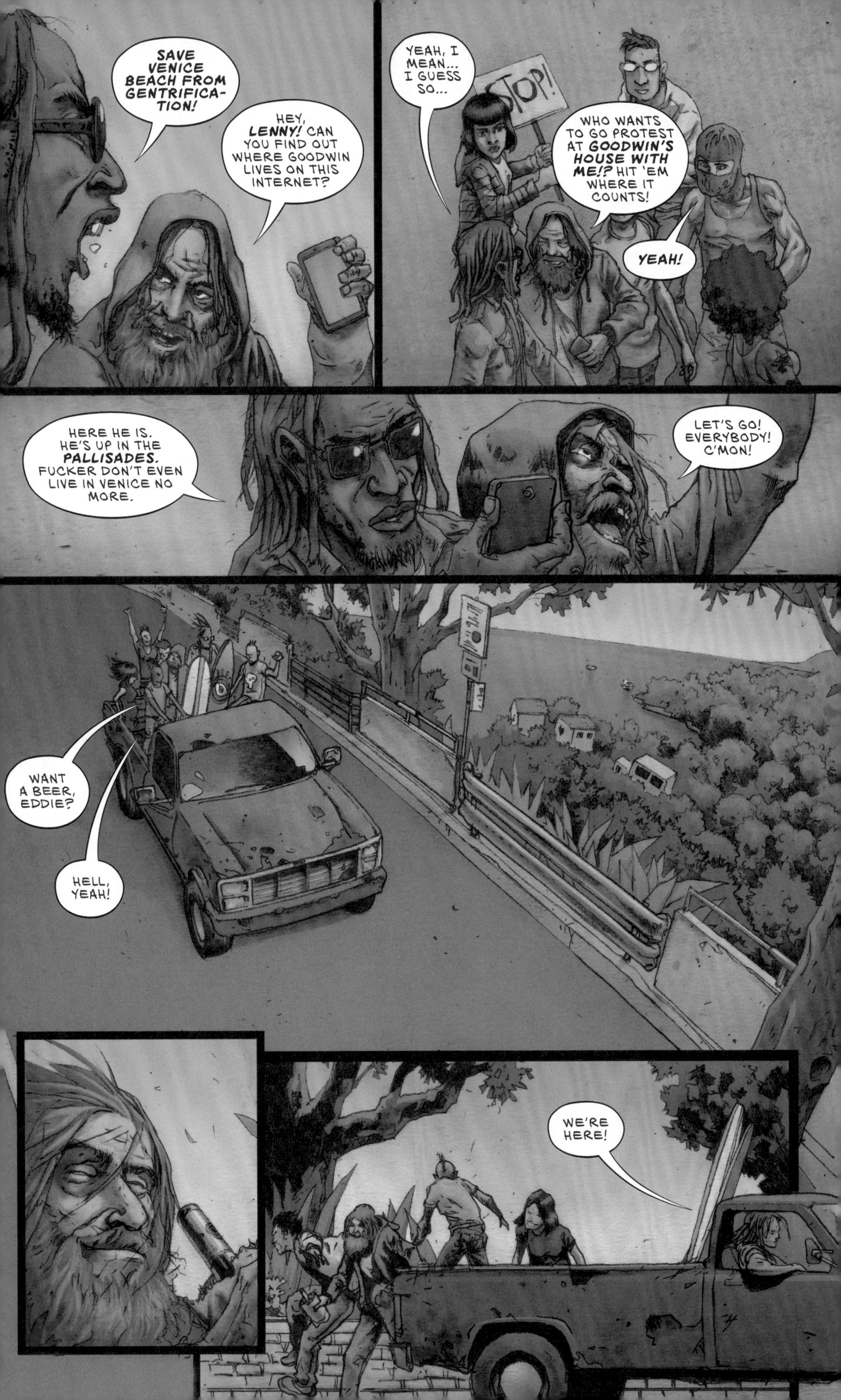
SAVE VENICE BEACH FROM GENTRIFICA-TION!
HEY, LENNY! CAN YOU FIND OUT WHERE GOODWIN LIVES ON THIS INTERNET?
YEAH, I MEAN... I GUESS SO...
STOP!
WHO WANTS TO GO PROTEST AT GOODWIN'S HOUSE WITH ME!? HIT 'EM WHERE IT COUNTS!
YEAH!
HERE HE IS. HE'S UP IN THE PALLISADES. FUCKER DON'T EVEN LIVE IN VENICE NO MORE.
LET'S GO! EVERYBODY! C'MON!
WANT A BEER, EDDIE?
HELL, YEAH!
WE'RE HERE!

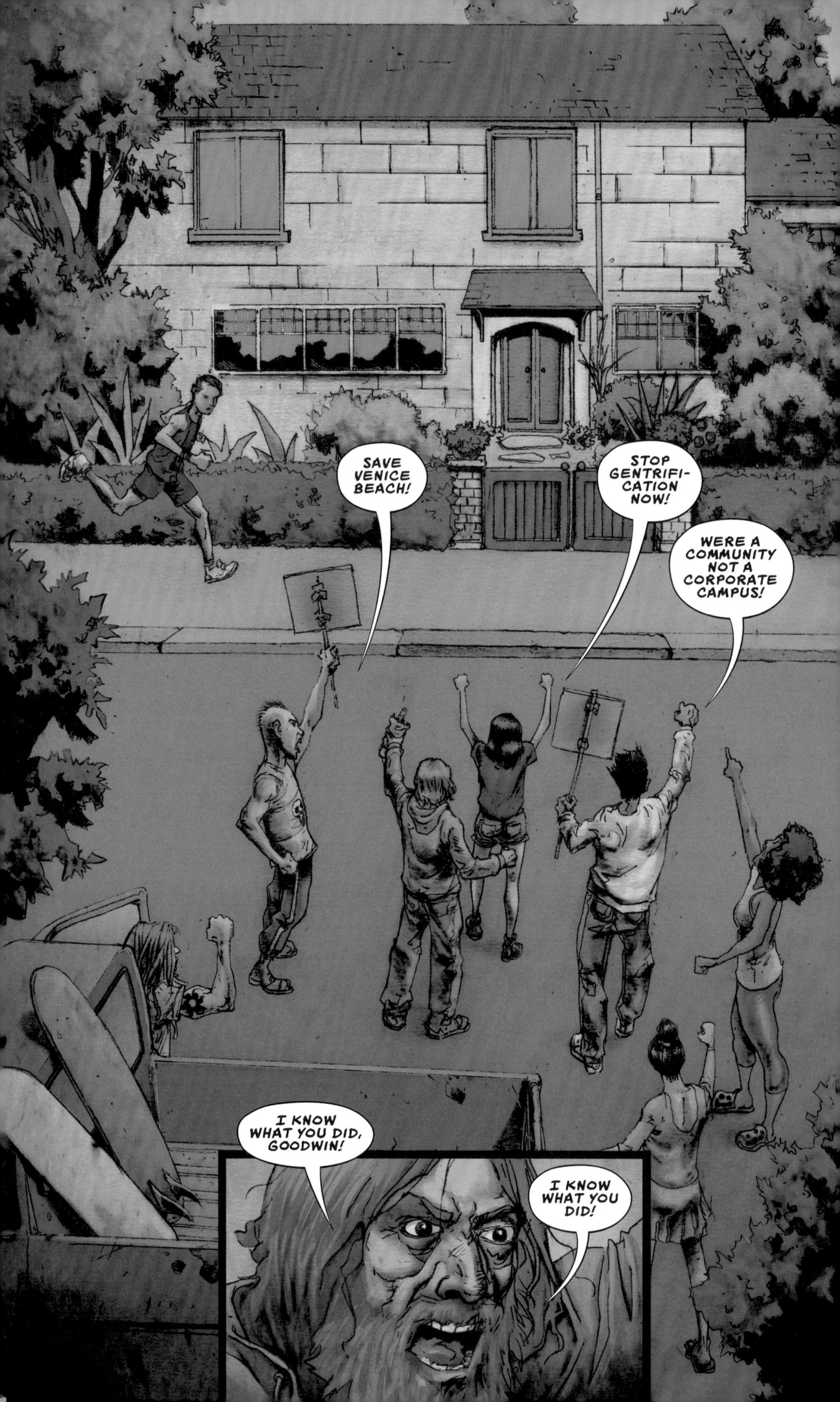
SAVE VENICE BEACH!
STOP GENTRIFI-CATION NOW!
WERE A COMMUNITY NOT A CORPORATE CAMPUS!
I KNOW WHAT YOU DID, GOODWIN!
I KNOW WHAT YOU DID!

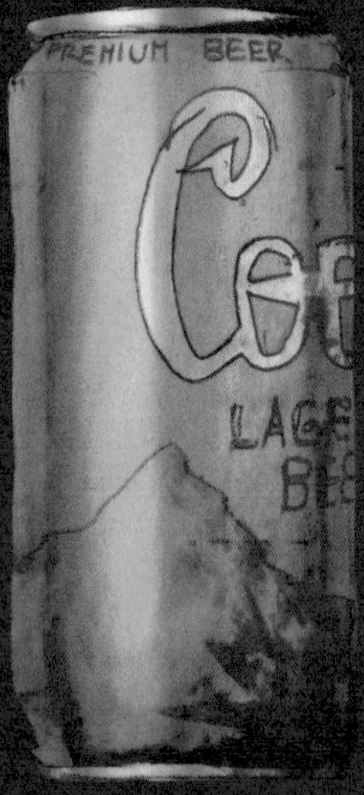
PREMIUM BEER

CHAPTER 5

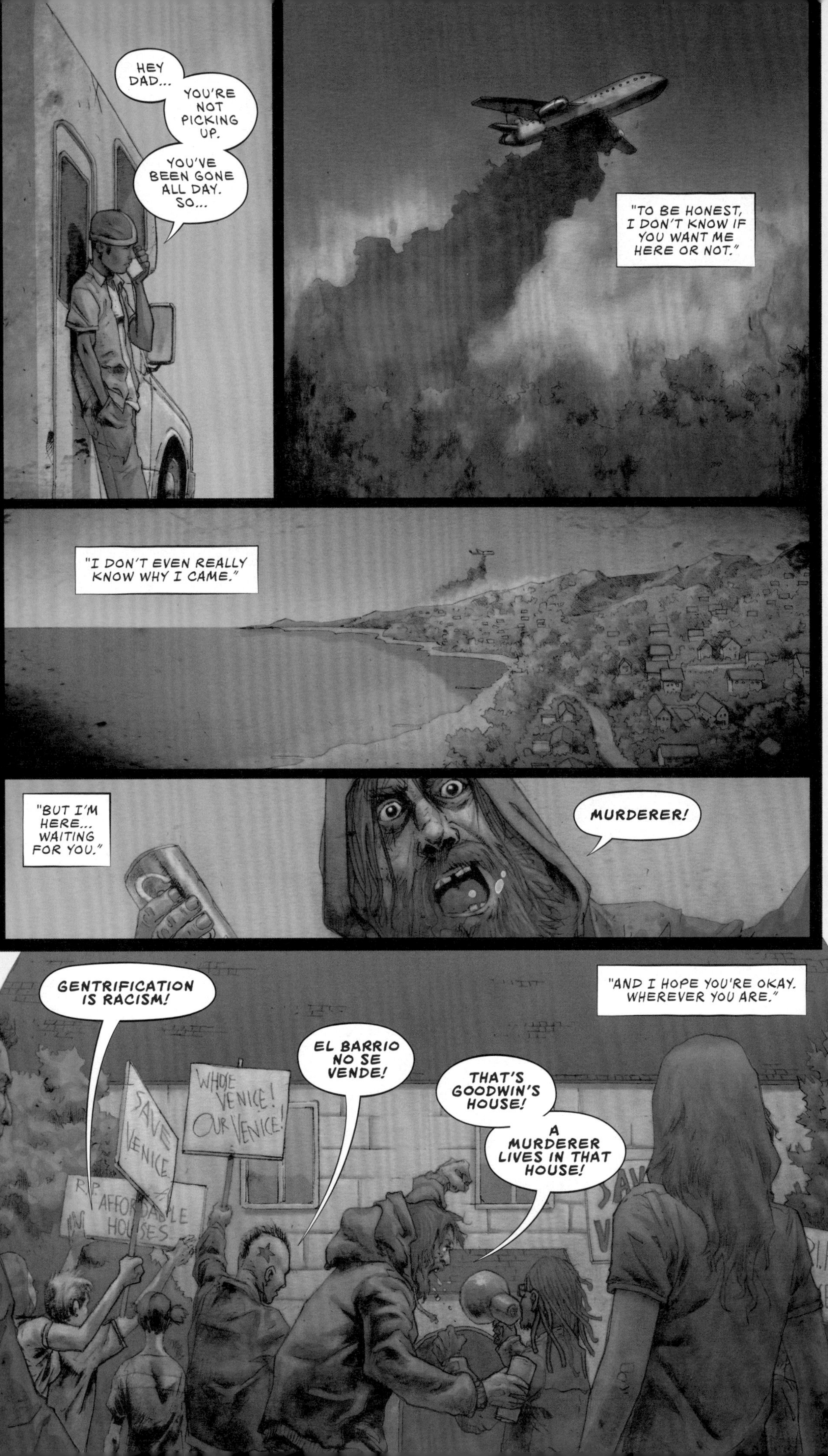
HEY DAD...
YOU'RE NOT PICKING UP.
YOU'VE BEEN GONE ALL DAY. SO...
"TO BE HONEST, I DON'T KNOW IF YOU WANT ME HERE OR NOT."
"I DON'T EVEN REALLY KNOW WHY I CAME."
"BUT I'M HERE... WAITING FOR YOU."
MURDERER!
GENTRIFICATION IS RACISM!
"AND I HOPE YOU'RE OKAY. WHEREVER YOU ARE."
SAVE VENICE
WHOSE VENICE! OUR VENICE!
R.I.P. AFFORDABLE HOUSES
EL BARRIO NO SE VENDE!
THAT'S GOODWIN'S HOUSE!
A MURDERER LIVES IN THAT HOUSE!

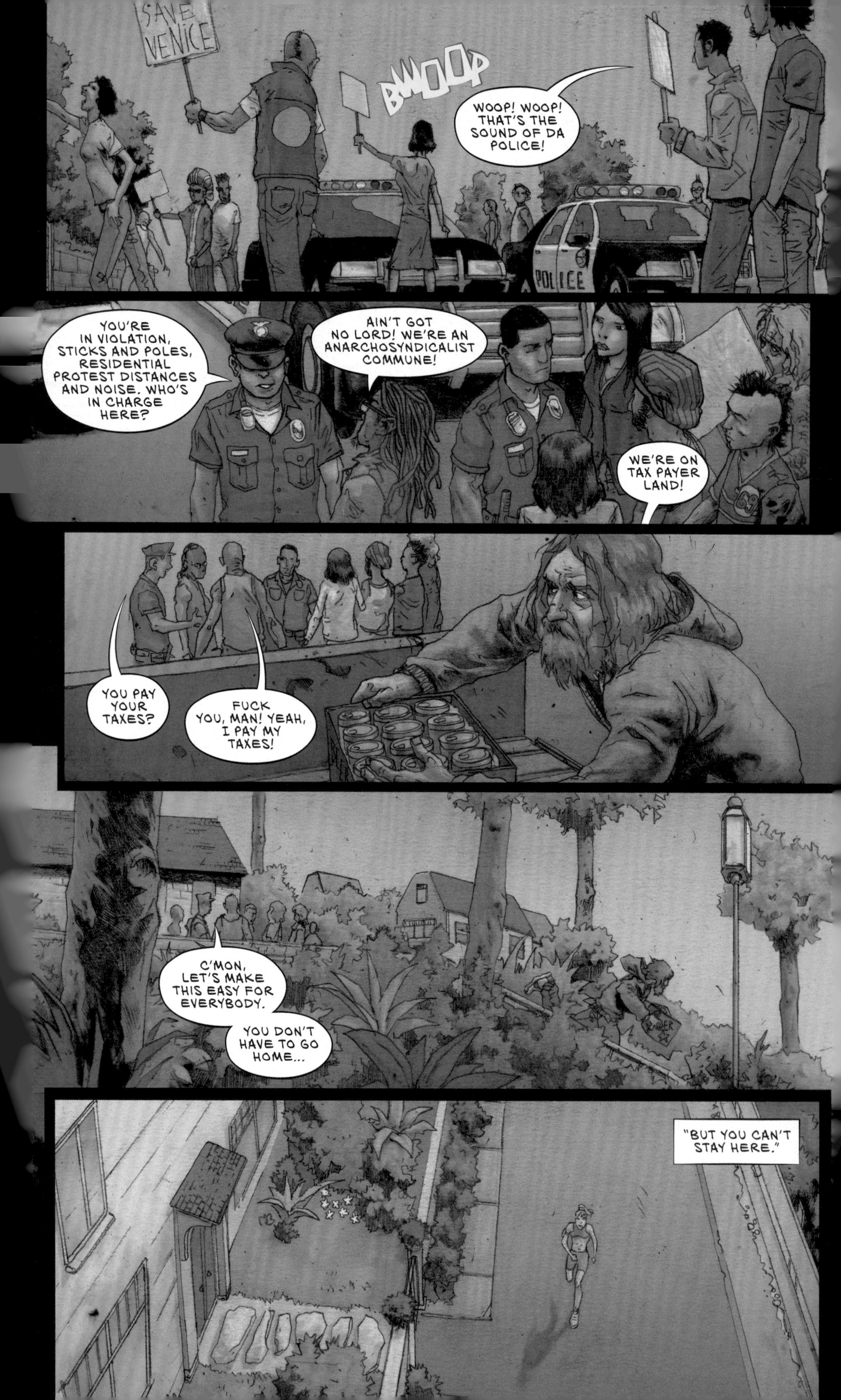
SAVE VENICE
BWOOP
WOOP! WOOP! THAT'S THE SOUND OF DA POLICE!
POLICE
YOU'RE IN VIOLATION, STICKS AND POLES, RESIDENTIAL PROTEST DISTANCES AND NOISE. WHO'S IN CHARGE HERE?
AIN'T GOT NO LORD! WE'RE AN ANARCHOSYNDICALIST COMMUNE!
WE'RE ON TAX PAYER LAND!
YOU PAY YOUR TAXES?
FUCK YOU, MAN! YEAH, I PAY MY TAXES!
C'MON, LET'S MAKE THIS EASY FOR EVERYBODY.
YOU DON'T HAVE TO GO HOME...
"BUT YOU CAN'T STAY HERE."

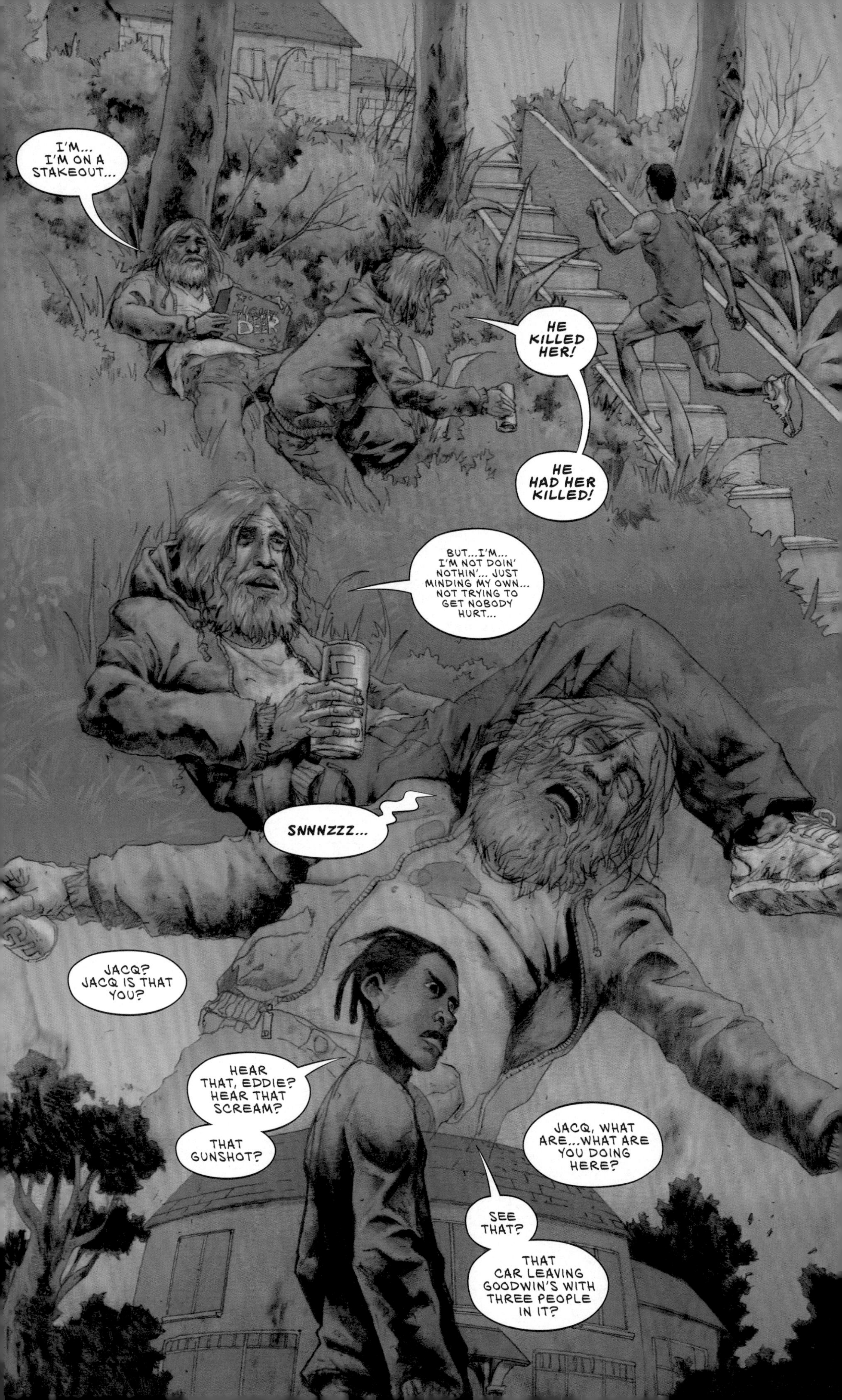

I'M... I'M ON A STAKEOUT...
HE KILLED HER!
HE HAD HER KILLED!
BUT...I'M... I'M NOT DOIN' NOTHIN'... JUST MINDING MY OWN... NOT TRYING TO GET NOBODY HURT...
SNNNZZZ...
JACQ? JACQ IS THAT YOU?
HEAR THAT, EDDIE? HEAR THAT SCREAM?
THAT GUNSHOT?
JACQ, WHAT ARE...WHAT ARE YOU DOING HERE?
SEE THAT?
THAT CAR LEAVING GOODWIN'S WITH THREE PEOPLE IN IT?

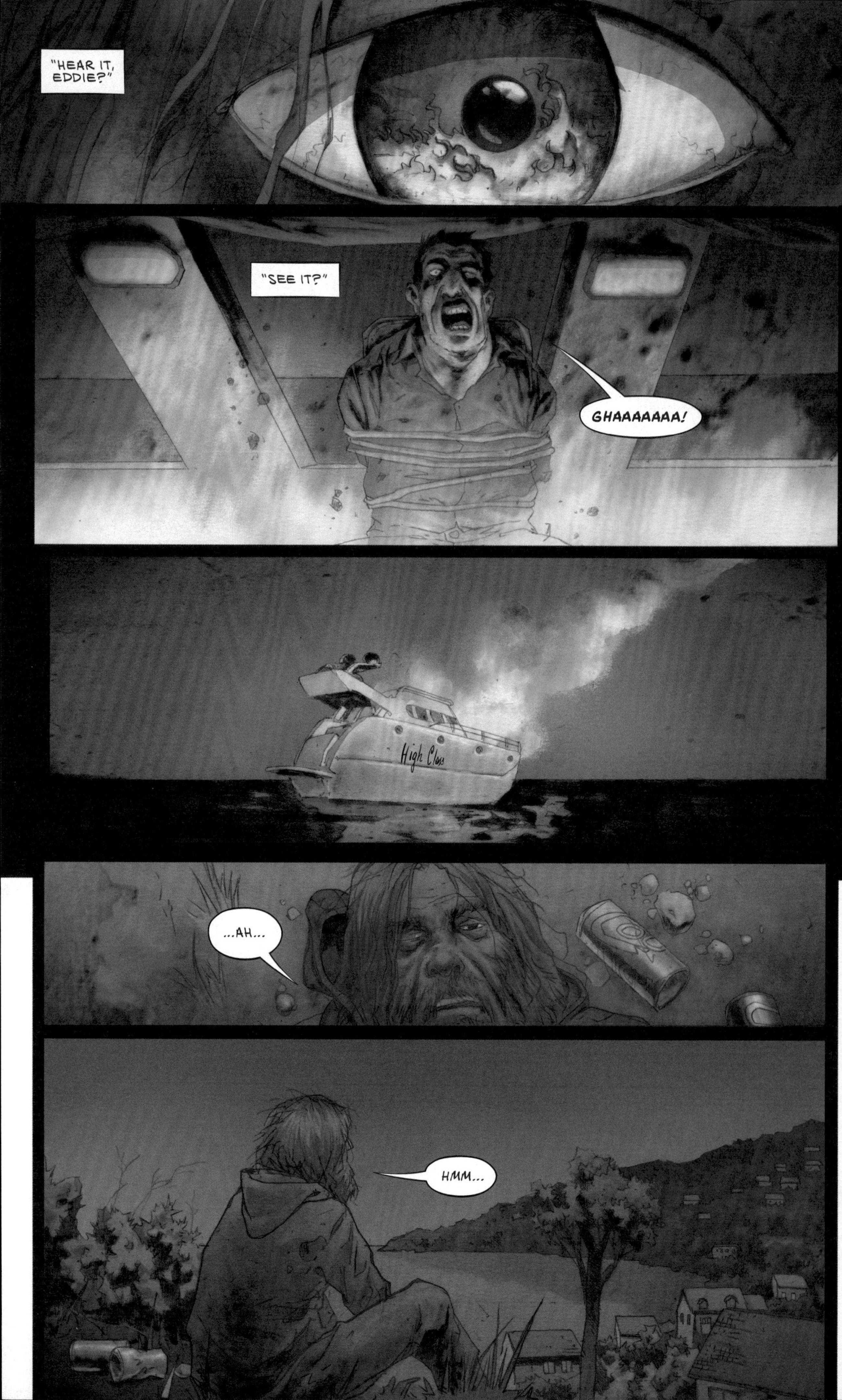
"HEAR IT, EDDIE?"
"SEE IT?"
GHAAAAAAA!
High Class
...AH...
HMM...

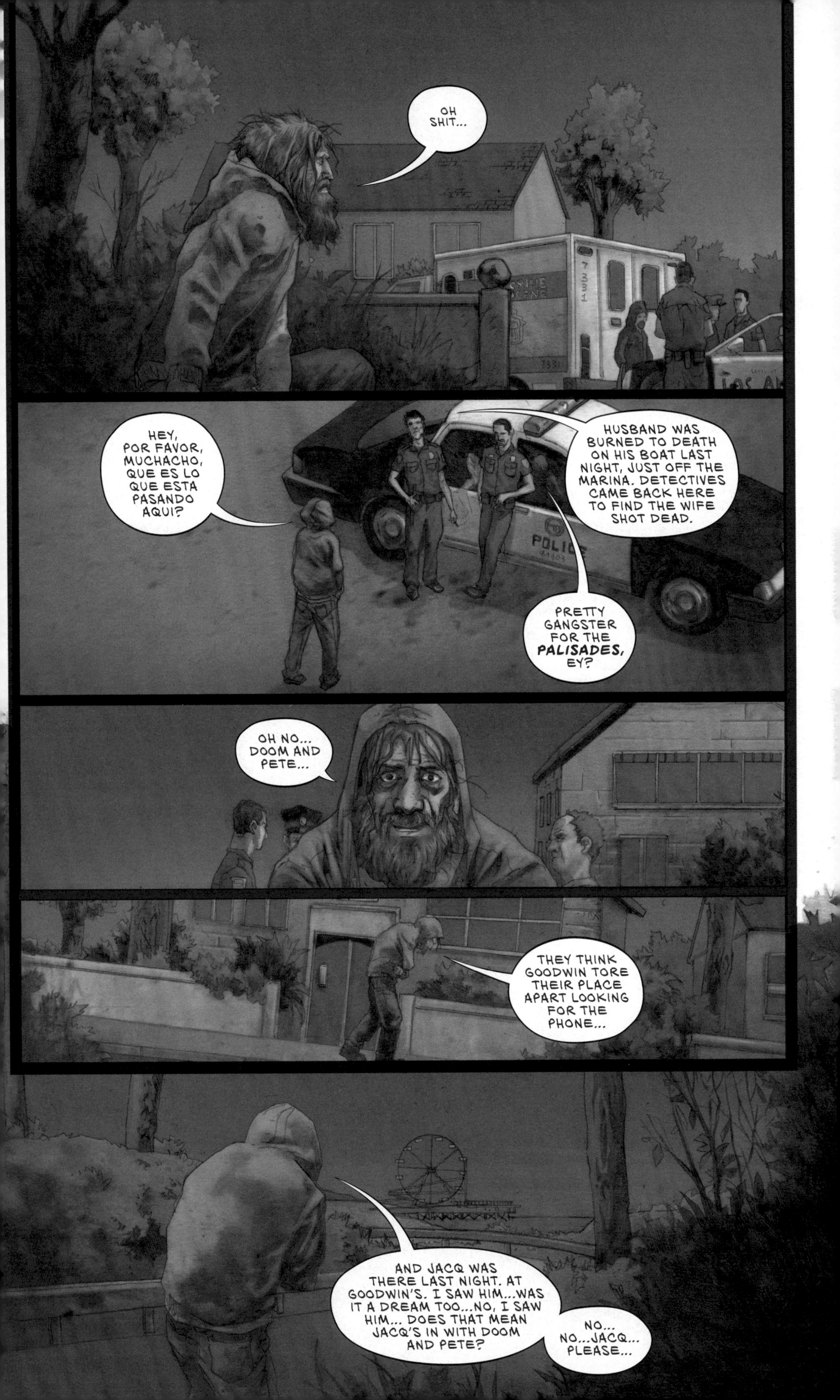
OH SHIT...
HEY, POR FAVOR, MUCHACHO, QUE ES LO QUE ESTA PASANDO AQUI?
HUSBAND WAS BURNED TO DEATH ON HIS BOAT LAST NIGHT, JUST OFF THE MARINA. DETECTIVES CAME BACK HERE TO FIND THE WIFE SHOT DEAD.
PRETTY GANGSTER FOR THE PALISADES, EY?
OH NO... DOOM AND PETE...
THEY THINK GOODWIN TORE THEIR PLACE APART LOOKING FOR THE PHONE...
AND JACQ WAS THERE LAST NIGHT. AT GOODWIN'S. I SAW HIM...WAS IT A DREAM TOO...NO, I SAW HIM... DOES THAT MEAN JACQ'S IN WITH DOOM AND PETE?
NO... NO...JACQ... PLEASE...

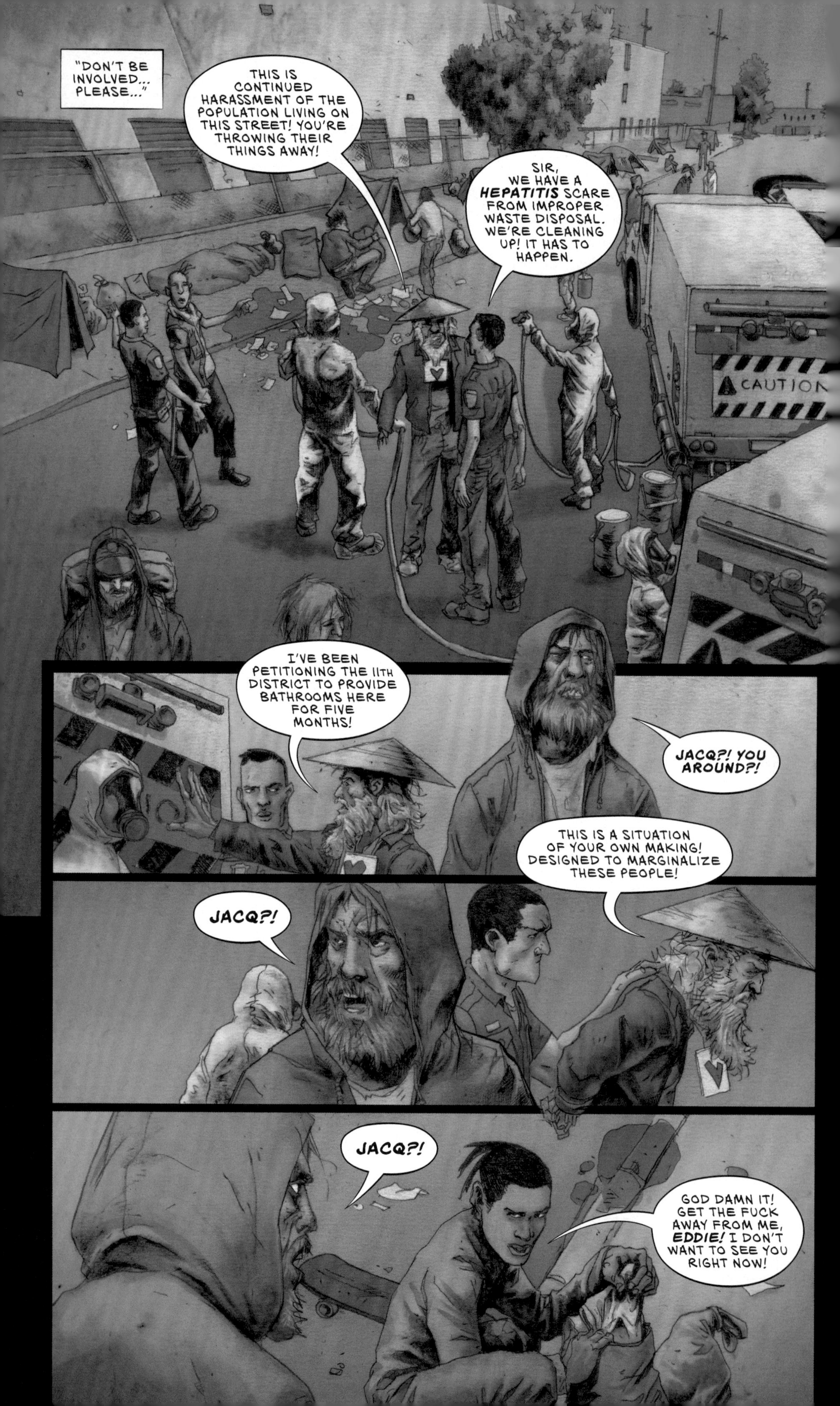
"DON'T BE INVOLVED... PLEASE..."
THIS IS CONTINUED HARASSMENT OF THE POPULATION LIVING ON THIS STREET! YOU'RE THROWING THEIR THINGS AWAY!
SIR, WE HAVE A HEPATITIS SCARE FROM IMPROPER WASTE DISPOSAL. WE'RE CLEANING UP! IT HAS TO HAPPEN.
CAUTION
I'VE BEEN PETITIONING THE 11TH DISTRICT TO PROVIDE BATHROOMS HERE FOR FIVE MONTHS!
JACQ?! YOU AROUND?!
THIS IS A SITUATION OF YOUR OWN MAKING! DESIGNED TO MARGINALIZE THESE PEOPLE!
JACQ?!
JACQ?!
GOD DAMN IT! GET THE FUCK AWAY FROM ME, EDDIE! I DON'T WANT TO SEE YOU RIGHT NOW!

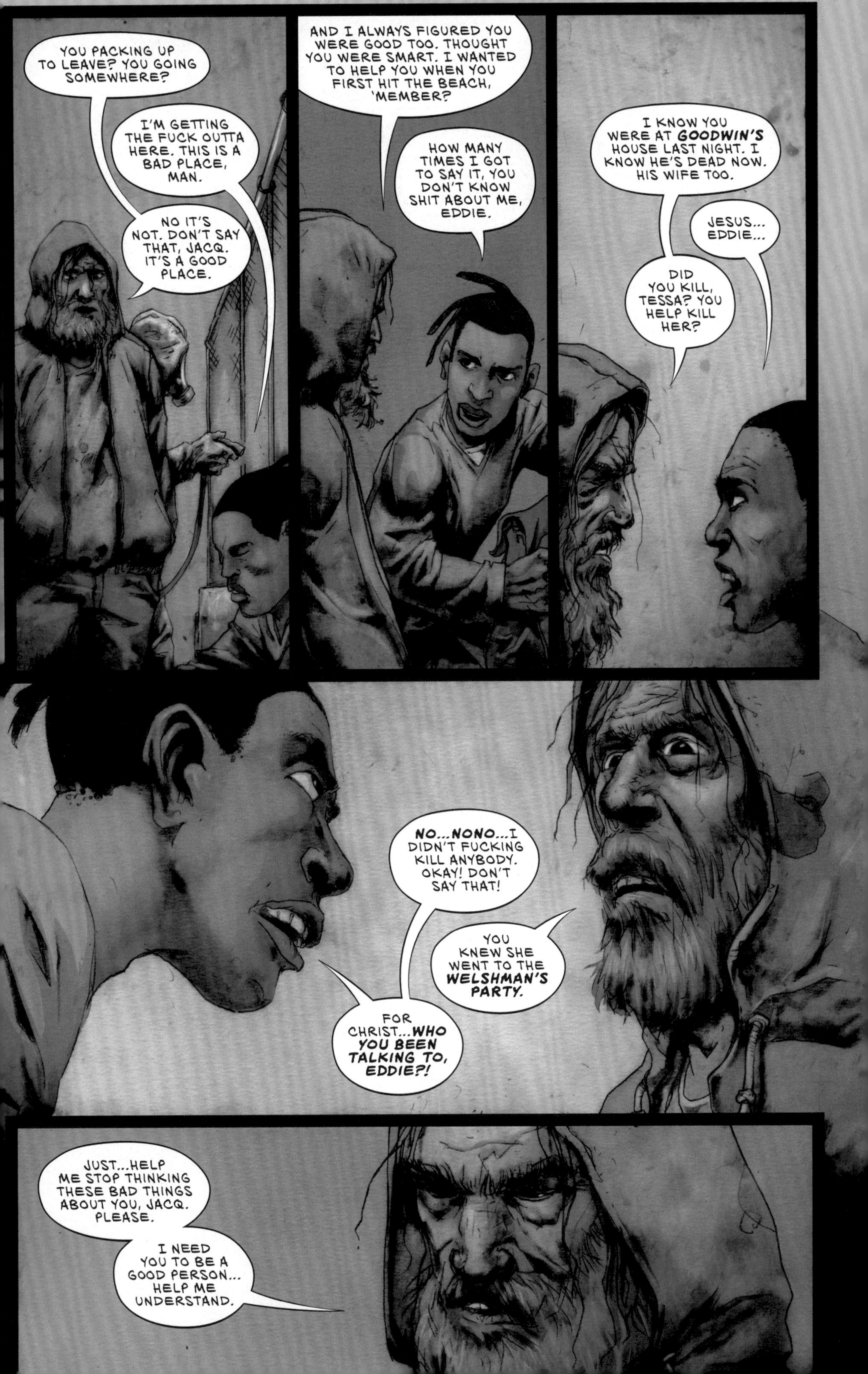

YOU PACKING UP TO LEAVE? YOU GOING SOMEWHERE?
I'M GETTING THE FUCK OUTTA HERE. THIS IS A BAD PLACE, MAN.
NO IT'S NOT. DON'T SAY THAT, JACQ. IT'S A GOOD PLACE.
AND I ALWAYS FIGURED YOU WERE GOOD TOO. THOUGHT YOU WERE SMART. I WANTED TO HELP YOU WHEN YOU FIRST HIT THE BEACH, 'MEMBER?
HOW MANY TIMES I GOT TO SAY IT, YOU DON'T KNOW SHIT ABOUT ME, EDDIE.
I KNOW YOU WERE AT **GOODWIN'S** HOUSE LAST NIGHT. I KNOW HE'S DEAD NOW. HIS WIFE TOO.
JESUS... EDDIE...
DID YOU KILL, TESSA? YOU HELP KILL HER?
NO...NONO...I DIDN'T FUCKING KILL ANYBODY. OKAY! DON'T SAY THAT!
YOU KNEW SHE WENT TO THE **WELSHMAN'S PARTY.**
FOR CHRIST...**WHO YOU BEEN TALKING TO, EDDIE?!**
JUST...HELP ME STOP THINKING THESE BAD THINGS ABOUT YOU, JACQ. PLEASE.
I NEED YOU TO BE A GOOD PERSON... HELP ME UNDERSTAND.

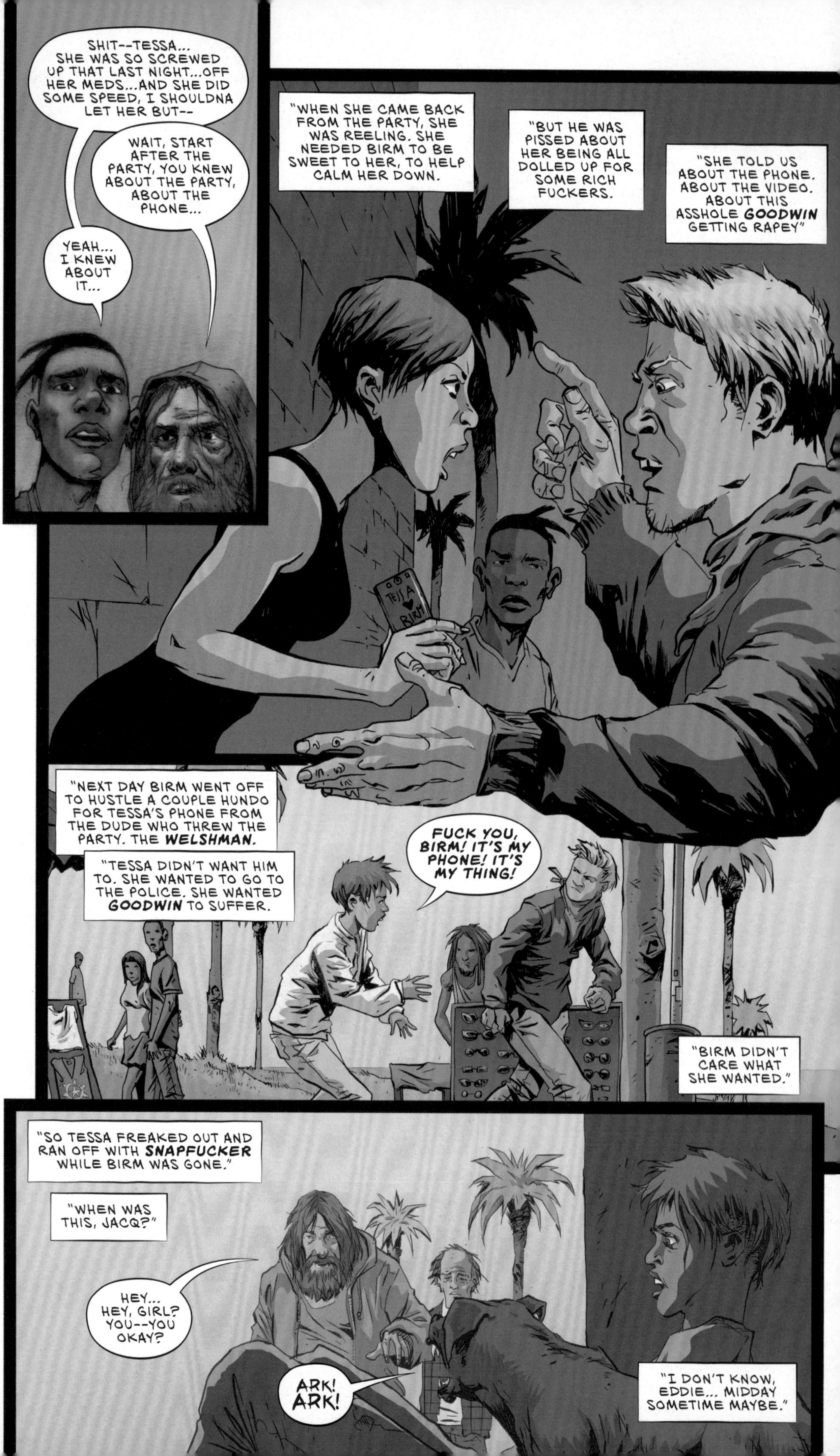

SHIT--TESSA... SHE WAS SO SCREWED UP THAT LAST NIGHT...OFF HER MEDS...AND SHE DID SOME SPEED, I SHOULDNA LET HER BUT--
WAIT, START AFTER THE PARTY, YOU KNEW ABOUT THE PARTY, ABOUT THE PHONE...
YEAH... I KNEW ABOUT IT...
"WHEN SHE CAME BACK FROM THE PARTY, SHE WAS REELING. SHE NEEDED BIRM TO BE SWEET TO HER, TO HELP CALM HER DOWN.
"BUT HE WAS PISSED ABOUT HER BEING ALL DOLLED UP FOR SOME RICH FUCKERS.
"SHE TOLD US ABOUT THE PHONE. ABOUT THE VIDEO. ABOUT THIS ASSHOLE GOODWIN GETTING RAPEY"
TESSA ♥ BIRM
"NEXT DAY BIRM WENT OFF TO HUSTLE A COUPLE HUNDO FOR TESSA'S PHONE FROM THE DUDE WHO THREW THE PARTY. THE WELSHMAN.
"TESSA DIDN'T WANT HIM TO. SHE WANTED TO GO TO THE POLICE. SHE WANTED GOODWIN TO SUFFER.
FUCK YOU, BIRM! IT'S MY PHONE! IT'S MY THING!
"BIRM DIDN'T CARE WHAT SHE WANTED."
"SO TESSA FREAKED OUT AND RAN OFF WITH SNAPFUCKER WHILE BIRM WAS GONE."
"WHEN WAS THIS, JACQ?"
HEY... HEY, GIRL? YOU--YOU OKAY?
ARK! ARK!
"I DON'T KNOW, EDDIE... MIDDAY SOMETIME MAYBE."

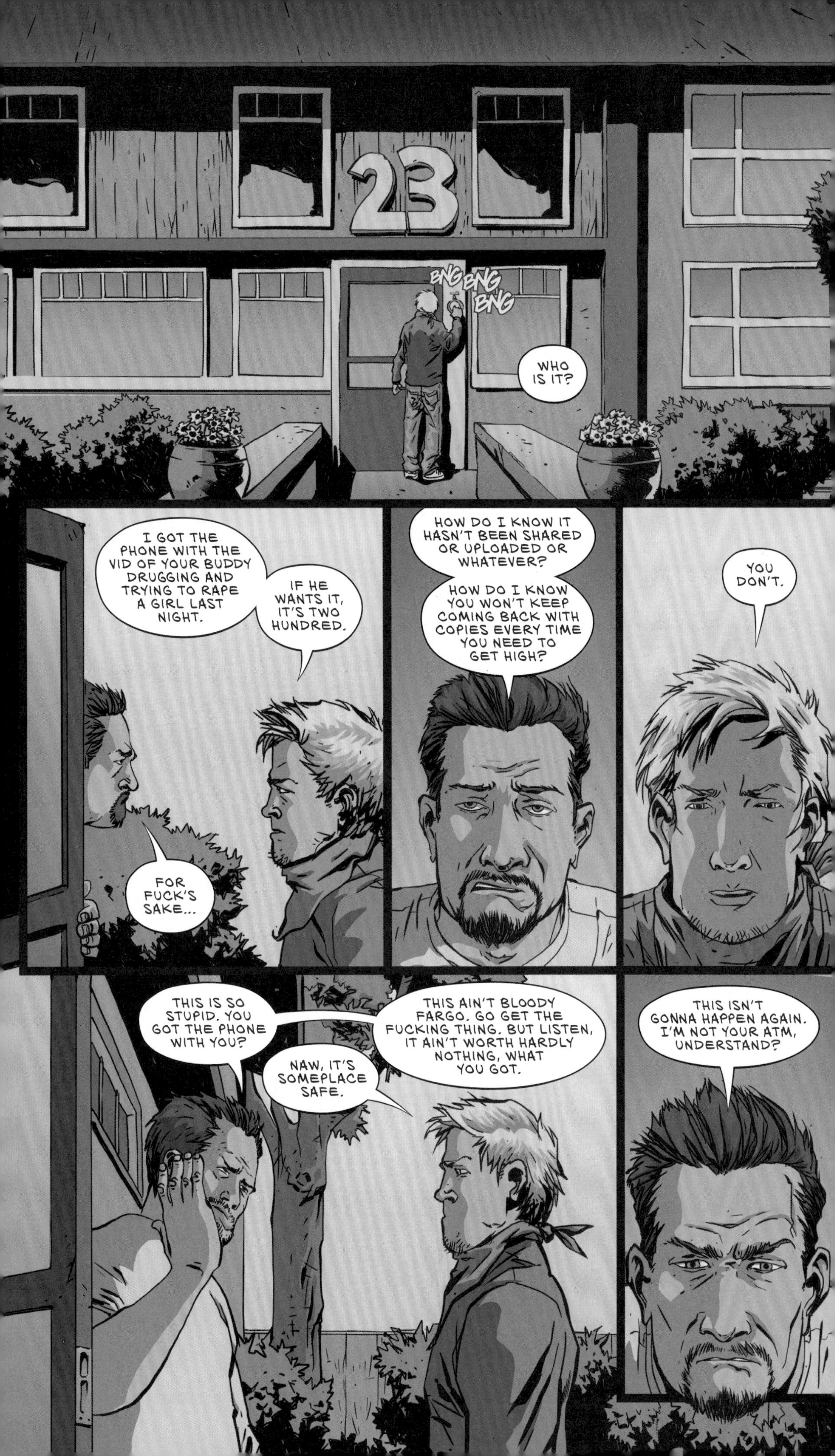
BNG BNG BNG
WHO IS IT?
I GOT THE PHONE WITH THE VID OF YOUR BUDDY DRUGGING AND TRYING TO RAPE A GIRL LAST NIGHT.
IF HE WANTS IT, IT'S TWO HUNDRED.
FOR FUCK'S SAKE...
HOW DO I KNOW IT HASN'T BEEN SHARED OR UPLOADED OR WHATEVER?
HOW DO I KNOW YOU WON'T KEEP COMING BACK WITH COPIES EVERY TIME YOU NEED TO GET HIGH?
YOU DON'T.
THIS IS SO STUPID. YOU GOT THE PHONE WITH YOU?
NAW, IT'S SOMEPLACE SAFE.
THIS AIN'T BLOODY FARGO. GO GET THE FUCKING THING. BUT LISTEN, IT AIN'T WORTH HARDLY NOTHING, WHAT YOU GOT.
THIS ISN'T GONNA HAPPEN AGAIN. I'M NOT YOUR ATM, UNDERSTAND?

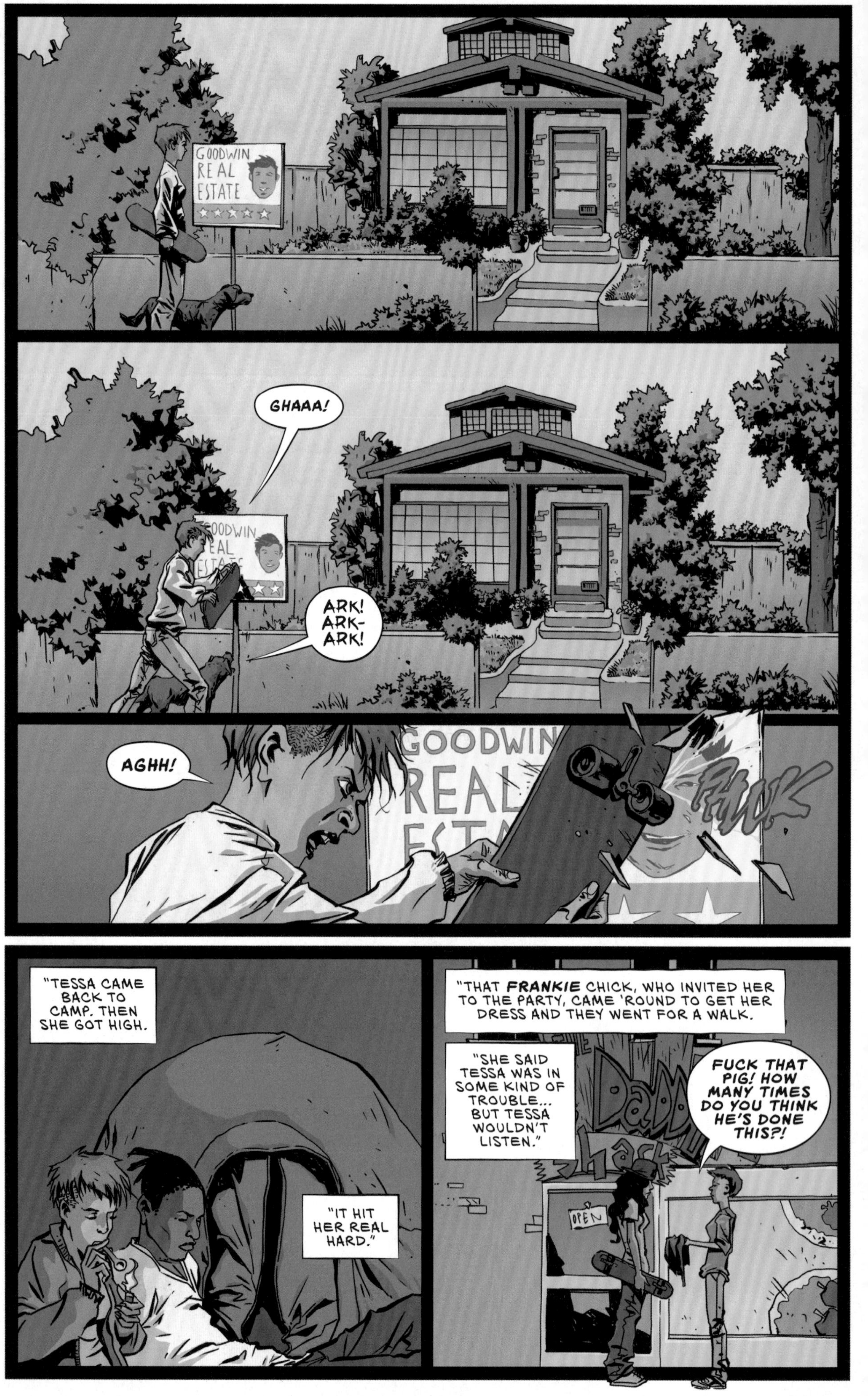
GOODWIN REAL ESTATE
GHAAA!
ARK! ARK-ARK!
AGHH!
"TESSA CAME BACK TO CAMP. THEN SHE GOT HIGH.
"IT HIT HER REAL HARD."
"THAT FRANKIE CHICK, WHO INVITED HER TO THE PARTY, CAME 'ROUND TO GET HER DRESS AND THEY WENT FOR A WALK.
"SHE SAID TESSA WAS IN SOME KIND OF TROUBLE... BUT TESSA WOULDN'T LISTEN."
FUCK THAT PIG! HOW MANY TIMES DO YOU THINK HE'S DONE THIS?!
OPEN

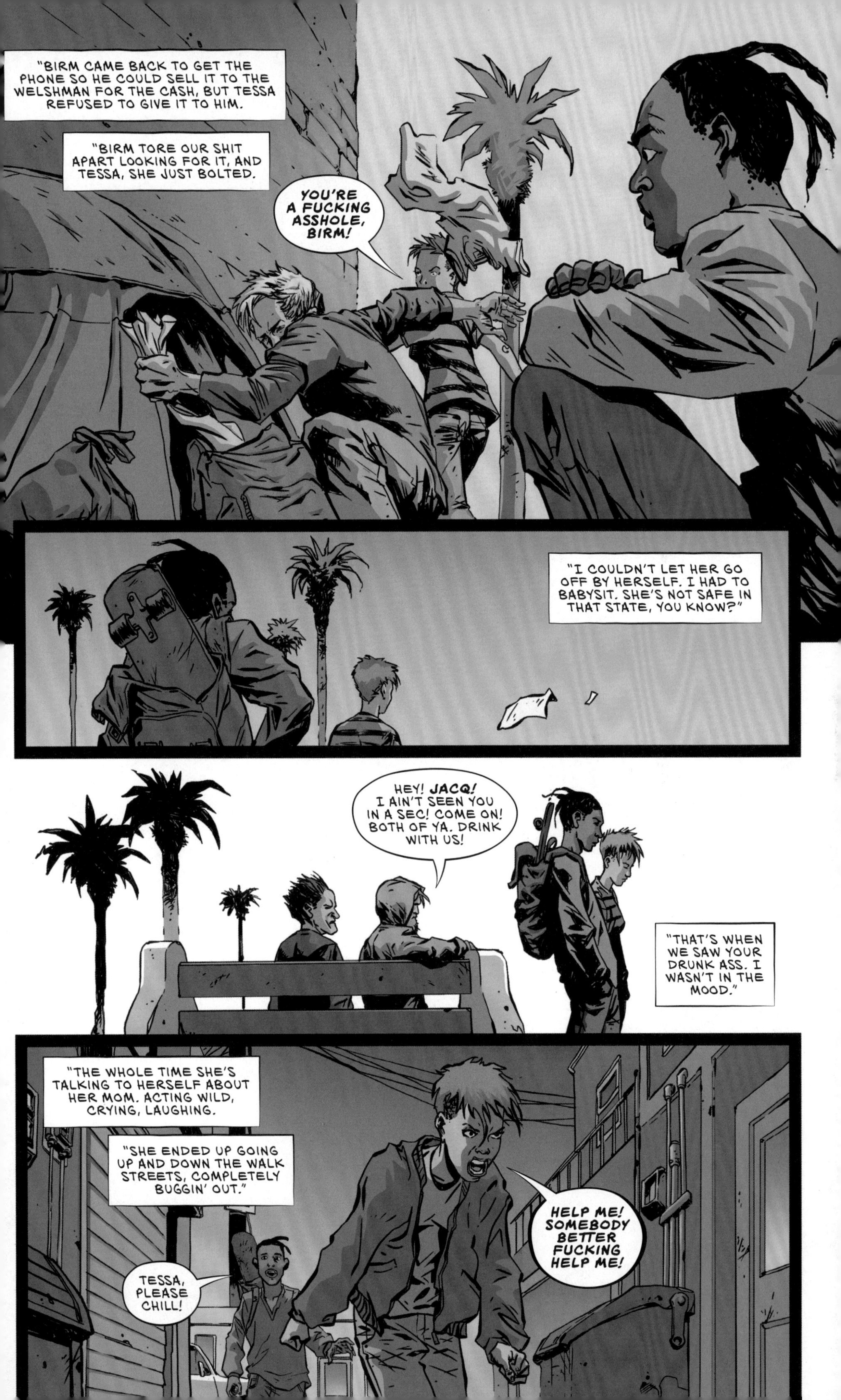
"BIRM CAME BACK TO GET THE PHONE SO HE COULD SELL IT TO THE WELSHMAN FOR THE CASH, BUT TESSA REFUSED TO GIVE IT TO HIM.
"BIRM TORE OUR SHIT APART LOOKING FOR IT, AND TESSA, SHE JUST BOLTED.
YOU'RE A FUCKING ASSHOLE, BIRM!
"I COULDN'T LET HER GO OFF BY HERSELF. I HAD TO BABYSIT. SHE'S NOT SAFE IN THAT STATE, YOU KNOW?"
HEY! JACQ! I AIN'T SEEN YOU IN A SEC! COME ON! BOTH OF YA. DRINK WITH US!
"THAT'S WHEN WE SAW YOUR DRUNK ASS. I WASN'T IN THE MOOD."
"THE WHOLE TIME SHE'S TALKING TO HERSELF ABOUT HER MOM. ACTING WILD, CRYING, LAUGHING.
"SHE ENDED UP GOING UP AND DOWN THE WALK STREETS, COMPLETELY BUGGIN' OUT."
HELP ME! SOMEBODY BETTER FUCKING HELP ME!
TESSA, PLEASE CHILL!

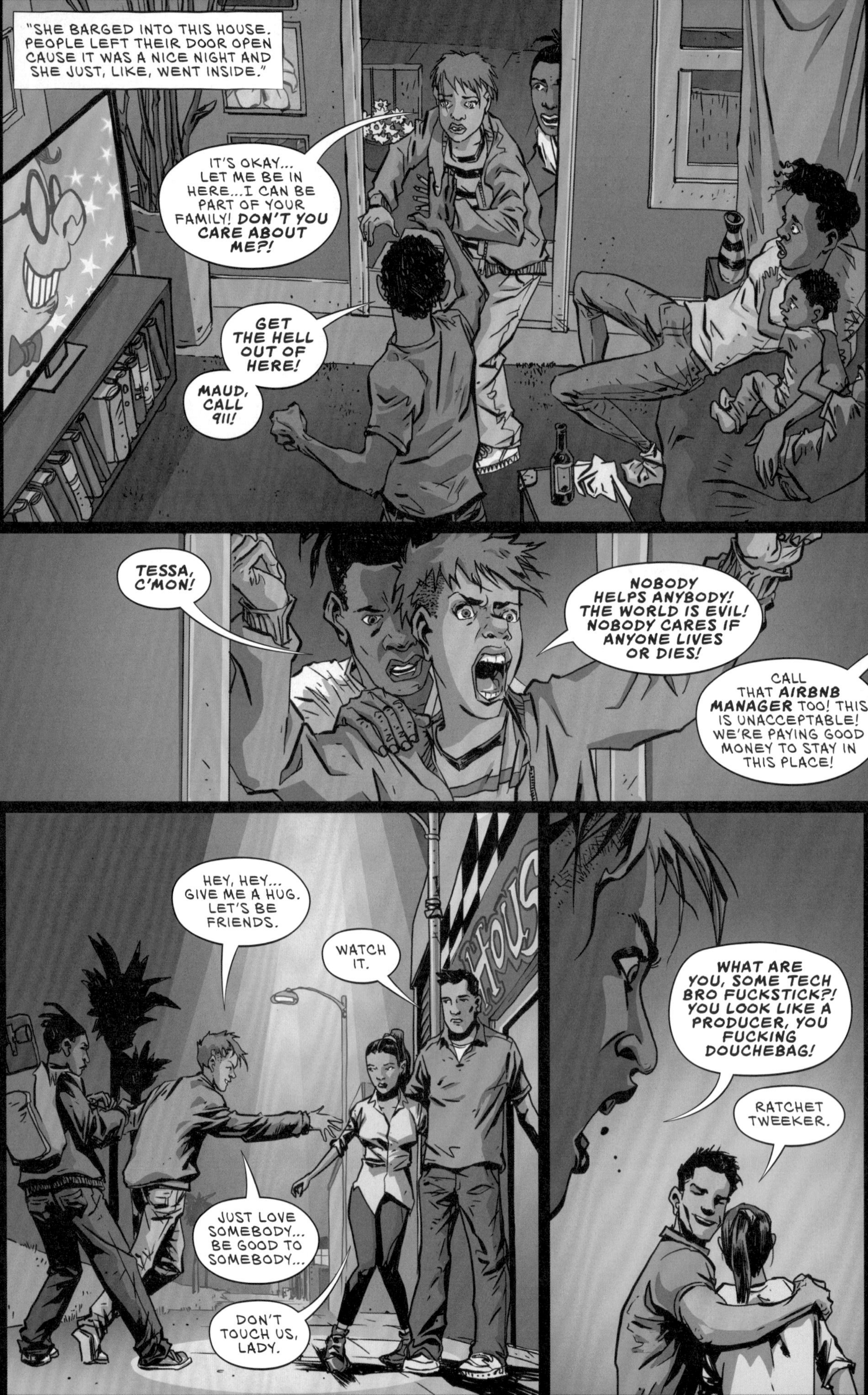
"SHE BARGED INTO THIS HOUSE. PEOPLE LEFT THEIR DOOR OPEN CAUSE IT WAS A NICE NIGHT AND SHE JUST, LIKE, WENT INSIDE."
IT'S OKAY... LET ME BE IN HERE...I CAN BE PART OF YOUR FAMILY! DON'T YOU CARE ABOUT ME?!
GET THE HELL OUT OF HERE!
MAUD, CALL 911!
TESSA, C'MON!
NOBODY HELPS ANYBODY! THE WORLD IS EVIL! NOBODY CARES IF ANYONE LIVES OR DIES!
CALL THAT AIRBNB MANAGER TOO! THIS IS UNACCEPTABLE! WE'RE PAYING GOOD MONEY TO STAY IN THIS PLACE!
HEY, HEY... GIVE ME A HUG. LET'S BE FRIENDS.
WATCH IT.
JUST LOVE SOMEBODY... BE GOOD TO SOMEBODY...
DON'T TOUCH US, LADY.
WHAT ARE YOU, SOME TECH BRO FUCKSTICK?! YOU LOOK LIKE A PRODUCER, YOU FUCKING DOUCHEBAG!
RATCHET TWEEKER.

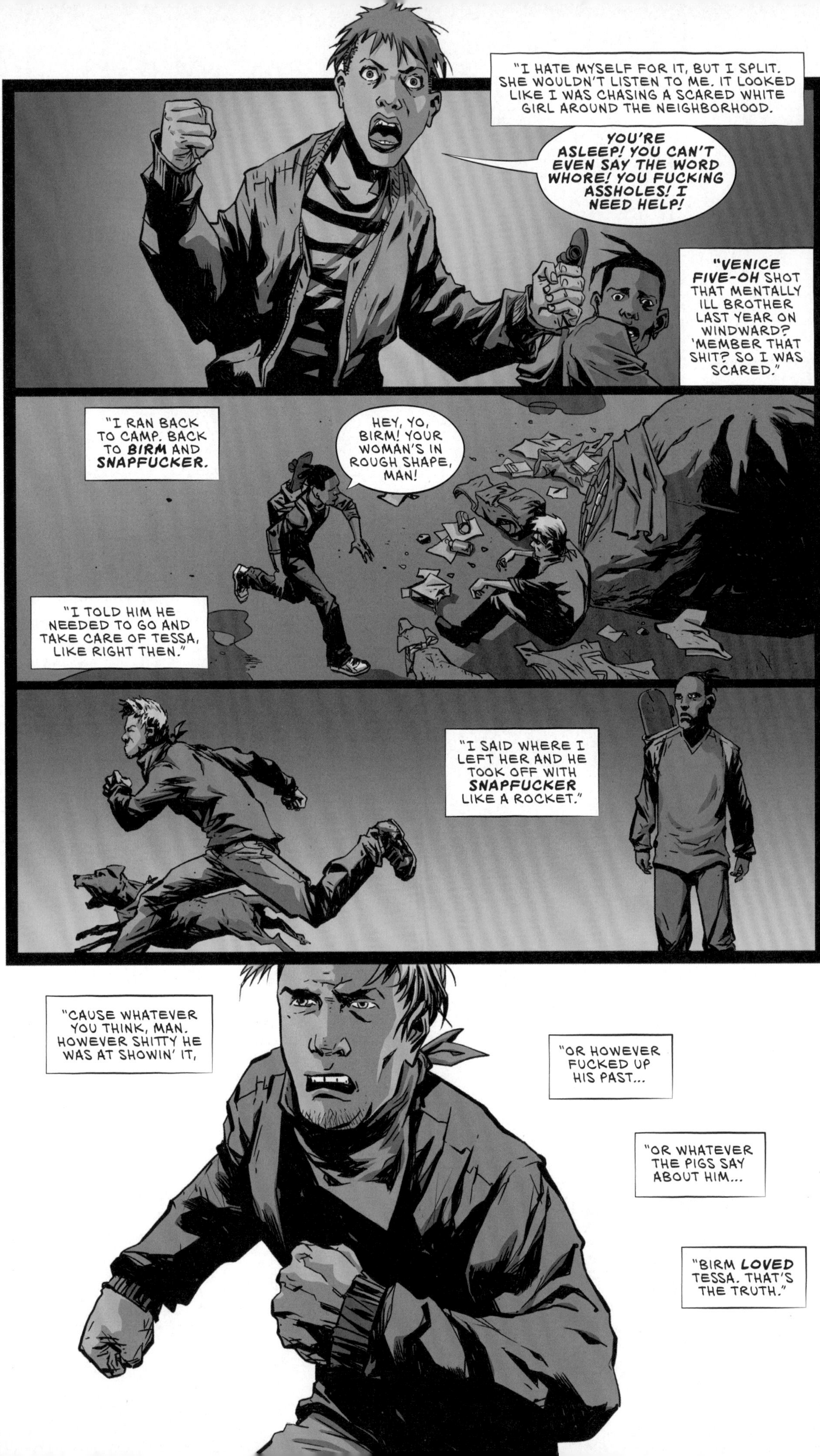
"I HATE MYSELF FOR IT, BUT I SPLIT. SHE WOULDN'T LISTEN TO ME. IT LOOKED LIKE I WAS CHASING A SCARED WHITE GIRL AROUND THE NEIGHBORHOOD.
YOU'RE ASLEEP! YOU CAN'T EVEN SAY THE WORD WHORE! YOU FUCKING ASSHOLES! I NEED HELP!
"VENICE FIVE-OH SHOT THAT MENTALLY ILL BROTHER LAST YEAR ON WINDWARD? 'MEMBER THAT SHIT? SO I WAS SCARED."
"I RAN BACK TO CAMP. BACK TO BIRM AND SNAPFUCKER.
HEY, YO, BIRM! YOUR WOMAN'S IN ROUGH SHAPE, MAN!
"I TOLD HIM HE NEEDED TO GO AND TAKE CARE OF TESSA, LIKE RIGHT THEN."
"I SAID WHERE I LEFT HER AND HE TOOK OFF WITH SNAPFUCKER LIKE A ROCKET."
"CAUSE WHATEVER YOU THINK, MAN. HOWEVER SHITTY HE WAS AT SHOWIN' IT,
"OR HOWEVER FUCKED UP HIS PAST...
"OR WHATEVER THE PIGS SAY ABOUT HIM...
"BIRM LOVED TESSA. THAT'S THE TRUTH."

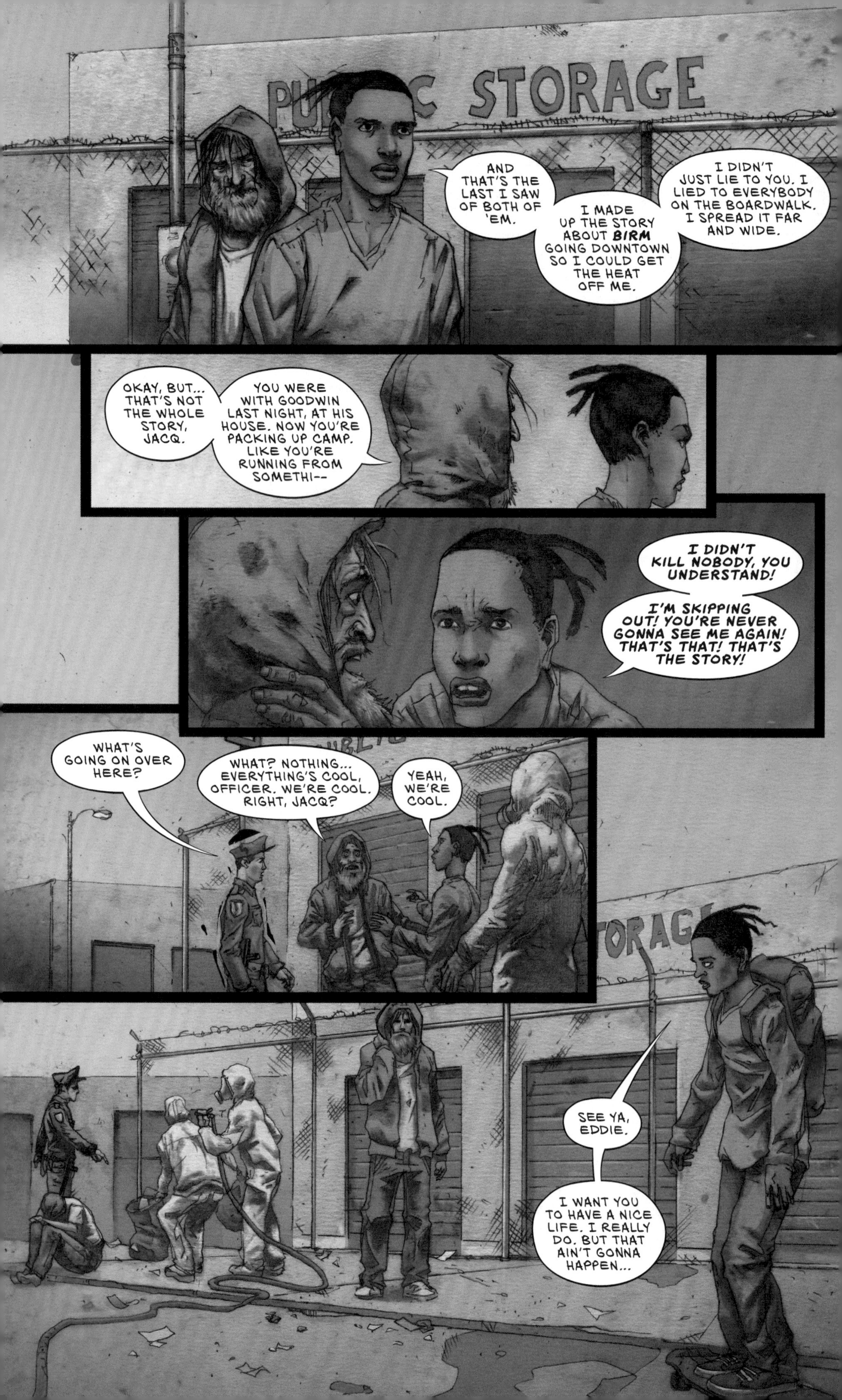
PUBLIC STORAGE
AND THAT'S THE LAST I SAW OF BOTH OF 'EM.
I MADE UP THE STORY ABOUT **BIRM** GOING DOWNTOWN SO I COULD GET THE HEAT OFF ME.
I DIDN'T JUST LIE TO YOU. I LIED TO EVERYBODY ON THE BOARDWALK. I SPREAD IT FAR AND WIDE.
OKAY, BUT... THAT'S NOT THE WHOLE STORY, JACQ.
YOU WERE WITH GOODWIN LAST NIGHT, AT HIS HOUSE. NOW YOU'RE PACKING UP CAMP. LIKE YOU'RE RUNNING FROM SOMETHI--
I DIDN'T KILL NOBODY, YOU UNDERSTAND!
I'M SKIPPING OUT! YOU'RE NEVER GONNA SEE ME AGAIN! THAT'S THAT! THAT'S THE STORY!
WHAT'S GOING ON OVER HERE?
WHAT? NOTHING... EVERYTHING'S COOL, OFFICER. WE'RE COOL. RIGHT, JACQ?
YEAH, WE'RE COOL.
TORAGE
SEE YA, EDDIE.
I WANT YOU TO HAVE A NICE LIFE. I REALLY DO. BUT THAT AIN'T GONNA HAPPEN...

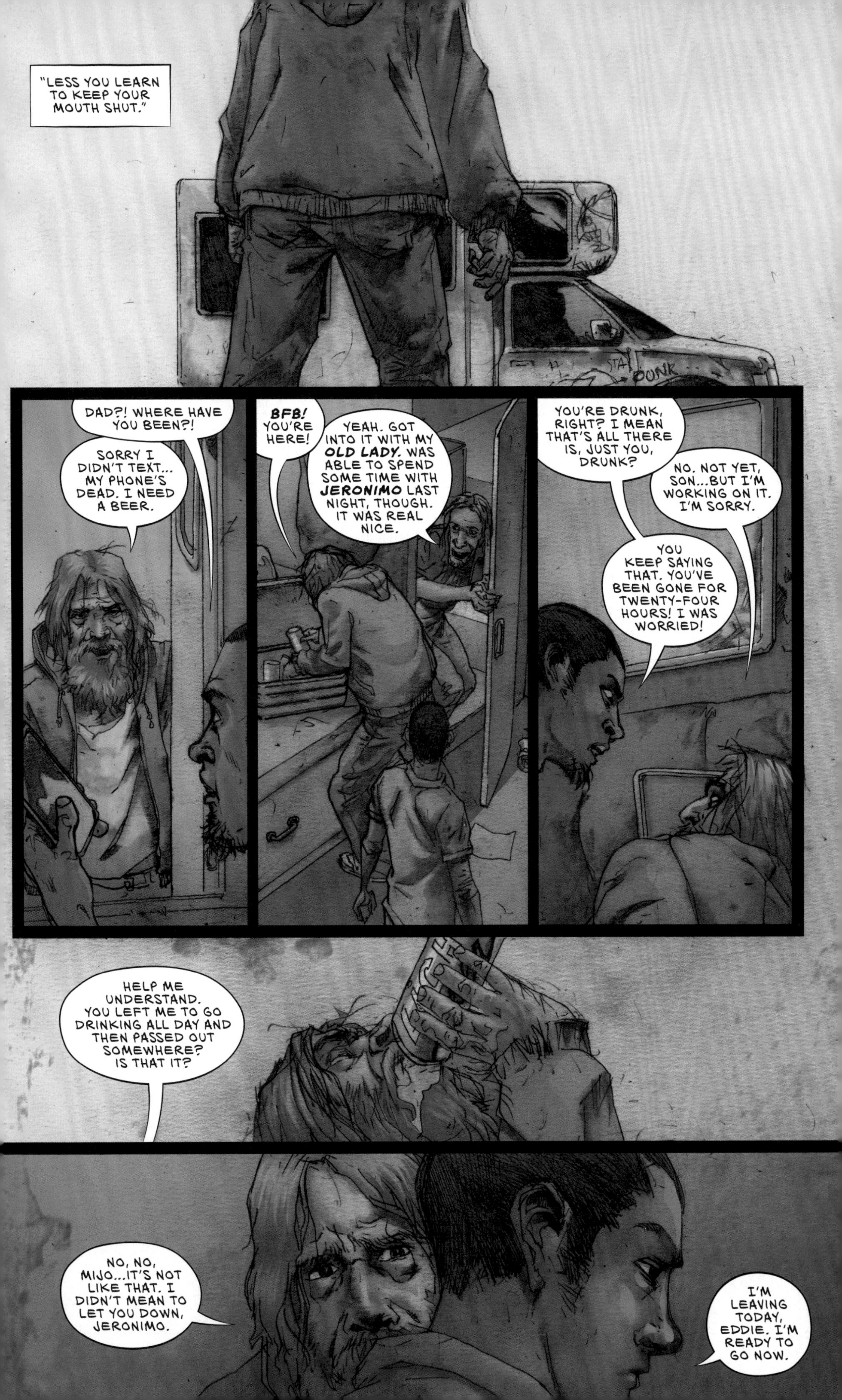
"LESS YOU LEARN TO KEEP YOUR MOUTH SHUT."
DAD?! WHERE HAVE YOU BEEN?!
SORRY I DIDN'T TEXT... MY PHONE'S DEAD. I NEED A BEER.
BFB! YOU'RE HERE!
YEAH. GOT INTO IT WITH MY OLD LADY. WAS ABLE TO SPEND SOME TIME WITH JERONIMO LAST NIGHT, THOUGH. IT WAS REAL NICE.
YOU'RE DRUNK, RIGHT? I MEAN THAT'S ALL THERE IS, JUST YOU, DRUNK?
NO. NOT YET, SON...BUT I'M WORKING ON IT. I'M SORRY.
YOU KEEP SAYING THAT. YOU'VE BEEN GONE FOR TWENTY-FOUR HOURS! I WAS WORRIED!
HELP ME UNDERSTAND. YOU LEFT ME TO GO DRINKING ALL DAY AND THEN PASSED OUT SOMEWHERE? IS THAT IT?
NO, NO, MIJO...IT'S NOT LIKE THAT. I DIDN'T MEAN TO LET YOU DOWN, JERONIMO.
I'M LEAVING TODAY, EDDIE. I'M READY TO GO NOW.

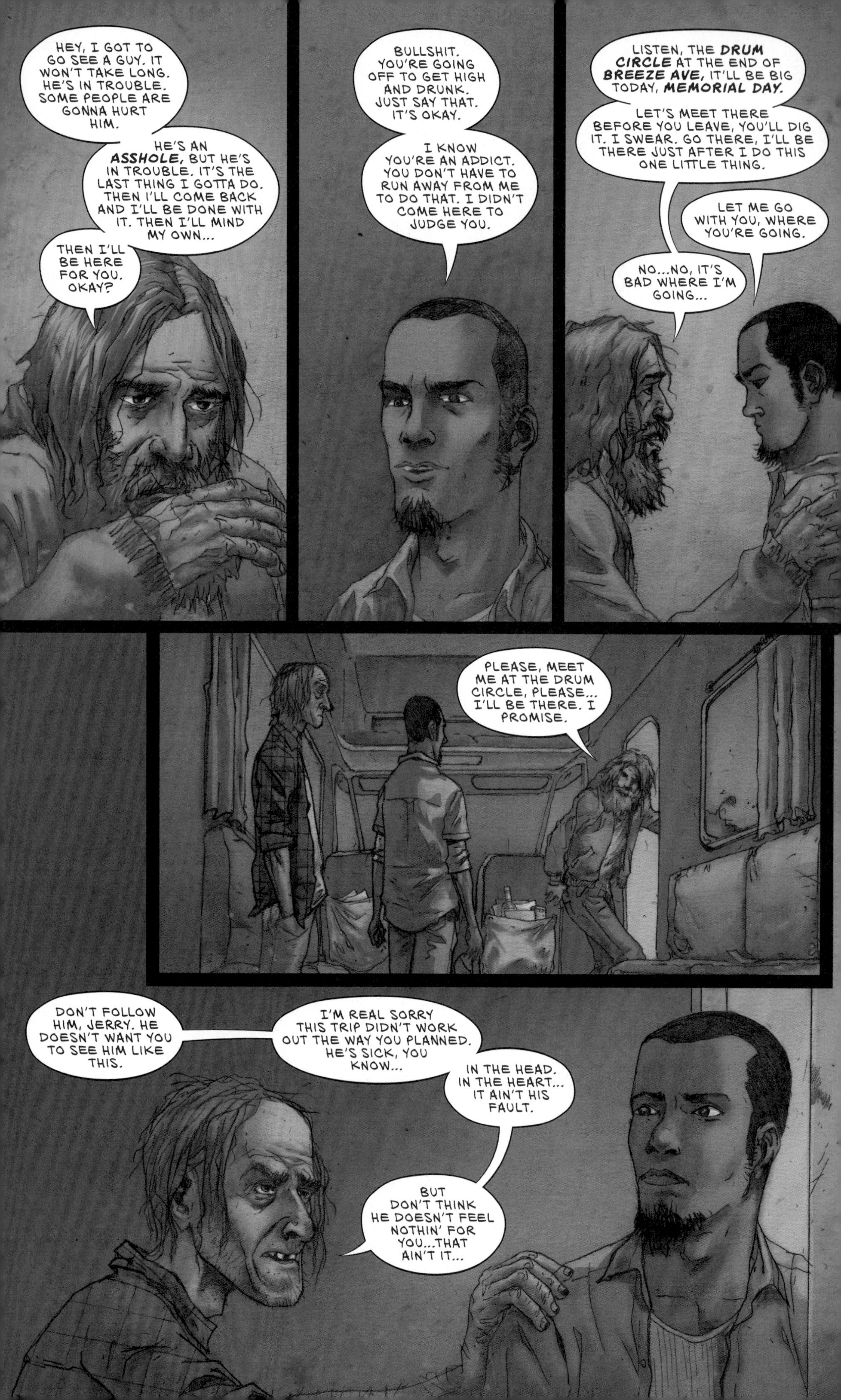
HEY, I GOT TO GO SEE A GUY. IT WON'T TAKE LONG. HE'S IN TROUBLE. SOME PEOPLE ARE GONNA HURT HIM.
HE'S AN **ASSHOLE,** BUT HE'S IN TROUBLE. IT'S THE LAST THING I GOTTA DO. THEN I'LL COME BACK AND I'LL BE DONE WITH IT. THEN I'LL MIND MY OWN...
THEN I'LL BE HERE FOR YOU. OKAY?
BULLSHIT. YOU'RE GOING OFF TO GET HIGH AND DRUNK. JUST SAY THAT. IT'S OKAY.
I KNOW YOU'RE AN ADDICT. YOU DON'T HAVE TO RUN AWAY FROM ME TO DO THAT. I DIDN'T COME HERE TO JUDGE YOU.
LISTEN, THE **DRUM CIRCLE** AT THE END OF **BREEZE AVE,** IT'LL BE BIG TODAY, **MEMORIAL DAY.**
LET'S MEET THERE BEFORE YOU LEAVE, YOU'LL DIG IT. I SWEAR. GO THERE, I'LL BE THERE JUST AFTER I DO THIS ONE LITTLE THING.
LET ME GO WITH YOU, WHERE YOU'RE GOING.
NO...NO, IT'S BAD WHERE I'M GOING...
PLEASE, MEET ME AT THE DRUM CIRCLE, PLEASE... I'LL BE THERE. I PROMISE.
DON'T FOLLOW HIM, JERRY. HE DOESN'T WANT YOU TO SEE HIM LIKE THIS.
I'M REAL SORRY THIS TRIP DIDN'T WORK OUT THE WAY YOU PLANNED. HE'S SICK, YOU KNOW...
IN THE HEAD. IN THE HEART... IT AIN'T HIS FAULT.
BUT DON'T THINK HE DOESN'T FEEL NOTHIN' FOR YOU...THAT AIN'T IT...

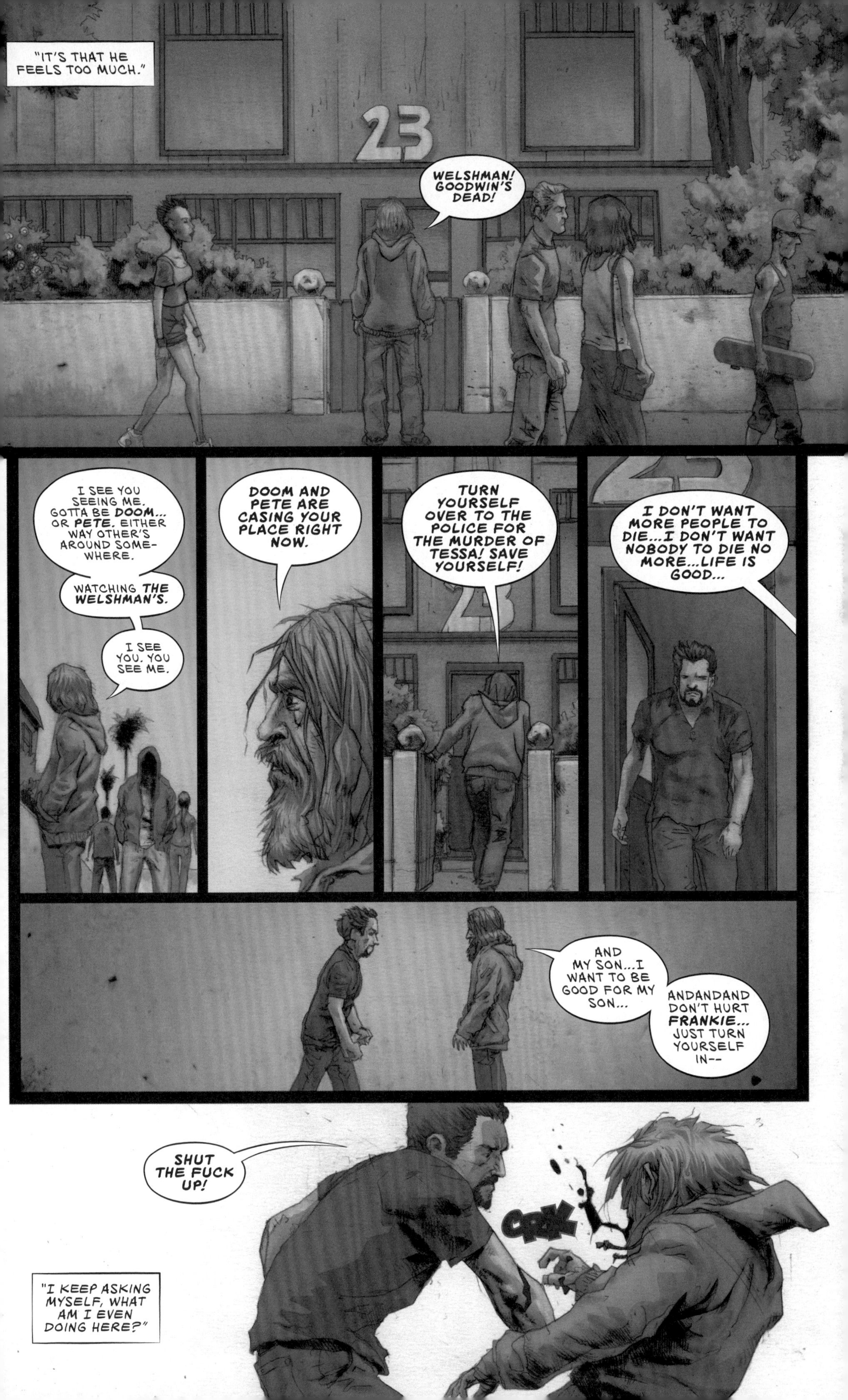
"IT'S THAT HE FEELS TOO MUCH."
WELSHMAN! GOODWIN'S DEAD!
I SEE YOU SEEING ME. GOTTA BE DOOM... OR PETE. EITHER WAY OTHER'S AROUND SOME-WHERE.
WATCHING THE WELSHMAN'S.
I SEE YOU. YOU SEE ME.
DOOM AND PETE ARE CASING YOUR PLACE RIGHT NOW.
TURN YOURSELF OVER TO THE POLICE FOR THE MURDER OF TESSA! SAVE YOURSELF!
I DON'T WANT MORE PEOPLE TO DIE...I DON'T WANT NOBODY TO DIE NO MORE...LIFE IS GOOD...
AND MY SON...I WANT TO BE GOOD FOR MY SON...
ANDANDAND DON'T HURT FRANKIE... JUST TURN YOURSELF IN--
SHUT THE FUCK UP!
CRAK
"I KEEP ASKING MYSELF, WHAT AM I EVEN DOING HERE?"

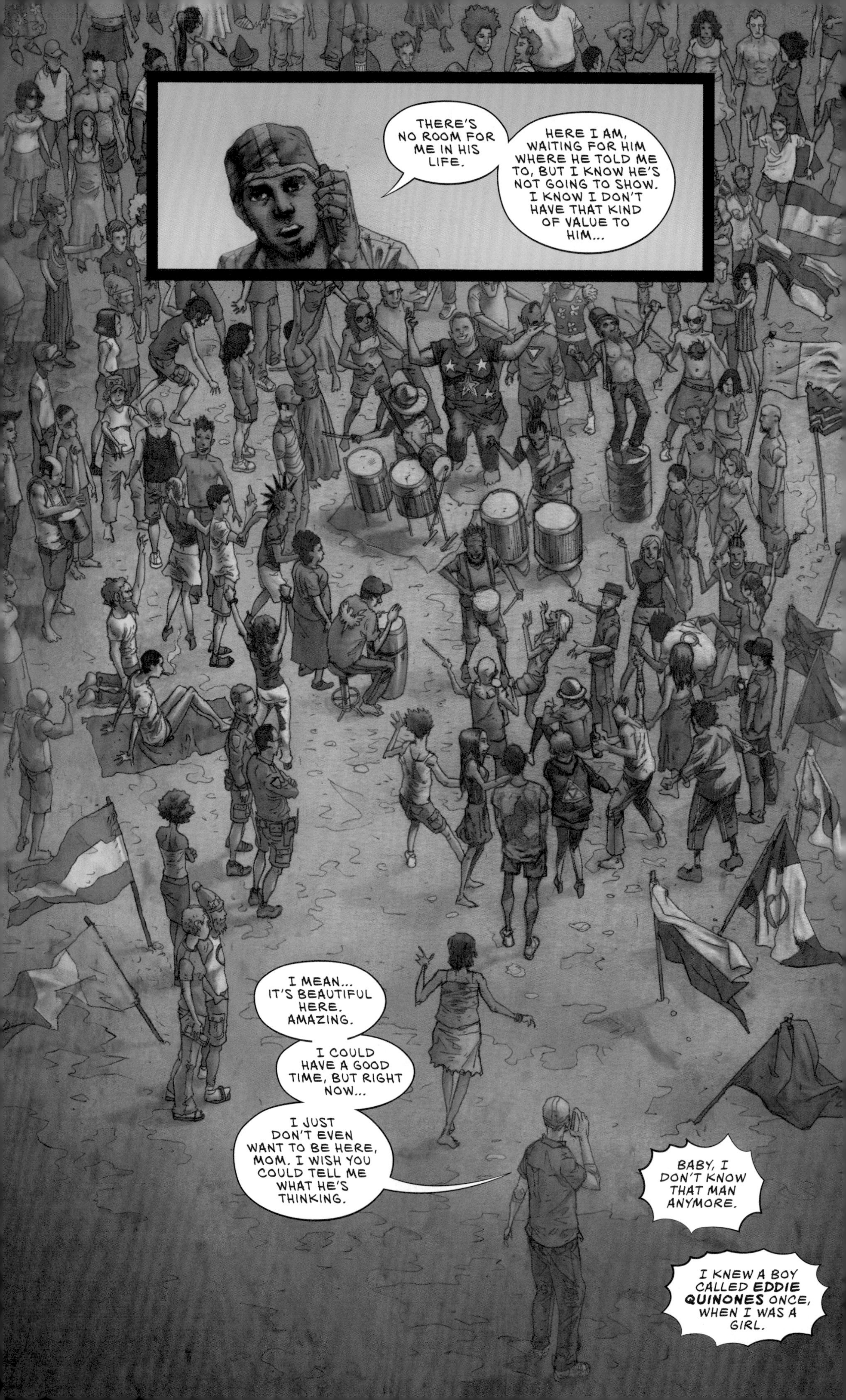
THERE'S NO ROOM FOR ME IN HIS LIFE.
HERE I AM, WAITING FOR HIM WHERE HE TOLD ME TO, BUT I KNOW HE'S NOT GOING TO SHOW. I KNOW I DON'T HAVE THAT KIND OF VALUE TO HIM...
I MEAN... IT'S BEAUTIFUL HERE. AMAZING.
I COULD HAVE A GOOD TIME, BUT RIGHT NOW...
I JUST DON'T EVEN WANT TO BE HERE, MOM. I WISH YOU COULD TELL ME WHAT HE'S THINKING.
BABY, I DON'T KNOW THAT MAN ANYMORE.
I KNEW A BOY CALLED **EDDIE QUINONES** ONCE, WHEN I WAS A GIRL.

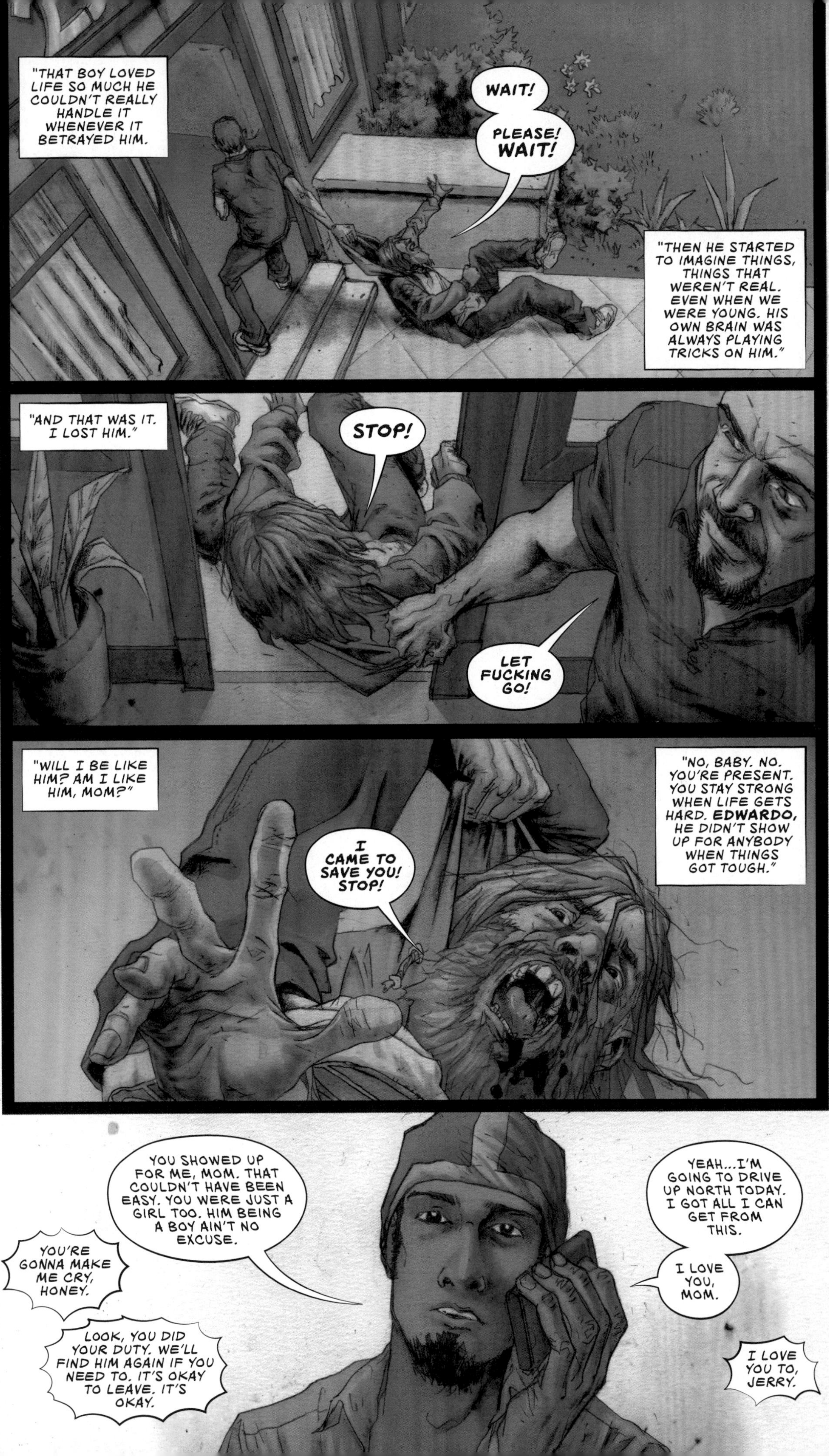

"THAT BOY LOVED LIFE SO MUCH HE COULDN'T REALLY HANDLE IT WHENEVER IT BETRAYED HIM.
WAIT!
PLEASE! WAIT!
"THEN HE STARTED TO IMAGINE THINGS, THINGS THAT WEREN'T REAL. EVEN WHEN WE WERE YOUNG. HIS OWN BRAIN WAS ALWAYS PLAYING TRICKS ON HIM."
"AND THAT WAS IT. I LOST HIM."
STOP!
LET FUCKING GO!
"WILL I BE LIKE HIM? AM I LIKE HIM, MOM?"
I CAME TO SAVE YOU! STOP!
"NO, BABY. NO. YOU'RE PRESENT. YOU STAY STRONG WHEN LIFE GETS HARD. EDWARDO, HE DIDN'T SHOW UP FOR ANYBODY WHEN THINGS GOT TOUGH."
YOU SHOWED UP FOR ME, MOM. THAT COULDN'T HAVE BEEN EASY. YOU WERE JUST A GIRL TOO. HIM BEING A BOY AIN'T NO EXCUSE.
YOU'RE GONNA MAKE ME CRY, HONEY.
LOOK, YOU DID YOUR DUTY. WE'LL FIND HIM AGAIN IF YOU NEED TO. IT'S OKAY TO LEAVE. IT'S OKAY.
YEAH...I'M GOING TO DRIVE UP NORTH TODAY. I GOT ALL I CAN GET FROM THIS.
I LOVE YOU, MOM.
I LOVE YOU TO, JERRY.

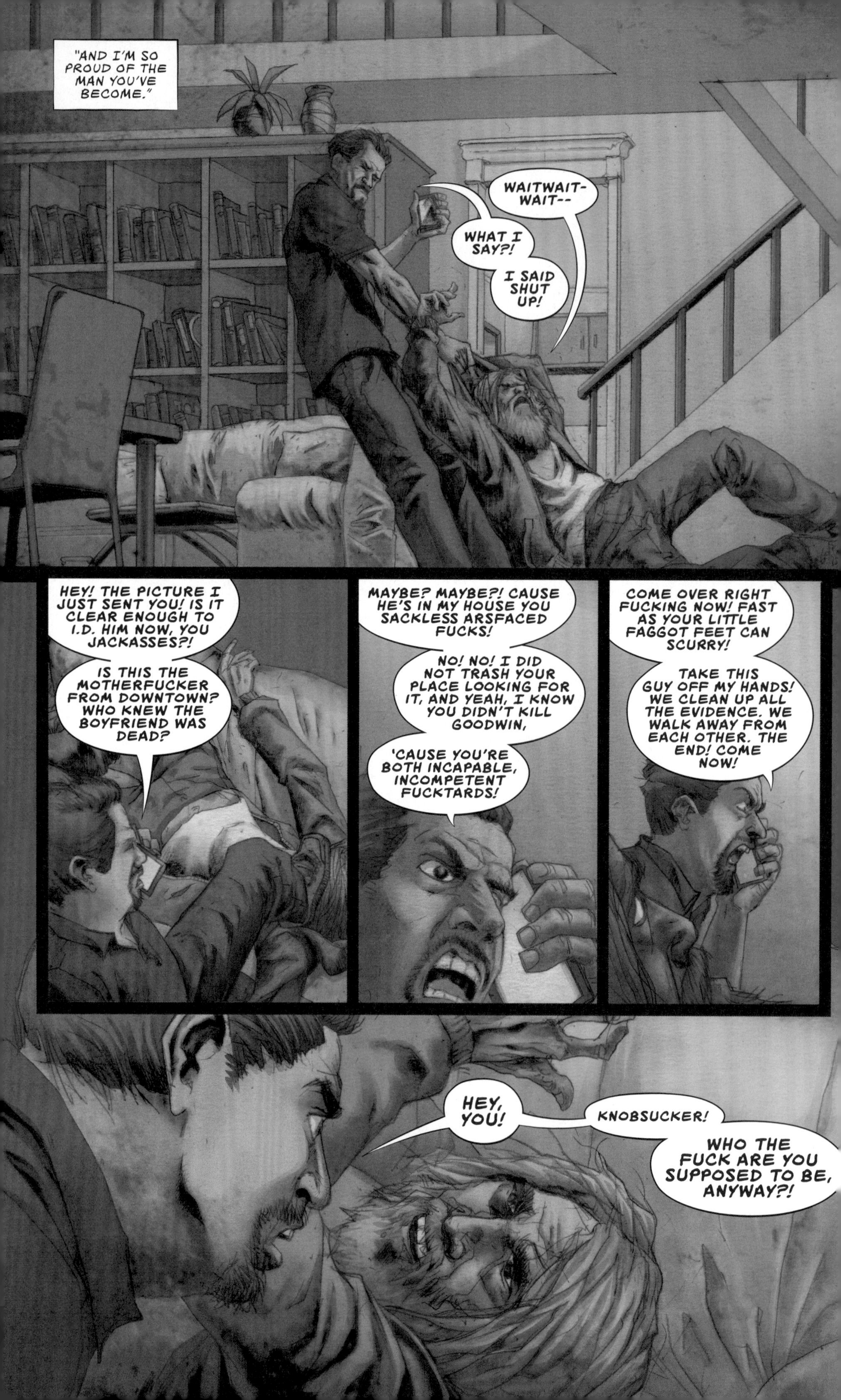
"AND I'M SO PROUD OF THE MAN YOU'VE BECOME."
WAITWAIT-WAIT--
WHAT I SAY?!
I SAID SHUT UP!
HEY! THE PICTURE I JUST SENT YOU! IS IT CLEAR ENOUGH TO I.D. HIM NOW, YOU JACKASSES?!
IS THIS THE MOTHERFUCKER FROM DOWNTOWN? WHO KNEW THE BOYFRIEND WAS DEAD?
MAYBE? MAYBE?! CAUSE HE'S IN MY HOUSE YOU SACKLESS ARSFACED FUCKS!
NO! NO! I DID NOT TRASH YOUR PLACE LOOKING FOR IT, AND YEAH, I KNOW YOU DIDN'T KILL GOODWIN,
'CAUSE YOU'RE BOTH INCAPABLE, INCOMPETENT FUCKTARDS!
COME OVER RIGHT FUCKING NOW! FAST AS YOUR LITTLE FAGGOT FEET CAN SCURRY!
TAKE THIS GUY OFF MY HANDS! WE CLEAN UP ALL THE EVIDENCE. WE WALK AWAY FROM EACH OTHER. THE END! COME NOW!
HEY, YOU!
KNOBSUCKER!
WHO THE FUCK ARE YOU SUPPOSED TO BE, ANYWAY?!

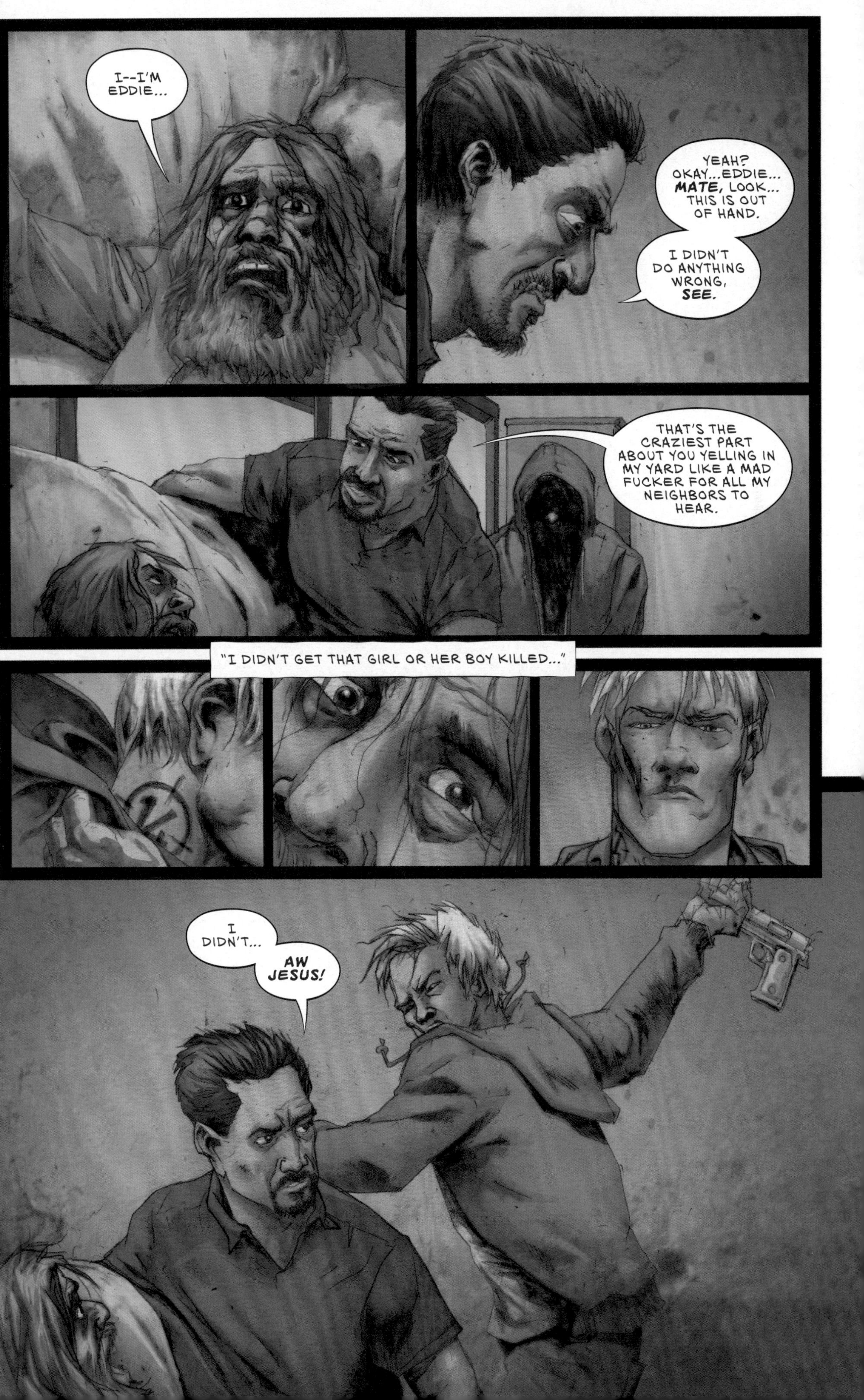

I--I'M EDDIE...
YEAH? OKAY...EDDIE... **MATE,** LOOK... THIS IS OUT OF HAND.
I DIDN'T DO ANYTHING WRONG, **SEE.**
THAT'S THE CRAZIEST PART ABOUT YOU YELLING IN MY YARD LIKE A MAD FUCKER FOR ALL MY NEIGHBORS TO HEAR.
"I DIDN'T GET THAT GIRL OR HER BOY KILLED..."
I DIDN'T...
AW JESUS!

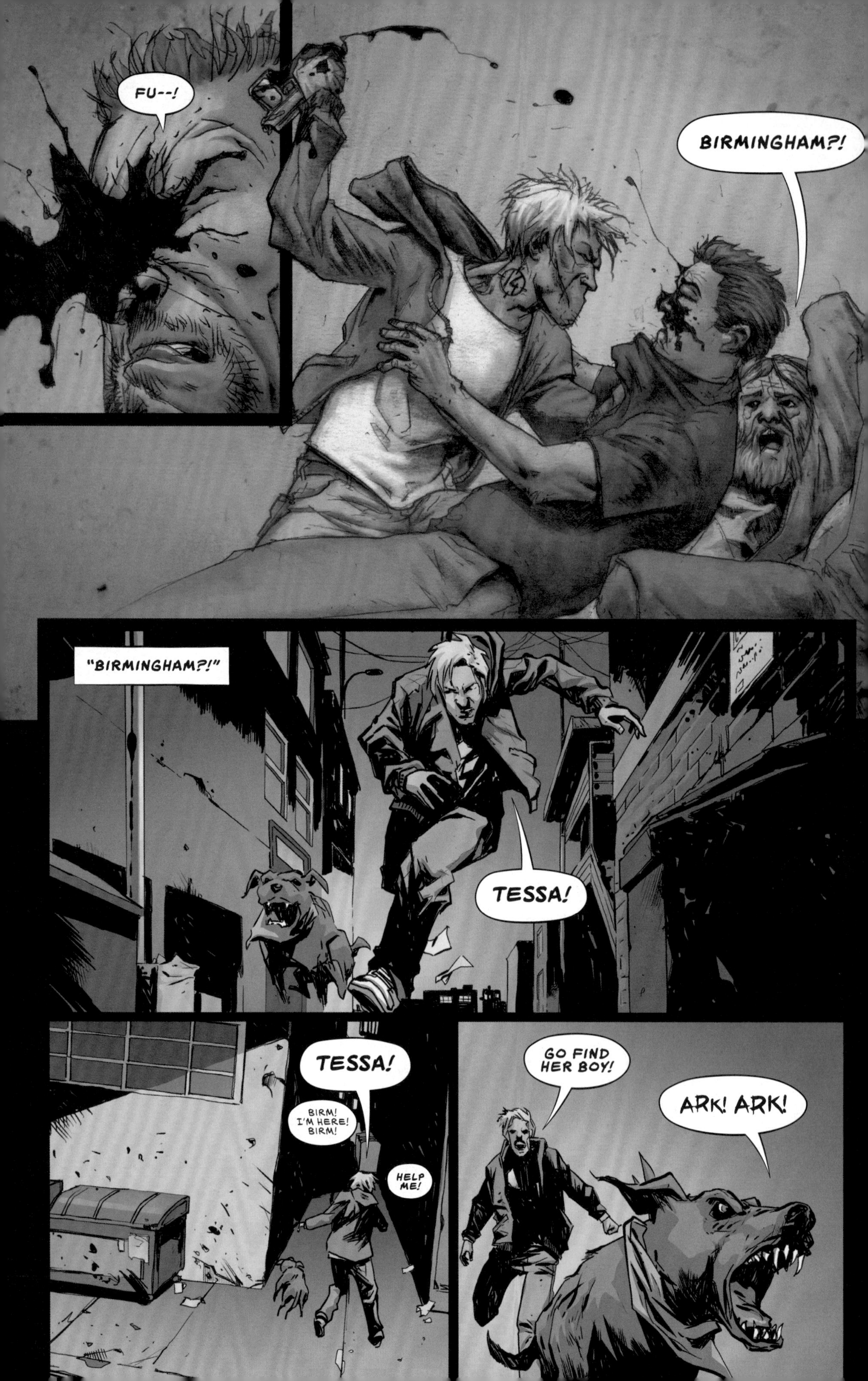
FU--!
BIRMINGHAM?!
"BIRMINGHAM?!"
TESSA!
TESSA!
BIRM! I'M HERE! BIRM!
HELP ME!
GO FIND HER BOY!
ARK! ARK!

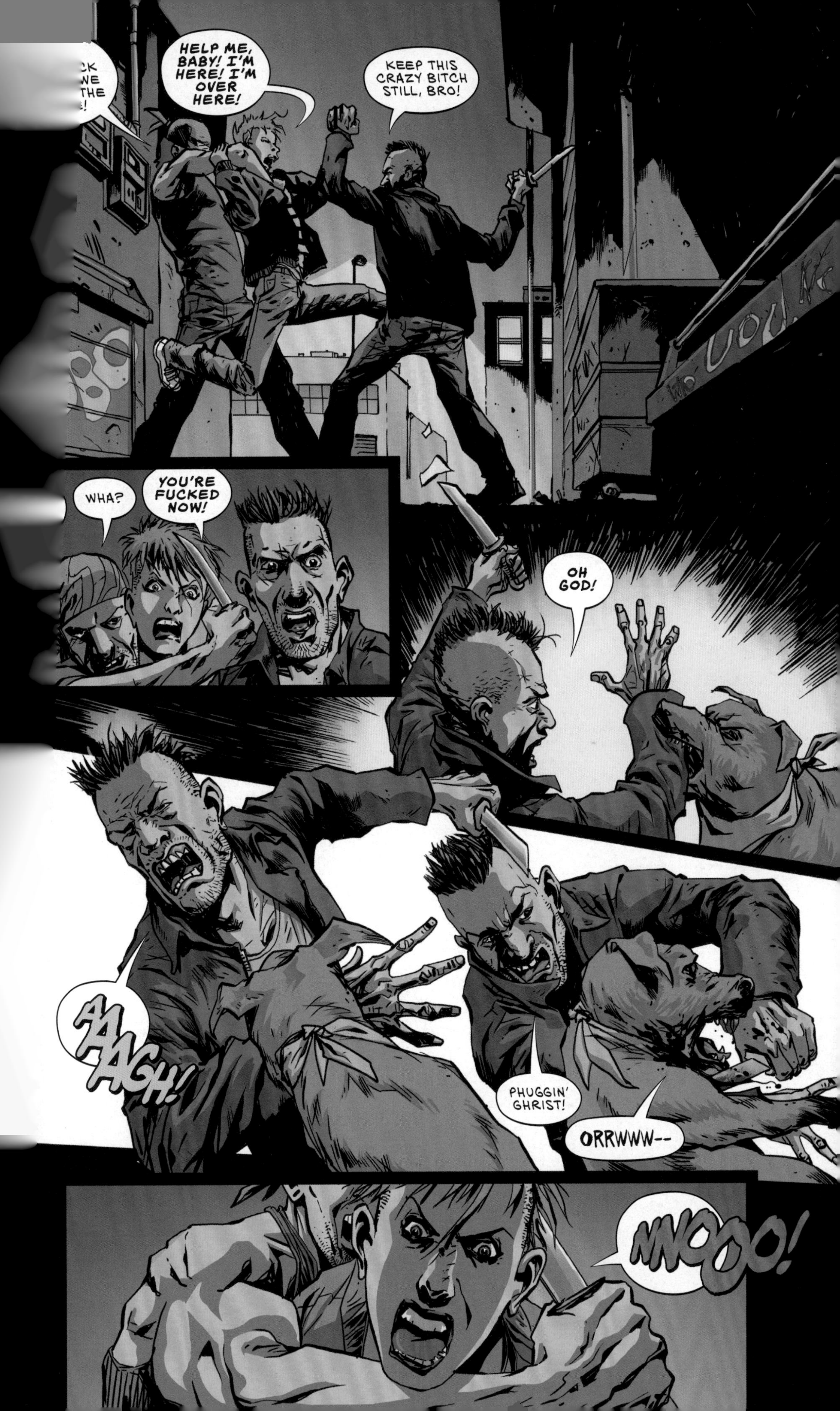
HELP ME, BABY! I'M HERE! I'M OVER HERE!
KEEP THIS CRAZY BITCH STILL, BRO!
WHA?
YOU'RE FUCKED NOW!
OH GOD!
AAAGH!
PHUGGIN' GHRIST!
ORRWWW--
NNOOOO!

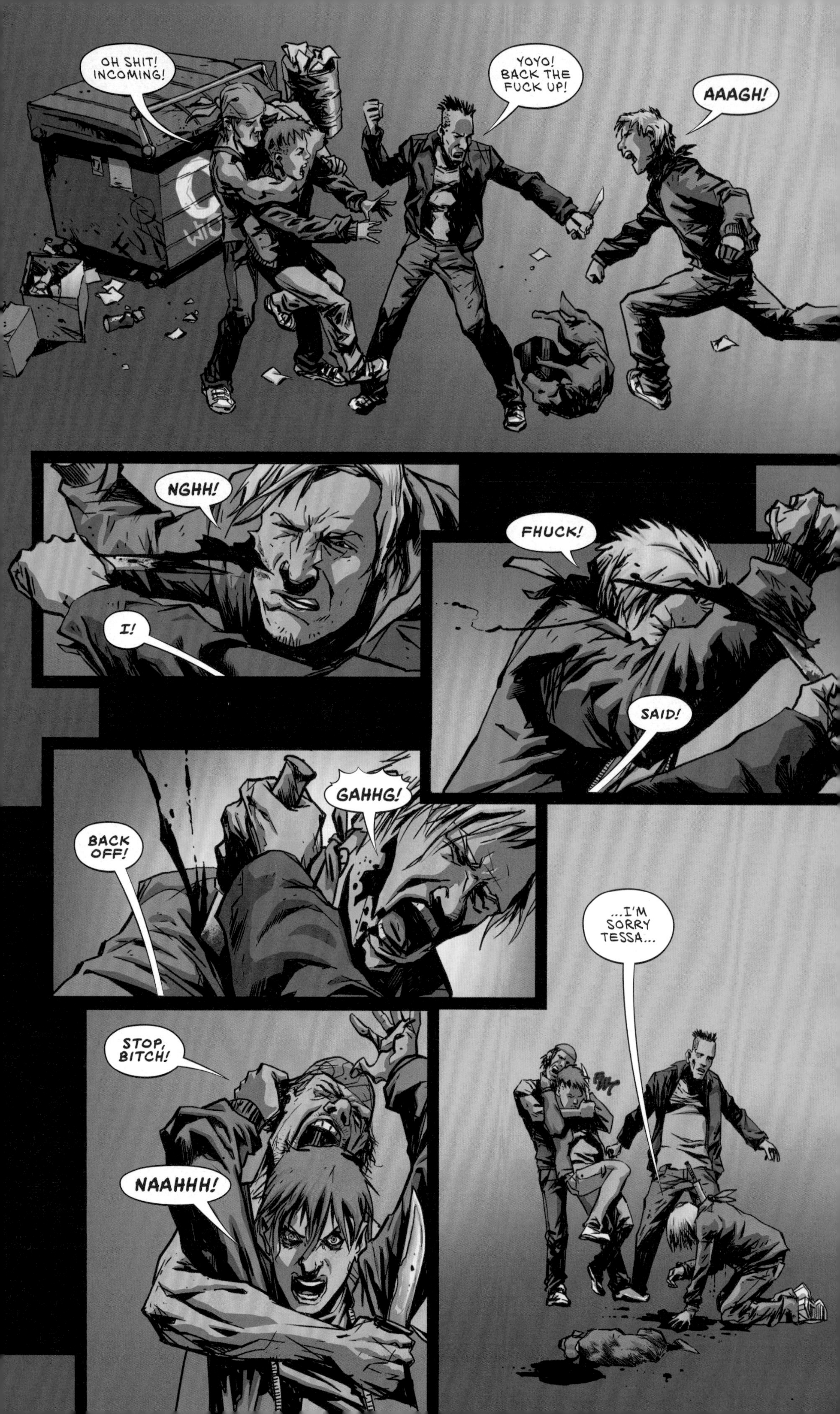
OH SHIT! INCOMING!
YOYO! BACK THE FUCK UP!
AAAGH!
NGHH!
I!
FHUCK!
SAID!
GAHHG!
BACK OFF!
...I'M SORRY TESSA...
STOP, BITCH!
NAAHHH!

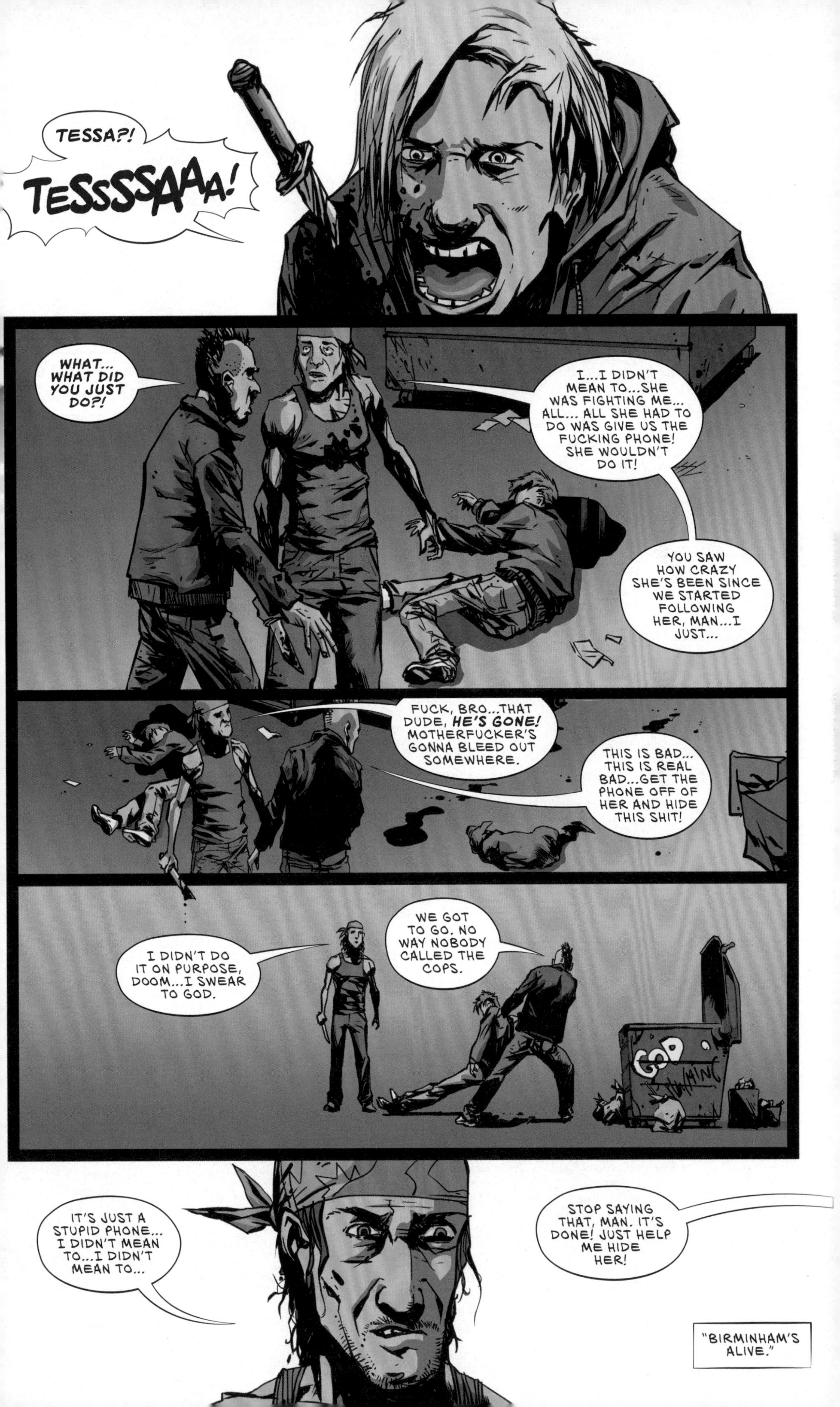
TESSA?!
TESSSSAAAA!
WHAT... WHAT DID YOU JUST DO?!
I...I DIDN'T MEAN TO...SHE WAS FIGHTING ME... ALL... ALL SHE HAD TO DO WAS GIVE US THE FUCKING PHONE! SHE WOULDN'T DO IT!
YOU SAW HOW CRAZY SHE'S BEEN SINCE WE STARTED FOLLOWING HER, MAN...I JUST...
FUCK, BRO...THAT DUDE, HE'S GONE! MOTHERFUCKER'S GONNA BLEED OUT SOMEWHERE.
THIS IS BAD... THIS IS REAL BAD...GET THE PHONE OFF OF HER AND HIDE THIS SHIT!
I DIDN'T DO IT ON PURPOSE, DOOM...I SWEAR TO GOD.
WE GOT TO GO. NO WAY NOBODY CALLED THE COPS.
GOD
IT'S JUST A STUPID PHONE... I DIDN'T MEAN TO...I DIDN'T MEAN TO...
STOP SAYING THAT, MAN. IT'S DONE! JUST HELP ME HIDE HER!
"BIRMINHAM'S ALIVE."

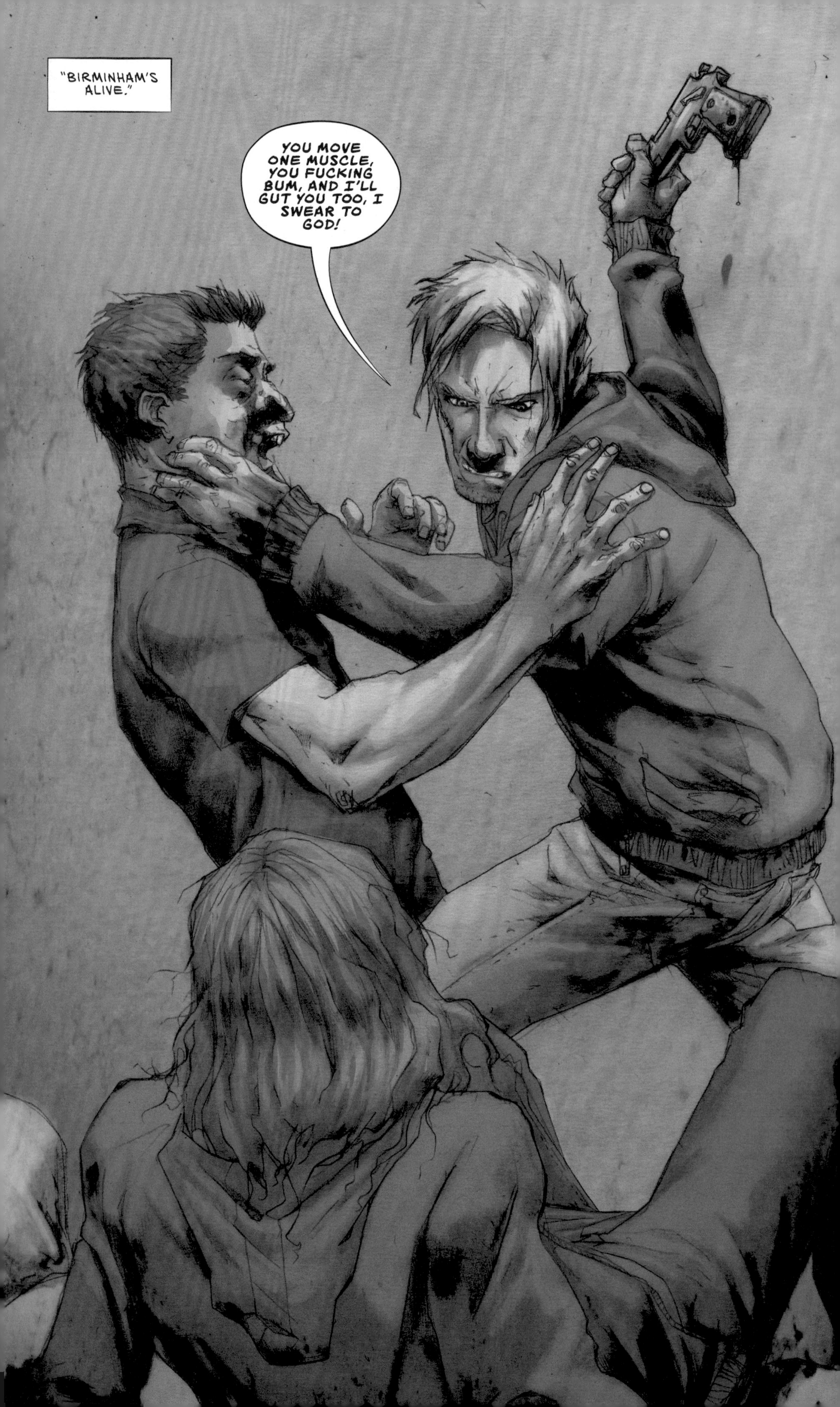

"BIRMINHAM'S ALIVE."
YOU MOVE ONE MUSCLE, YOU FUCKING BUM, AND I'LL GUT YOU TOO, I SWEAR TO GOD!

CHAPTER 6

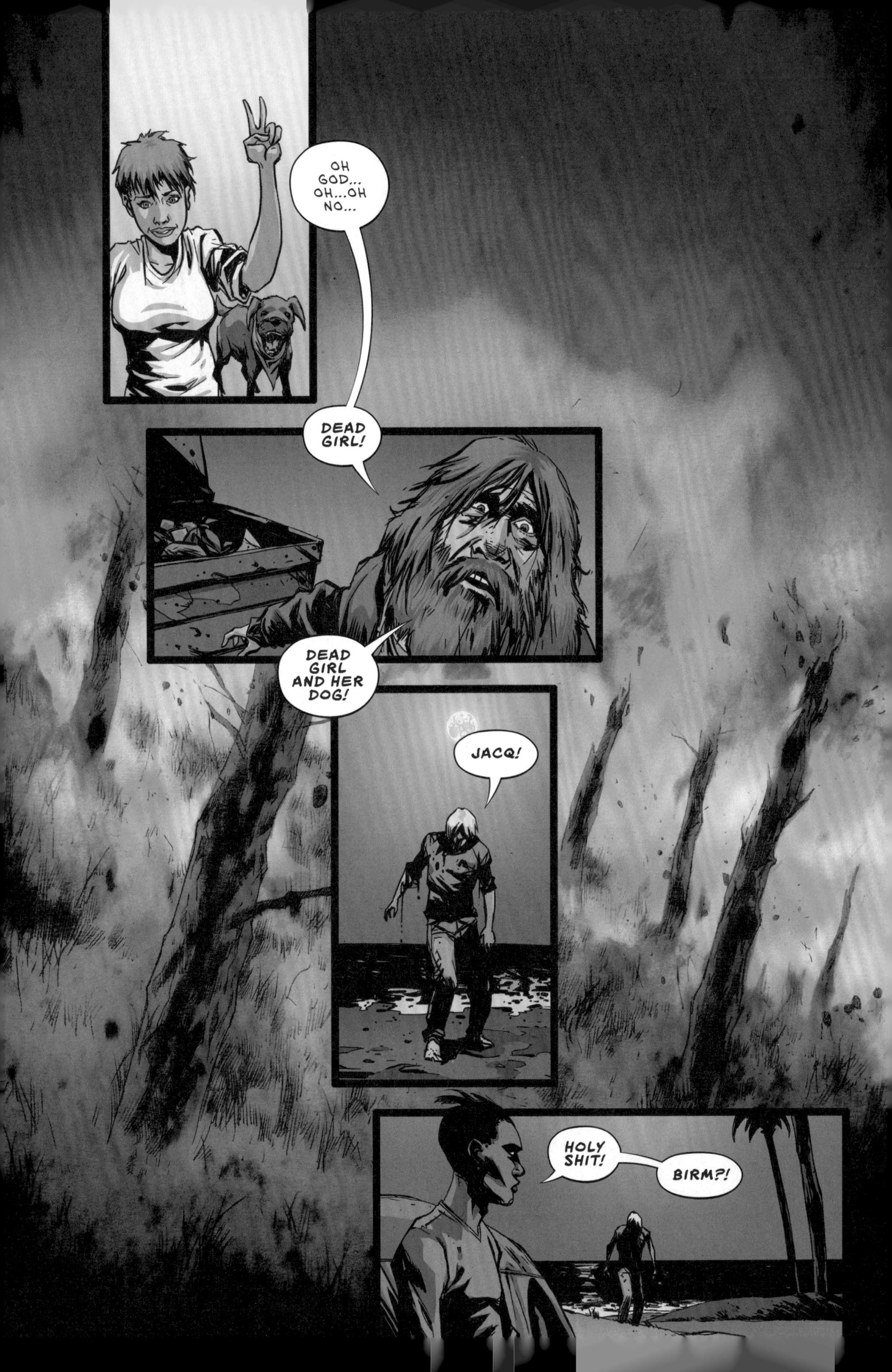
OH GOD... OH...OH NO...
DEAD GIRL!
DEAD GIRL AND HER DOG!
JACQ!
HOLY SHIT!
BIRM?!

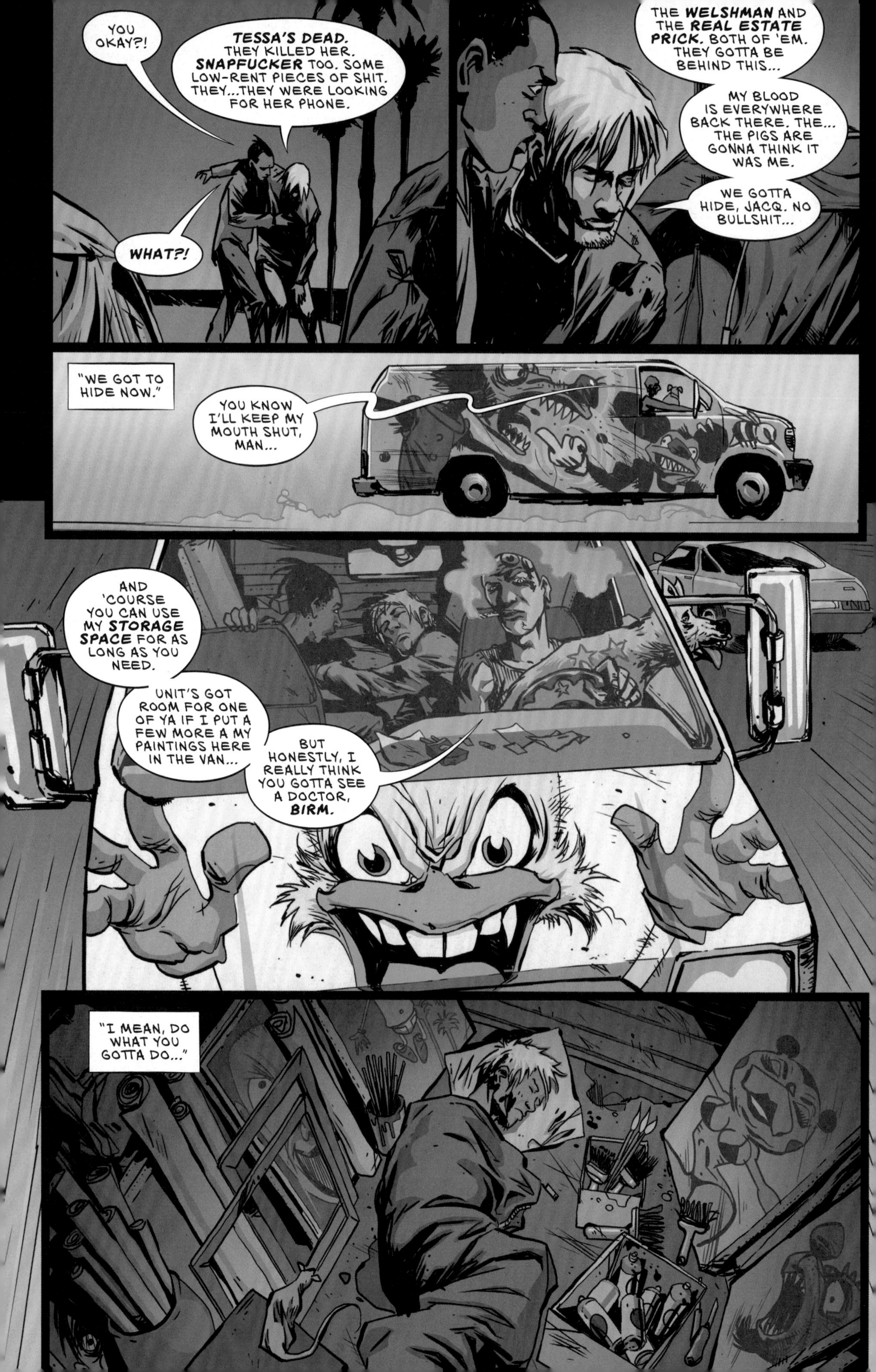
YOU OKAY?!
TESSA'S DEAD. THEY KILLED HER. SNAPFUCKER TOO. SOME LOW-RENT PIECES OF SHIT. THEY... THEY WERE LOOKING FOR HER PHONE.
WHAT?!
THE WELSHMAN AND THE REAL ESTATE PRICK. BOTH OF 'EM. THEY GOTTA BE BEHIND THIS...
MY BLOOD IS EVERYWHERE BACK THERE. THE... THE PIGS ARE GONNA THINK IT WAS ME.
WE GOTTA HIDE, JACQ. NO BULLSHIT...
"WE GOT TO HIDE NOW."
YOU KNOW I'LL KEEP MY MOUTH SHUT, MAN...
AND 'COURSE YOU CAN USE MY STORAGE SPACE FOR AS LONG AS YOU NEED.
UNIT'S GOT ROOM FOR ONE OF YA IF I PUT A FEW MORE A MY PAINTINGS HERE IN THE VAN...
BUT HONESTLY, I REALLY THINK YOU GOTTA SEE A DOCTOR, BIRM.
"I MEAN, DO WHAT YOU GOTTA DO..."

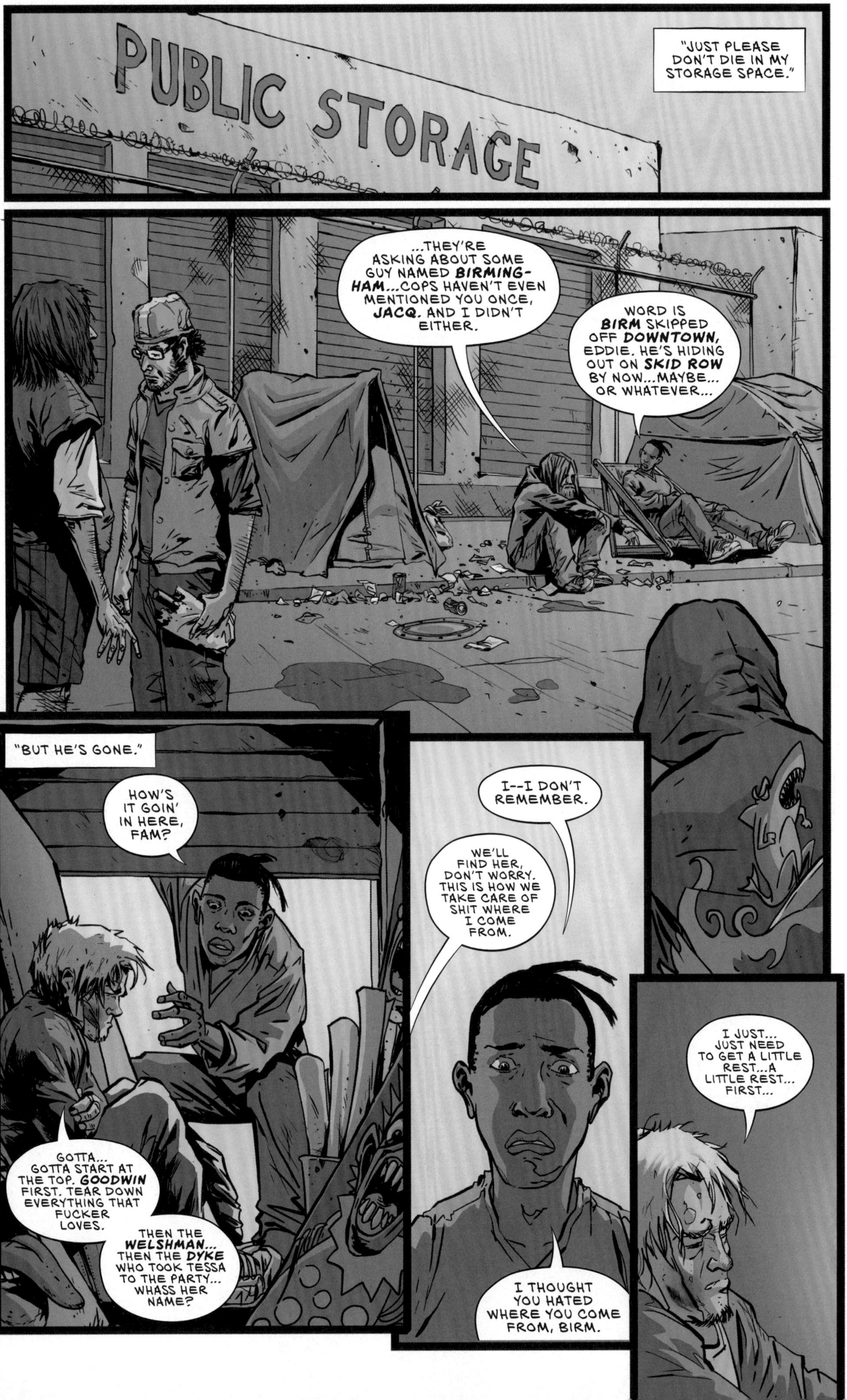
PUBLIC STORAGE
"JUST PLEASE DON'T DIE IN MY STORAGE SPACE."
...THEY'RE ASKING ABOUT SOME GUY NAMED BIRMING-HAM...COPS HAVEN'T EVEN MENTIONED YOU ONCE, JACQ. AND I DIDN'T EITHER.
WORD IS BIRM SKIPPED OFF DOWNTOWN, EDDIE. HE'S HIDING OUT ON SKID ROW BY NOW...MAYBE... OR WHATEVER...
"BUT HE'S GONE."
HOW'S IT GOIN' IN HERE, FAM?
GOTTA... GOTTA START AT THE TOP. GOODWIN FIRST. TEAR DOWN EVERYTHING THAT FUCKER LOVES.
THEN THE WELSHMAN... THEN THE DYKE WHO TOOK TESSA TO THE PARTY... WHASS HER NAME?
I--I DON'T REMEMBER.
WE'LL FIND HER, DON'T WORRY. THIS IS HOW WE TAKE CARE OF SHIT WHERE I COME FROM.
I THOUGHT YOU HATED WHERE YOU COME FROM, BIRM.
I JUST... JUST NEED TO GET A LITTLE REST...A LITTLE REST... FIRST...

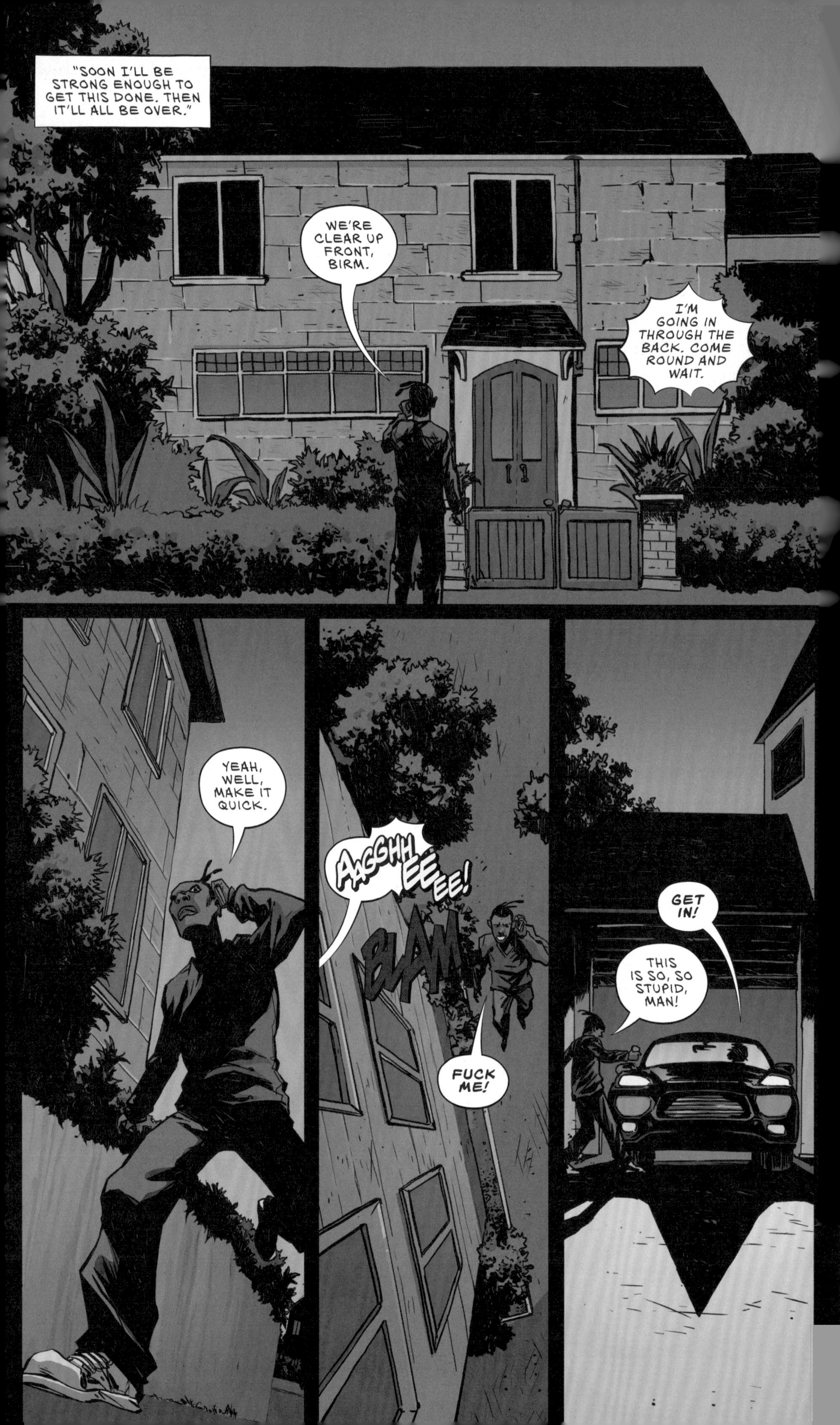
"SOON I'LL BE STRONG ENOUGH TO GET THIS DONE. THEN IT'LL ALL BE OVER."
WE'RE CLEAR UP FRONT, BIRM.
I'M GOING IN THROUGH THE BACK. COME ROUND AND WAIT.
YEAH, WELL, MAKE IT QUICK.
AAGGHHEEEEE!
BLAM
FUCK ME!
GET IN!
THIS IS SO, SO STUPID, MAN!

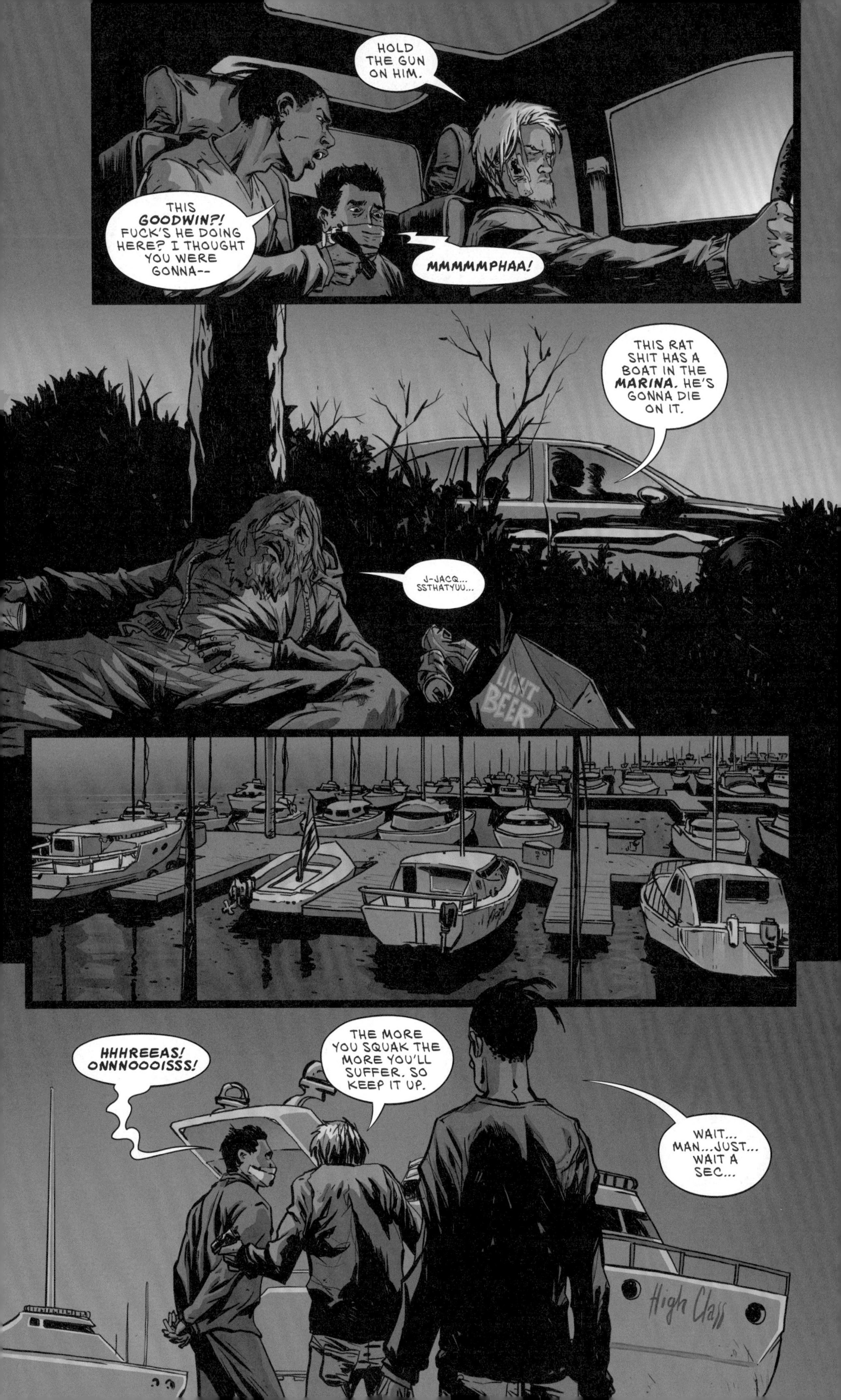
HOLD THE GUN ON HIM.
THIS GOODWIN?! FUCK'S HE DOING HERE? I THOUGHT YOU WERE GONNA--
MMMMMPHAA!
THIS RAT SHIT HAS A BOAT IN THE MARINA. HE'S GONNA DIE ON IT.
J-JACQ... SSTHATYUU...
LIGHT BEER
HHHREEAS! ONNNOOOISSS!
THE MORE YOU SQUAK THE MORE YOU'LL SUFFER. SO KEEP IT UP.
WAIT... MAN...JUST... WAIT A SEC...
High Class

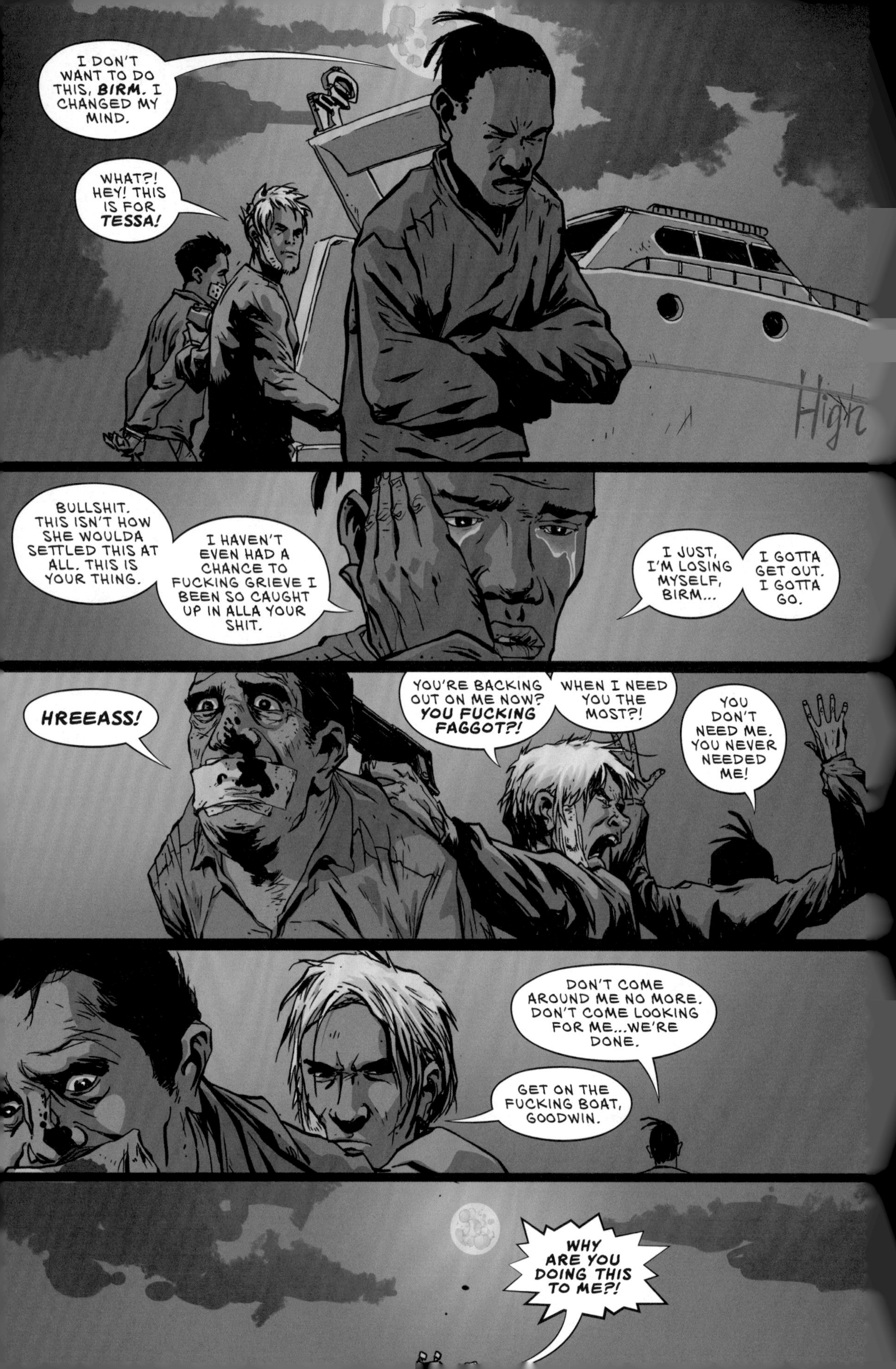
I DON'T WANT TO DO THIS, **BIRM.** I CHANGED MY MIND.
WHAT?! HEY! THIS IS FOR ***TESSA!***
High
BULLSHIT. THIS ISN'T HOW SHE WOULDA SETTLED THIS AT ALL. THIS IS YOUR THING.
I HAVEN'T EVEN HAD A CHANCE TO FUCKING GRIEVE I BEEN SO CAUGHT UP IN ALLA YOUR SHIT.
I JUST, I'M LOSING MYSELF, BIRM...
I GOTTA GET OUT. I GOTTA GO.
HREEASS!
YOU'RE BACKING OUT ON ME NOW? ***YOU FUCKING FAGGOT?!***
WHEN I NEED YOU THE MOST?!
YOU DON'T NEED ME. YOU NEVER NEEDED ME!
DON'T COME AROUND ME NO MORE. DON'T COME LOOKING FOR ME...WE'RE DONE.
GET ON THE FUCKING BOAT, GOODWIN.
WHY ARE YOU DOING THIS TO ME?!

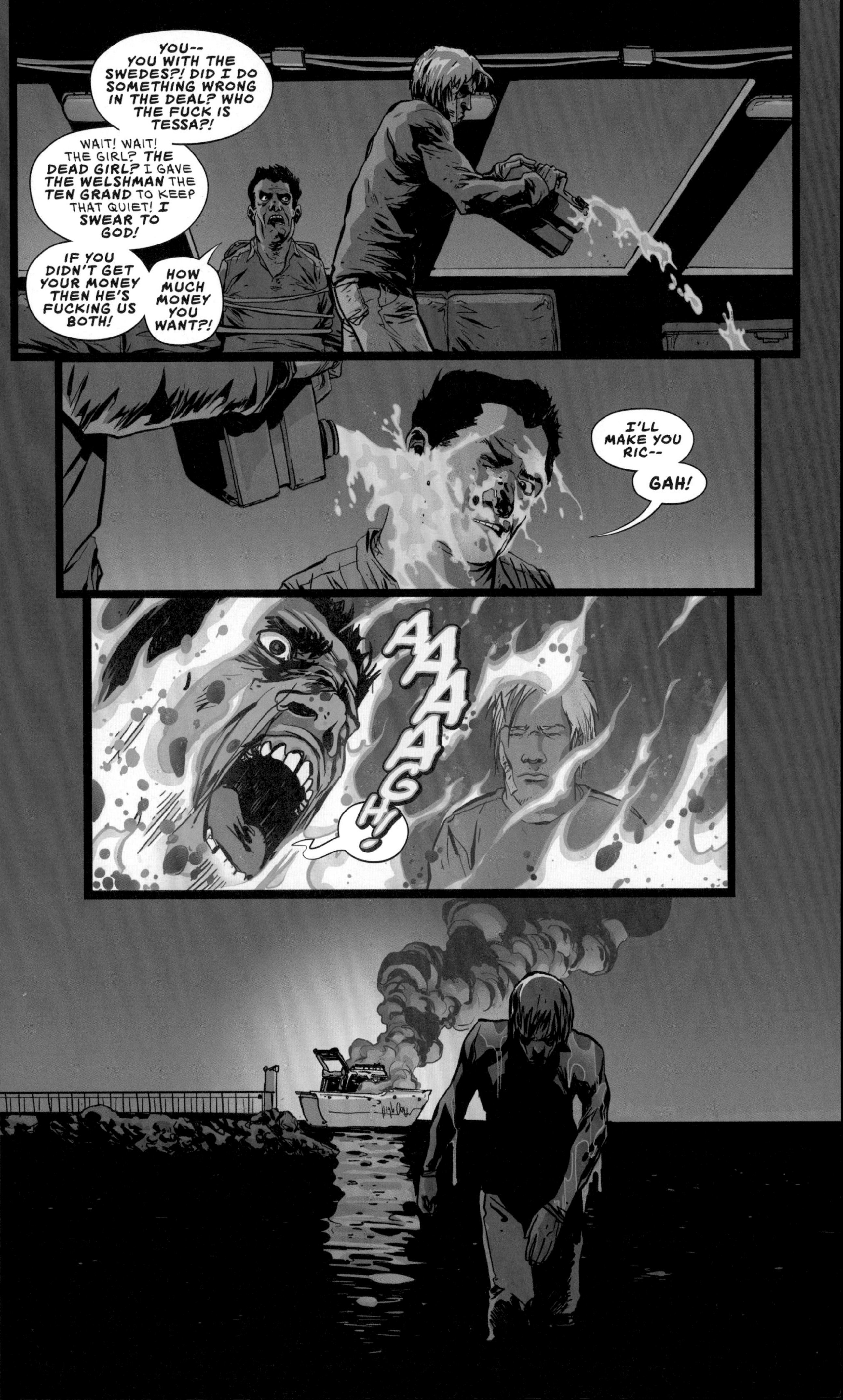
YOU-- YOU WITH THE SWEDES?! DID I DO SOMETHING WRONG IN THE DEAL? WHO THE FUCK IS TESSA?!
WAIT! WAIT! THE GIRL? THE DEAD GIRL? I GAVE THE WELSHMAN THE TEN GRAND TO KEEP THAT QUIET! I SWEAR TO GOD!
IF YOU DIDN'T GET YOUR MONEY THEN HE'S FUCKING US BOTH!
HOW MUCH MONEY YOU WANT?!
I'LL MAKE YOU RIC--
GAH!
AAAAAGH!

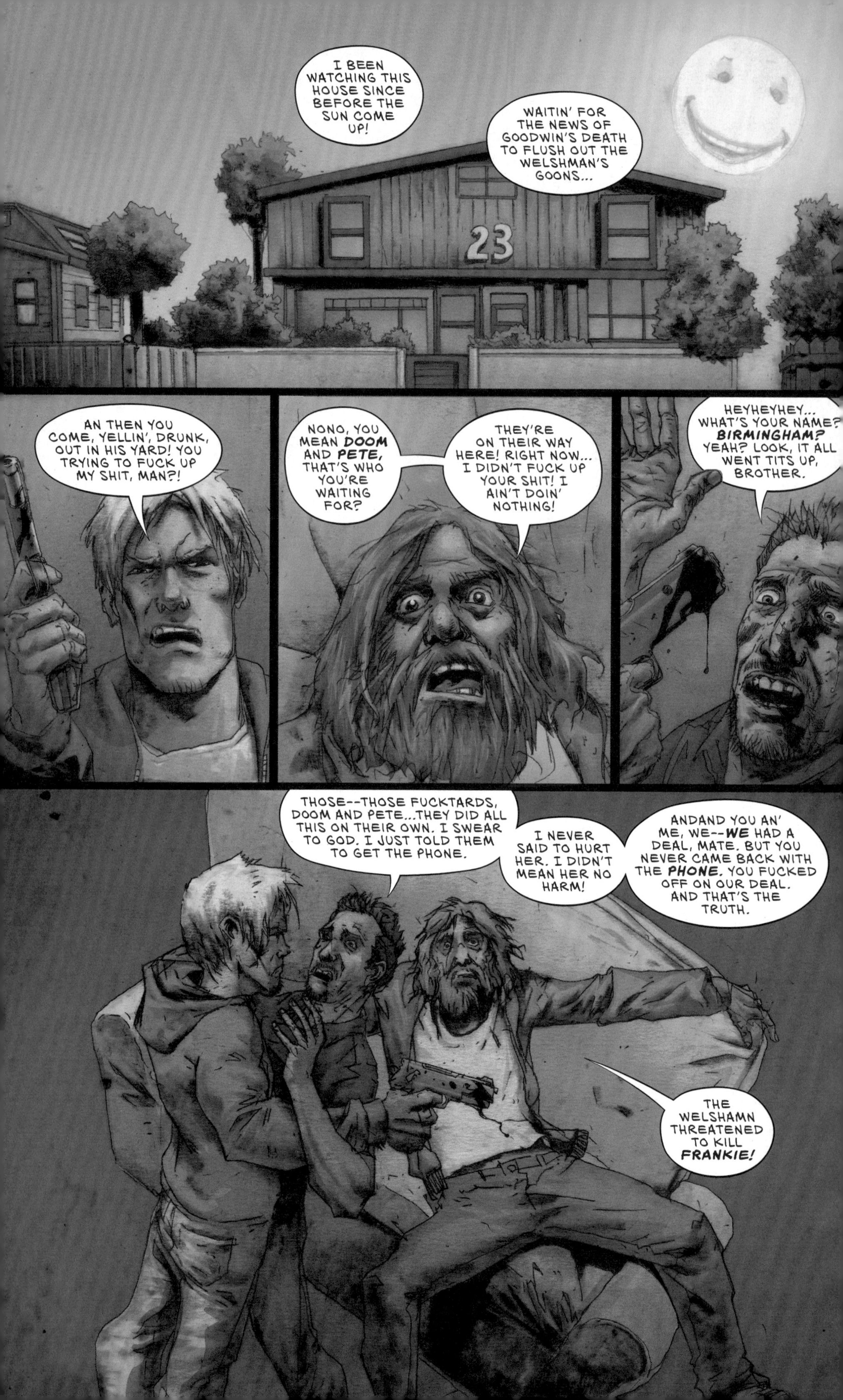
I BEEN WATCHING THIS HOUSE SINCE BEFORE THE SUN COME UP!
WAITIN' FOR THE NEWS OF GOODWIN'S DEATH TO FLUSH OUT THE WELSHMAN'S GOONS...
23
AN THEN YOU COME, YELLIN', DRUNK, OUT IN HIS YARD! YOU TRYING TO FUCK UP MY SHIT, MAN?!
NONO, YOU MEAN **DOOM** AND **PETE**, THAT'S WHO YOU'RE WAITING FOR?
THEY'RE ON THEIR WAY HERE! RIGHT NOW... I DIDN'T FUCK UP YOUR SHIT! I AIN'T DOIN' NOTHING!
HEYHEYHEY... WHAT'S YOUR NAME? ***BIRMINGHAM?*** YEAH? LOOK, IT ALL WENT TITS UP, BROTHER.
THOSE--THOSE FUCKTARDS, DOOM AND PETE...THEY DID ALL THIS ON THEIR OWN. I SWEAR TO GOD. I JUST TOLD THEM TO GET THE PHONE.
I NEVER SAID TO HURT HER. I DIDN'T MEAN HER NO HARM!
ANDAND YOU AN' ME, WE--**WE** HAD A DEAL, MATE. BUT YOU NEVER CAME BACK WITH THE **PHONE.** YOU FUCKED OFF ON OUR DEAL. AND THAT'S THE TRUTH.
THE WELSHAMN THREATENED TO KILL **FRANKIE!**

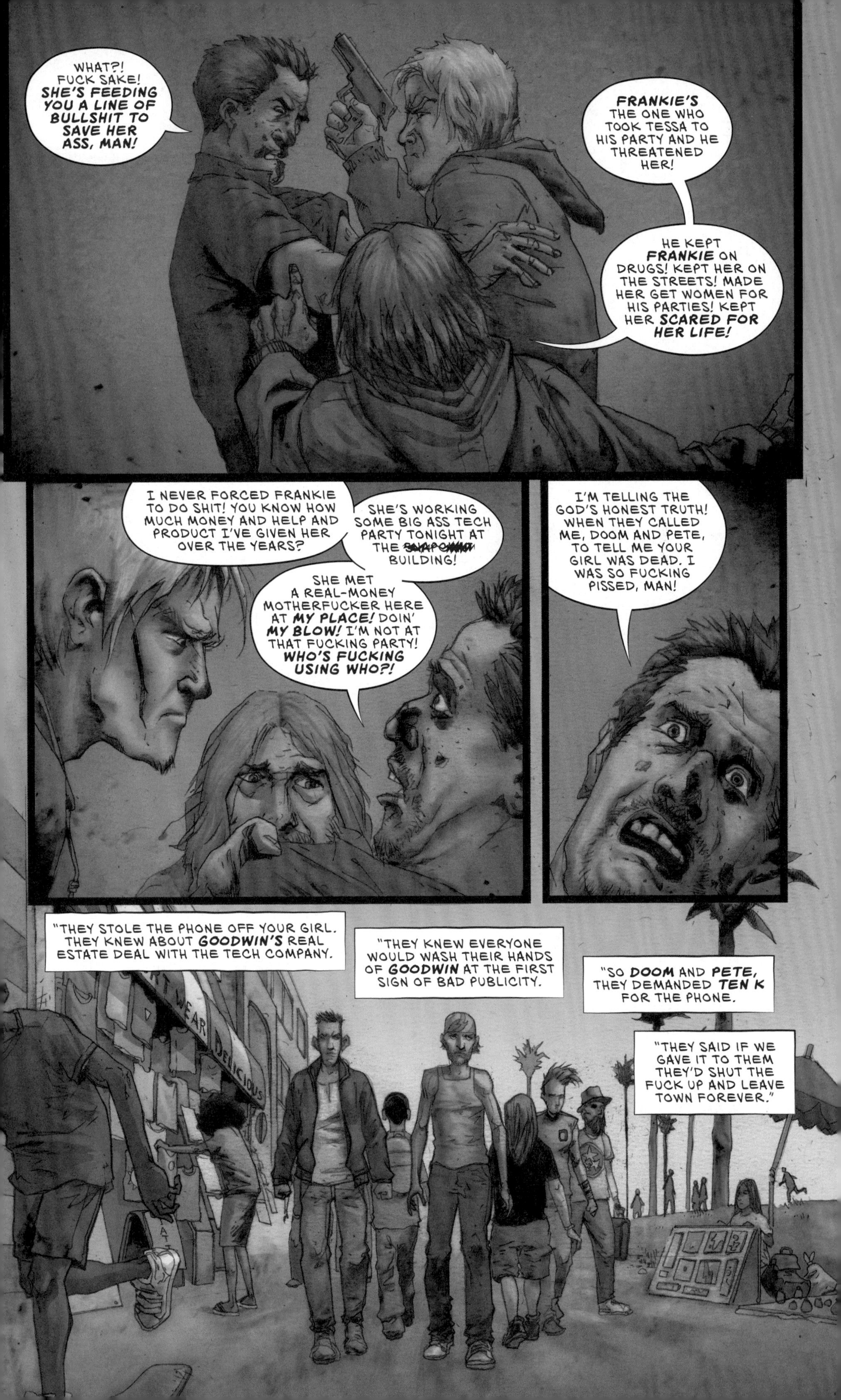
WHAT?! FUCK SAKE! SHE'S FEEDING YOU A LINE OF BULLSHIT TO SAVE HER ASS, MAN!
FRANKIE'S THE ONE WHO TOOK TESSA TO HIS PARTY AND HE THREATENED HER!
HE KEPT FRANKIE ON DRUGS! KEPT HER ON THE STREETS! MADE HER GET WOMEN FOR HIS PARTIES! KEPT HER SCARED FOR HER LIFE!
I NEVER FORCED FRANKIE TO DO SHIT! YOU KNOW HOW MUCH MONEY AND HELP AND PRODUCT I'VE GIVEN HER OVER THE YEARS?
SHE'S WORKING SOME BIG ASS TECH PARTY TONIGHT AT THE [redacted] BUILDING!
SHE MET A REAL-MONEY MOTHERFUCKER HERE AT MY PLACE! DOIN' MY BLOW! I'M NOT AT THAT FUCKING PARTY! WHO'S FUCKING USING WHO?!
I'M TELLING THE GOD'S HONEST TRUTH! WHEN THEY CALLED ME, DOOM AND PETE, TO TELL ME YOUR GIRL WAS DEAD. I WAS SO FUCKING PISSED, MAN!
"THEY STOLE THE PHONE OFF YOUR GIRL. THEY KNEW ABOUT GOODWIN'S REAL ESTATE DEAL WITH THE TECH COMPANY.
"THEY KNEW EVERYONE WOULD WASH THEIR HANDS OF GOODWIN AT THE FIRST SIGN OF BAD PUBLICITY.
"SO DOOM AND PETE, THEY DEMANDED TEN K FOR THE PHONE.
"THEY SAID IF WE GAVE IT TO THEM THEY'D SHUT THE FUCK UP AND LEAVE TOWN FOREVER."
DELICIOUS

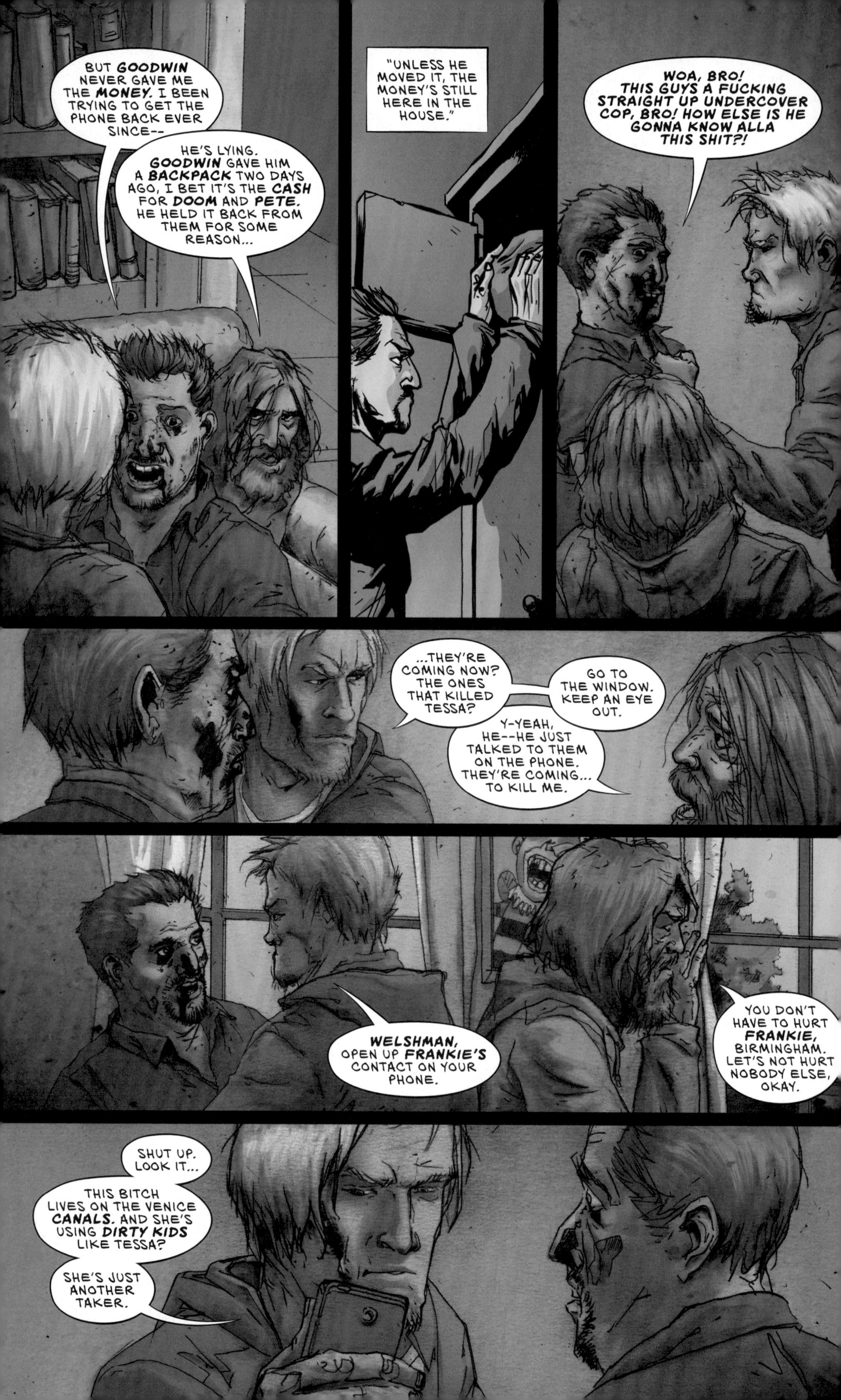
BUT GOODWIN NEVER GAVE ME THE MONEY. I BEEN TRYING TO GET THE PHONE BACK EVER SINCE--
HE'S LYING. GOODWIN GAVE HIM A BACKPACK TWO DAYS AGO, I BET IT'S THE CASH FOR DOOM AND PETE. HE HELD IT BACK FROM THEM FOR SOME REASON...
"UNLESS HE MOVED IT, THE MONEY'S STILL HERE IN THE HOUSE."
WOA, BRO! THIS GUYS A FUCKING STRAIGHT UP UNDERCOVER COP, BRO! HOW ELSE IS HE GONNA KNOW ALLA THIS SHIT?!
...THEY'RE COMING NOW? THE ONES THAT KILLED TESSA?
GO TO THE WINDOW. KEEP AN EYE OUT.
Y-YEAH, HE--HE JUST TALKED TO THEM ON THE PHONE. THEY'RE COMING... TO KILL ME.
WELSHMAN, OPEN UP FRANKIE'S CONTACT ON YOUR PHONE.
YOU DON'T HAVE TO HURT FRANKIE, BIRMINGHAM. LET'S NOT HURT NOBODY ELSE, OKAY.
SHUT UP. LOOK IT...
THIS BITCH LIVES ON THE VENICE CANALS. AND SHE'S USING DIRTY KIDS LIKE TESSA?
SHE'S JUST ANOTHER TAKER.

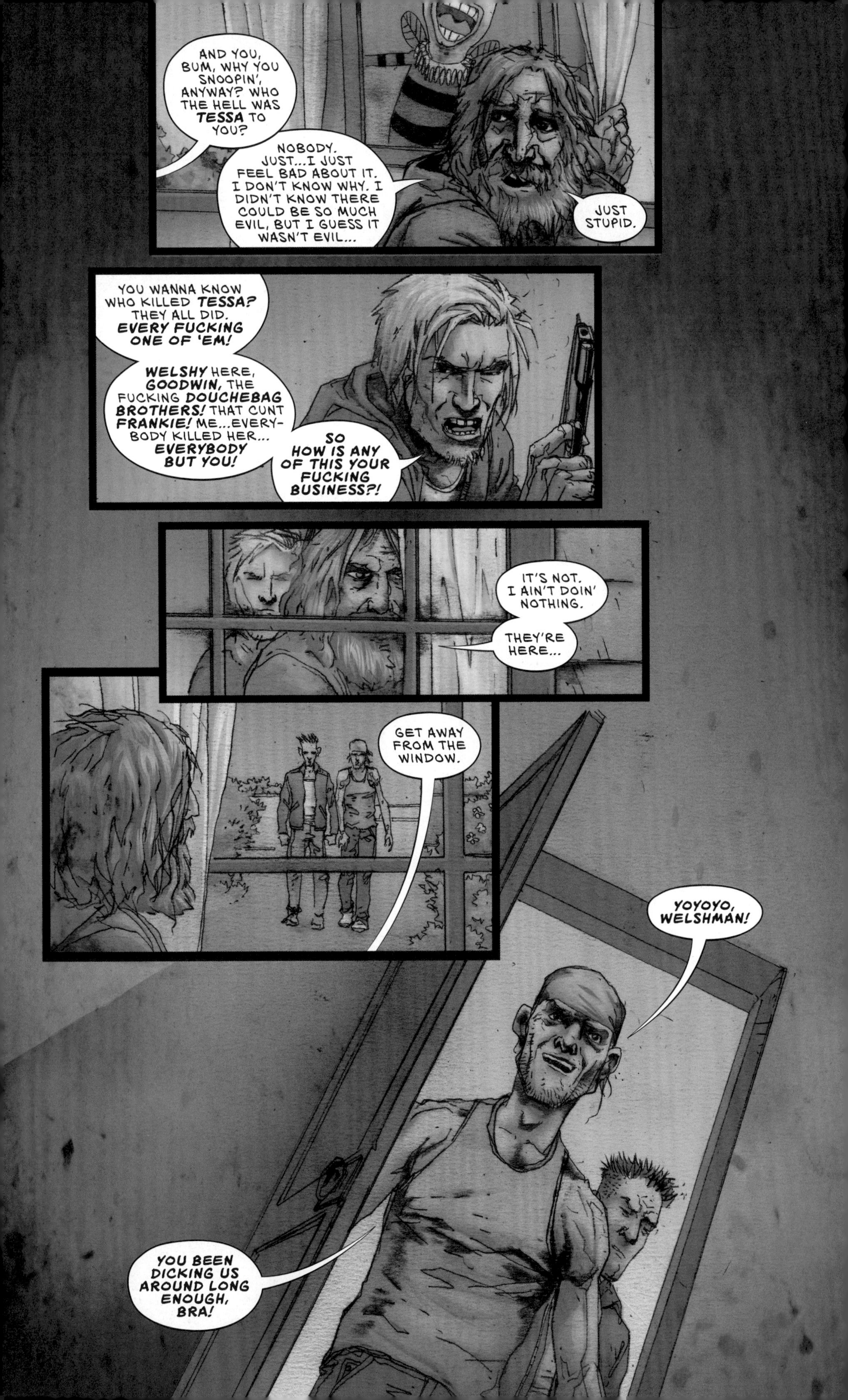
AND YOU, BUM, WHY YOU SNOOPIN', ANYWAY? WHO THE HELL WAS TESSA TO YOU?
NOBODY. JUST...I JUST FEEL BAD ABOUT IT. I DON'T KNOW WHY. I DIDN'T KNOW THERE COULD BE SO MUCH EVIL, BUT I GUESS IT WASN'T EVIL...
JUST STUPID.
YOU WANNA KNOW WHO KILLED TESSA? THEY ALL DID. EVERY FUCKING ONE OF 'EM!
WELSHY HERE, GOODWIN, THE FUCKING DOUCHEBAG BROTHERS! THAT CUNT FRANKIE! ME...EVERYBODY KILLED HER... EVERYBODY BUT YOU!
SO HOW IS ANY OF THIS YOUR FUCKING BUSINESS?!
IT'S NOT. I AIN'T DOIN' NOTHING.
THEY'RE HERE...
GET AWAY FROM THE WINDOW.
YOYOYO, WELSHMAN!
YOU BEEN DICKING US AROUND LONG ENOUGH, BRA!

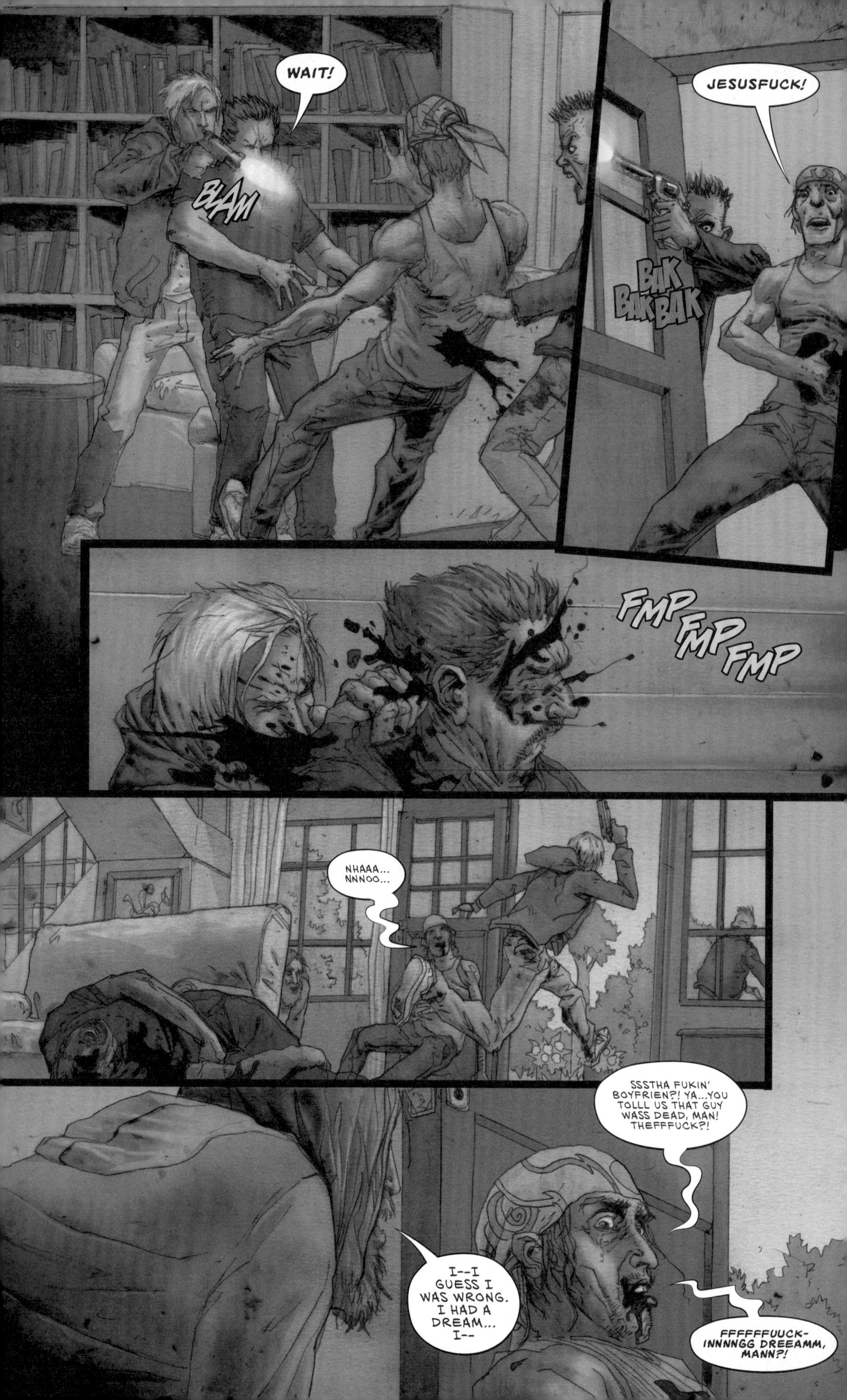
WAIT!
BLAM
JESUSFUCK!
BAK BAK BAK
FMP FMP FMP
NHAAA... NNNOO...
SSSTHA FUKIN' BOYFRIEN?! YA...YOU TOLLL US THAT GUY WASS DEAD, MAN! THEFFFUCK?!
I--I GUESS I WAS WRONG. I HAD A DREAM... I--
FFFFFFUUCK-INNNNGG DREEAMM, MANN?!

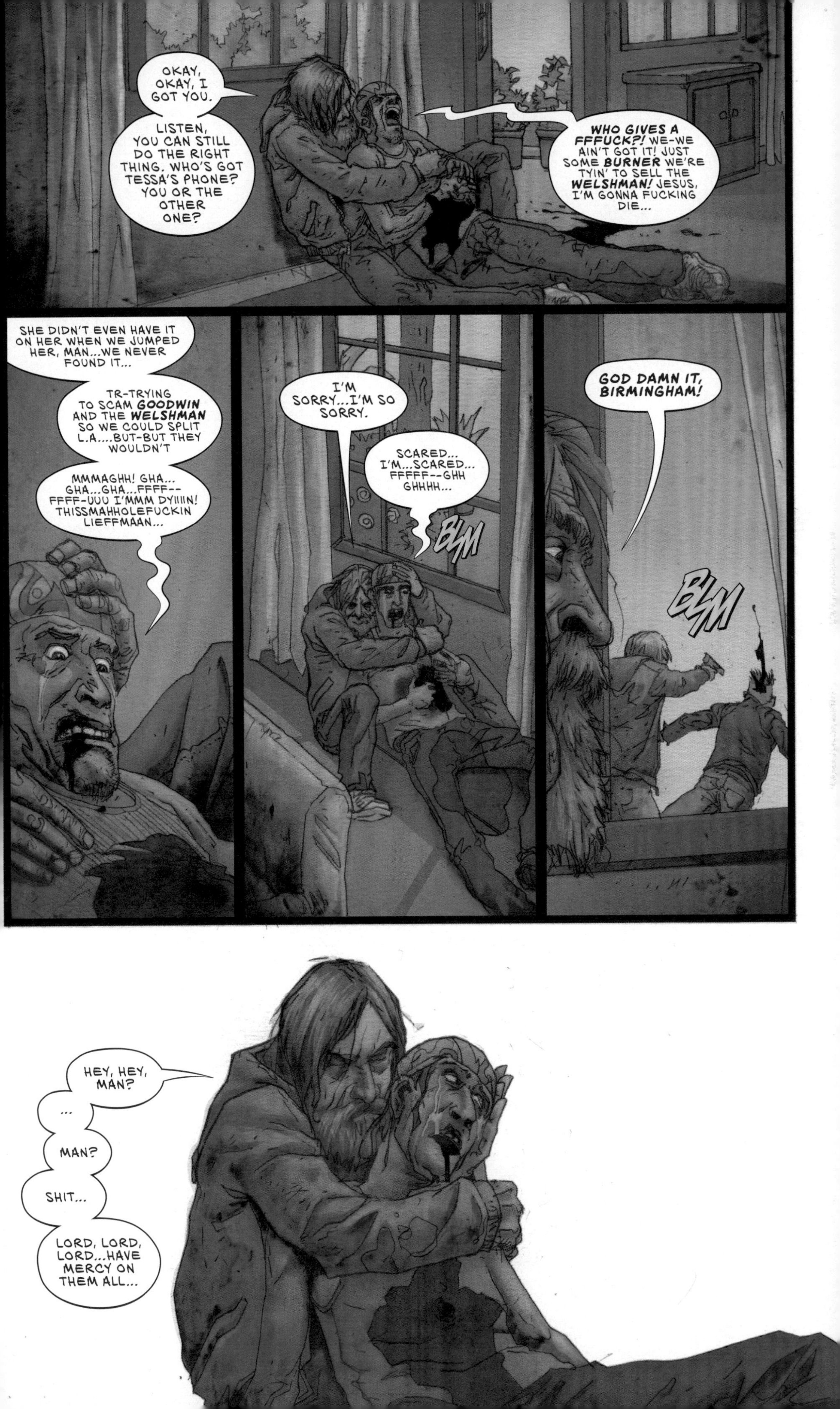
OKAY, OKAY, I GOT YOU.
LISTEN, YOU CAN STILL DO THE RIGHT THING. WHO'S GOT TESSA'S PHONE? YOU OR THE OTHER ONE?
WHO GIVES A FFFUCK?! WE-WE AIN'T GOT IT! JUST SOME BURNER WE'RE TYIN' TO SELL THE WELSHMAN! JESUS, I'M GONNA FUCKING DIE...
SHE DIDN'T EVEN HAVE IT ON HER WHEN WE JUMPED HER, MAN...WE NEVER FOUND IT...
TR-TRYING TO SCAM GOODWIN AND THE WELSHMAN SO WE COULD SPLIT L.A....BUT-BUT THEY WOULDN'T
MMMAGHH! GHA... GHA...GHA...FFFF-- FFFF-UUU I'MMM DYIIIIN! THISSMAHHOLEFUCKIN LIEFFMAAN...
I'M SORRY...I'M SO SORRY.
SCARED... I'M...SCARED... FFFFF--GHH GHHHH...
BLM
GOD DAMN IT, BIRMINGHAM!
BLM
HEY, HEY, MAN?
...
MAN?
SHIT...
LORD, LORD, LORD...HAVE MERCY ON THEM ALL...

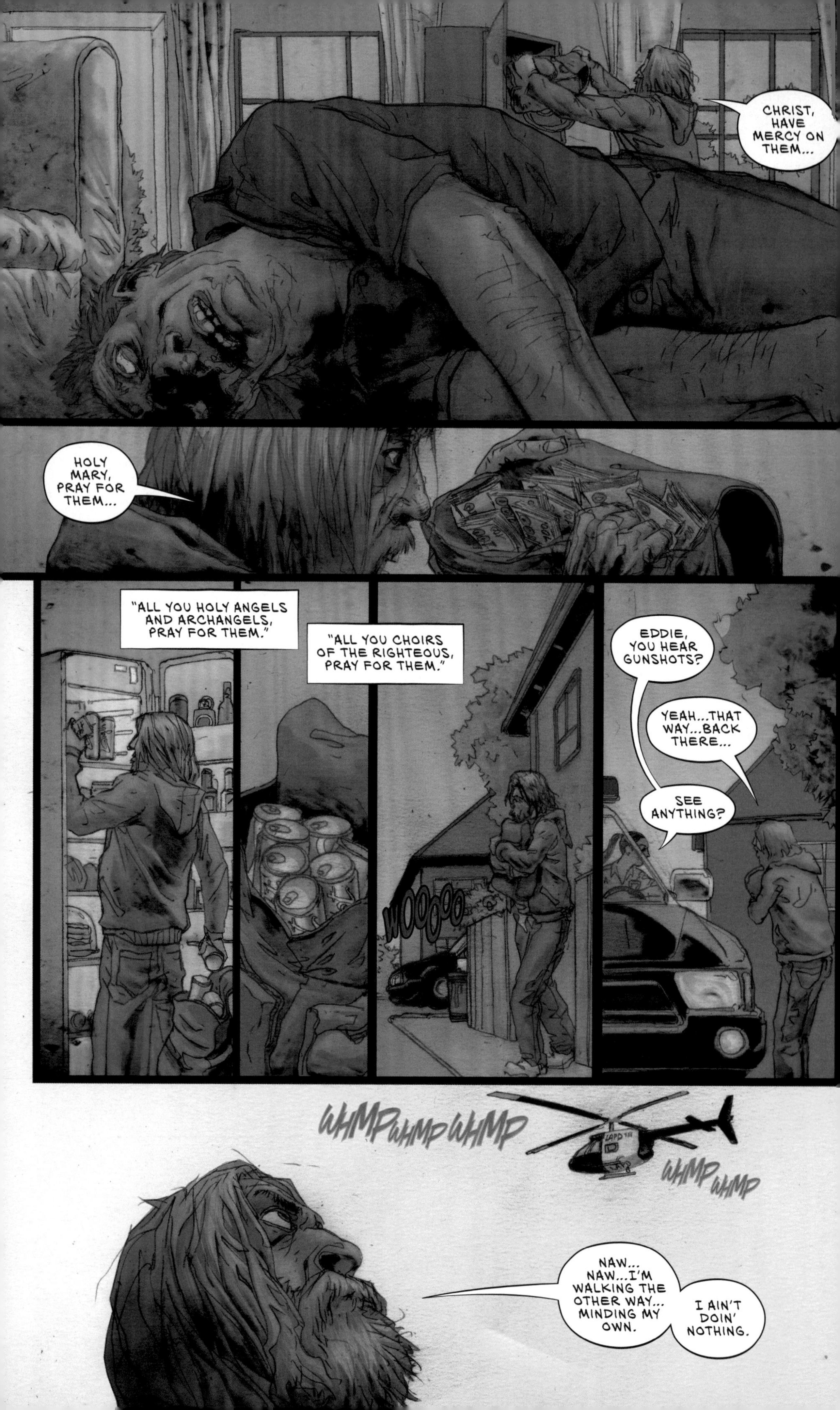
CHRIST, HAVE MERCY ON THEM...
HOLY MARY, PRAY FOR THEM...
"ALL YOU HOLY ANGELS AND ARCHANGELS, PRAY FOR THEM."
"ALL YOU CHOIRS OF THE RIGHTEOUS, PRAY FOR THEM."
WOOOOO
EDDIE, YOU HEAR GUNSHOTS?
YEAH...THAT WAY...BACK THERE...
SEE ANYTHING?
WHMP WHMP WHMP
WHMP WHMP
NAW... NAW...I'M WALKING THE OTHER WAY... MINDING MY OWN.
I AIN'T DOIN' NOTHING.

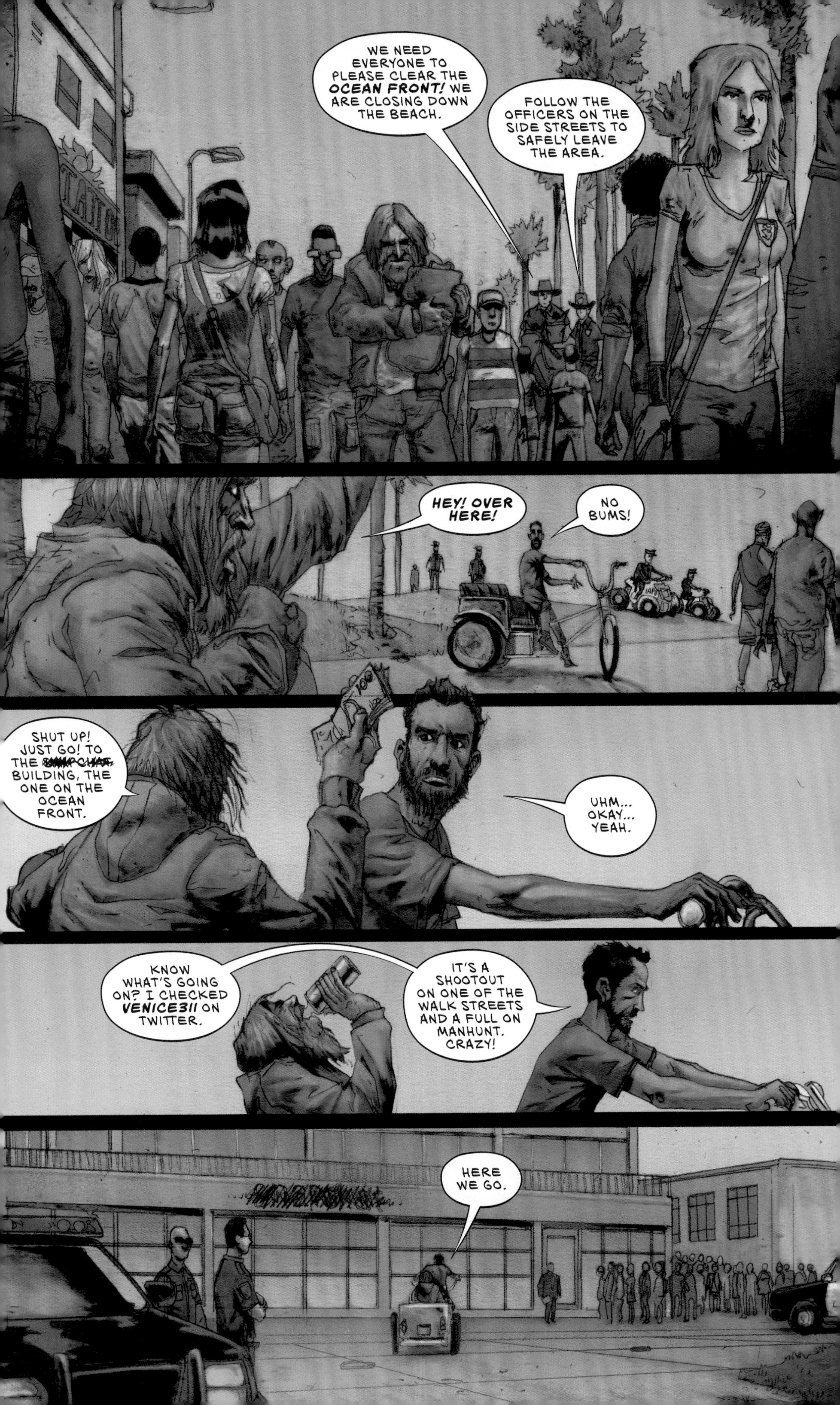
WE NEED EVERYONE TO PLEASE CLEAR THE **OCEAN FRONT!** WE ARE CLOSING DOWN THE BEACH.
FOLLOW THE OFFICERS ON THE SIDE STREETS TO SAFELY LEAVE THE AREA.
HEY! OVER HERE!
NO BUMS!
SHUT UP! JUST GO! TO THE [redacted] BUILDING, THE ONE ON THE OCEAN FRONT.
UHM... OKAY... YEAH.
KNOW WHAT'S GOING ON? I CHECKED **VENICE311** ON TWITTER.
IT'S A SHOOTOUT ON ONE OF THE WALK STREETS AND A FULL ON MANHUNT. CRAZY!
HERE WE GO.

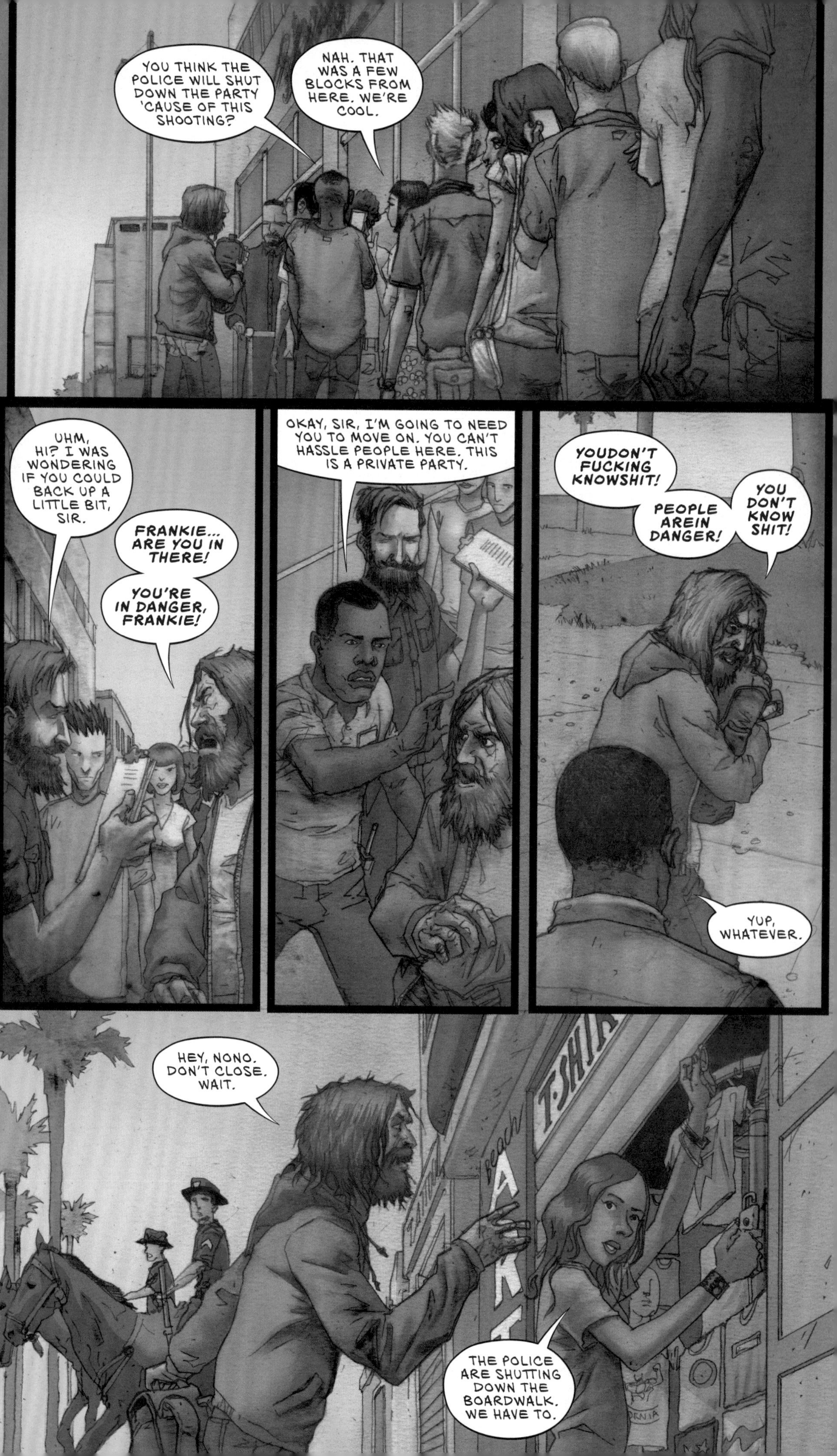
YOU THINK THE POLICE WILL SHUT DOWN THE PARTY 'CAUSE OF THIS SHOOTING?
NAH. THAT WAS A FEW BLOCKS FROM HERE. WE'RE COOL.
UHM, HI? I WAS WONDERING IF YOU COULD BACK UP A LITTLE BIT, SIR.
FRANKIE... ARE YOU IN THERE!
YOU'RE IN DANGER, FRANKIE!
OKAY, SIR, I'M GOING TO NEED YOU TO MOVE ON. YOU CAN'T HASSLE PEOPLE HERE. THIS IS A PRIVATE PARTY.
YOUDON'T FUCKING KNOWSHIT!
PEOPLE AREIN DANGER!
YOU DON'T KNOW SHIT!
YUP, WHATEVER.
HEY, NONO. DON'T CLOSE. WAIT.
T-SHIR
THE POLICE ARE SHUTTING DOWN THE BOARDWALK. WE HAVE TO.

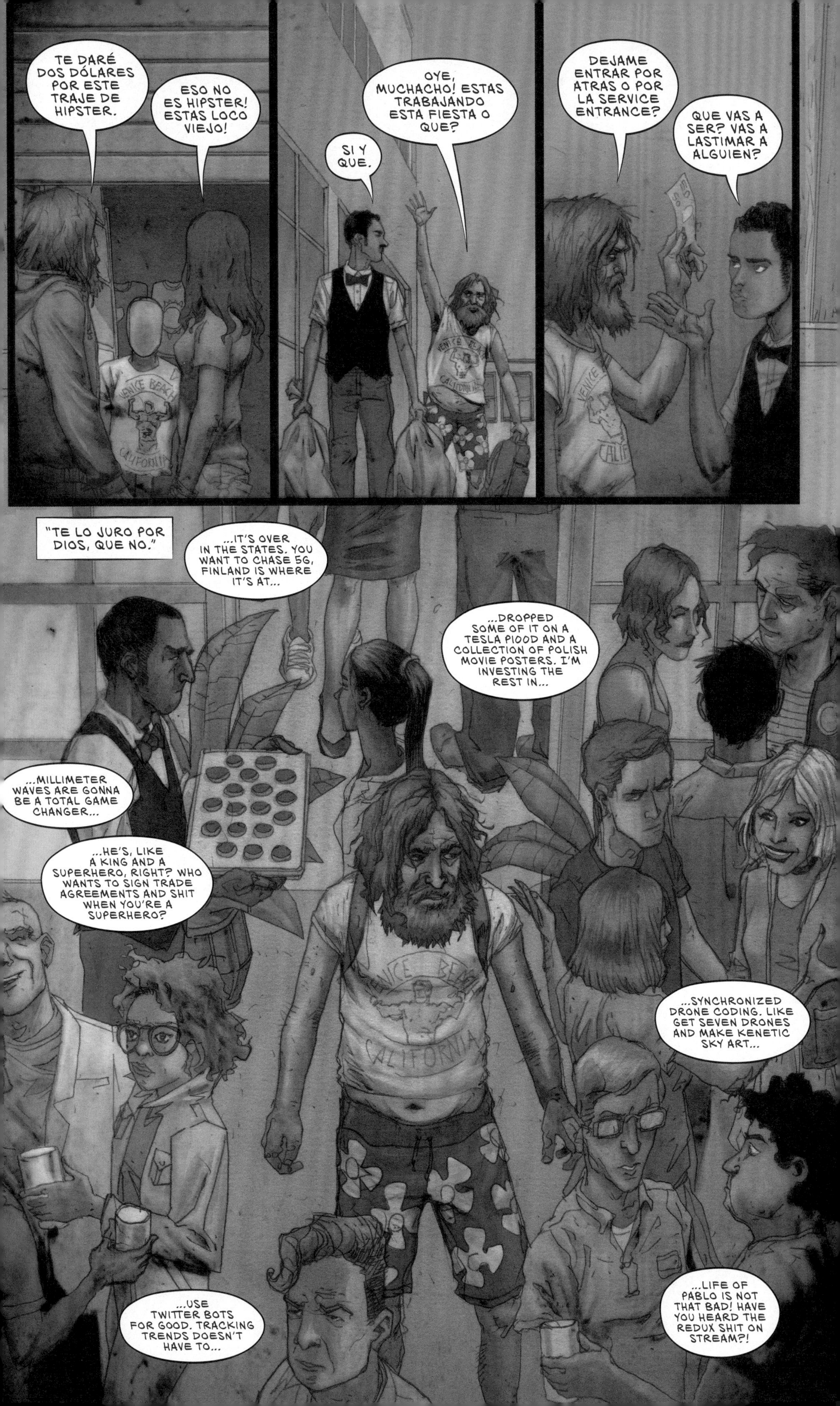
TE DARÉ DOS DÓLARES POR ESTE TRAJE DE HIPSTER.
ESO NO ES HIPSTER! ESTAS LOCO VIEJO!
OYE, MUCHACHO! ESTAS TRABAJANDO ESTA FIESTA O QUE?
SI Y QUE.
DEJAME ENTRAR POR ATRAS O POR LA SERVICE ENTRANCE?
QUE VAS A SER? VAS A LASTIMAR A ALGUIEN?
"TE LO JURO POR DIOS, QUE NO."
...IT'S OVER IN THE STATES. YOU WANT TO CHASE 5G, FINLAND IS WHERE IT'S AT...
...DROPPED SOME OF IT ON A TESLA P100D AND A COLLECTION OF POLISH MOVIE POSTERS. I'M INVESTING THE REST IN...
...MILLIMETER WAVES ARE GONNA BE A TOTAL GAME CHANGER...
...HE'S, LIKE A KING AND A SUPERHERO, RIGHT? WHO WANTS TO SIGN TRADE AGREEMENTS AND SHIT WHEN YOU'RE A SUPERHERO?
...SYNCHRONIZED DRONE CODING. LIKE GET SEVEN DRONES AND MAKE KENETIC SKY ART...
...USE TWITTER BOTS FOR GOOD. TRACKING TRENDS DOESN'T HAVE TO...
...LIFE OF PABLO IS NOT THAT BAD! HAVE YOU HEARD THE REDUX SHIT ON STREAM?!

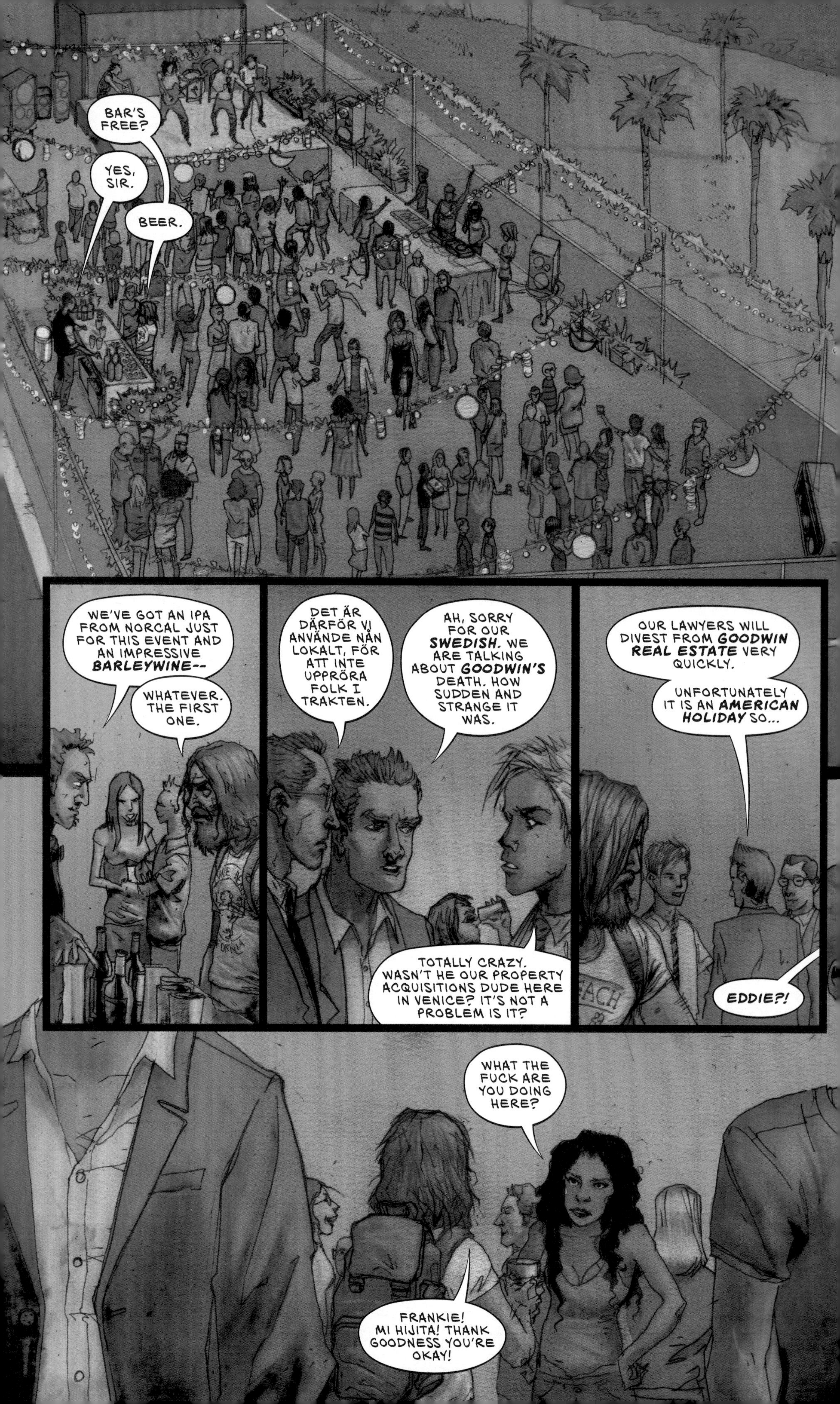
BAR'S FREE?
YES, SIR.
BEER.
WE'VE GOT AN IPA FROM NORCAL JUST FOR THIS EVENT AND AN IMPRESSIVE BARLEYWINE--
WHATEVER. THE FIRST ONE.
DET ÄR DÄRFÖR VI ANVÄNDE NÅN LOKALT, FÖR ATT INTE UPPRÖRA FOLK I TRAKTEN.
AH, SORRY FOR OUR SWEDISH. WE ARE TALKING ABOUT GOODWIN'S DEATH. HOW SUDDEN AND STRANGE IT WAS.
TOTALLY CRAZY. WASN'T HE OUR PROPERTY ACQUISITIONS DUDE HERE IN VENICE? IT'S NOT A PROBLEM IS IT?
OUR LAWYERS WILL DIVEST FROM GOODWIN REAL ESTATE VERY QUICKLY.
UNFORTUNATELY IT IS AN AMERICAN HOLIDAY SO...
EDDIE?!
WHAT THE FUCK ARE YOU DOING HERE?
FRANKIE! MI HIJITA! THANK GOODNESS YOU'RE OKAY!

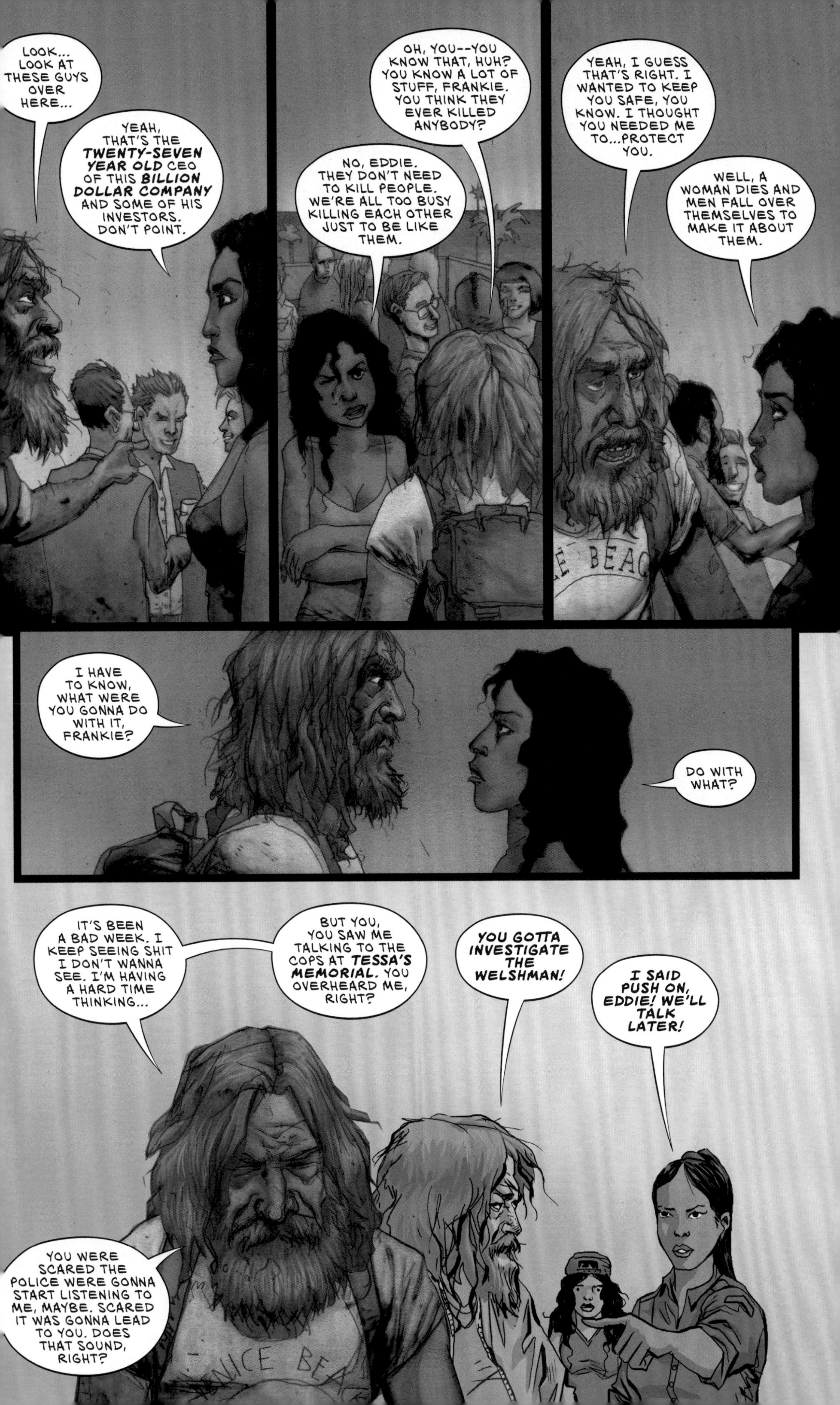
LOOK... LOOK AT THESE GUYS OVER HERE...
YEAH, THAT'S THE TWENTY-SEVEN YEAR OLD CEO OF THIS BILLION DOLLAR COMPANY AND SOME OF HIS INVESTORS. DON'T POINT.
OH, YOU--YOU KNOW THAT, HUH? YOU KNOW A LOT OF STUFF, FRANKIE. YOU THINK THEY EVER KILLED ANYBODY?
NO, EDDIE. THEY DON'T NEED TO KILL PEOPLE. WE'RE ALL TOO BUSY KILLING EACH OTHER JUST TO BE LIKE THEM.
YEAH, I GUESS THAT'S RIGHT. I WANTED TO KEEP YOU SAFE, YOU KNOW. I THOUGHT YOU NEEDED ME TO...PROTECT YOU.
WELL, A WOMAN DIES AND MEN FALL OVER THEMSELVES TO MAKE IT ABOUT THEM.
I HAVE TO KNOW, WHAT WERE YOU GONNA DO WITH IT, FRANKIE?
DO WITH WHAT?
IT'S BEEN A BAD WEEK. I KEEP SEEING SHIT I DON'T WANNA SEE. I'M HAVING A HARD TIME THINKING...
BUT YOU, YOU SAW ME TALKING TO THE COPS AT TESSA'S MEMORIAL. YOU OVERHEARD ME, RIGHT?
YOU GOTTA INVESTIGATE THE WELSHMAN!
I SAID PUSH ON, EDDIE! WE'LL TALK LATER!
YOU WERE SCARED THE POLICE WERE GONNA START LISTENING TO ME, MAYBE. SCARED IT WAS GONNA LEAD TO YOU. DOES THAT SOUND, RIGHT?

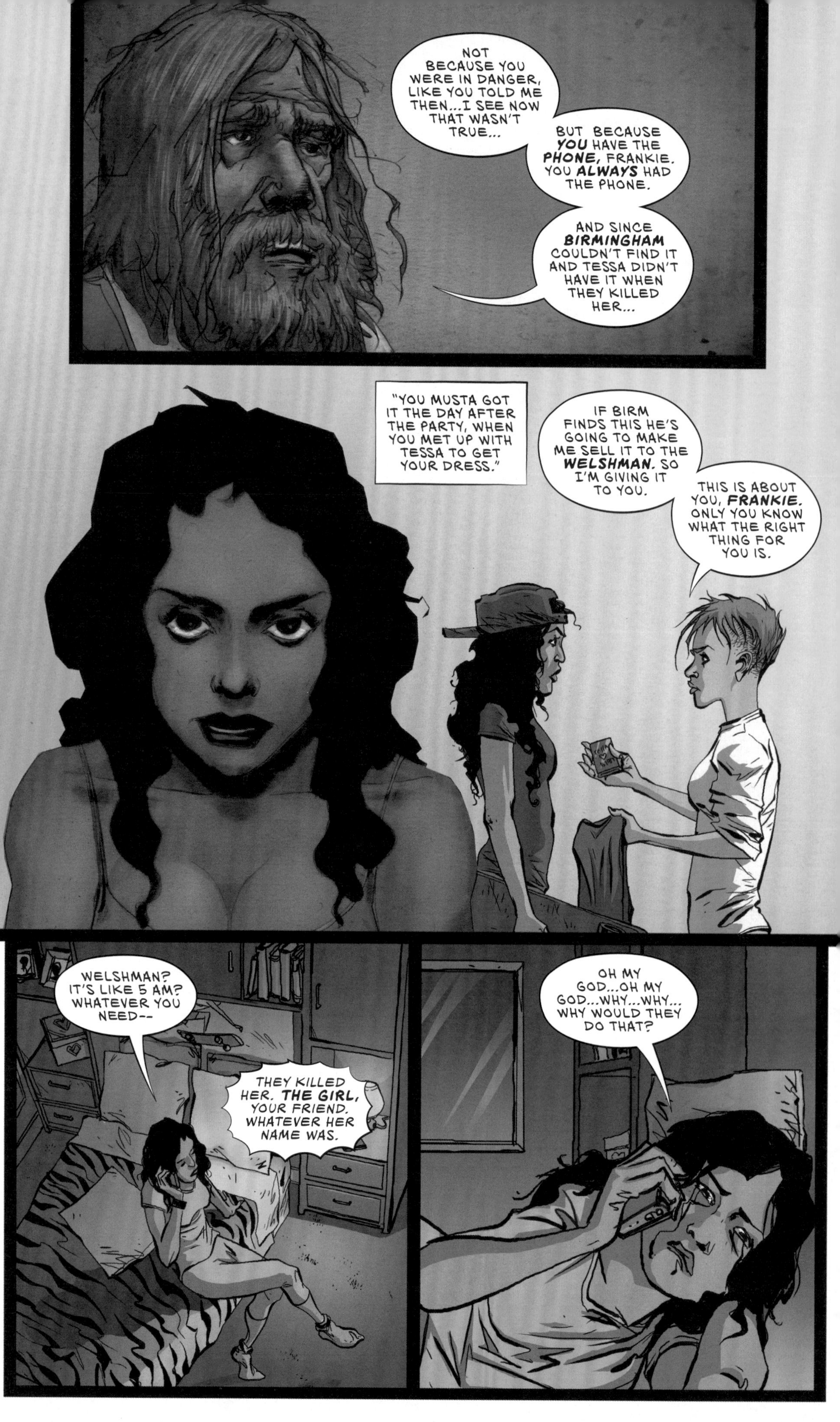
NOT BECAUSE YOU WERE IN DANGER, LIKE YOU TOLD ME THEN...I SEE NOW THAT WASN'T TRUE...
BUT BECAUSE **YOU** HAVE THE **PHONE,** FRANKIE. YOU **ALWAYS** HAD THE PHONE.
AND SINCE **BIRMINGHAM** COULDN'T FIND IT AND TESSA DIDN'T HAVE IT WHEN THEY KILLED HER...
"YOU MUSTA GOT IT THE DAY AFTER THE PARTY, WHEN YOU MET UP WITH TESSA TO GET YOUR DRESS."
IF BIRM FINDS THIS HE'S GOING TO MAKE ME SELL IT TO THE **WELSHMAN.** SO I'M GIVING IT TO YOU.
THIS IS ABOUT YOU, **FRANKIE.** ONLY YOU KNOW WHAT THE RIGHT THING FOR YOU IS.
WELSHMAN? IT'S LIKE 5 AM? WHATEVER YOU NEED--
THEY KILLED HER. **THE GIRL,** YOUR FRIEND. WHATEVER HER NAME WAS.
OH MY GOD...OH MY GOD...WHY...WHY... WHY WOULD THEY DO THAT?

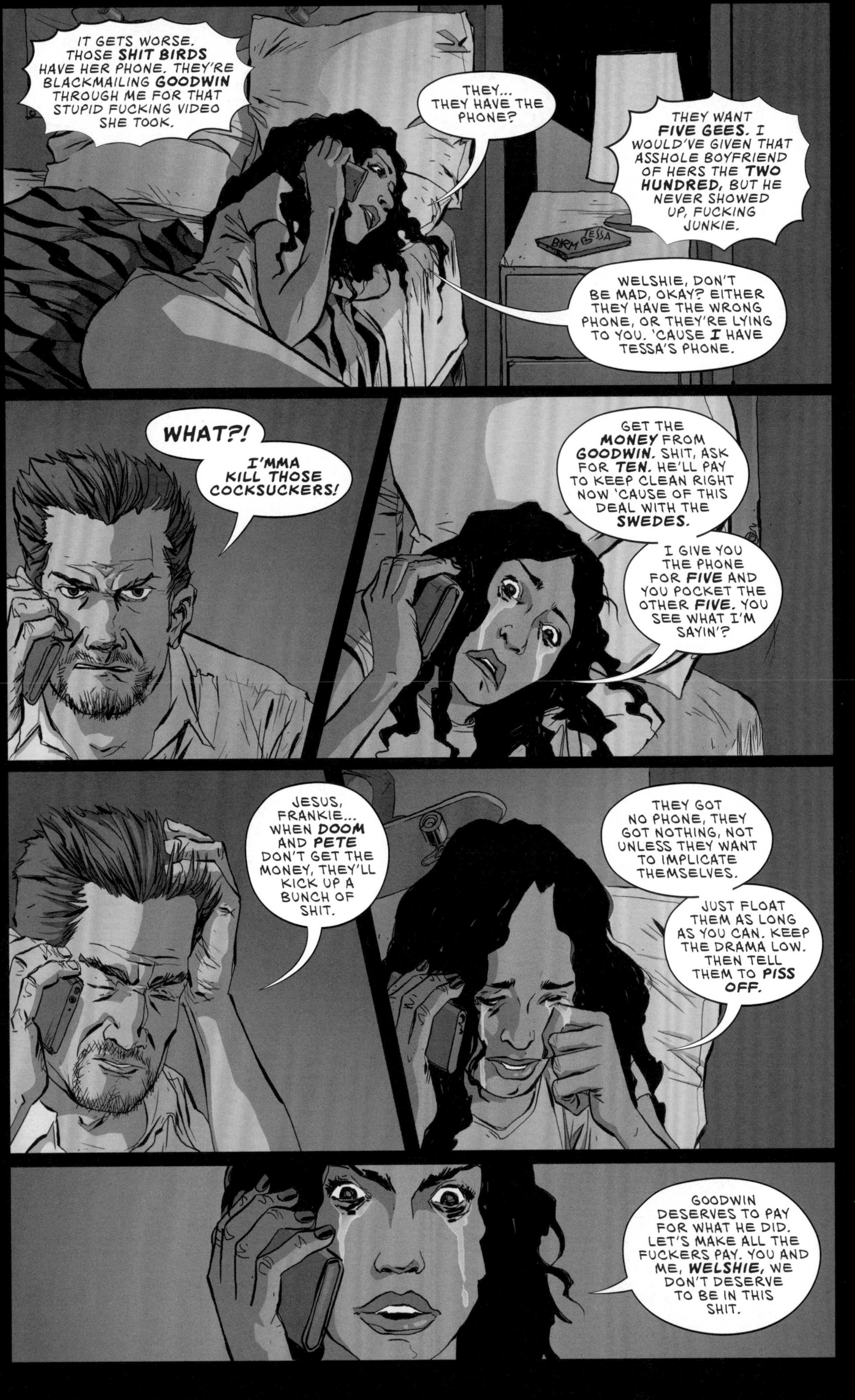

IT GETS WORSE. THOSE SHIT BIRDS HAVE HER PHONE. THEY'RE BLACKMAILING GOODWIN THROUGH ME FOR THAT STUPID FUCKING VIDEO SHE TOOK.
THEY... THEY HAVE THE PHONE?
THEY WANT FIVE GEES. I WOULD'VE GIVEN THAT ASSHOLE BOYFRIEND OF HERS THE TWO HUNDRED, BUT HE NEVER SHOWED UP, FUCKING JUNKIE.
BIRM TESSA
WELSHIE, DON'T BE MAD, OKAY? EITHER THEY HAVE THE WRONG PHONE, OR THEY'RE LYING TO YOU. 'CAUSE I HAVE TESSA'S PHONE.
WHAT?!
I'MMA KILL THOSE COCKSUCKERS!
GET THE MONEY FROM GOODWIN. SHIT, ASK FOR TEN. HE'LL PAY TO KEEP CLEAN RIGHT NOW 'CAUSE OF THIS DEAL WITH THE SWEDES.
I GIVE YOU THE PHONE FOR FIVE AND YOU POCKET THE OTHER FIVE. YOU SEE WHAT I'M SAYIN'?
JESUS, FRANKIE... WHEN DOOM AND PETE DON'T GET THE MONEY, THEY'LL KICK UP A BUNCH OF SHIT.
THEY GOT NO PHONE, THEY GOT NOTHING, NOT UNLESS THEY WANT TO IMPLICATE THEMSELVES.
JUST FLOAT THEM AS LONG AS YOU CAN. KEEP THE DRAMA LOW. THEN TELL THEM TO PISS OFF.
GOODWIN DESERVES TO PAY FOR WHAT HE DID. LET'S MAKE ALL THE FUCKERS PAY. YOU AND ME, WELSHIE, WE DON'T DESERVE TO BE IN THIS SHIT.

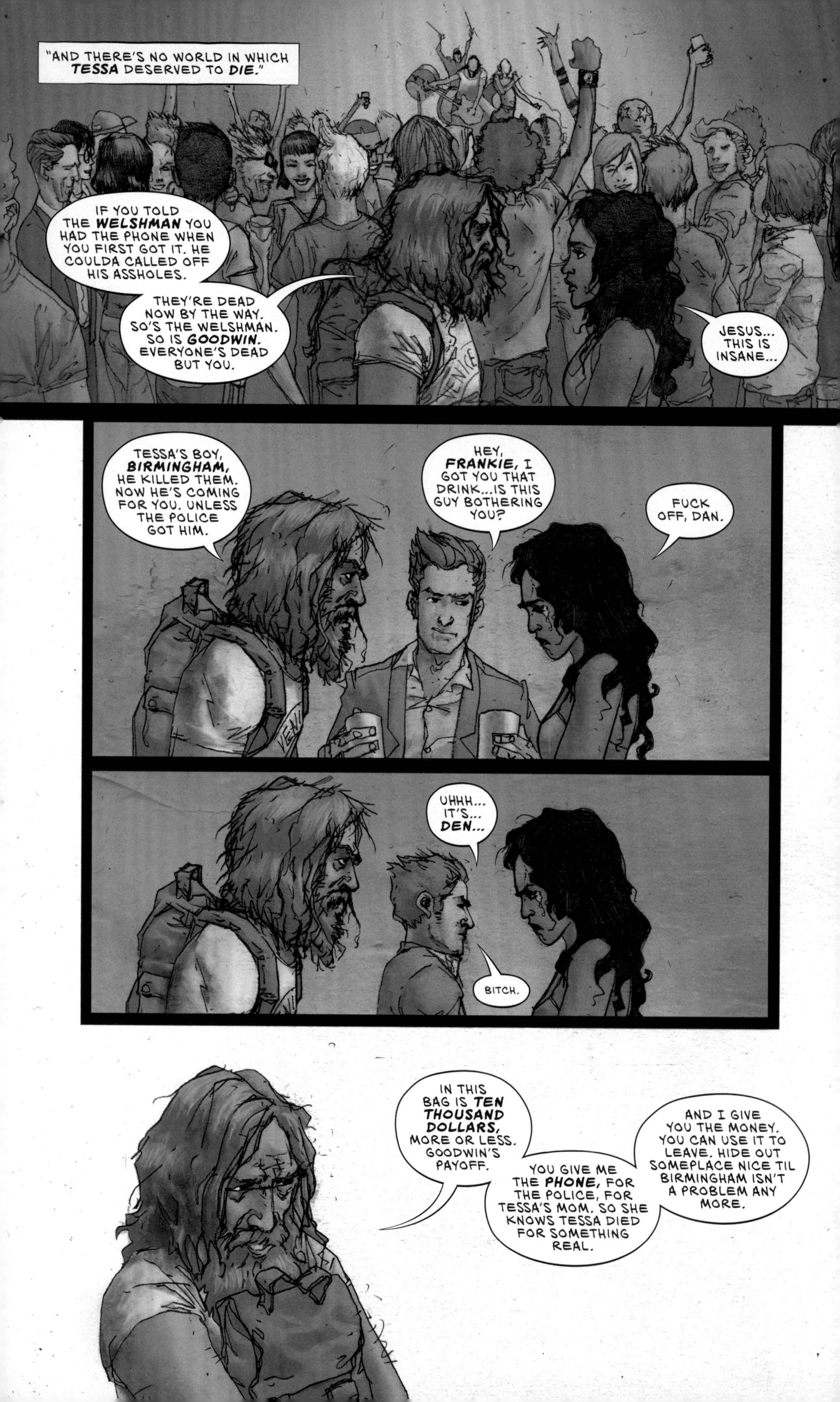
"AND THERE'S NO WORLD IN WHICH TESSA DESERVED TO DIE."
IF YOU TOLD THE WELSHMAN YOU HAD THE PHONE WHEN YOU FIRST GOT IT. HE COULDA CALLED OFF HIS ASSHOLES.
THEY'RE DEAD NOW BY THE WAY. SO'S THE WELSHMAN. SO IS GOODWIN. EVERYONE'S DEAD BUT YOU.
JESUS... THIS IS INSANE...
TESSA'S BOY, BIRMINGHAM, HE KILLED THEM. NOW HE'S COMING FOR YOU. UNLESS THE POLICE GOT HIM.
HEY, FRANKIE, I GOT YOU THAT DRINK...IS THIS GUY BOTHERING YOU?
FUCK OFF, DAN.
UHHH... IT'S... DEN...
BITCH.
IN THIS BAG IS TEN THOUSAND DOLLARS, MORE OR LESS. GOODWIN'S PAYOFF.
YOU GIVE ME THE PHONE, FOR THE POLICE, FOR TESSA'S MOM. SO SHE KNOWS TESSA DIED FOR SOMETHING REAL.
AND I GIVE YOU THE MONEY. YOU CAN USE IT TO LEAVE. HIDE OUT SOMEPLACE NICE TIL BIRMINGHAM ISN'T A PROBLEM ANY MORE.

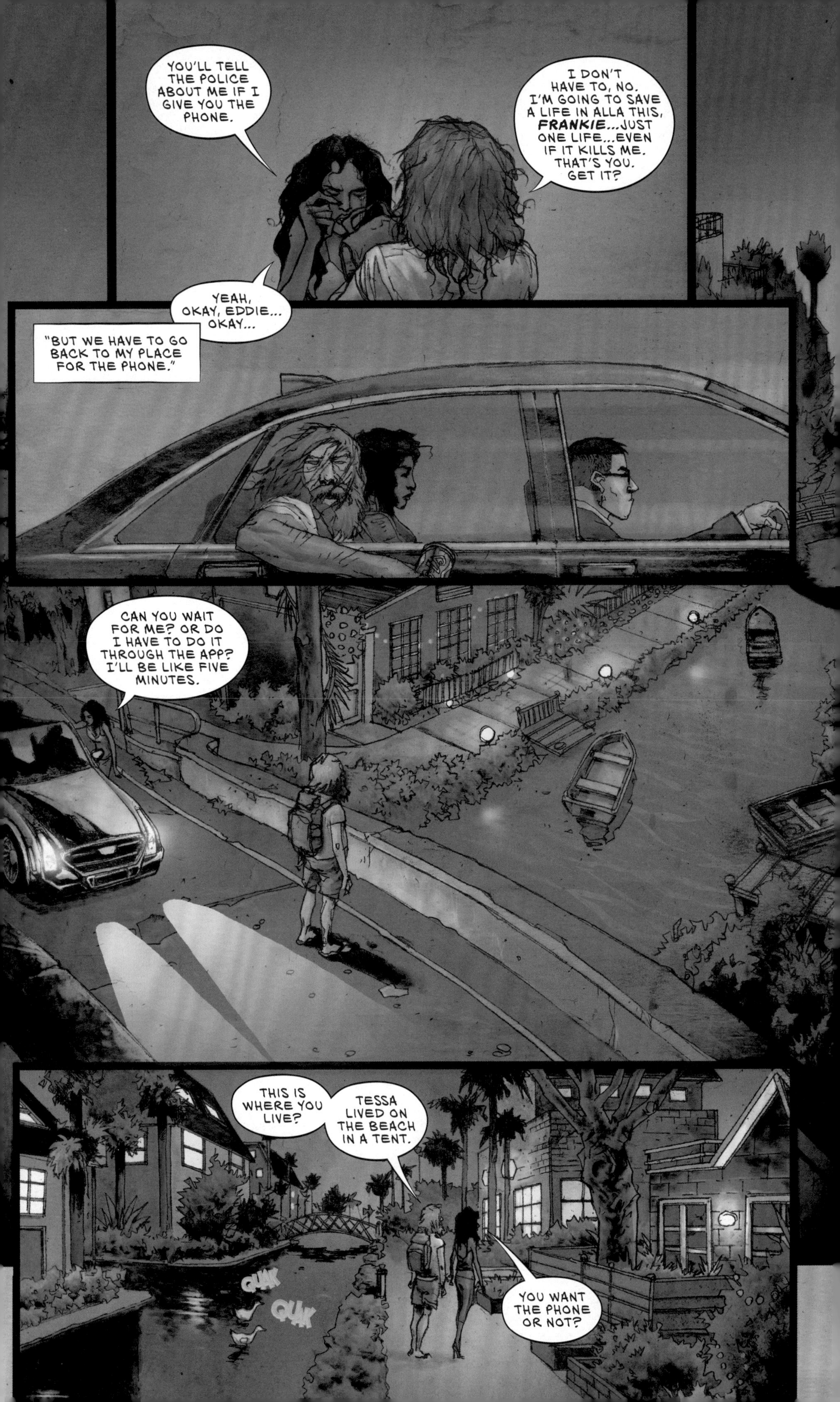
YOU'LL TELL THE POLICE ABOUT ME IF I GIVE YOU THE PHONE.
I DON'T HAVE TO, NO. I'M GOING TO SAVE A LIFE IN ALLA THIS, FRANKIE...JUST ONE LIFE...EVEN IF IT KILLS ME. THAT'S YOU. GET IT?
YEAH, OKAY, EDDIE... OKAY...
"BUT WE HAVE TO GO BACK TO MY PLACE FOR THE PHONE."
CAN YOU WAIT FOR ME? OR DO I HAVE TO DO IT THROUGH THE APP? I'LL BE LIKE FIVE MINUTES.
THIS IS WHERE YOU LIVE?
TESSA LIVED ON THE BEACH IN A TENT.
QUAK
QUAK
YOU WANT THE PHONE OR NOT?

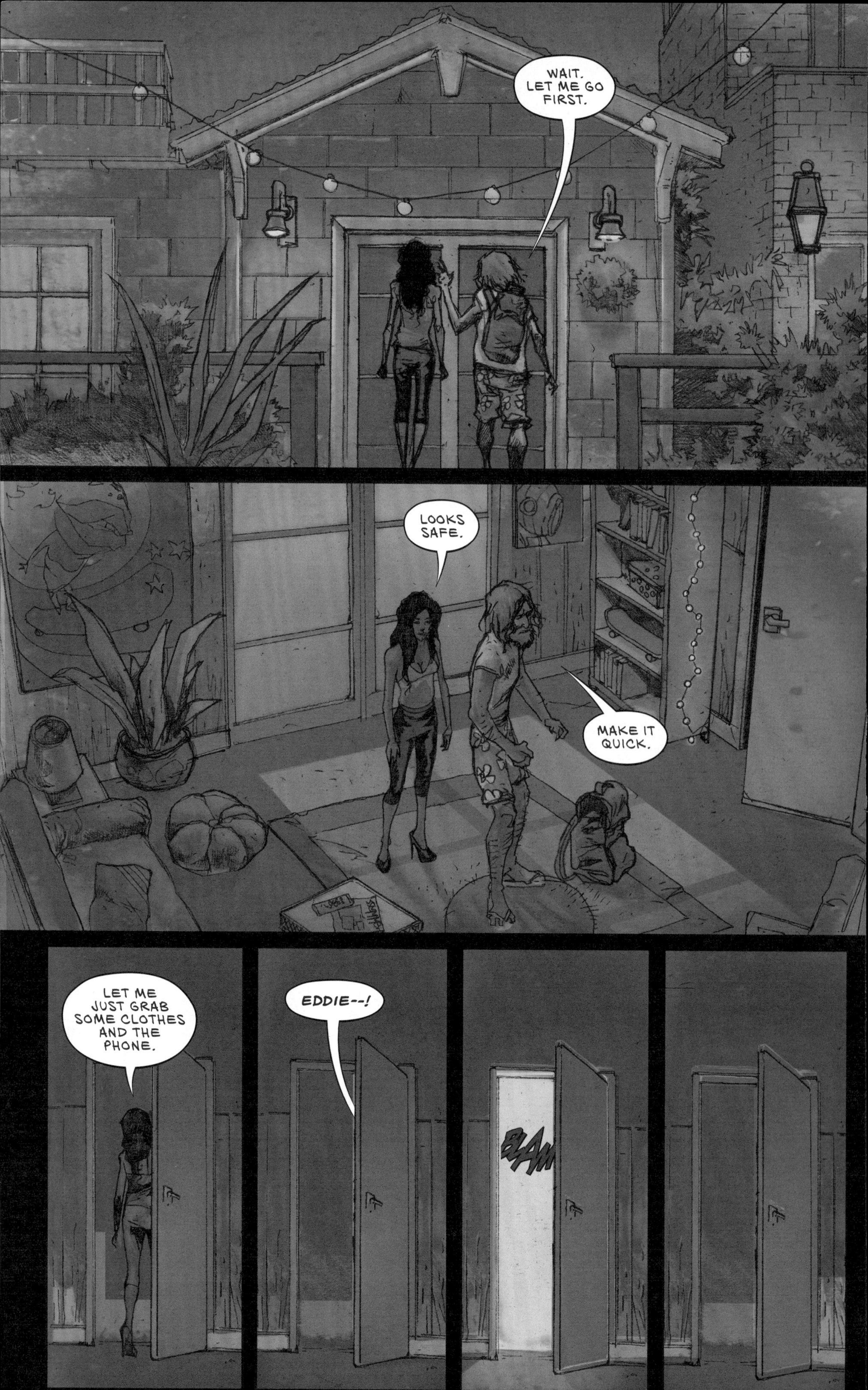
WAIT. LET ME GO FIRST.
LOOKS SAFE.
MAKE IT QUICK.
LET ME JUST GRAB SOME CLOTHES AND THE PHONE.
EDDIE--!
BLAM

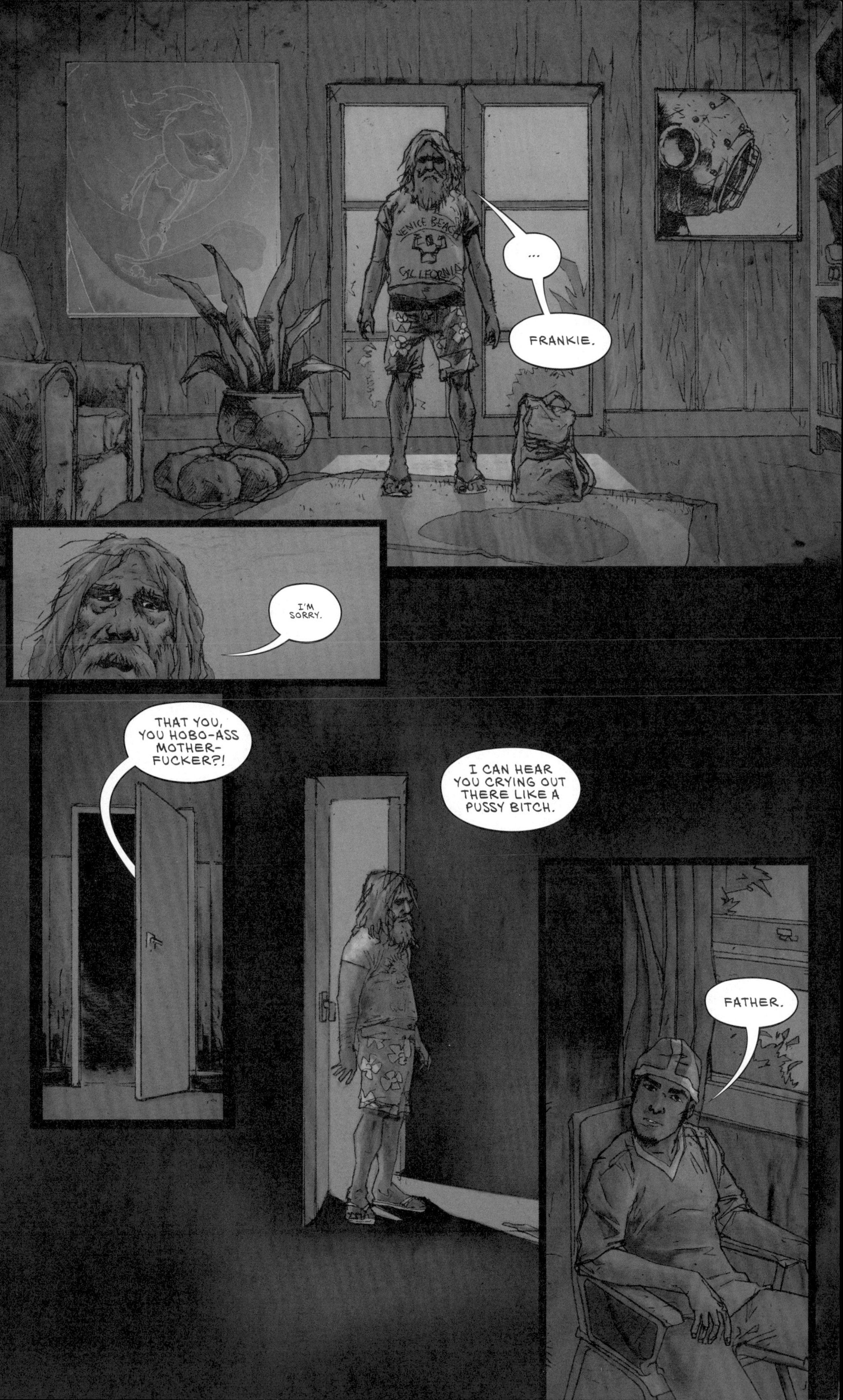

...
FRANKIE.
I'M SORRY.
THAT YOU, YOU HOBO-ASS MOTHER-FUCKER?!
I CAN HEAR YOU CRYING OUT THERE LIKE A PUSSY BITCH.
FATHER.

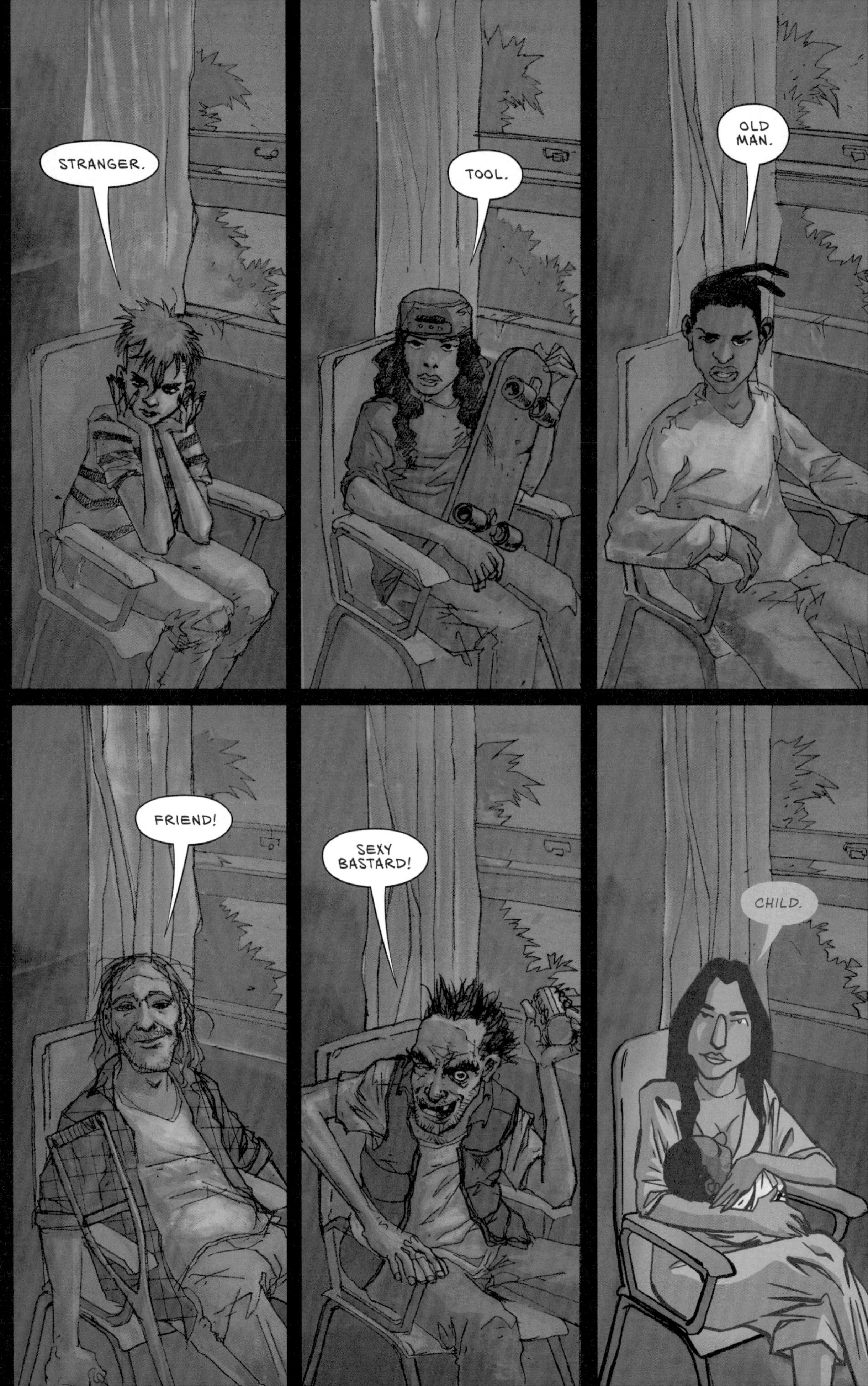
STRANGER.
TOOL.
OLD MAN.
FRIEND!
SEXY BASTARD!
CHILD.

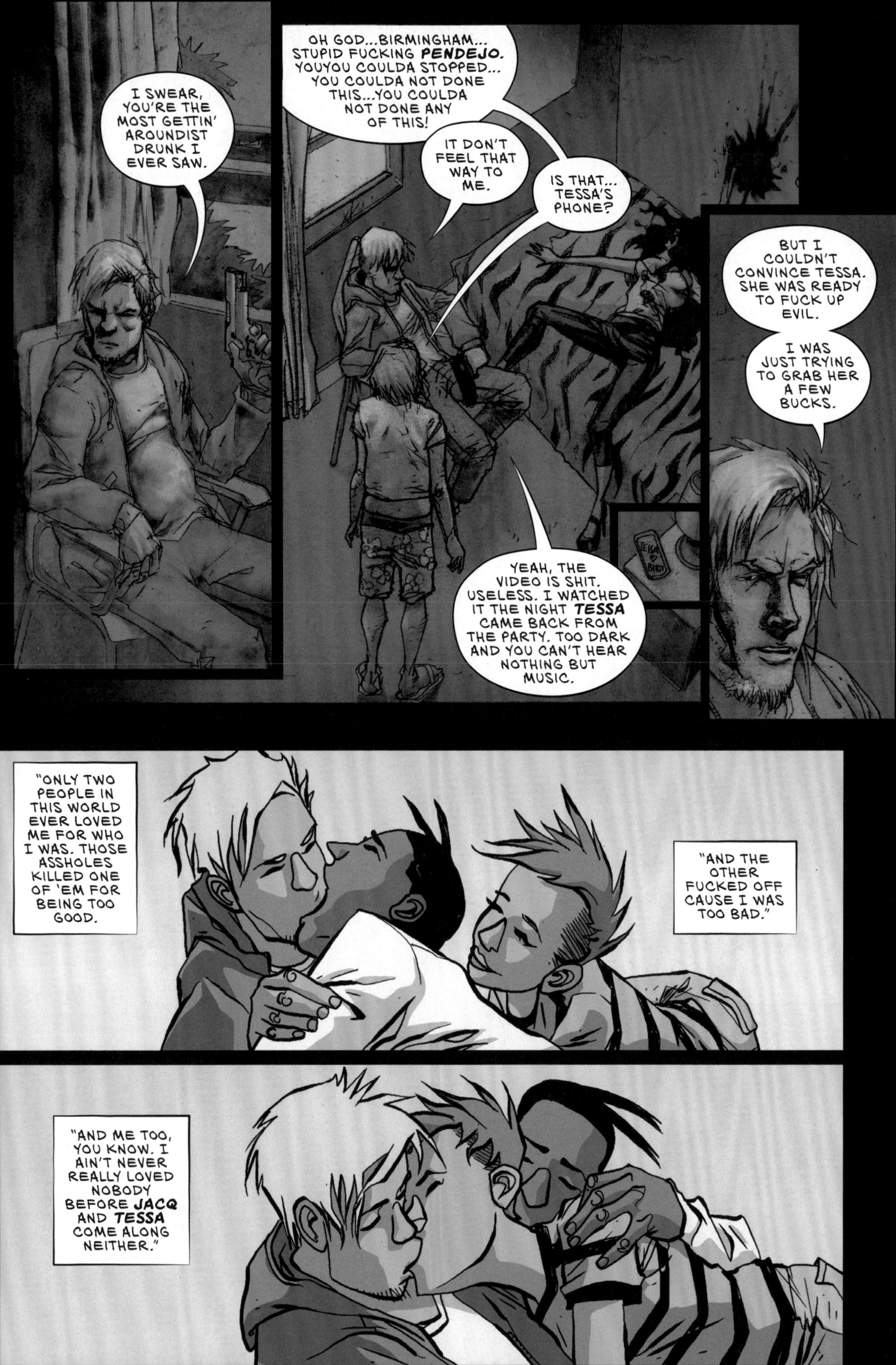
I SWEAR, YOU'RE THE MOST GETTIN' AROUNDIST DRUNK I EVER SAW.
OH GOD...BIRMINGHAM... STUPID FUCKING PENDEJO. YOUYOU COULDA STOPPED... YOU COULDA NOT DONE THIS...YOU COULDA NOT DONE ANY OF THIS!
IT DON'T FEEL THAT WAY TO ME.
IS THAT... TESSA'S PHONE?
YEAH, THE VIDEO IS SHIT. USELESS. I WATCHED IT THE NIGHT TESSA CAME BACK FROM THE PARTY. TOO DARK AND YOU CAN'T HEAR NOTHING BUT MUSIC.
BUT I COULDN'T CONVINCE TESSA. SHE WAS READY TO FUCK UP EVIL.
I WAS JUST TRYING TO GRAB HER A FEW BUCKS.
"ONLY TWO PEOPLE IN THIS WORLD EVER LOVED ME FOR WHO I WAS. THOSE ASSHOLES KILLED ONE OF 'EM FOR BEING TOO GOOD.
"AND THE OTHER FUCKED OFF CAUSE I WAS TOO BAD."
"AND ME TOO, YOU KNOW. I AIN'T NEVER REALLY LOVED NOBODY BEFORE JACQ AND TESSA COME ALONG NEITHER."

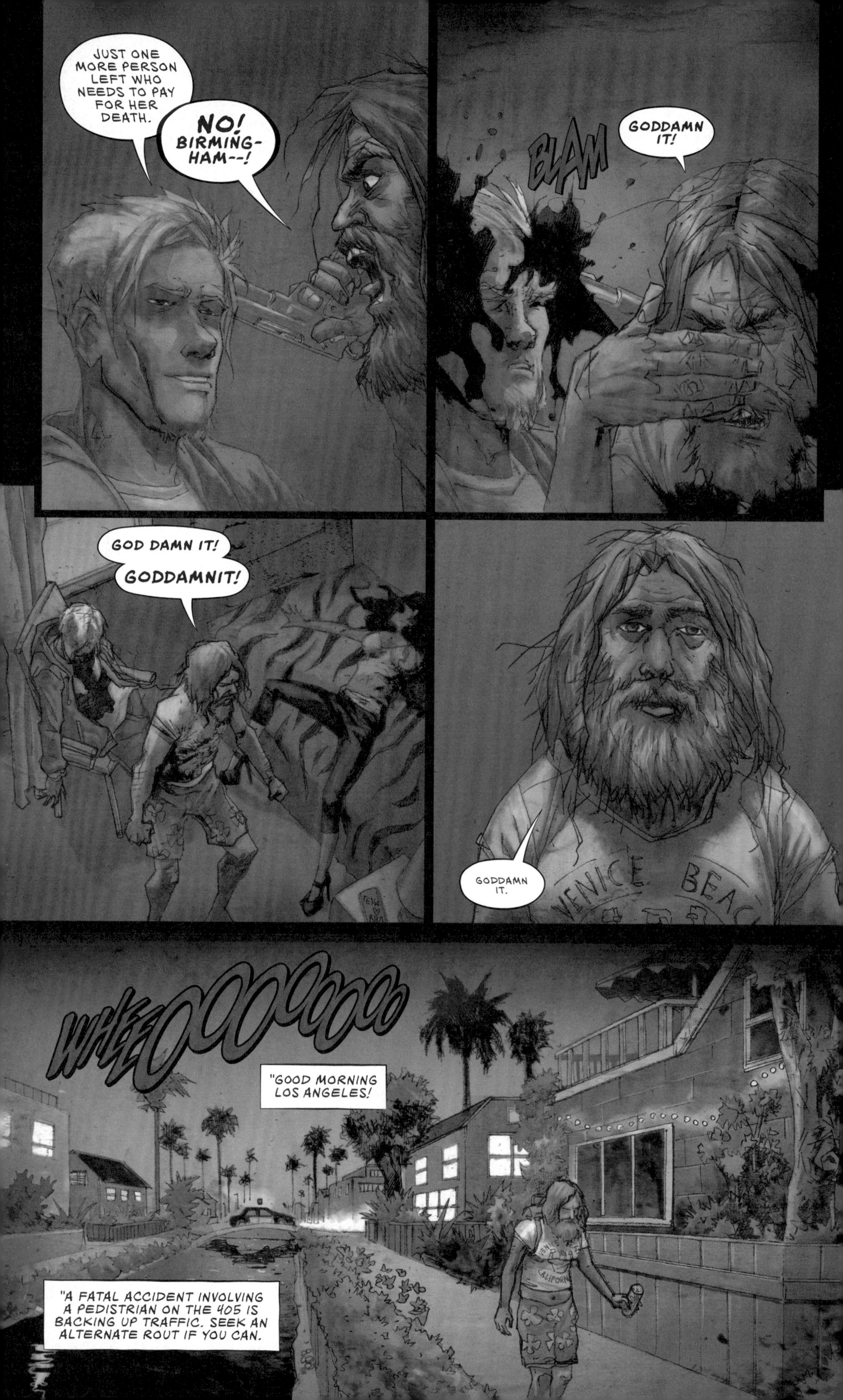
JUST ONE MORE PERSON LEFT WHO NEEDS TO PAY FOR HER DEATH.
NO! BIRMING-HAM--!
BLAM
GODDAMN IT!
GOD DAMN IT!
GODDAMNIT!
GODDAMN IT.
VENICE BEAC
WHEEOOOOOOO
"GOOD MORNING LOS ANGELES!
"A FATAL ACCIDENT INVOLVING A PEDISTRIAN ON THE 405 IS BACKING UP TRAFFIC. SEEK AN ALTERNATE ROUT IF YOU CAN.

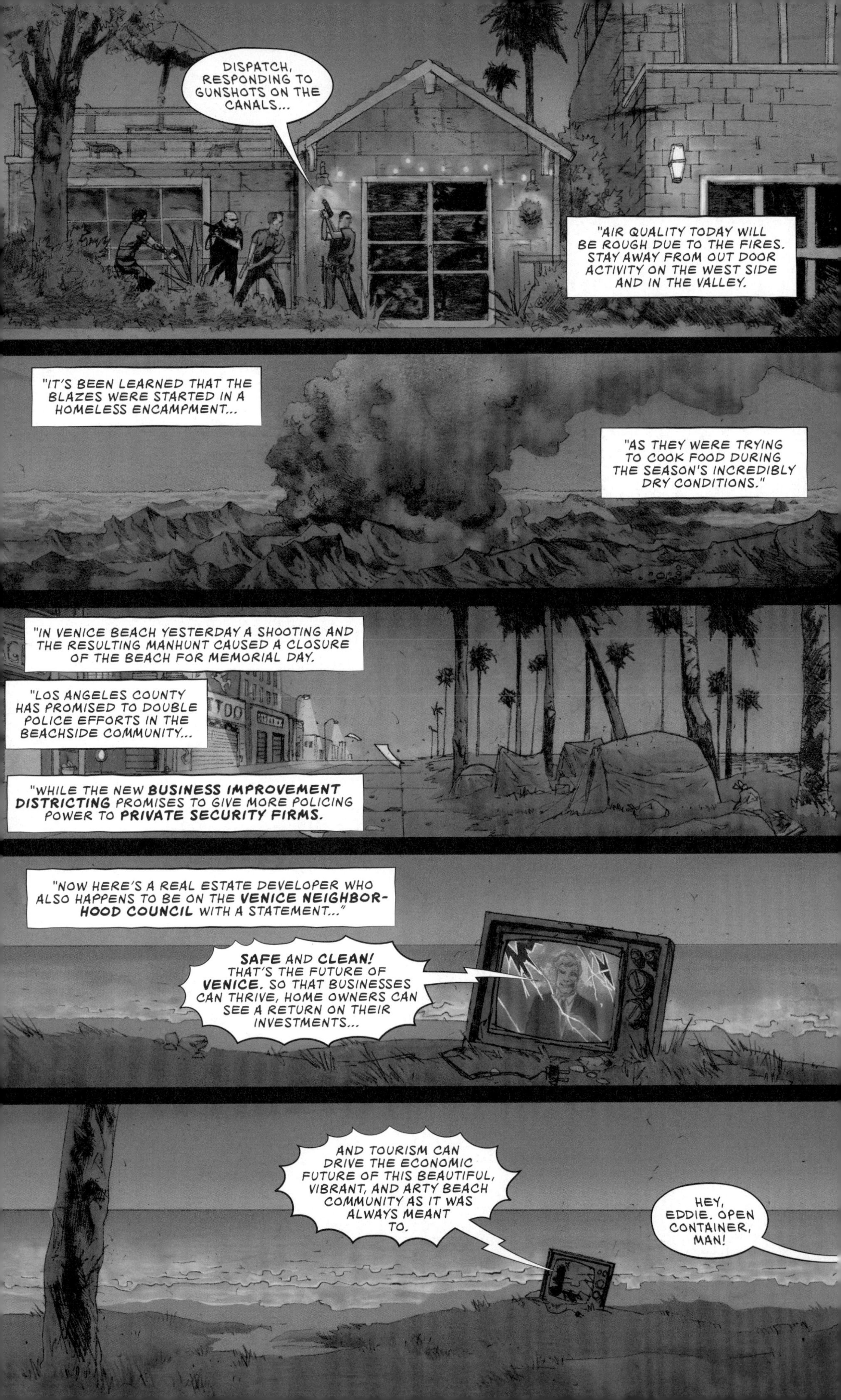

DISPATCH, RESPONDING TO GUNSHOTS ON THE CANALS...
"AIR QUALITY TODAY WILL BE ROUGH DUE TO THE FIRES. STAY AWAY FROM OUT DOOR ACTIVITY ON THE WEST SIDE AND IN THE VALLEY.
"IT'S BEEN LEARNED THAT THE BLAZES WERE STARTED IN A HOMELESS ENCAMPMENT...
"AS THEY WERE TRYING TO COOK FOOD DURING THE SEASON'S INCREDIBLY DRY CONDITIONS."
"IN VENICE BEACH YESTERDAY A SHOOTING AND THE RESULTING MANHUNT CAUSED A CLOSURE OF THE BEACH FOR MEMORIAL DAY.
"LOS ANGELES COUNTY HAS PROMISED TO DOUBLE POLICE EFFORTS IN THE BEACHSIDE COMMUNITY...
"WHILE THE NEW **BUSINESS IMPROVEMENT DISTRICTING** PROMISES TO GIVE MORE POLICING POWER TO **PRIVATE SECURITY FIRMS.**
"NOW HERE'S A REAL ESTATE DEVELOPER WHO ALSO HAPPENS TO BE ON THE **VENICE NEIGHBOR-HOOD COUNCIL** WITH A STATEMENT..."
SAFE AND **CLEAN!** THAT'S THE FUTURE OF **VENICE.** SO THAT BUSINESSES CAN THRIVE, HOME OWNERS CAN SEE A RETURN ON THEIR INVESTMENTS...
AND TOURISM CAN DRIVE THE ECONOMIC FUTURE OF THIS BEAUTIFUL, VIBRANT, AND ARTY BEACH COMMUNITY AS IT WAS ALWAYS MEANT TO.
HEY, EDDIE. OPEN CONTAINER, MAN!

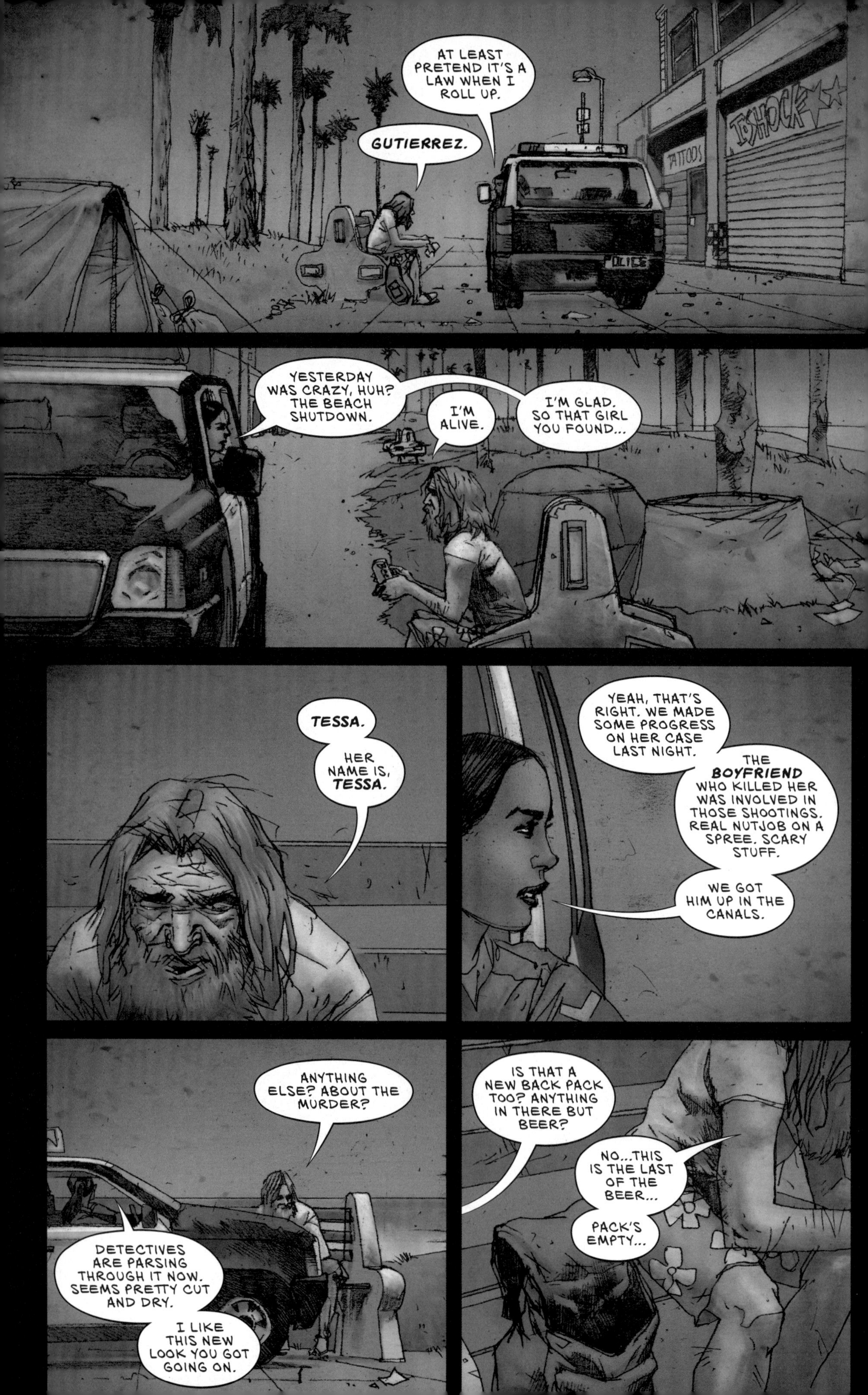

AT LEAST PRETEND IT'S A LAW WHEN I ROLL UP.
GUTIERREZ.
TATTOOS
POLICE
YESTERDAY WAS CRAZY, HUH? THE BEACH SHUTDOWN.
I'M ALIVE.
I'M GLAD. SO THAT GIRL YOU FOUND...
TESSA.
HER NAME IS, TESSA.
YEAH, THAT'S RIGHT. WE MADE SOME PROGRESS ON HER CASE LAST NIGHT.
THE BOYFRIEND WHO KILLED HER WAS INVOLVED IN THOSE SHOOTINGS. REAL NUTJOB ON A SPREE. SCARY STUFF.
WE GOT HIM UP IN THE CANALS.
ANYTHING ELSE? ABOUT THE MURDER?
DETECTIVES ARE PARSING THROUGH IT NOW. SEEMS PRETTY CUT AND DRY.
I LIKE THIS NEW LOOK YOU GOT GOING ON.
IS THAT A NEW BACK PACK TOO? ANYTHING IN THERE BUT BEER?
NO...THIS IS THE LAST OF THE BEER...
PACK'S EMPTY...

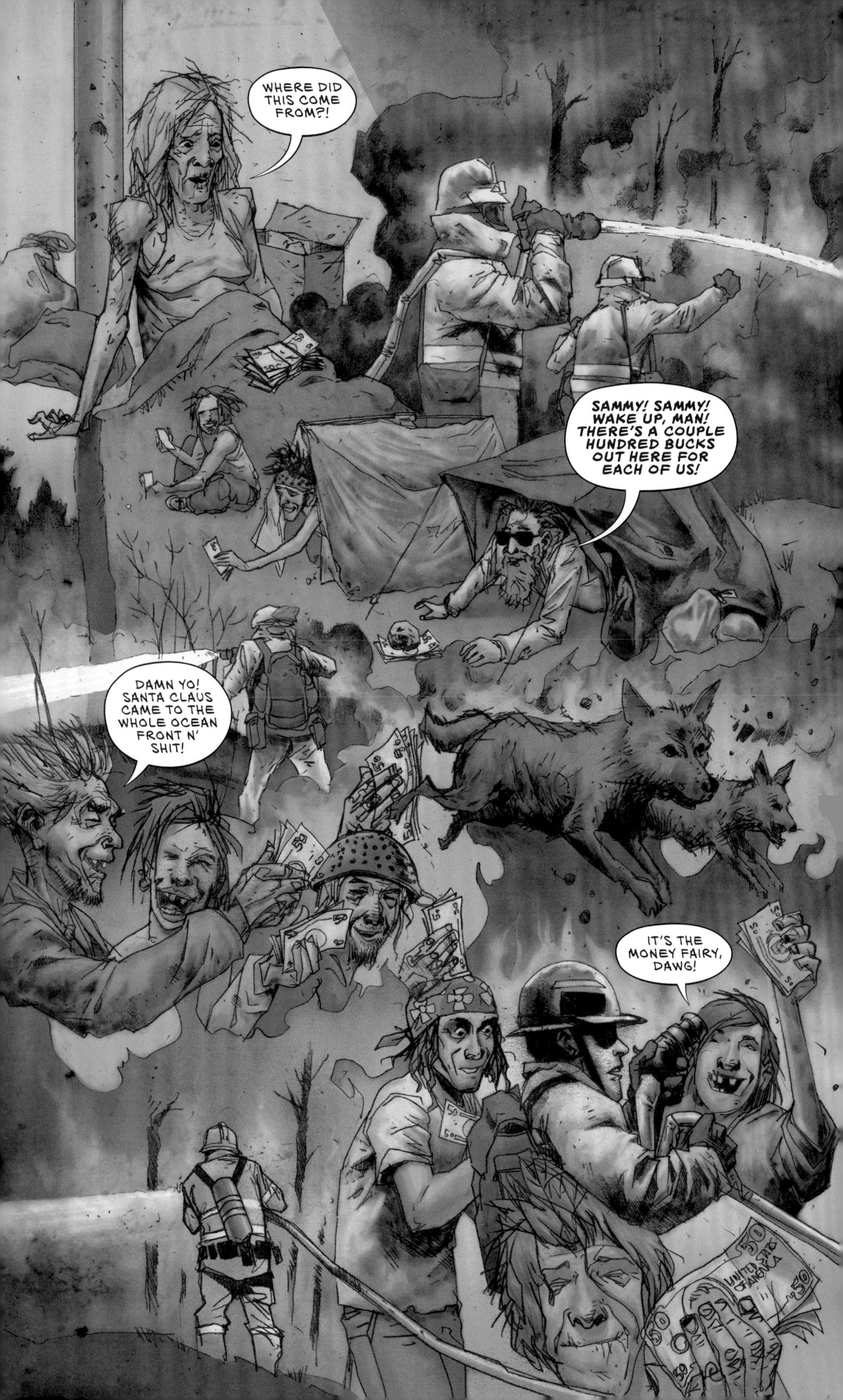
WHERE DID THIS COME FROM?!
SAMMY! SAMMY! WAKE UP, MAN! THERE'S A COUPLE HUNDRED BUCKS OUT HERE FOR EACH OF US!
DAMN YO! SANTA CLAUS CAME TO THE WHOLE OCEAN FRONT N' SHIT!
IT'S THE MONEY FAIRY, DAWG!

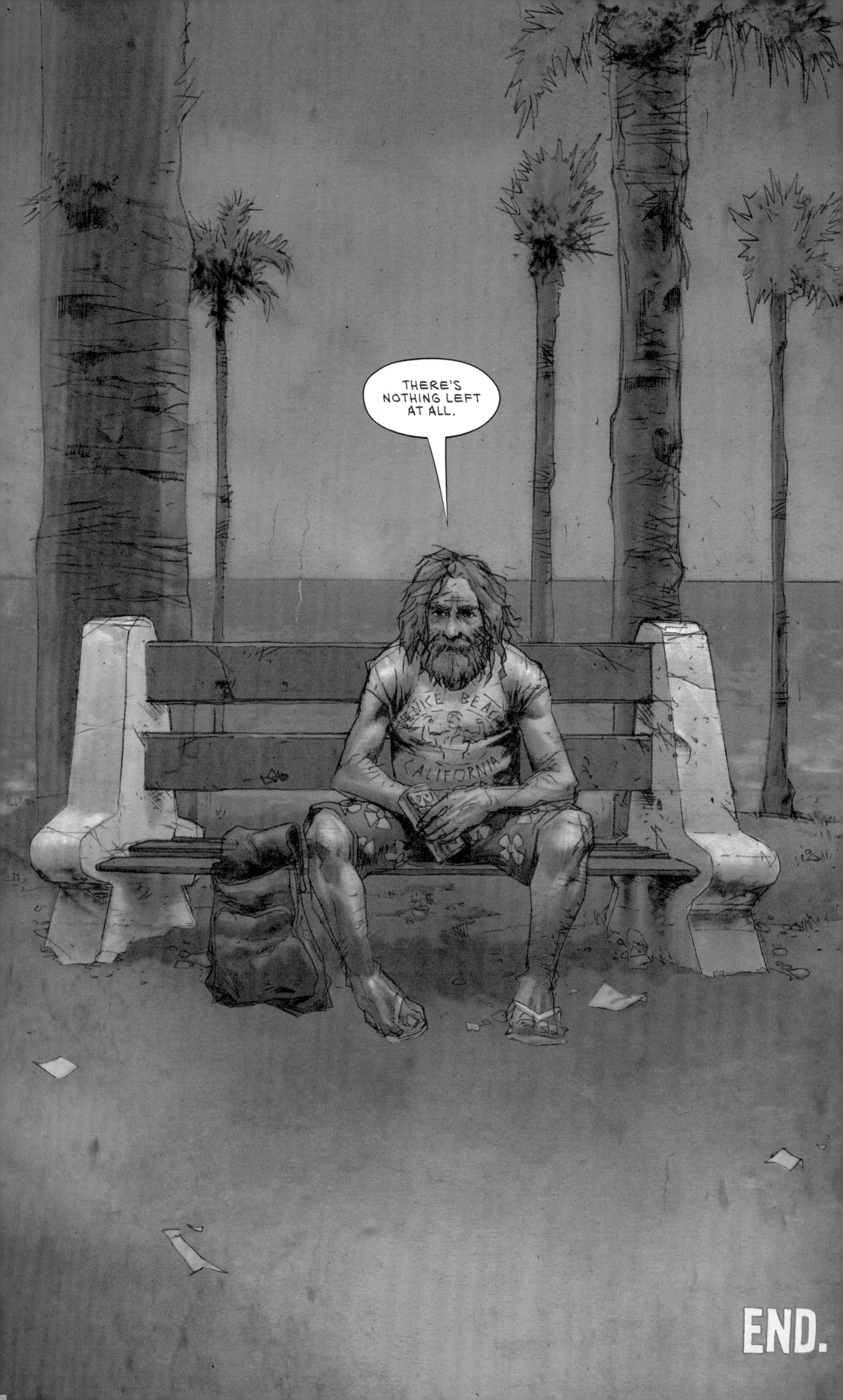
THERE'S NOTHING LEFT AT ALL.
CALIFORNIA
END.

CREATORS

JOSHUA DYSART | WRITER

Joshua Dysart is a multiple Eisner-nominated writer of books such as HELLBOY, SWAMP THING, CONAN, HARBINGER, BLOODSHOT, BPRD, and VIOLENT MESSIAHS. He wrote the critically-acclaimed UNKNOWN SOLDIER for Vertigo, as well as a graphic novel based on Neil Young's album "Greendale." It spent two weeks at #3 on the New York Times Best-Seller list. In 2017, Dysart received the Dick Giordano Humanitarian Award for his work bringing stories from destabilized regions of the world to comic books.

ALBERTO PONTICELLI | ARTIST

Alberto Ponticelli is Eisner-nominated artist known for his work on UNKNOWN SOLDIER, FRANKENSTEIN, ANIMAL MAN. He recently worked on HUNGRY GHOSTS, written by the late Anthony Bourdain. He is the author of BLATTA, a graphic novel which won several prizes. A longtime collaborator of Josh Dysart, Ponticelli travelled to California and took thousands of photographs to build the world of GOODNIGHT PARADISE.

GIULIA BRUSCO | COLOR ARTIST

Giulia Brusco is Italian and lives in London. She has colored comic books since 2000, working on titles such as SCALPED, DJANGO UNCHAINED, and THE GIRL WITH THE DRAGON TATTOO.

STEVE WANDS | LETTERER

STEVE WANDS is a Comic Book Letterer, Artist, and Indie author. He works on top titles at DC Comics, Vertigo, Image, and Random House. He's the author of the STAY DEAD series, co-author of TRAIL OF BLOOD, and is a writer of short stories. When not working he spends time with his wife and sons in New Jersey.

SEBASTIAN GIRNER | EDITOR

Sebastian Girner is a German-born, American-raised comic editor and writer. His editing includes such series as DEADLY CLASS, SOUTHERN BASTARDS and THE PUNISHER. He lives and works in Brooklyn with his wife.